T0306185

RESPONSIBLE BUSINESS

THE TEXTBOOK FOR MANAGEMENT LEARNING, COMPETENCE AND INNOVATION

RESPONSIBLE BUSINESS

The Textbook for Management Learning, Competence and Innovation

Oliver Laasch and **Roger Conaway**

Routledge
Taylor & Francis Group

LONDON AND NEW YORK

PRME Principles for Responsible
Management Education

Greenleaf Publishing/PRME Book Series –
For Responsibility in Management Education

First published 2016 by Greenleaf Publishing Limited

Published 2017 by Routledge
2 Park Square, Milton Park, Abingdon, Oxon OX14 4RN
711 Third Avenue, New York, NY 10017, USA

Routledge is an imprint of the Taylor & Francis Group, an informa business

Cover by Sadie Gornall-Jones

A special thank-you goes to Marlenne Patlan-Montalvo who has contributed to
both the first and second editions of this book.

The authors gratefully acknowledge the support by the Tecnológico de Monterrey based on the
earlier ebook edition available on www.ebookstec.com and in the iTunes Store.

British Library Cataloguing in Publication Data:
 A catalogue record for this book is available from the British Library.
  ISBN-13: 9781783535057 [pbk]
  ISBN-13: 9781783534869 [hbk]

Contents

Figures viii

Tables xi

Foreword to the first edition *by Jonas Haertle* xiii

Introduction to the second edition xiv

A. Contextualizing

1. **The state of the planet** 3
    The planet as a sick organism 4
    The economy–society–environment system 5
    The planet's most pressing issues and crises 8
    Appendix 16

2. **A history of business, society and environment** 25
    The classic period: setting the stage 26
    The modern period: formalizing 30
    The progressive period: mainstreaming 32
    Appendix 43

B. Conceptualizing

3. **Sustainability** 57
    Understanding sustainable development 57
    Sectoral contributions to sustainable development 62

4. **Responsibility** 73
    From responsible business and management to sustainable
        business and development 74
    Background frameworks of responsible business 76

5.   **Ethics**... 86
     What is business ethics?.. 86
     Normative business ethics: making right decisions............................. 88

C. Managing

6.   **Responsible management process**....................................... 101
     Three-dimensional management for the triple bottom line................ 101
     The responsible management process 105
     Picking the right responsible management instrument 112

7.   **Practice norms**.. 127
     United Nations norms 128
     International Organization for Standardization (ISO) guidelines 133
     Appendix 142

D. Strategizing

8.   **Envisioning responsible business**...................................... 155
     Primary motivations for becoming a responsible business 156
     Development strategies for becoming a responsible business............ 160
     Making responsible business commitments.................................... 164

9.   **Strategic management**.. 172
     Analyzing the status quo.. 172
     Strategic management processes... 178
     Business models 183
     Appendix 192

E. Implementing

10. **Implementation basics**.. 195
     Good implementation practices... 195
     Mainstream responsible management instruments and business
        functions 199

11. **Main business functions** 207
     Logistics 207
     Operations and production... 210
     Customer relationship management: marketing, sales, service........... 214

12. **Business support functions**... 222
     Law and compliance 222
     Accounting... 224
     Finance... 228
     Organizational structure and design....................................... 231

Human resources management 233
Research, development and innovation 237

13. **Supply chain management** 245
Defining sustainable supply chains 247
Stages of sustainable supply chain management 250
Sustainable supply chain management tools 251

F. Communicating

14. **Communication in responsible business** 261
Communicating with stakeholders 262
Responsible communication formats 263
Integrated stakeholder communication 267
Communication purposes and the right formats................. 269

15. **Communication challenges** 286
Dealing with critical attitudes... 286
Greenwashing 289

G. Innovating

16. **Innovation for change**...................................... 299
Objects and purposes of innovation 302
Who innovates and how?... 306

17. **Individual change** 314
Unsustainable attitudes, behaviors and their origins 315
Sustainable development, lifestyles and income................ 319
Changing lifestyle and consumption 321
Activism and change agency... 326

18. **Organizational change**.................................... 336
Developing sustainable business 337
Transformational approaches.. 343
Entrepreneurial approaches 353

19. **Systemic change** 364
Changing systems 365
Transforming subsystems 372
The role of public policy in systems change...................... 378

Glossary 390

References... 406

About the authors... 427

Figures

1.1   Planetary mega-issues overview 10

2.1   Historic periods in the relationship between business, society, and
      environment 26

3.1   Main graphic concepts of sustainable development 58
3.2   Characteristics necessary to achieve sustainability 60
3.3   Sectoral contributions to sustainable development 63

4.1   Dynamics and definitions of responsible business, responsible
      management, sustainable business, and sustainable development 75

5.1   Domains of business ethics 87

6.1   Three-dimensional management and the triple bottom line 102
6.2   The responsible management process trinity 105
6.3   Specialized responsible management instruments 113
6.4   The stakeholder management process 114
6.5   Typical stakeholder map of a taco restaurant 115
6.6   The physical product life-cycle 118

7.1   Classifying responsible business norms 128
7.2   Main components of the GRI guidelines 131

8.1   Primary motivation for responsible business 156
8.2   Development strategy for responsible business 161
8.3   Responsible business categories 165
8.4   Responsible business self-assessment 165

9.1   Responsible business SWOT analysis 173
9.2   Materiality assessment for a taco business 175
9.3   Dynamics of responsible business planning and mainstream
      strategic management components 178
9.4   Sustainability scorecards applied to Unilever's sustainable living
      plan 183
9.5   Questions to be asked when designing business models for
      responsible business 184
9.6   Feedback loops in the TOMS business model activity system 185
9.7   Responsible business model blank canvas 192

10.1 Mapping a responsible management subsystem 198
10.2 Mainstream management functions in a company's value chain 199

11.1 Applying the "four Ps" to LOHAS and BoP markets 216

12.1 Classifications of hard law relevant to responsible management 224
12.2 Basic elements of the sustainability accounting process 226
12.3 Responsible management topics throughout the financial
      management process 230
12.4 Elements of organizational structure 232
12.5 Symbiosis of human resources and responsible business 236
12.6 Simplified employee life-cycle 236

13.1 Sustainable supply chain management model 247

15.1 Stakeholder perceptions and subsequent outcomes 290

16.1 The sixth wave of innovation 300
16.2 Concepts of innovation covered in this chapter 301
16.3 How to become a serial management innovator? 307

17.1 Classic approaches to explaining human behavior 316
17.2 Kuznets curves and sustainable development 320
17.3 Sustainability of lifestyle and consumption styles 323
17.4 Individual activism throughout roles and vehicles 327

18.1 Sustainable business practice and overall output model 339
18.2 Profiles of leaders, managers, and entrepreneurs 345
18.3 Complementary change approaches 350
18.4 Categorizing projects by responsibility and sustainability criteria 351
18.5 Characteristics of entrepreneurship 353

19.1 Elements, interrelations, and embeddedness of the economic system ... 366
19.2 Approaches to system change for sustainability 371

19.3   Industrial ecosystem mechanisms 374
19.4   Resource cascading and revalorization 374
19.5   Policies and political actors for sustainable development 378
19.6   The Overton window for selected responsible business topics 382

Tables

1.1   Exemplary global development frameworks 9

2.1   Historic events in the relationship between business, society, and
       environment 43

3.1   UN Sustainable Development Goals 2015 62

5.1   Applying pluralistic ethical decision-making to the NoW case 92

6.1   Classifying value creation into internal, external, social,
       environmental, and economic.. 103
6.2   Elements and management instruments of typical responsible
       management activities 107
6.3   Types of organizational actor and their main characteristics 108
6.4   Typical stakeholders and their characteristics 110
6.5   Stakeholder categories 116
6.6   Typical impacts throughout the life-cycle 120

7.1   Overview of responsible business norms 142

9.1   Excerpt from Tacos de la Esquinita's responsible business portfolio 177
9.2   Integrating mainstream and responsible business across the
       strategic guidance instruments.. 180

10.1   Responsible management instruments used in a company's
        functions in order of appearance in this book... 201

11.1   Comparing strategic, operations, and production management 211
11.2   Operations approaches to responsible management................................. 213

14.1   Overview of responsibility communication formats 264
14.2   Stages of behavior change 273
14.3   Competences for responsible business 274
14.4   Types of cause-related marketing 276

15.1   Negative attributions to responsible business conduct 288

16.1   Typical innovations combining distinct purposes and objects 305

18.1   Barriers in the way of sustainable business 342

19.1   Prominent types of sustainable economic subsystem 372

Foreword to the first edition

Jonas Haertle, Head Principles for Responsible Management Education (PRME) Secretariat, UN Global Compact Office

Today, sustainability ranks high on the corporate agenda as an increasing number of executives around the world recognize the growing relevance and urgency of global environmental, social, and economic challenges. Regardless of size, location, or sector, businesses are looking beyond the traditional drivers of financial performance, seeing how sustainability issues can affect their bottom line. Market disturbances, civil unrest, or natural resource constraints can indeed have wide-ranging and material impacts. But sustainability issues are not only viewed from a risk management perspective. Increasingly, business leaders discover the tangible benefits and opportunities of greater sustainability.

With corporate sustainability becoming a strategic issue for companies, there also comes the demand for management education to adapt to this new reality. The Principles for Responsible Management Education (PRME), written in 2007 and now endorsed by over 400 business schools and management-related academic institutions from over 60 countries, serve as guidelines for management education providers to enhance curricula, pedagogy, research, and incentives to prepare organizational leaders who will balance economic and societal goals.

The book's important characteristics are its international perspective, featuring cases from countries all around the world, its strong theoretical basis, and the integration of sustainability, ethics, and responsibility topics. The book also covers a wide variety of tools for change on individual, company, and systemic levels. It provides a useful resource to support PRME signatory schools as well as other interested institutions.

Jonas Haertle
New York, March 27, 2012

Introduction to the second edition

Much has happened in the areas of responsible business and management since the first edition of this book was published in 2012. Relevant changes have happened not only regarding content, but also in terms of responsible management practice and educational methods.

New topics

In terms of the **responsible business and management topics**, we have updated the book to include the most up-to-date material. Content added to the conceptual basis of this book includes a new chapter on innovation, a new section on business models, and an evidence-based management approach based on the planetary boundaries framework. Several responsible management norms have also changed since the first edition. We have included the new United Nations Sustainable Development Goals; a section on integrated reporting; and the new G4 sustainability reporting guidelines.

From education to responsible management learning

When it comes to **responsible management practice**, we have observed that an increasing number of executives learn about responsible business and management on the job. We have encountered hardly any managers who have had a formal education on how to manage sustainability, responsibility, and ethically. As a consequence, this book has been designed as a tool for responsible management learning, be it in an educational program or on the job. Materials for self-directed learning are scarce and often either shallow in their coverage, or inadequate in contents. This is why we have restructured this second edition as a textbook/handbook. The first edition of this book already featured highly practitioner-relevant contents, such as hands-on management process descriptions, responsible business norms and standards, and illustrative real-life cases.

New chapter structure

Additionally, we have now restructured the book by converting the often long and content-heavy chapters into shorter more easily accessible chapters, each centered on one specific topic. Several chapters have additional tools, such as the responsible management norm checklist or a blank responsible business model canvas, in their appendixes. The sections mirror important management tasks on the learning journey toward responsible business and management:

- Contextualizing
- Conceptualizing
- Managing
- Strategizing
- Implementing
- Communicating
- Innovating

We hope that this new structure makes the contents more accessible for both students using the book as a textbook, and executives using it as a handbook and resource for their respective learning journeys.

From knowledge to competence

In terms of the **development of educational methods** for responsible management education, it becomes increasingly clear that teaching knowledge is of limited effectiveness. It does not lead to the type of resourceful and competent responsible manager we need, to make the transition toward sustainable, responsible, and ethical business happen. This has led to the development of an increasing appreciation of a "competence-based approach" to responsible management education (Laasch, 2014). Such an approach aims to actively go beyond teaching domain knowledge, and toward facilitating learning across the sub-competence areas of knowing, thinking, doing, relating, and being. In this second edition we have acknowledged both this shift in educational method and the need for self-directed, on-the-job learning materials mentioned above. Accordingly, each chapter in this book has a new exercises section with at least one task for training each of these five competence areas. Each exercise includes a feedback and self-assessment section in order for students, executives, and educators alike to check progress toward mastering responsible management, and toward becoming a responsible manager.

Using the book

A word of caution: the end-of-chapter exercises might look quite short and "harmless." However, most of them require a quite extensive self-coordinated effort and self-organization. Most exercises are problem-based and with a loose structure. Some of them are designed to be completed outside your comfort zone, to facilitate truly transformative learning. If you are an educator, it is up to you to add additional material or other preparatory elements, or to customize the exercises to make them fit your course. If you are a learner, please make sure you find the right balance between accepting a challenge and not going too far out of your comfort zone.

So how to make best use of this book? If you are an executive, we would propose you start with the section of the book that most suits your current need in responsible management learning. For instance, if you are currently immersed in a strategic task, the strategizing section might be most relevant. If you are involved in effecting change for responsible business, the change section makes sense. If you are an educator using this book as a textbook for your course, you might want to pick the most relevant chapters based on your course description. You might also want to review and possibly customize some of the end-of-chapter exercises to achieve a perfect fit. If you are a student, you have probably been told which parts of the book you are meant to cover. However, please do not let this fact keep you from browsing through the rest of the book. There are many things in here that you might find exciting, and you might even find that some of the exercises are quite fun!

Responsible business for sustainable development: our normative assemblage

"**Responsible business for sustainable development,**" the underlying theme of this second edition, reflects a strong normative orientation that is carried through the whole book. Responsible business and management, as framed here, ought to lead to sustainable business, and ultimately to sustainable development. We are well aware that this "ought" is not a universal truth. For instance, in our other textbook we approached responsible management as a less narrowly focused umbrella term for management practices equally related to sustainability, responsibility, and ethics (Laasch and Conaway, 2015). However, in this book we have chosen the rather narrow normative framing of "responsible business for sustainable development" to create an educational material that equips future and current mangers with the responsible management competences necessary for tackling what is probably the greatest challenge of our age: sustainable development.

Using distinct, but not contradictory, definitions of responsible management might make us vulnerable to accusations of definitional ambiguity. In our defense, we have thought about this point very thoroughly. We believe that there are many viable combinations or assemblages of sustainability, responsibility, ethics, and other social cares and concerns. So there is no universal truth about the relationship between these topics and, vice versa, no single "true" definition.

A **normative assemblage** is a whole of heterogeneous normative elements (such as sustainability, responsibility, and ethics) reflecting the social cares and concerns of the actors involved in establishing the assemblage. The heterogeneous elements of such assemblages are typically aligned along powerful normative orientations, which in our case is sustainable development. Normative assemblages are context-bound, and also reflect the historical heritage of past developments. In the case of our book, "responsible business for sustainability," the context and history are a mixture of the increasing academic integration of these topics (Hansen *et al.*, 2014) and the growing practitioner tendency to frame corporate responsibility as an instrument to achieve corporate sustainability. This is also reflected in the fairly new ISO 26000 norm, which describes sustainable development as the goal of organizational responsibility. Also, the United Nations Global Compact and Principles for Responsible Management Education initiatives have focused on sustainable development as the overarching normative "ought" of responsibility. This is the context that makes corporate social responsibility for sustainable development (just) one (out of many) "true" normative assemblages. In another context, be it that of a particular company or culture, responsible business and management might mean something completely different—a different, but no less "true," normative assemblage.

We hope you will find good use for this book and that it may support you on your personal learning journey toward responsible business and management competence. Please feel free to let us know how it went, any time!

Oliver Laasch
Assistant Professor of Strategy,
The University of Nottingham, Ningbo, China
Founder, Center for Responsible Management Education
Roger N. Conaway
Professor of International Business, Tecnológico de
Monterrey, Mexico, Campus San Luis Potosí

A.
CONTEXTUALIZING

1
The state of the planet

What I hear in my dreams is generations in the future screaming back to us in time saying "What are you doing? Don't you see?"

Paul E. Stamets, biologist, in *The 11th Hour* (Conners and Conners Petersen, 2007)

What is a responsible business? A responsible business is one that assumes its responsibilities in the social, environmental, and economic dimensions, ultimately contributing to sustainable development. Sustainable development is a development that "meets the needs of the present without compromising the ability of future generations" (United Nations, 1987, p. 24), and it is intrinsically linked with the state of our planet. Only if we live on a planet that provides the full human population (society) with the necessary (environmental) resources through an economic system that does not deplete these resources will we reach sustainable development. Thus, responsible business is at the heart of the relationship between business, society, and environment. The concept of responsible business is aimed at achieving a positive fit: a situation where businesses achieve a positive impact on society, environment, and the overall economy, without forfeiting profitability. However, there may be companies that can never achieve such a positive fit, due to the underlying nature of their business. Some of the terms used in relation to responsible business are "business sustainability," "corporate citizenship," "corporate social responsibility," and "business ethics." These terms comprise necessary background theories to responsible business, which will be explained in more detail in subsequent chapters.

Responsible business pioneer

If there was a red carpet for responsible businesses, the company InterfaceFlor, with its founder the late Ray Anderson, would have walked it many times. As early as 1973 the company started producing carpet tiles, which had a considerably reduced environmental impact compared with the more usual one-piece carpets. Interface pioneered carpet recycling, is a leader in employee diversity programs, and has committed to reducing its environmental impact to—lo and behold!—zero by 2020. They even branded this goal as "Mission Zero." InterfaceFlor has also grown successfully as a business, fueled by the differentiation provided by its outstanding environmental performance in the carpet industry, which is generally characterized as an economic sector that is particularly harmful to the natural environment (InterfaceFlor, 2010, 2016).

The planet as a sick organism

The problems faced by humanity are hard to ignore, yet many people, organizations, and even governments do still ignore them to a certain extent. In the mid-1960s, former NASA scientist James Lovelock developed the Gaia Hypothesis, which sees Earth as a self-regulating organism, a sick organism which is trying to fight off a harmful parasite: humankind (Lovelock, 1979, 2006). Lovelock's theory of considering Earth, or Gaia (Gaia was the ancient Greek Earth goddess), as a living organism has been questioned; the more conventional perspective of Earth as an imbalanced system of environmental, social, and economic subsystems is possibly more helpful in explaining today's issues and crisis-stricken planet. Issues such as global warming, poverty, and the water and food crises are highly interlinked and, therefore, more difficult to solve. This section presents an overview of the various social, environmental, and economic issues, or symptoms, of the Earth crisis. This understanding of the state of the Earth will provide a sound basis for appreciating

Human climate relicts

Climate relicts are small populations of species that survived past eras of climate change in geographic pockets, protecting them from the hardships of changing conditions (Zimmer, 2011). Human beings might become the next climate relicts. In *The Vanishing Face of Gaia: A Final Warning*, Lovelock (2009) makes the case for the human population surviving climate change in pockets, such as in some parts of Canada. Human beings might also have the ability to create human-made climate pockets.

what responsible business should contribute to improving the health of the planet and the wellbeing of the people living on it.

We often hear the phrase "saving the planet." However, whom we are really trying to save is us, humanity. This concern is reflected in the very first definition of sustainable development: a development that "meets the needs of the present without compromising the ability of future generations to meet their own needs" (United Nations, 1987, p. 24). Sustainable development aims to preserve the planet, not primarily for the sake of itself, but for the sake of future generations to come.

The economy–society–environment system

The issues and crises described here should not be limited to just one of the three dimensions of society, environment, or economy. For instance, many people tend to see poverty as a purely social problem, but there are inherent connections to environmental factors as well. On the one hand, the root and very definition of poverty, the absence of wealth or money, reveals the economic component of the issue. Programs tackling poverty, therefore, often have as many economic components (micro-entrepreneurship, financial support, etc.) as they have social components (health, nutrition, education). On the other hand, while the socio-economic link seems more obvious, the link to the environmental dimension is nonetheless important. The World Bank (2001), in its document describing its environmental strategy, extensively illustrates the dynamics of environment and poverty. Deteriorating environmental conditions tend to negatively affect the poor overproportionately. People in poorer populations often earn their livelihoods in direct interaction with ecosystems, such as by working in food industries, such as fishery and agriculture. The poor are often more vulnerable to natural disasters, such as drought, hurricanes, and floods, which can often be related to environmental degradation.

Cooking up diseases

Increased temperatures mean that people are more likely to get sick. High temperatures cause an increase in parasites, bacteria, and viruses. The changing weather stimulates what were once season-specific diseases to occur at any time of the year (Vanguardia, 2011).

Economy and society

The relationship between economy and society is laden with conflicts, but it also has enormous benefits for both sides. The economic system relies on society for production activities. On the other hand, society fuels the economy with purchasing power.

Economic activity has immense effects on society. Economic growth, when distributed equally, leads to increased welfare and prosperity. The economy, single industries, or companies can also have negative effects on society. For example, an economic system has an inherent tendency to increase consumer behavior by massive marketing efforts. There is criticism of the pattern of unnecessary consumption, which creates artificial and often destructive wants, which distract from society's real needs. Secondary effects of economic activity on the natural environment often ultimately negatively impact on society. A notable example is the negative health effect of air pollution, which often affects heavily industrialized areas.

Economy and environment

Natural resources, such as oil, ore, minerals, water, timber, plants, and animals, underpin the most basic level of economic activity. Without natural resources, economic activity would stop. Throughout the history of modern economic activity, natural resources have been over-used. An interesting example is given by the book *The Last Hours of Ancient Sunlight* (Hartman, 2001), which explains how the economic system is based on unsustainably using up "ancient sunlight" in the form of fossil fuels, such as coal and petroleum, which were formed by solar energy millions of years ago. Economic activity is increasingly shifting from nonrenewable to renewable sources of energy and raw material. The costs of switching to a low-carbon economy are estimated to be much lower (1–2% of the annual world GDP) than the costs caused by the consequences of continuing with the current CO_2 production patterns (5–20% of the annual world GDP) and further fueling climate change (Stern, 2006).

However, the economy is exerting a damaging influence on the world's natural environment. The continued use of limited natural resources and the creation of emissions and waste put enormous strain on the world's ecosphere. Increasingly, though, it has been suggested that economic activity must not always result in a negative environmental impact. For instance, the movements of environmental entrepreneurship and natural capitalism aim to create a basis for economic activity with added value for the environment (Hawken *et al.*, 1999). Secondary effects of the economy on the environment include the environmental impact of society's consumption of goods and services produced by economic systems.

Society and environment

Strictly speaking, the global human society is just one more species in the community of living things forming the world's biosphere. Nevertheless, the impact of society on the environment by far exceeds the impact of any other species that has ever lived on the planet. The reasons are linked to both quantity and quality of human subsistence. Fueled by exploitative production methods and techno-logical progress, the quantity of human beings living on Earth has by far exceeded the planet's biological carrying capacity. The equivalent of 1.5 Earths was needed to sustainably provide enough space for the global population in 2007. It is esti-mated that by 2050 this number will increase to two Earths (WWF, 2010), with the global population predicted to rise to over 10 billion.

Behavior patterns harmful to the natural environment are also qualitatively unsustainable. Especially in fully economically developed countries, the amount of natural resources being consumed to sustain these developed societies by far exceeds basic necessities. Developing countries, with a growing middle class, follow suit in copying the unsustainable behavior patterns of developed coun-tries. Environmental awareness, spirituality, and connection to living things are often replaced by consumerist preferences.

Future consumption heavyweights

Due to their impressive quantitative growth, China and India are at the center of both economists' and sustainability scholars' attention. The qualitative development might even matter more than the mere population growth. For instance, India expects its middle class to grow from 5% to 40% of the population, becoming the world's fifth-largest consumer economy by 2025 (Ablett *et al.*, 2007).

The natural environment provides many services to society. The Millennium Ecosystem Assessment (MA) (2005) gives an extensive overview of how human wellbeing depends on the integrity of biomes, the major types of ecosystem that constitute the planet's ecosphere. Ecosystems influence human beings by providing a wide variety of ecosystem services. The four main categories of ecosystem services as drafted by the MA are:

1. **Provisioning services:** providing food, water, timber, fiber, etc.
2. **Regulating services:** regulating climate, floods, disease, wastes, water quality, etc.
3. **Cultural services:** influencing culture by providing recreational, aesthetic, and spiritual benefits, etc.
4. **Supporting services:** providing necessary support for the other three catego-ries, for example soil formation, photosynthesis, nutrient cycling, etc.

An evaluation of the overall value of ecosystem services, conducted as early as 1987, estimated that the planet's 16 main ecosystems provide services with an average annual value of US$33 trillion to society and the economy. At that time, the global GDP was a mere US$18 trillion (Costanza *et al.*, 1997). Comparing these two facts, one easily comes to the conclusion that our society and the economic system providing the goods and services to satisfy society's need are highly inef-ficient. For every dollar of purchasing power created, two dollars of ecosystem services are used. Another eye-opening interpretation of these numbers is that ecosystems are actually providing more value to society than the economy does. The logical question is: Why is society supporting growth of the economy and destroying the basis for the larger value created by the natural environment?

Probably the most complete description of how "successful" we as humanity have been in destroying our own habitat comes from the thinking around "planetary boundaries" (Rockström et al., 2009). A multidisciplinary team of scientists outlined the "safe operating space for humanity" by looking at the critical values that our Earth system should not exceed for humanity to be able to live on Earth in the long run. These planetary boundaries were expressed in ten quantified thresholds:

1. Climate change
2. Rate of biodiversity loss
3. Nitrogen cycle (part of a boundary with the phosphorus cycle)
4. Phosphorus cycle (part of a boundary with the nitrogen cycle)
5. Stratospheric ozone depletion
6. Ocean acidification
7. Global fresh water use
8. Change in land use
9. Atmospheric aerosol loading
10. Chemical pollution

The planet's most pressing issues and crises

As depicted in Table 1.1, many frameworks have been developed to describe, control, and solve the global social, environmental, and economic issues and crises. The United Nations Sustainable Development Goals are a list of 17 goals reflecting areas of critical importance for humanity and the planet. Agenda 21 tackles the problems from a more generalized perspective, focusing on the necessary actions to ensure global sustainability (United Nations, 2011a). The World Development Indicators, published annually by the World Bank, provide an extensive quantitative description of the state of the world (World Bank, 2016). "The state of the world" is also the title of the annual collection of articles on the changing topic of sustainable development issued by the Worldwatch Institute (Worldwatch Institute, 2016).

A difficult aspect of the issues and crises faced by the world is their highly complex structure, so targeting economic, social, and environmental development separately is an easy mistake. However, the complex structure of the world's mega-issues has five crucial characteristics:

Table 1.1: Exemplary global development frameworks

Framework	Institution	Issues covered
Sustainable Development Goals	United Nations	1. Poverty 2. Hunger and food security 3. Health 4. Education 5. Gender equality and women's empowerment 6. Water and sanitation 7. Energy 8. Economic growth 9. Infrastructure, industrialization 10. Inequality 11. Cities 12. Sustainable consumption and production 13. Climate change 14. Oceans 15. Biodiversity, forests, deforestation 16. Peace and justice 17. Partnerships
World Development Indicators	World Bank	**People:** e.g., wealth and consumption distribution, education, nutrition, health, labor **Environment:** e.g., agriculture, deforestation, biodiversity, air pollution, energy, water **Economy:** e.g., economic output, sectoral structure (manufacturing, commerce, services), consumption and investment, monetary indicators **States and markets:** e.g., business environment, stock market, tax policies, public services (military, transport, communication) **Global links:** e.g., trade, debt, commodities, financial flows, development aid, travel and tourism
Agenda 21	United Nations	1. Social and economic dimensions 2. Conservation and management of resources for development 3. Strengthening the role of major groups 4. Means of implementation

1. **Interlinked:** issues are mutually interlinked and reinforcing
2. **Systemic:** issues are not isolated incidents, but rather based on systemic flaws in the relationship between business, society, and environment
3. **Global:** issues cannot be isolated locally, but are global in both impact and potential solutions
4. **Resilient:** issues have been threatening and known for a considerable amount of time, but remained strong in spite of considerable solution efforts
5. **Convergent:** joint issues development moving toward a planetary mega-crisis, a showdown

As early as 1989, the Brundtland report by the World Commission on Environment and Development used the image of interlocked crises to create awareness of the unique threatening structure of global issues:

> ... the various global "crises" that have seized public concern, particularly over the past decade. These are not separate crises: an environmental crisis, a development crisis, an energy crisis: they are all one. (United Nations, 1987, p. 20)

In order to achieve holistic, sustainable development, it is crucial to understand the main global issues and their mutual interconnectedness. Some of the most critical global issues and crises are described in Figure 1.1. Of course, such a summary can only provide a basic, and inevitably fragmentary, working knowledge of the most important challenges faced by humanity. Each topic constitutes an extensive domain of specialized knowledge acquired by managers who want to contribute to the mitigation and solution of the respective issue to be addressed by responsible business conduct: see this chapter's appendix for more information.

Figure 1.1: Planetary mega-issues overview

I. Demographics	II. Poverty	III. Environment	IV. Resources	V. Economic & political system
• Overpopulation • Educational challenges • Cultural differences	• Extreme poverty • Extreme hunger • Human health • Global pandemics	• Climate change • Waste disposal • Biodiversity loss • Ocean crisis • Natural disasters	• Energy crisis • World water crisis • Food insecurity • Soil loss and desertification	• Economic system flaws • Wealth distribution • Globalization and trade system issues • Corruption

Exercises

Know

Use the multiple choice questions below to test your knowledge. Answers may be right or wrong and there are up to four right or wrong answers per question:

1. Responsible business …

    a. … aims for a positive fit, a situation achieving positive social and environmental impact. If necessary, a business may have to accept that achieving this positive impact may not be profitable.
    b. … is related to terms such as corporate citizenship and business ethics.
    c. … aims to contribute to sustainable development.
    d. … aims to manage the relationship between business, society, and environment.

2. The most severe issues and crises threatening life on Planet Earth …

    a. … are described in many frameworks such as the Sustainable Development Goals (SDGs) and the World Development Indicators (WDI).
    b. … should be solved one by one.
    c. … include poverty as one of the typical resource issues.

3. The Gaia Hypothesis …

    a. … considers Earth as an imbalanced mother system of environmental, social and economic subsystems.
    b. … blames missing governmental inventions as the main cause of the Gaia phenomenon.
    c. … was developed by the ancient Greek philosopher Plato. He referred to Gaia, the ancient Greek Earth goddess.
    d. … has been proven wrong.

B. Think

Look at this chapter's appendix, which illustrates a set of planetary mega-issues in depth. Imagine a (feasible) scenario, a possible chain of events, where issues interact in a way that immediately threatens the survival of humanity on Planet Earth.

C. Do

Think about one small thing you could do to stop being part of the problem and start being part of the solution to one of the planetary mega-issues. Then do it!

D. Relate

Have a conversation with someone on one of the issues illustrated in this chapter's appendix. Try to find out together what should be done to solve the issue in question. Document the position of your conversation partner(s).

E. Be

Watch a movie on the state of the planet such as *The 11th Hour* or *An Inconvenient Truth*. Write a short essay on how what you see relates to you and how it makes you feel.

Feedback

A. Know

Question 1

a. Right: positive fit aims to achieve a positive social, environmental, and economic system impact while being profitable. However, there may be companies that can never achieve such a positive fit, due to the underlying nature of their business.

b. Right: these terms are important background theories of responsible business.

c. Right: the ultimate purpose of responsible business as framed in the context of this book is to contribute to sustainable development by becoming a sustainable business.

d. Right: the paragraph describing responsible business describes it as having the business–society–environment relationship at its heart.

Question 2

a. Right: SDG and WDI are frameworks for the description of the worldwide issues and crises.

b. Wrong: due to their interlinked structure, these issues and crises cannot be solved one by one.

c. Wrong: in this chapter's appendix, poverty has been included under "poverty issues."

Question 3

a. Right: the Gaia Hypothesis describes the Earth as a sick mother system or organism.

b. Wrong: the Gaia Hypothesis blames human society in general.

c. Wrong: although the word "Gaia" does come from ancient Greek, Plato was not involved in the development of the hypothesis referring to the sickening planet. The Gaia Hypothesis was developed by the scientists Lovelock and Margulis in the mid-1960s.

d. Wrong: the Gaia Hypothesis has not been proven wrong, but contested and complemented by other systemic approaches to the Earth system.

B. Think

Level	Anticipatory thinking	Notes
+	Feasible scenario of multiple issues described reveals a profound level of anticipatory thinking	
=	Feasible scenario involving multiple issues	
–	No scenario of interacting issues has been developed, or the scenario is not feasible, either in terms of its threat-evoking mechanisms, or in terms of its potential to wipe out humanity	

C. Do

Level	Taking initiative	Notes
+	Initiative taken which is highly relevant to the mitigation of the issue: "If everyone would do this, the issue would be solved"	
=	Initiative taken, but it is not very relevant to the issue chosen	
–	No initiative taken	

D. Relate

Level	Collaborative problem-solving	Notes
+	A solution has been developed based on a process that involves meaningful input from both conversation partners	
=	A solution has been developed, but it is mainly based on one dominant person's input	
–	Conversation has not happened or no solution to the problem has been achieved	

E. Be

Level	Emotional awareness	Notes
+	Profound description of one's emotions regarding the state of the planet	
=	Basic awareness of one's emotions regarding the state of the planet	
−	No or little insight into one's emotions regarding the state of the planet	

Appendix

1. Demographic Issues

Overpopulation

- **Not anymore, Asia.** A region other than the huge East has for the first time taken the lead in population growth. By 2050 it is estimated that 25.5% of the world population will live in Africa, a continent where 42.7% of the population subsists on less than US$1.25 per day.
  https://esa.un.org/unpd/wpp/Publications/Files/Key_Findings_WPP_2015.pdf
  http://www.afdb.org/fileadmin/uploads/afdb/Documents/Publications/Working_Paper_223_
  -_Eliminating_Extreme_Poverty_in_Africa_Trends_Policies_and_the_Role_of_International_
  Organizations.pdf

- **FYI.** Only nine countries will account for half of the world's population growth (in descending order): India, Nigeria, Pakistan, the Democratic Republic of the Congo, Ethiopia, the United Republic of Tanzania, the U.S.A., Indonesia, and Uganda.
  https://esa.un.org/unpd/wpp/Publications/Files/Key_Findings_WPP_2015.pdf

- **Vintage is trendy.** By 2050 the world population will grow by 2.376 billion to reach a total of 9.725 billion people. Of this increase, 46.2% will be 60 years old or more.
  http://www.un.org/en/development/desa/population/publications/pdf/popfacts/PopFacts_
  2014-4Rev1.pdf
  https://esa.un.org/unpd/wpp/Publications/Files/Key_Findings_WPP_2015.pdf

- **XXL.** In 2014, more people (54%) already lived in the urban areas of the world, making the challenges of sustainable development even more tangible. Tokyo will for some time remain the most populous city, with 38 million inhabitants (equivalent to the total population of Poland).
  https://esa.un.org/unpd/wup/Publications/Files/WUP2014-Highlights.pdf
  http://data.worldbank.org/indicator/SP.POP.TOTL

Educational challenges

- **Stop the boom.** Two years after the start of the civil war in Syria, the out-of-school population rose from 300,000 to 1.8 million (39.48% of children and adolescents). Syria had enjoyed universal primary enrollment since 2000.
  http://www.uis.unesco.org/Education/Documents/fs-31-out-of-school-children-en.pdf

- **Counter clockwise.** There are 2.4 million more children out of school since 2010. Half of the 59 million children that lack primary education in the world live in sub-Saharan Africa.
  http://www.uis.unesco.org/Education/Documents/fs-31-out-of-school-children-en.pdf

- **Sustainable struggle.** In order to achieve universal primary enrollment by 2030, 25.8 million teachers would need to be recruited (3.2 million alone for new positions). Furthermore, US$40 billion of funding would be required, meaning donors would have to increase their support by 600%.
  http://www.uis.unesco.org/Education/Documents/fs-31-out-of-school-children-en.pdf
  http://www.uis.unesco.org/Education/Documents/fs33-2015-teachers.pdf

Cultural and ethnic issues

- **The root cause.** Ethnic conflicts in Africa have been well documented in Rwanda, the Democratic Republic of the Congo, Burundi, Uganda, Chad, and Nigeria. These countries were all in the bottom 30 of the world ranking for GDP per capita in 2014.
  http://www2.hu-berlin.de/transcience/Vol6_No2_26_37.pdf

- **Broadening the definition of homeless.** In 2014, the number of refugees was four times that of the previous year, and 51% of the 19.5 million in total were under 18 years old. Three countries generated 53% of the world's refugees: Syria, Afghanistan, and Somalia.
http://www.unhcr.org/figures-at-a-glance.html
http://www.unhcr.org/news/latest/2015/6/558193896/worldwide-displacement-hits-all-time
-high-war-persecution-increase.html

- **A Western problem.** Race was the most frequent source of job discrimination allegations in 2015 in the U.S.A. Race (47%), religion (18.6%), and sexual orientation (18.6%) were the most frequent motives for assaults perpetrated in the U.S.A. in 2014.
https://www.eeoc.gov/eeoc/statistics/enforcement/charges.cfm
https://www.fbi.gov/news/stories/2015/november/latest-hate-crime-statistics-available

2. Poverty issues

Extreme poverty

- **Not enough incentives.** In developing countries, 30% of the workforce (about 839 million people) survives on US$1.25–2.00 per day; 14.7% of those who live on US$1.25 or less per day are actually engaged in a wage-based job.
http://www.ilo.org/wcmsp5/groups/public/---dgreports/---dcomm/documents/publication/
wcms_243961.pdf

- **Less poor yet severe.** In 2015, the poor population decreased by 2.4 million compared with 2010. There is still a long way to go when countries in Africa have over 60% of their population in severe poverty.
http://hdr.undp.org/sites/default/files/2015_human_development_report.pdf

- **Accuracy is not what matters.** In line with the World Bank's forecast in 2015, extreme poverty almost "fell below 10% for the first time" with 800 million living in extreme poverty: that's only 5 million more than the 795 million undernourished people in the world.
http://www.worldbank.org/en/news/press-release/2015/10/04/world-bank-forecasts-global
-poverty-to-fall-below-10-for-first-time-major-hurdles-remain-in-goal-to-end-poverty-by-2030

Extreme hunger

- **The importance of deadlines.** In 1996, the World Food Summit expected to the number of undernourished people to halve from 991 to 495 million by 2015, yet 20 years later the figure remains 795 million, including 161 million children under the age of five. In terms of infant mortality, 45% is caused by poor nutrition.
http://www.fao.org/3/a4ef2d16-70a7-460a-a9ac-2a65a533269a/i4646e.pdf
http://www.un.org/millenniumgoals/2014%20MDG%20report/MDG%202014%20English%20
web.pdf

- **Wrong delivery address.** In 2015, almost 13% of the population of developing countries was undernourished, while 33% of the food produced worldwide went to waste. Nearly 115 kg/year is estimated to be wasted per capita in Europe and North America alone.
http://www.fao.org/docrep/014/mb060e/mb060e00.pdf
https://www.wfp.org/hunger/stats

- **Eat everything on your plate, including the ugly carrot.** Besides the food loss that takes place before human consumption, esthetics may account for a further 25–30% of waste when vegetables are discarded if they are blemished or the wrong length or shape.
http://www.fao.org/docrep/014/mb060e/mb060e00.pdf

Human health issues

- **Polluted air causes deaths and costs money.** In 2012 alone, 6,974,000 deaths related to toxicity were registered, of which 73% occurred in South-East Asia and the western Pacific region. In 2014 the monetary impact of air pollution was US$3.5 trillion annually.
  http://www.unep.org/yearbook/2014/PDF/chapt7.pdf

- **A chameleonic condition.** Hidden hunger is highly present in all regions of the world. Micronutrient deficiency affected 2 billion people worldwide in 2015, both under- and overweight, and made children and pregnant women in sub-Saharan Africa and South Asia especially vulnerable. The loss in economic productivity is estimated to be as much as US$2.1 trillion.
  https://www.ifpri.org/sites/default/files/ghi/2014/feature_1818.html

- **To be born in the darkness.** The poorest 20% of the world's population has only a 49% service coverage for maternal and child health. In addition, health is jeopardized by the condition of health facilities: in the Democratic Republic of the Congo, for instance, 91% of health facilities lack a power source and 63% have no improved water source.
  http://apps.who.int/iris/bitstream/10665/200009/1/9789241565110_eng.pdf
  http://apps.who.int/iris/bitstream/10665/85761/2/9789240690837_eng.pdf

Global pandemics

- **The privilege of prevention.** Over 60% of annual deaths were caused by noncommunicable (chronic) diseases in 2015. This group of diseases, which includes cardiovascular and chronic respiratory conditions, cancer, and diabetes, can be significantly reduced with management but kills some 29 million people a year in low- and middle-income countries.
  http://www.who.int/features/factfiles/noncommunicable_diseases/en/

- **The future of zoonoses.** The latest outbreak of mosquito-borne disease, in the form of the Zika virus, has alerted the world to preparing to face a future pandemic. Indeed, 75% of diseases in the 21st century are zoonotic (communicated from animals to humans): 60 countries and territories have mosquito-borne transmission; and 11,310 out of the 28,616 people infected with Ebola had died by 2015.
  https://www.usaid.gov/news-information/fact-sheets/emerging-pandemic-threats-program
  http://www.who.int/csr/disease/ebola/en/
  http://www.who.int/emergencies/zika-virus/en/

- **Consciousness matters.** Some 37 million people live with HIV; 36.85% of those affected received treatment in 2015 compared with 2.16% in 2003, saving 7.6 million lives. Two-thirds of new infections occur in sub-Saharan Africa where one in 20 adults has the virus.
  http://www.who.int/topics/millennium_development_goals/diseases/en/
  http://www.un.org/millenniumgoals/2015_MDG_Report/pdf/MDG%202015%20rev%20 (July%201).pdf

- **It's getting hotter.** Climate change will mean another risk to health in the coming years with 250,000 additional deaths predicted by 2030, mostly due to diarrhea and malaria; 250 million people in Africa will be exposed to water stress, and harvests fed by rain might be halved by 2020.
  http://hdr.undp.org/sites/default/files/2015_human_development_report.pdf

3. Environmental threats and degradation

Climate change

- **2016: a record year ...** For the first time since worldwide records began, the CO_2 ppm monthly indicator reached 404.36 in May 2016, and Mexico City registered the most dangerous air quality for 14 years when the Air Quality Metropolitan Index, which measures O_3, SO_2, NO_2, CO, and small particulates, registered 203 on a >200 point scale—it only requires 150 points to trigger a Climate Contingency Phase I alert.
  http://climate.nasa.gov/vital-signs/carbon-dioxide
  http://www.aire.cdmx.gob.mx/default.php?opc='ZaBhnml='&dc=Zw==

- **Beyond our expectations.** Not only do mankind's current consumption levels in 2016 require 1 ha per capita more than the Earth's actual capacity for production and disposal, but 85% of the world's population lives in a country that lacks the regenerative capacity for its usage level of natural resources.
  http://www.footprintnetwork.org/ar/index.php/GFN/page/living_planet_report_2014_facts/
  http://awsassets.panda.org/downloads/wwf_lpr2014_low_res_full_report.pdf

- **Hot wheels.** The expectation that automobile usage will triple by 2050 has a number of implications. On the one hand, transport will be responsible for 57% of global CO_2 emissions by that time. On the other, both sea and air transport have the potential to be 75% and 100% more fuel-efficient respectively, with ships alone saving up to 255 million tonnes of carbon emissions. Sustainability will also be profitable, as 3.8 trillion jobs could be created by an increase in low-emission vehicle manufacturing, enough to provide employment to just over one-third of the world's population in 2050.
  http://ee.ricardo.com/cms/assets/Uploads/DFID-Low-carbon-summary-sheets/DFID_low_carbon_development_transport.pdf

Waste disposal

- **A 4 billion tonne trash can, please.** it is estimated that 3 billion people lack the means of proper waste disposal, meaning that less than 50% of solid waste is properly disposed of. Regionally, Africa has the poorest level of waste collection, as low as 25% in some countries.
  http://www.unep.org/ietc/Portals/136/Publications/Waste%20Management/GWMO%20report/GWMO_report.pdf

- **You didn't watch it on the news.** Screens were the largest single-item group of electronic waste produced in 2014 (15%) with a total of 41.8 million tonnes, 16 million tonnes of which were generated in Asia. Europe continues to have the highest per capita waste with 15.6 kg/person, compared with 1.7 kg/person in Africa.
  http://www.unep.org/ietc/Portals/136/Publications/Waste%20Management/GWMO%20report/GWMO_report.pdf

- **Forever and ever.** Plastic represents a major threat for the oceans. In 2014, some 200 species were observed to suffer from entanglement in marine debris. Even if not physically impaired, other marine species suffer from eating microplastic particles. With a current production of 299 million tonnes in 2013, recycling plastic would generate a revenue of US$12.7 billion; it currently represents a US$13 billion natural capital cost annually.
  http://www.unep.org/ietc/Portals/136/Publications/Waste%20Management/GWMO%20report/GWMO_report.pdf

Biodiversity loss

- **Darwin knows best.** The current levels of greenhouse gases in the atmosphere are reshaping ecosystems and habitats for all species. Although animals have been noted to change their behavior and geographic range in response, it is estimated that some species, such as rodents and primates, will not move fast enough to keep up with the effects of climate change by the end of the century.
http://awsassets.panda.org/downloads/wwf_lpr2014_low_res_full_report.pdf

- **Get your waterproof camera ready.** In 2014, it was reported that the populations of 3,038 species of mammals, birds, reptiles, amphibians, and fish had halved since the 1970s. Only 24% of the population remains for fish and other marine species.
http://awsassets.panda.org/downloads/wwf_lpr2014_low_res_full_report.pdf

- **Missing!** In the same report, South America registered the worst biodiversity loss both on land and in the sea, with 56% of its animal population having disappeared. Exploitation (37%) and habit degradation/change (31.4%) were the main causes.
http://awsassets.panda.org/downloads/wwf_lpr2014_low_res_full_report.pdf

Ocean crisis

- **Floating graves.** Since 1985, some water zones have been detected around the world with an oxygen level of less than 2 mg/liter, so low that virtually no species can survive. By 2015, the total surface area of the 500 dead zones registered around the world had increased to 245,000 km^2, the size of the U.K.

- **Things are getting spicy.** Over the past 200 years, the acidity level of the oceans has increased by 30%; by 2100, this rate of acidification is expected to rise to 150%. In the best-case scenario, only a third of coral reefs will survive the severe damage.
https://www.iaea.org/ocean-acidification/download/8%20June%202015/CSM-Ocean_Acidification_Web.pdf
http://awsassets.panda.org/downloads/wwf_lpr2014_low_res_full_report.pdf

- **The luxury of tuna.** Fishing, which contributes US$274 billion to GDP annually, is the industry most threatened by climate change, due to rising temperatures, acidification, overexploitation, and droughts. This is particularly the case in developing countries, where the greatest biodiversity loss is occurring and where 96% of those involved in fishing live.
http://www.fao.org/3/bbd8940c-825d-4eea-9192-701ea41df9d8/i4398e.pdf
https://www.iaea.org/ocean-acidification/download/8%20June%202015/CSM-Ocean_Acidification_Web.pdf

Natural disasters

- **Nature in its own language.** Extreme weather conditions overtake the natural disaster ranking from 2005 to 2014 by a 6:10 ratio. Floods alone account for half the total disasters registered and, in 2014 alone, 87% of disasters were climate-related.
https://www.unisdr.org/we/inform/disaster-statistics

- **You could make something with that sum.** The total economic loss from 2005 to 2014 due to natural disasters was US$1.4 trillion, equal to ten years' budget cuts by the U.S. government. The most expensive year was 2011, which cost US$364 billion.
https://www.unisdr.org/we/inform/disaster-statistics
http://www.ronjohnson.senate.gov/public/_cache/files/b61bc3d5-a0e9-4d48-ba25-17d4b1f238b6/1.4trillioninsavings.pdf

4. Resource issues

Energy crisis

- **One step closer.** Between 2010 and 2015, 400 million people gained access to electricity. However encouraging this number is, there is still an urgent need to accelerate worldwide coverage because 1.1 billion people still rely on wood, coal, charcoal, or animal waste to obtain energy for their basic needs, with all the health risks such fuels imply.
  http://blogs.worldbank.org/opendata/sustainable-development-and-demand-energy

- **Take a deep breath, or not.** Some 81% of the world's energy use still depends on fossil fuels. Renewable energy consumption has decreased in comparison to 2000 but only in developing countries: for example, renewable energy only accounts for a meager 2% of consumption in the Middle East and North Africa.
  http://blogs.worldbank.org/opendata/sustainable-development-and-demand-energy

- **To move lighter.** Current oil prices are delaying the transition to sustainable energy as the return on investment takes longer if vehicles and industries continue to run on cheap fuel. Projections to 2040 estimate that efficiency improvements could be made to the value of US$800 billion.
  https://www.iea.org/Textbase/npsum/WEO2015SUM.pdf

World water crisis

- **Not for everyone.** Safe drinking water coverage has reached 96% and 84% in urban and rural communities respectively. Yet 663 million people still relied on unimproved sources of drinking water in 2015. A major part of the unpaid work done by women is the 200 million hours a day spent in Africa collecting water.
  http://hdr.undp.org/sites/default/files/2015_human_development_report.pdf

- **For cleaner cities.** Adequate sanitation is a further goal to be achieved, with 2.4 billion people currently lacking access. In slums alone, 700 million people use unimproved sanitation facilities. With a projected 40% growth in urban areas, health conditions in cities will be a major challenge.
  http://hdr.undp.org/sites/default/files/2015_human_development_report.pdf

- **Not our imagination.** Water crisis was identified as the #1 threat to business and society at the 2015 World Economic Forum. By 2050, about 40% of the population (some 4 billion) will experience water stress. Without proper awareness, people will not appreciate the real value of water if subsidies mean it is sold at 7.3% of the production cost, as occurs in Saudi Arabia.
  http://www.siwi.org/wp-content/uploads/2015/09/2015-WWW-report-digital.pdf

Food insecurity

- **Out of league.** In territories where there are protracted crises, rates of malnutrition are 25% higher than in other developing countries. In 2016, 366 million people in 24 countries are expected to struggle with hunger crisis for longer than anticipated by the SDGs because of little or no government control. People in territories where there are protracted crises are "acutely vulnerable to death, disease and disruption of livelihoods."
  http://www.fao.org/3/a4ef2d16-70a7-460a-a9ac-2a65a533269a/i4646e.pdf

- **A country-size loss.** Europe's use of 25% extra cultivated land per capita, land-exhausting agricultural practices cannot have a good outcome. The volatility of food prices is a threat for practically all nations: African countries are the most vulnerable as, in 2016, poor people spend 50–80% of their income on food. If prices were to double, China would suffer an economic loss of US$161 billion, equal to the whole GDP of New Zealand.
  http://www.footprintnetwork.org/en/index.php/GFN/page/china_and_indias_gdp_will_be_hit_hardest_by_global_food_price_shock/

Soil loss and desertification

- **Você têm água?** A total of 849 million ha (similar to the entire surface area of Brazil) will be degraded by 2050. In the most optimistic of scenarios, the improvement of land practices could prevent only 319 million ha from loss of fertility.
http://www.unep.org/newscentre/default.aspx?DocumentID=2758&ArticleID=10697

- **A different kind of foe.** Up to 700 million people will be displaced by 2030 due to severe water scarcity; 14 times the number of climate refugees in 2010. Water (or the lack of it) nearly displaced as many people as armed conflict in 2015.
http://www.unccd.int/Lists/SiteDocumentLibrary/Publications/Desertification_The%20 invisible_frontline.pdf
http://www.unhcr.org/figures-at-a-glance.html

- **Tic toc.** Depending on how fast you read, in the time you go through this page 23 ha will be permanently damaged by drought or desertification (every 60 seconds).
http://www.un.org/sustainabledevelopment/biodiversity/

5. Economic and political system issues

Flaws in the economic system

- **Overshoot.** The world first started using more resources than were available in the 1970s, and the point in the year at which this happens occurs ever quicker. In 2015, Overshoot Day occurred on August 13, and in 2016 it was expected to happen on August 8; if business continues as usual, by 2030 the world will start consuming the following year's resources on June 28. Economic losses for the business externalities of the top 3,000 companies account for 4% of the world GDP, or US$2.1 trillion; by 2050, resource degradation, pollution, greenhouse emissions, and waste will cost US$28.6 trillion every year.
http://www.footprintnetwork.org/en/index.php/GFN/page/earth_overshoot_day_2015_ press_release/
http://awsassets.panda.org/downloads/wwf_lpr2014_low_res_full_report.pdf

- **When it is not enough.** One aspect of the current economic system—consumerism— is increasingly harshly criticized. A national survey by the German Environment Agency revealed that the number of domestic appliances and gadgets being replaced during the first five years of use rose from 7% to 13% in 2013. The survey also showed that, in 2012, 60% of discarded televisions were still functional. Planned obsolescence is a concept that, among other endangering factors, is analyzed in relation to the fashion industry in the 2015 documentary *The True Cost* (https://www.youtube.com/watch?v=OaGp5_Sfbss).
http://www.umweltbundesamt.de/en/press/pressinformation/obsolescence-fact-check

- **Speaking of competitiveness.** More energy-efficient use and a reduction in consumption of oil-intensive energy are the main reasons behind the outstanding 50% reduction in oil dependence by the world GDP in 2015. However, in the same year coal and oil received the highest percentages of subsidies—3.9 and 1.8% of the world's GDP respectively compared with 0.6% for natural gas—making it hard for sustainable energy sources to achieve a global presence in the short term.
https://www.imf.org/external/pubs/ft/wp/2015/wp15105.pdf

Wealth inequalities

- **The oldest inequality.** Opportunity cost is the translation into monetary terms of certain conditions that prevent a group of individuals from pursuing a certain activity. Wealth inequality is one of the most important, as well as gender discrimination. The misuse of economic potential in the female population of developing countries is a particular topic of discussion. For example, if women were given the same access to agricultural resources as men, the number of hungry people in the world could be reduced by 150 million.
http://www.un.org/sustainabledevelopment/hunger/

- **Is it called growth?** The wealth concentration of the richest 1% in the U.S.A. increased from 8% of the national income to almost 20% in the 30-year period to 2015, the sharpest increase on record. Among the OECD members that year, the U.S.A. was the third most unequal nation, just after Mexico and Chile.
http://reports.weforum.org/outlook-global-agenda-2015/top-10-trends-of-2015/1-deepening
-income-inequality/
http://www.oecd.org/forum/issues/oecd-forum-2015-income-inequality-in-figures.htm

- **A wider perspective.** In 2015, 83.5% of the world's wealth was held by ten countries, six of which had poverty percentages lower than the OECD average.
http://www.oecd.org/forum/issues/oecd-forum-2015-income-inequality-in-figures.htm

Globalization and trade system issues

- **Chess board.** In 2014, foreign direct investment (FDI) decreased by 16% compared with the previous year, primarily as a result of the insecure global environment: acute geopolitical risks and the fragile economy were decisive factors in the most important reduction in investment since 2008.
http://unctad.org/en/PublicationsLibrary/wir2015_en.pdf

- **Exotic investments.** Increased attention from the world media, sources of labor, and illicit flows of money are all consequences of the presence of multinational companies in Africa. The persistent misuse of international laws and tax breaks has prevented billions of dollars of revenue from being reinvested in the African nations. In 2012, tax breaks in Sierra Leone were eight times its health budget; 60% of the Nigerian population lives on less than US$1 per day, yet the country is the world's fourth-largest uranium producer.
https://www.oxfam.org/sites/www.oxfam.org/files/world_economic_forum_wef.africa_
rising_for_the_few.pdf

Corruption

- **Bigger breadcrumbs than usual.** More than 210,000 companies were mentioned in the Panama Papers leaked at the beginning of 2016 by the German newspaper *Süddeutsche Zeitung*. Mossack Fonseca was the firm, along with financial institutions such as HSBC Private Bank, accused of creating offshore companies for worldwide clients that ranged from monarchs to celebrities. Citizens for Tax Justice estimates that more than US$2 trillion of funds are hidden in tax havens around the world.
http://ctj.org/pdf/offshoreshell2014.pdf

- **Harsh times.** The Corruption Perception Index 2015 showed an average score of 43/100, two points lower than that of 2010; some of the most corrupt countries were at the same time some of the least developed, including Sudan, South Sudan, Afghanistan, and Guinea-Bissau; and sub-Saharan Africa showed no improvement in 40 out of 46, including the lowest score in Somalia.
http://www.transparency.org/cpi2015

- **Be careful what you import.** Countries that account for 20.5% of world exports and comprise half of the signatories to the OECD Convention on Combating Foreign Bribery are actually violating the agreement. Ten percent of OECD members are listed in the worst half of the Corruption Perception Index.
  http://www.transparency.org/news/pressrelease/20_major_exporting_countries_violate_international_law_obligations
  http://www.transparency.org/exporting_corruption
  https://issuu.com/transparencyinternational/docs/2015_exportingcorruption_oecdprogre/11?e=2496456/14890701

2

A history of business, society and environment

Unless more of our business leaders learn to exercise their powers and responsibilities with a definitely increased sense of responsibility [...] our civilization may well head for one of its periods of decline.

Wallace B. Donham, Dean,
Harvard Business School (1927, p. 406)

The historical development of responsible business is a valuable source of understanding and information for applying responsible management. For example, it is surprising to many practitioners to discover that the popular term "greenwashing" can be understood in depth when related to the classic Greek virtue ethics. Stakeholder theory, which is the management instrument of choice in a socially responsible business, was designed as a profit-seeking strategic management instrument. Who would have guessed that the attractiveness of the LOHAS (Lifestyles of Health and Sustainability) market segment has a strong basis in the hippie movement? Sound knowledge of the historical landmark events of business, society, and environment is essential to achieving a thorough understanding of responsible business.

Landmark historical facts are found mainly in economic history, general social history, labor history, and environmental history. The latter describes the interaction between human activity and the environment. In the following, historical events and developments will be described and analyzed in the light of responsible business. For responsible business to develop into what we know it as today,

Figure 2.1: Historic periods in the relationship between business, society, and environment

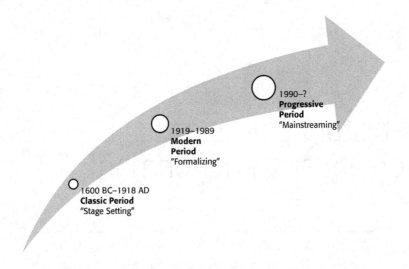

1990–?
**Progressive
Period**
"Mainstreaming"

1919–1989
**Modern
Period**
"Formalizing"

1600 BC–1918 AD
Classic Period
"Stage Setting"

the relationship between business, society, and environment had to pass through three main phases of development (Fig. 2.1):

1. The classic period
2. The modern period
3. The progressive period

The classic period: setting the stage

The roots of business culture and responsible business

The stage was set for responsible business during the classic period. The holy books of world religions, such as the Bible (c.1600 BC–AD 100) and the Quran (c.AD 610–32), are still defining elements of regional business culture and the values applied in business conduct. The values promoted by the Bible are a basic driver of business philanthropy in the Americas and many regions of the Old World, while the Quran has largely influenced the practices of Islamic finance, which is one of the quickly emerging ethical and socially responsible investment trends (IMF, 2007). Islamic values are defining for businesses in the Middle East and large parts of South-East Asia, but some Islamic values are not in accordance with Western ideologies of responsible management. For instance, diversity policies promoting gender equality, popular in Western responsible businesses, contradict certain Islamic ideologies.

The thinking of Confucianism [c.551–478 BC] provides a common value construct for East Asian business culture. Confucianism's point of departure and most important value is the wellbeing of people or humanity as a whole. This very basic insight makes Confucianism highly conducive to the implementation of social responsibilities. The second dominant Confucian core value, righteousness, is positively related to responsible business (Sprunger, 2011). With the rise of globalization, a contemporary challenge for responsible business is to adjust responsible business practices from regional or religious approaches to a truly global practice.

An emergent responsible investment megatrend

Islamic finance is limited to financial relationships involving entrepreneurial investment subject to the moral prohibition of interest earnings or usury (*riba*); money lending; and direct or indirect association with lines of business involving anything forbidden (*haram*) (IMF, 2007, p.4).

The origins of (business) ethics

Ethical thinking, as it is applied today in business, is the basis of responsible business. It is rooted in the ancient Greek philosophical thought. The "band of three" (c.469–322 BC), meaning the three most influential Greek philosophers, Plato, Socrates, and Aristotle, lay the foundation for non-consequentialist ethics: this strand of ethics judges right or wrong actions, not based on the outcome, but on the factors influencing the way the decision was made. Non-consequentialist ethics, often called deontological ethics, includes the main streams of thought of virtue ethics, ethics of duties, and ethics of rights and justice. Virtue ethics judges the righteousness of the character of the actor and finds its roots in the thinking of Plato and Aristotle. The first formulation of Emmanuel Kant's 1785 categorical imperative states "I ought never to conduct myself except so that I could also will that my maxim become a universal law" (Kant *et al.*, 2002, p. 18). Kant's work is often called the modern deontology (as opposed to classical Greek deontology) or ethics of duty. Kant describes the ultimate duty of acting as good as if one's action should become generally applicable law (Hursthouse, 1999). John Locke's work

An extreme perspective on citizenship

Aristotle famously expressed that the one who does not take part in a community's affairs is either a beast or a god (Aristotle, 2005). The philosopher's call for active citizenship can be seen as representative of the ancient Greek contribution to today's individual civic activities and corporate citizenship. What then should we consider of companies who do not contribute to the community?

(1689–95) on the ethics of rights refers to the unalienable entitlements of people (Chappel, 1994). These will be described in greater detail below in the context of the human rights movement.

John Rawls' 1971 theory of justice led to the ethics of justice, which promotes fairness in both the process leading to a decision and the outcome of the decision (Rawls, 1999). It is, therefore, a hybrid construction between consequentialist and non-consequentialist ethics. Outstanding streams of thought in consequentialist ethics (judging the outcome of an action) are capitalist egoism based on Adam Smith (1776) and on utilitarian thinking by John Stewart Mills (1863).

Adam Smith, in *The Wealth of Nations* (Smith, 2008), draws a picture of a profit-maximizing and, therefore, egoist business. Egoist ethics is ethics for the pursuit of self-interest. Egoism is the basis for today's discussion about what businesses should strive for: egoist profit maximization or profit optimization that benefits all involved stakeholders (Thielemann and Wettstein, 2008). Profit optimization reflects a utilitarian ethics, as proposed by John Stewart Mills in *Utilitarianism* (Mills, 2008). Utilitarian ethics pursues the greatest amount of happiness possible, a rationale which is reflected in current stakeholder management practices. These main streams of ethical thinking are the philosophical basis of business ethics.

The historical roots of today's unsustainability

To understand today's economic world order and its effects on society and environment, historical phases of economic world history are of crucial importance. The age of discovery and colonization (1419–1660) was the starting point of today's wealth inequality between the Northern and Southern hemispheres, and of exploitative relationships between the First and the developing worlds. It is the root of the necessity for today's sustainable and responsible supply chain management practices. The first industrial revolution (1730–70) brought economic growth, which in turn caused a welfare increase for workers employed in the booming new industries. This increase in welfare allowed for constant and rapid population growth, which is the basis for overpopulation and unsustainability today. The second industrial revolution (1860–1914) not only brought an additional boost of world economic activity and a negative impact on the environment, but also served as a breeding ground for two of the most important characteristics of the problems being caused by today's economic activity.

First, it gave birth to today's fossil fuel-based industry with the introduction of the internal combustion engine and petroleum-based plastics. Responsible business aims to achieve independence from fossil fuels by means of technologies such as solar energy, alternative engines, or kinetic local energy sourced from wind, water, or even human movements. Responsible business practice also includes the constant reduction of the negative impact of petroleum-based plastics, including reduction in material and packaging, usage of plastics derived from renewable biomass, and recycling and biodegradability technologies.

The second development is the birth of mass production, most notably made possible by Henry Ford's development of the conveyor belt-based assembly line.

Mass production is the technological basis of cheap products and the necessary condition for unsustainable consumerist behavior. Responsible management aims to foster responsible, sustainable, and ethical consumption patterns based on real needs rather than on superficial consumerist trends.

Ancient unsustainability

Human beings acted unsustainably long before the introduction of the fossil fuel-based economy. The farming activity of irrigation in ancient Mesopotamia, for example, increased the soil salinity to such levels that, by the year 1700 BC, yields had decreased over 60%. As a result, wheat cultivation was abandoned completely (Tammilehto, 2008). Easter Island's ancient civilization, famous for its giant head-shaped stone sculptures, is also supposed to have become extinct because of the unsustainable use of a crucial scarce island resource: wood (Foot, 2004).

The development of human and labor rights

Current responsible management standards, such as the Global Compact framework and ISO 26000, strongly focus on human rights. The secondary field of labor rights reflects the responsibility to one of business's most important interest groups: the employees. Human rights and citizen rights have been developed in a long line of historical events, documents, and streams of thought. At least three classic statements of human rights lie in the English Bill of Rights (1689), the U.S. Declaration of Independence (1776), and the French Declaration on the Rights of Man and of the Citizen (1789). These statements enable an understanding of the field of corporate citizenship, because they illustrate basic civic rights and duties which can be applied to corporate citizens as well as individual citizens. The field of labor rights and standards has been developed by transferring human rights to the workplace and matching them with Marx's 1867 criticism of the capitalist system exploiting the working masses, as described in *Capital* (Marx, 2000).

The birth of ecology

Human and labor rights, as part of the social component of responsible business, gained early public recognition. By contrast, the environmental component of responsible business was not discussed in mainstream culture until the 19th century. Inspired by Darwin's evolutionary theories, the German biologist and philosopher, Ernst Haeckel, created the term "ecology" in 1866 to describe the relationship between living organisms and their natural environment (Haeckel, 1988).

In 1854, a Native American prophecy first highlighted the harmful effects that human activity might have on ecology. The full Cree prophecy draws an impressive early picture of the environmental unsustainability of especially Western cultures. The prophecy deals with the consequences of ("white men's") greed, which can be interpreted as the search for profit maximization and consumerism. It describes a future state of environmental destruction characterized by the "earth being ravaged and polluted, the forests being destroyed, the birds would fall from the air, the waters would be blackened, the fish being poisoned in the streams, and the trees would no longer be" (Bird Clan of East Central Alabama, 2004). The prophecy even draws on the modern understanding of the environment being a necessary precondition for human survival when stating that "mankind as we would know it would all but cease to exist." The positive outlook of the prophecy was the advent of the so-called "rainbow warriors," who would lead the world to a sustainable situation when "all the peoples of all the tribes would form a New World of Justice, Peace, Freedom and recognition of the Great Spirit [of nature]." This prophecy was later adopted by the environmentalist movement. In retrospect, it provides a very concise account of today's problems and potential solutions. As early as 1798 the British economist, Thomas Malthus, provided a more scientific interpretation of humanity's future issues. His work on the world's demography suggests that constant population growth will exceed the Earth's carrying capacity, and mentioned poverty and famine as potential consequences (Malthus, 2011).

The modern period: formalizing

The modern period of responsible management is characterized by an increasing formalization of responsible management in the form of international institutions, research, and practice applications. Important civic movements, such as racial equality, and the hippie and the environmentalist movements bring the relationship between business, society, and environment to the attention of broader society.

Civic movements

The late outliers of the second industrial revolution changed agriculture in such a profound way that it was called the "green revolution." In the middle of the 20th century (c.1940–60), the world witnessed a drastic increase in agricultural production based on new technologies and practices such as irrigation, fertilizers, and pesticides. The two latter practices especially sparked an early environmental movement, which had long-lasting influences on later environmental activism. Rachel Carson's book *Silent Spring* criticized the negative environmental and health effects of pesticides, one of the main enablers of the green revolution. The book's title in fact refers to the loss of biodiversity, most noticeable in the absence of birdsongs during springtime (Carson, 2002). The African-American civil rights movement (1955–68) marked the beginning of various nondiscrimination movements, which later expanded to include gender, sexual orientation, race/ethnicity, religion, physical handicaps, and age. In today's responsible business, the topic is called "diversity management". The hippie movement (1960–70) integrated the environmental and equality movements, combining the aspects of a liberal mind-set, harmony with nature, respect, tolerance, and a search for spirituality. This spirituality and quest for holistic living reflects actual consumer tendencies toward sustainable living.

Activist with credentials

Born in 1907, Rachel Carson studied marine biology, received her MS in zoology, and worked for the U.S. Bureau of Fisheries. She became one of the most influential people of the 20th century after publishing several books on nature, such as the famous *Silent Spring*, in which she calls "for a change in the way humankind viewed the natural world" (Lear, 1998).

Development of a global institutional infrastructure

To manage a responsible business, it is crucial to understand the international and regional norms and organizations that provide an institutional framework for management conduct. As early as 1919, the International Labour Organization (ILO) was founded to promote workers' rights and wellbeing. ILO documents are still the most important landmark standards for getting the employee stakeholder relationship right. The Universal Declaration of Human Rights (1948) is the modern version of the classically developed citizen rights. For the first time in history, the declaration proposed a set of universally valid entitlements for all human beings on Earth. The declaration was developed by the United Nations and has served as a basis for the development of most of the subsequent standards applied in responsible business. In 1968, the Club of Rome, an alliance of high-impact business, society, academic, and political leaders, was founded with the purpose of fighting the unsustainability of human activity on Earth. An explosion of institutional infrastructure for responsible management then took place throughout the subsequent progressive period (see below).

Development of practice tools and of the academic discipline

Today's primary responsible business management tools began to be developed in the late 1960s. The tool of product life-cycle assessment illustrates, measures, and manages the environmental, social, and economic impacts of a product from sourcing and production, through usage, and to the end of the useful life-cycle. Product life-cycle assessment was first applied in a study by Teastley with the Coca-Cola Company in 1969 (U.S. Environmental Protection Agency, 2006; AGA, 2010). Corporate ethics was formalized as an academically accepted stream of applied ethics in the 1970s and widely taught, primarily in U.S. business schools. The field of stakeholder management received broad academic attention with Edward Freeman's 1984 publication *Strategic Management: A Stakeholder Approach* (Freeman, 2010). Stakeholder management was later adopted as the main management tool of the responsible business movement.

The academic understanding of responsible business evolved in parallel with the responsible business practice tools. According to Carroll, the publication of the book *Social Responsibilities of the Businessman* by Howard Bowen in 1953 is recognized as the first publication explicitly describing responsible business (Carroll, 1999). After a slow start to academic coverage of responsible business, Nobel Prize-winning economist Milton Friedman drew attention to corporate social responsibility in both business and academic circles (Friedman, 1970). His questioning of social business responsibilities in general is probably the most widely discussed statement in responsible business and still receives academic coverage more than four decades after its publication in the *New York Times Magazine* in 1970.

Only a few years later, the modern sustainability movement was born. In 1972, the Club of Rome published *The Limits to Growth*, which reconnected to Malthus's classic forecasts of coming overpopulation (Malthus, 2011). The publication was the starting point for public recognition and academic coverage of the concept of sustainable development, as defined by the report of the UN World Commission on Environment and Development, also known as the Brundtland Commission (Brundtland, 1987). In the same year, Edward Barbier (1987) laid the groundwork for the popular Venn diagram which defines the three dimensions—later the three pillars—of sustainable development as being social, environmental, and economic development. The generation of the concept of sustainable development was very timely given that, for the first time ever, in 1975 humanity's ecological impact on the Earth overtook the planet's carrying capacity during this modern period (WWF, 2010).

The progressive period: mainstreaming

Throughout the progressive period of responsible management, the relationship between business, society, and environment moved from being an accepted side topic to a mainstream consideration for businesses, governments, and society. At the end of the progressive period, responsible business had become a worldwide social and business megatrend.

Issue, scandals, and crises

That responsible business was able to become mainstream can be attributed to a series of publicly highlighted business issues, crises, and scandals. The multi-national shoe manufacturer Nike was in a constant struggle with civil society actors for alleged use of cheap and exploitative, sweatshop labor. This struggle went on for more than 20 years and served as a constant reminder of the harm that irresponsible business practices can do to a company and its reputation (Waller and Conaway, 2011). Another prominent example is the issue surrounding the Brent Spar oil storage buoy operated by Shell (1995). Greenpeace activists occupied Brent Spar to protest against the planned dumping of the platform into the Atlantic Ocean. Worldwide public attention rose to such a degree that Shell service stations were boycotted on a large scale, and one service station was even physically attacked in an arson attempt (Greenpeace, 2007). The Enron and Worldcom bankruptcies, due to fraudulent accounting practices (2001–2002), not only brought down both companies, but also the world-renowned accounting firm Arthur Anderson (USA Today, 2005). The world financial and economic crisis of 2007 had severe social consequences globally. Recession, destruction of companies, subsequent job loss, and an increase in poverty were only the most obvious consequences. The reason for the crisis was behavior that could have been avoided by good ethics and responsible business practices in the banking sector, coupled with a massive problem with the repayment of subprime loans, mortgages that could be sold at a higher price due to the considerably higher risk of payback.

The "green pop culture"

In contrast to the negative coverage of social, environmental, and economic issues, the progressive period has also seen the development in mainstream "pop culture" of responsible management and issues related to it. Most prominently, former U.S. Vice President Al Gore received global public attention with his 2006 movie *An Inconvenient Truth*, which raised awareness of climate change and its consequences (Guggenheim, 2006); the movie won two Academy Awards the following year. Leonardo DiCaprio followed suit with *The 11th Hour*, providing an extensive overview of the issues that threaten mankind's survival on Earth (Conners and Conners Petersen, 2007). These two Hollywood productions had been preceded by a long line of movies criticizing the negative impact of businesses on society and environment. In 2003, the movie and book, both titled *The Corporation: The Pathological Pursuit of Profit and Power*, translated the classic business ethics criticism of profit maximization into a fashionable and

---

Last call

The 11th Hour is a film documentary, with contributions from more than 50 world leaders, that describes the endangered natural state of the Earth. Narrated by Leonardo DiCaprio, the film points to technology, social responsibility, and conservation as key factors in finding a solution to the problem, although it is almost too late (Conners and Conners Petersen, 2007).

mass-accessible format (Achbar and Abbott, 2003). The filmmaker Michael Moore produced three business-critical blockbusters in a period of 20 years. The Moore movie, *Capitalism: A Love Story*, covers the dubious role of the financial sector in the 2007 world economic crisis (Moore, 2009). The movie *Super Size Me* became a modern classic by criticizing the fast-food industry for pursuing profits by promoting poor nutrition (Spurlock, 2004).

Powered by broad public attention of social and environmental issues, the sustainable, ethical, and responsible living movement went mainstream around the start of the millennium, as the LOHAS (Lifestyles of Health and Sustainability) market segment, and with it sustainable consumption, became a large-scale trend (NMI, 2010, 2011).

One first sign of responsible business and products becoming mainstream happened when Toyota launched the first mass-produced hybrid car, the Prius, in 1997. Again, it was pop culture pushing sustainable behavior and sales. Pictures of celebrities such as DiCaprio, Sting, or Cameron Diaz posing with a Prius at the gas station were extremely influential in the commercial success of more than 2 million cars sold in 2010. Another example is the RED product line, promoted by the singer Bono. RED encourages mainstream corporations to introduce a co-branded RED product, which donates a certain percentage of sales to the fight against Aids in Africa (RED, 2015). RED was the first product-customized and global cause-related marketing campaign.

Development of high-impact institutions

During the modern period of responsible business, the institutional influence on responsible business behavior moved from marginalized initiatives to well-accepted, high-impact mainstream institutions. The Foundation of the World Business Council for Sustainable Development (WBCSD) in 1990 is probably the best example of how seriously responsible business began to be taken by major businesses. Today, WBCSD is a global sustainability player, led by the CEOs of around 200 companies, including Toyota, Unilever, and Shell (Timberlake, 2006).

The governmental sector also started to take the topic very seriously. The 1992 Rio convention, known as the Earth Summit, attracted representatives from over 172 governments, including 108 heads of state. The outcomes were broad commitments to solving the world's most pressing problems, summarized in Agenda 21. A total of 178 governments voted to adopt Agenda 21 and to follow a set of development goals, divided into various socioeconomic factors. These factors include poverty, sustainable consumption and health, environmental factors, the strengthening of groups central to sustainable development, and the measures necessary for implementation. Another important outcome of the Rio conference was the Rio Declaration on Environment and Development, which summarizes the actions to be implemented to reach sustainable development as defined in 27 principles (United Nations, 1997). In the follow-up conference in 1997, the Kyoto protocol, the first global agreement for the global reduction of greenhouse gases, was signed.

The International Organization for Standardization (ISO) mainstreamed the topic of environmental business responsibility by launching the now widely accepted ISO 14000 standard for environmental management in 1996. The subsequent ISO 26000 norm (2010) gives guidance on social responsibilities and is expected to further facilitate the implementation of responsible management for mainstream businesses and organizations of every kind. From 1999 onward, the United Nations increasingly focused on promoting responsible business. The Global Compact (GC), a voluntary initiative which includes a self-commitment to ten responsible business principles, was launched in 2000, and by 2010 GC had more than 6,000 members, including many of the largest multinational companies. The United Nations Environment Programme supported the foundation of the Global Reporting Initiative (GRI) by the Coalition for Environmentally Responsible Economies (Ceres), which developed the GRI standard for sustainability reporting. GRI annual reports are now available for most of the world's biggest enterprises and various other organizations.

The eight Millennium Development Goals (MDGs) were launched in 2005 and were quickly accepted as guidance for sustainable development. In 2015 the MDGs were substituted by the new Sustainable Development Goals (SDG). Sustainability also made headway into the educational sector. In the UN Decade of Education for Sustainable Development (2005–14), extensive efforts were made to give people the necessary mind-set and skills to live more sustainable lives (DESD, 2011). With the founding of the Principles for Responsible Management Education (PRME) in 2007, the United Nations identified management education as a crucial factor in shaping responsible businesses and focused on creating managers who can be change agents for a sustainable and inclusive economic system (PRME, 2011). The European Union also became an entity at the forefront of the responsible business movement. Among other things, the EU Corporate Social Responsibility Strategy and the EU Multi Stakeholder Forum have become role models for regional initiatives for responsible business on a worldwide scale (Commission of the European Communities, 2006).

Training responsible managers

In 2007 the Principles for Responsible Management Education were developed, by deans, university presidents, and representatives of leading educational institutions, with the support of the United Nations. By 2016, over 500 academic institutions had joined this initiative to educate a new generation of leaders to responsibly manage business for the good of the planet (PRME, 2016).

Megatrends of flat globalization and interactive transparency

The *New York Times* author and triple Pulitzer Prize-winner Thomas L. Friedman described globalization in the 21st century as a flat globalization, where companies of any kind and size are able to compete on an international scale (Friedman, 2005). Such a type of globalization increases the importance of internationally recognized and applied responsible business standards. A crucial factor in a flat world is information technology. The information age began with the mass production of personal computers, but gained importance for responsible business when the internet, from 1995 on, became a mass phenomenon. The internet has been a driver of responsible business for two specific reasons. First, it facilitates an almost instant transparency about companies' positive and/or negative impacts. In combination with mobile-phone-based photography and internet connectedness, news about an oil spill or an unethical remark by a frontline employee can travel across the world instantly. Second, the internet makes it easier for companies to actively report social and environmental performance. Most companies have online, downloadable sustainability, responsibility, and citizenship reports that follow the Global Reporting Initiative standards. In 2004, the term "Web 2.0" was coined by Tim O'Reilly to describe a new internet age characterized by a wide variety of new features such as interactivity, user-created content, and social networking. Web 2.0 enables a cheap and highly effective form of stakeholder dialogue, which is the very basis of a successful responsible business (O'Reilly, 2005).

Focus topic of management practice and theory

Archie B. Carroll's (1991) pyramid of corporate social responsibility clearly categorized for the first time the different types of responsibility a company should fulfill. The four categories described are:

1. Economic responsibilities
2. Legal responsibilities
3. Ethical responsibilities
4. Philanthropic/discretionary responsibilities

The pyramid was a principal component of a stream of research defining the different types of responsible business conduct, such as corporate social performance and corporate social responsiveness. Carroll's work is the basis for the contemporary theoretical understanding and practical implementation of responsible business. The moment that showed the extent to which responsible business had become a mainstream topic occurred when the godfather of strategic management, Michael Porter, and his co-author, NGO specialist Marc Kramer, published the article "Strategy and society" (Porter and Kramer, 2006) in the prestigious journal *Harvard Business Review*, which is appreciated equally by practitioners and academics. Another academic and business practitioner, Philip Kotler, a renowned academic in the marketing field, had already integrated the responsible business topics of social and cause-related marketing into several textbooks, and in 2004, he co-authored the bestselling book *Corporate Social Responsibility: Doing the Most Good for Your Company and Your Cause* (Kotler and Lee, 2004).

Each of these key publications showed the integration of responsible business into classic business functions (strategy and marketing). They also gave rise to a general awareness of the business case for responsible business, describing the various ways companies can benefit from behaving responsibly. Another milestone for the mainstreaming of responsible business models is Muhammad Yunus winning the Nobel Peace Prize in 2006, the first time that this prestigious award was given for a business model. The micro-banking model, represented by Yunus's Grameen Bank, profitably gave credits to millions of poor people in order to reduce poverty. The Grameen Bank is often seen as an example of Prahalad's bottom-of-the-pyramid theory, which postulates that businesses can tap into the potential of the poor and profitably integrate them into the market economy as suppliers, workers, and consumers (Prahalad, 2010).

Exercises

A. Know

Use the multiple choice questions below to test your knowledge. Each answer may be wrong or right and there may be zero to four right or wrong answers per question:

1. The classic period of the relationship between business, society, and environment ...
    a. ... among other things, comprises the time of the industrial revolution.
    b. ... was a time of major importance for the development of human and labor rights.
    c. ... mainly unfolded during the period between 1930 and 1950.
    d. ... is also called the era of "mainstreaming."

2. The modern period of the relationship between business, society, and environment ...
    a. ... was the time of the African-American civil rights movement.
    b. ... was when the foundation of the World Business Council for Sustainable Development (WBCSD) took place.
    c. ... was the period between 1919 and 1990.
    d. ... is the era of mainstreaming the relationship between business, society, and environment.

3. The progressive period of the relationship between business, society, and environment ...
    a. ... gave birth to "the green revolution," a legendary movement of the major multinational businesses going "green."
    b. ... is not over yet.
    c. ... was when the central responsible business tool life-cycle assessment was developed.
    d. ... is the period when topics related to business, society, and environment began moving mainstream.

4. Today's unsustainability ...
    a. ... is not a new phenomenon. Already in ancient Mesopotamia unsustainable agricultural practices caused problems in food production.
    b. ... is, among other things, caused by early discovery and colonization activities, as these activities have led to unsustainable migratory movements from the Northern to the Southern hemisphere.
    c. ... is partly due to the birth of mass production, which enabled unsustainable consumption patterns.
    d. ... is partly due to a welfare increase during the first industrial revolution.

5. During the time when responsible business became a focus topic of management ...

   a.   ... Michael Porter developed the corporate social responsibility pyramid, which categorizes economic, legal, ethical, and philanthropic (discretionary) responsibilities.

   b.   ... Marc Kramer was one of the co-authors of the article that highlighted the relationship between business and society.

   c.   ... Muhammad Yunus won the Nobel Prize in Economic Science for his work with the Grameen Bank.

   d.   ... awareness of the business case for responsible business was increased.

B. Think

Rewriting history: imagine what the world around you would look like if you lived 50 years in the future. Creatively write a fictitious history time-line from today to this imagined future.

C. Do

If you were in her shoes: think about one point in time where the action of a person could have changed the course of history in a way that would have carried us into a more sustainable present. Describe the problem this person might have solved or the opportunity possibly realized, and the actions you would have taken if you had been this person.

D. Relate

Open a conversation with someone you know about one of the historic events mentioned in this chapter. Exchange and document your knowledge and views on the meaning of these events with this person in order to understand this event better.

E. Be

How does this make you feel? Reflect on your internal reactions to the history of business, society, and environment presented in this chapter. Try to capture how it makes you feel and what attitudes you have to the overall development or to single events. Can your reactions be expressed in feelings, motivations, moods, or attitudes? Do you react differently to different events or types of event in this history? How do you explain your reactions?

Feedback

A. Know

Question 1

a.   Right: the first and the second industrial revolution as well as the agricultural "green revolution" fall into the classic period of the relationship between business, society, and environment.

b.   Right: the basics of human and labor rights can be found throughout the early British and French documents constituting basic citizen and human rights, as well as Marx's works on the exploitation of workers by the capitalist system.

c.   Wrong: 1930 to 1950 is the last stage of the classic period, but only represents a minor fraction of the overall period roughly ranging from 600 BC to AD 1950.

d.   Wrong: it is the progressive period that is characterized by a mainstreaming of the relationship between business, society, and environment, while the classic period can be characterized by the term "stage-setting."

Question 2

a.   Right: the main phase of the African-American civil rights movement roughly took place between 1955 and 1968.

b.   Wrong: the WBCSD was founded at the very beginning of the progressive period.

c.   Right: these years reflect the progressive period.

d.   Wrong: the era of mainstreaming is the progressive period.

Question 3

a.   Wrong: the "green revolution" is related to efficiency improvements in food production due to improved agricultural methods during the early modern period.

b.   Right: the progressive period and the "mainstreaming" of the relationship between business, society, and environment began in 1990 and is in full process.

c.   Wrong: life-cycle assessment was developed during the modern period, together with business ethics and stakeholder management.

d.   Right: it is also called the era of "mainstreaming."

Question 4

a.   Right: the irrigation practices in ancient Mesopotamia proved unsustainable and finally led to the abandonment of wheat cultivation.

b.   Wrong: discovery and colonization activities have contributed to today's global unsustainability, but mainly by the creation of wealth inequalities between the Northern and Southern hemispheres.

c.   Right: mass production led to a decrease in prices and a higher consumption potential of people.

   d.   Right: economic growth during the first industrial revolution increased
        people's welfare, which in turn supported a constant population growth
        based on improved living conditions.

Question 5

   a.   Wrong: the pyramid was developed by Archie B. Carroll.
   b.   Right: the article was co-authored with Michael Porter as first author.
   c.   Wrong: in spite of being a finance professor, Yunus won the Nobel Peace
        Prize, not the Nobel Prize in Economics.
   d.   Right: awareness of the positive business benefits from responsible
        business practices was increased by manifold publications such as
        "Strategy and society" by Porter and Kramer (2006).

B. Think

Level	Future-oriented thinking competence	Notes
+	Illustration of a convincing future scenario and strong connection to today's situation through fictitious key events and developments	
=	Illustration of a possible future in depth	
−	Little evidence of the ability to imagine a possible future in detail	

C. Do

Level	Problem and opportunity skills	Notes
+	Feasible plan of action based on the recognition of a significant historic problem or opportunity	
=	Plan of action based on the recognition of a historic problem or opportunity	
−	No plan of action and/or no recognition of a historic problem or opportunity	

D. Relate

Level	Collaborative knowledge creation competence	Notes
+	Highly integrated shared knowledge about the event which attributes the origin of individual elements to the respective conversation partner	
=	Equitable account of knowledge of all conversation partners, but little integration and attribution of individual elements to the respective conversation partner	
–	Biased or unilateral account of knowledge	

E. Be

Level	Introspection competence	Notes
+	Deep and thoughtful insight into internal states and processes, appreciating their causes	
=	Basic insight into own internal states and processes	
–	Little or no evidence of the ability to monitor and express insight into internal states and processes	

Appendix

Table 2.1: Historic events in the relationship between business, society, and environment

Legend

Symbols used in the table divide the historical events and developments into the following three groups:

◆ Major developments in world history impacting on responsible business and management

● Scientific developments impacting on responsible business and management

✳ Institutional developments impacting on responsible business and management, including norms and organizations

Period	Event	Summary	Topic areas
Classic period: stage-setting			
1600 BC–AD 100	Bible [◆]	The scripture of the Bible defines values still prevalent in the morality of many Western businesses.	Business philanthropy
551–478 BC	Confucianism [◆]	Confucianist thinking dominates business morality mostly in East Asia.	Welfare thinking
469–322 BC	Ancient Greek philosophy and citizenship [●]	Ancient Greek philosophers such as Plato, Aristotle, and Socrates are the grandfathers of modern ethical thinking. Also, the Greek "polis" in its understanding of the city-state and community of citizens is the root of democracy and the understanding of citizenship.	Virtue ethics Corporate citizenship
AD 610–32	Establishment of the contents of the Quran [◆]	The Quran's value construct largely influences the business morality in Middle Eastern and many South-East Asian countries.	Islamic business Islamic finance Gender inequality
1215	Magna Carta [✳]	The Magna Carta limited the arbitrary punishment powers of the king and conceded a basic freedom to "freemen."	Citizen Rights Human rights
1419–1660	The age of discovery and establishment of colonial empires [◆]	The exploration and subsequent colonial exploitation of the Americas, Africa, and Asia has led to many elements of today's worldwide imbalances in welfare.	Third-world poverty and exploitation Racism Sustainable supply chain management

Period	Event	Summary	Topic areas
1689	English Bill of Rights [✱]	This extended the rights of English citizens based on liberal thinking.	Citizen rights Human rights
1730–70 (approx.)	First industrial revolution [◆]	The industrial revolution's technological achievements led to increased welfare among workers and a subsequent explosion of the Earth's population. Also allowed the technological achievement for a large-scale exploitation and pollution of natural resources.	Overpopulation Pollution Unsustainable economic development
1776	Publication of the book *The Wealth of Nations* by Adam Smith [●]	Adam Smith's book is often seen as the basis for economic thinking, capitalism, and an incentive-based market economy. In his earlier book, *The Theory of Moral Sentiments*, Smith first used the term "the invisible hand" to describe the forces of markets, and also defines "self-love" (egoism) as the first motive for morality (Smith, 2008).	(Economic) egoist ethics Market economy Incentives
1785	Initiation of Kant's categorical imperative [●]	In his work *Groundwork of the Metaphysics of Morals*, Kant proposes the "categorical imperative" as the ultimate decision-making instrument for defining moral behavior based on one's duties (Kant et al., 2002).	Ethics of duties The categorical imperative of sustainability
1789	French Declaration on the Rights of Man and of the Citizen [✱]	This shifted the approach to universal rights from being purely citizen-based to a human rights approach, which grants natural right to any human being.	Citizenship rights Human rights
1798	Thomas Malthus publishes *An Essay on the Principle of Population* [●]	Malthus argued that a rise in the population would lead to an oversupply of labor and subsequent reduction of wages, which in turn creates poverty (Malthus, 2011).	Social unsustainability Overpopulation Poverty

Period	Event	Summary	Topic areas
1854	Cree prophecy [●]	The Cree prophecy has been attributed to either an old native American woman of the Cree tribe or to Chief Seattle, eponym of the city Seattle. It states that due to the "white men's" greed destroying nature, there would be a time when mankind would almost cease to exist (Bird Clan of East Central Alabama, 2004).	Environmentalism Unsustainability of "Western" lifestyles
1860–1914	Second industrial (technology) revolution [◆]	This sparked unprecedented economic growth fueled by inventions such as the assembly line, the internal combustion engine, and the use of electricity. The petroleum industry was also born in this period. The increase in production efficiency created the necessary precondition for cheap mass production, which in turn raised average people's consumption potential.	Mass production Consumerism and materialism Fossil fuel-based industry
1863	Publication of the book *Utilitarianism* by John Steward Mills [●]	Mills describes utilitarianism and the greatest overall happiness caused by a behavior as the main end of ethical decision-making. Mills bases his arguments on the central idea of welfare and the "greatest happiness principle" proposed by Bentham (Mills, 2008).	Utilitarian ethics Welfare thinking
1866	Ecology (Ernst Haeckel) [●]	Haeckel coined the term "ecology," describing the interrelation of the natural environment's elements, which served as a basis for the modern understanding of the term (Haeckel, 1988).	Environmental management Environmental unsustainability
1867	Publication of the book *Capital: Critique of Political Economy* by Karl Marx [●]	Marx sees the exploitation of labor as the main motivation of capitalist behavior and therefore capitalism as intrinsically unsocial (Marx, 2000).	Criticism of capitalism Fair labor conditions Exploitative labor

Period	Event	Summary	Topic areas
Modern period: formalizing			
1919	Foundation of the International Labour Organization (ILO) [✻]	The ILO was founded after World War I for humanitarian, economic, and political reasons. The ILO has set the labor standards which are reference documents for the development of most of the current norms for responsible business (ILO, 2000).	International labor standards
1920	External effects and social costs by Pigou in the book *The Economics of Welfare* [●]	With his work on external effects, Pigou laid the ground for the development of welfare and environmental economics, which are the economic theories that analyze the social and environmental effects of economic activity (Pigou, 2005).	(Social) welfare economics Environmental economics Taxation of externalities
1940–60	The green revolution [◆]	During the this period, agricultural production experienced a dramatic increase in productivity based on automation and the use of chemical substances.	Unsustainable food supply Biodiversity loss
1943	Publication of Abraham Maslow's needs pyramid in *A Theory of Human Motivation* [●]	Maslow's hierarchical needs pyramid explains the basic motivations of human beings (Maslow, 1943). Understanding Maslow's pyramid is fundamental to analyzing and changing consumerist behavior toward more sustainable ways.	Consumerism Sustainable living
1948	Universal Declaration of Human Rights [✻]	Developed after World War II, this is still the main reference document for the understanding of international, universal human rights.	Human rights
1953	Publication of the book *Social Responsibilities of the Businessman* by Howard Bowen [●]	Bowen's book constitutes the point of departure for the modern understanding of corporate social responsibility (Bowen, 1953).	Corporate social responsibility

Period	Event	Summary	Topic areas
1955–68	African-American civil rights movement [◆]	This has been a milestone for the achievement of the goal of racial nondiscrimination and served as the basis for the general nondiscrimination movement.	Workplace diversity and inclusion Civil rights
1960	Coase theorem [●]	The Coase theorem describes how to internalize external costs by attributing property rights to externalities, thereby creating a market for externalities (Coase, 1960). A prominent example is "emission trading," where companies are given a certain maximum right to pollute. If the business does not use up this maximum amount, it can sell the unused emission rights to other businesses that have exceeded their own emission limit.	Environmental economics (Social) welfare economics Emission trading Market-based solutions
1960–70	Hippie movement [◆]	With its promotion of liberal values, spirituality, proximity to nature, and nondiscrimination, this has been an important basis for many of the values pursued in responsible business. The modern Lifestyles of Health and Sustainability (LOHAS) movement has much in common with the hippie mind-set.	Environmentalism LOHAS markets Diversity and inclusion
1962	Publication of the book *Silent Spring* by Rachel Carson [●]	Rachel Carson criticizes the negative environmental and health effects of the green revolution in the agricultural sector (Carson, 2002).	Environmentalism
1968	Foundation of the Club of Rome [✱]	This brought together a group of diplomats, industry and civil society leaders, and academics concerned about economic and social activity overshooting the planet's environmental limits.	Sustainable development Overpopulation Footprinting
1969	Birth of the product life-cycle assessment methodology [●]	A tool centrally applied in responsible management, this first took place in a project headed by the researcher Teastley for the Coca-Cola Company (U.S. Environmental Protection Agency, 2006).	Product life-cycle impact assessment Cradle to cradle Recycling

Period	Event	Summary	Topic areas
1970	Publication of Milton Friedman's *New York Times* article, "The social responsibility of business is to increase its profits" [●]	Friedman criticized the social responsibility of a business from both an economic and ideological perspective. A company as being a lifeless entity cannot have a responsibility, while companies' managers might have a responsibility, but should not allocate financial resources to social causes as this means "stealing" money from business owners, employees, and consumers (Friedman, 1970).	Corporate social responsibility Philanthropy Greenwashing Principal–agent theory
1970–80	Development of business (corporate) ethics [●]	This made the topic an academically recognized field of applied ethics, which led to increased coverage of business ethics and the related topic of corporate governance throughout the business school curriculum.	Business ethics Corporate governance
1971	Publication of the book *A Theory of Justice* by John Rawls [●]	This formalized the philosophical stream of thinking of ethics of justice, searching for fair decision-making procedures and outcomes (Rawls, 1999).	Ethics of justice
1972	Publication of the book *The Limits to Growth* by the Club of Rome [●]	This became a world best seller by calling attention to the impending "overshoot," a situation where world economy and society will be forced into decline by the resource limits of the planet (Meadows *et al.*, 2005).	Sustainable development
1975	Humanity's footprint on Earth exceeds the ecological carrying capacity [◆]	This happened when world society was barely aware of the problem. Corrective measures have not been taken sufficiently and humanity's ecological footprint kept growing, by far exceeding what Earth can bear in the long run.	Unsustainability Environmental footprint

Period	Event	Summary	Topic areas
1984	Publication of the book *Strategic Management: A Stakeholder Approach* by Edward Freeman [●]	This introduced the tool of stakeholder management, which is at the heart of managing responsible business. Freeman argued that a business cannot be successful without fulfilling the needs of "groups and individuals that can affect or are affected" by the business's activities, i.e. stakeholders (Freeman, 2010, p. 25).	Stakeholders Business case for responsible business
1987	Brundtland report [●]	The report by the UN World Commission on Environment and Developments, officially titled *Our Common Future*, delivered the popular definition for sustainable development as a "development that meets the needs of the present without compromising the ability of future generations to meet their own needs" (United Nations, 1987).	Sustainable development
1987	Edward Barbier's pillar model of sustainable development [●]	This formalized the three dimensions of sustainable development being social, environmental, and economic development (Barbier, 1987).	Sustainable development

Progressive period: mainstreaming

Period	Event	Summary	Topic areas
1990–2001	Nike sweatshop issue [◆]	Nike being accused of employing sweatshop labor conditions in subsidiaries' factories was picked up as a major issue by social activist groups. It showcased that companies' responsibilities do not end "at the factory door."	Sustainable supply chain management Exploitative labor Social activism
1990	Foundation of the World Business Council for Sustainable Development (WBCSD) [✱]	This institutionalized the commitment of high-level business leaders for a business contribution to sustainable development. WBCSD designed the environmental management tool "eco-efficiency," aiming to simultaneously reduce the environmental impact and costs of a business's operations. WBCSD also proposed *Vision 2050*, a roadmap toward a sustainable world economic system (Timberlake, 2006).	Eco-efficiency Business case

Period	Event	Summary	Topic areas
1991	Archie B. Carroll's responsibility pyramid [●]	This structured business responsibilities into the four categories of economic, legal, ethical, and philanthropic/discretionary responsibility (Carroll, 1991).	Corporate social responsibility
1992	Rio Summit and Agenda 21 [✳]	The United Nations Conference on Environment and Development (UNCED), also called the Rio Summit, served as breeding ground for several landmark institutions for sustainable development, such as the Rio Declaration on Environment and Development, Agenda 21, and the Framework Convention on Climate Change (United Nations, 1997).	Sustainable development Climate change
1995	Brent Spar [◆]	Triggered by the Greenpeace's activist opposition to the deep-sea dumping of the Brent Spa oil buoy, Shell received worldwide opposition to their business activities (Greenpeace, 2007).	Activism Environmentalism
1995	Beginning of the "information age" as the internet becomes public [◆]	The broad availability of the internet created the necessary conditions for a new transparency, including information on companies' responsible or irresponsible behavior.	Transparency Stakeholder engagement
1996	Publication of the ISO 14000 standards for environmental management [✳]	ISO 14000 supports the implementation of environmental management systems, and puts companies' environmental impact on the management agenda.	Environmental management
1997	Kyoto protocol [✳]	This was the first internationally accepted agreement on the reduction of the emission of greenhouse gases, signed by the majority of the world's governments (UNFCCC, 2011).	Climate change

Period	Event	Summary	Topic areas
1997	Toyota launches the mass-produced Prius hybrid car [♦]	The first mass-produced alternative engine-powered car, the Prius is an important milestone as it shows that industries can reduce their dependence on the fossil fuel-based model, while increasing their competitiveness and creating new markets.	Sustainable innovation Fossil fuel-based industry Green technologies
1999	Foundation of the Global Reporting Initiative [✱]	This created a standardized framework for reporting social, environmental, and economic performance (GRI, 2016).	Institutionalization Sustainability reporting
2000	Launch of the Global Compact [✱]	This provides businesses with a United Nations-backed platform to improve their social and environmental impacts based on ten core principles (UNGC, 2011b).	Institutionalization Issues and causes
2000	Documentation of the LOHAS market segment [●]	The Lifestyles of Health and Sustainability (LOHAS) market is segmented into clearly defined submarkets such as sustainable living and eco-tourism (LOHAS Magazine, 2010).	Sustainable consumption Cause-related marketing
2000	Bursting of the "Dot.com Bubble" [♦]	This and the massive economic damage done due to speculative stock market mechanisms highlighted the financial markets as one of the systemic problems of the capitalist system.	Economic system malfunctions
2000	Start of the era of "flat" globalization [♦]	Thomas Friedman's description of the "flat world," where globalization becomes mass-accessible (Friedman, 2005), enabling a new type of global social and environmental entrepreneurship.	Sustainable entrepreneurship Supply-chain responsibility
2001–2002	Enron and Worldcom scandals [♦]	These triggered the collapse of several corporate giants due to unethical accounting and governance practices.	Economic system malfunctions Organizational governance
2004	Web 2.0 [♦]	The shift from the rather static internet 1.0 to the interactive Web 2.0 provides a platform highly conducive to enhanced stakeholder engagement (O'Reilly, 2005).	Stakeholder engagement Transparency

Period	Event	Summary	Topic areas
2004	Publication of the book *The Fortune at the Bottom of the Pyramid* by C.K. Prahalad [●]	This cast light on the possibility of including poor people in the economic system, either as customers, employees, or suppliers (Prahalad, 2010).	Inclusive business
2005–14	UN Decade of Education for Sustainable Development [✱]	This highlights the importance of educating people in their private and professional life for sustainable behavior patterns (DESD, 2011).	Institutionalization Sustainability education
2005–15	UN Millennium Development Goals [✱]	These summarize the most important goals necessary to combat poverty were adopted by the majority of the world's national governments (United Nations, 2011c).	Sustainable development Issues and causes
2006	EU Corporate Social Responsibility Strategy [✱]	This has served as the role model for many regional initiatives and clusters of responsible business. The strategy's definition of corporate social responsibility has been widely adopted (Commission of the European Communities, 2006).	Corporate social responsibility Responsible business clusters
2006	Publication of the *Harvard Business Review* article "Strategy and society" by Michael Porter and Marc Kramer [●]	This showcased how responsible businesses can create value for both business and society when strategically aligned (Porter and Kramer, 2006).	Business case Strategic corporate social responsibility
2006	Nobel Peace Prize for Muhammad Yunus and his Grameen Bank's microfinance program [✱]	This drew international attention to how innovative social business models can solve and/or mitigate social and environmental issues profitably.	Microfinance Social business Poverty alleviation Business case

Period	Event	Summary	Topic areas
2006	Release of Al Gore's movie *An Inconvenient Truth*, which wins two Oscars [◆]	This movie educates about, and calls for action against, climate change and its world-threatening consequences (Guggenheim, 2006).	Climate change
2006	Launch of Product RED, the first mass-customized cause-related marketing campaign [◆]	Product RED provides the platform for businesses to introduce "RED" product lines under their own brand names. A percentage of sales revenue from RED-branded products goes toward fighting Aids in Africa (RED, 2015).	Sustainable consumption Cause-related marketing
2007	World financial and economic crisis [◆]	The crisis and its social and economic consequences was caused by the immoral business practice of "subprime lending," selling loans with a high probability of not being paid back.	Economic system failures
2007	Launch of the UN Principles for Responsible Management Education (PRME) [✱]	The PRME is a quickly growing alliance of business schools worldwide, devoted to educating responsible managers who are committed to promoting sustainable development through their vocational activity (PRME, 2011).	Sustainability education
2010	Publication of the ISO 26000 standards for social responsibility [✱]	ISO 26000 provides guidance to organizations on implementing social responsibility.	Institutionalization Norms
2015	UN Sustainable Development Goals [✱]	These consist of 17 goals to be achieved for globally sustainable development.	Global goals for sustainable development

B.
CONCEPTUALIZING

3
Sustainability

The first message we want to convey is that the present pattern of development cannot continue and must be changed. A second message—and one of hope—is that change is not only necessary—it is also possible.

Gro Harlem Brundtland, former prime minister of Norway (1987, p. 1)

Understanding sustainable development

The attentive reader of Chapter 1, which described the state of the world with all its issues, crises, human suffering, and environmental degradation, might arrive at some very fundamental questions: What can we do? Will we be able to stabilize and reverse the damaged state of the Earth? What is the cure?

Similar questions have led to the creation of the concept of sustainable development as an answer to the most pressing issues of the planet. According to the Brundtland definition, a sustainable development is one which balances resources for the future. What are these resources? What is this capital that we have to sustain for future generations to live well?

Barbier (1987) first described the three dimensions of sustainable development as social, environmental, and economic. These dimensions are made up of different types of capital: social, environmental, and economic. The economy is at the heart of a model of concentric circles that describes the interdependence of these three dimensions (Fig. 3.1). The model shows how economic activity is restricted by the borders of society (the next bigger circle). If a company exceeds the borders of what society allows as acceptable economic activity, it will lose its license to operate, meaning that society will force it to restrict its activity.

A pragmatic definition

The Brundtland report defines sustainability with a strong focus on intergenerational justice, or, as the U.S.A.'s first lady, Michelle Obama, put it in a speech in the White House, sustainable development has to do with "the most important job—being a mom—and, like mothers and fathers everywhere, the health and safety of our children is our top priority. This is what it is all about: the future" (Phillips, 2009).

This might happen, for instance, when consumers boycott a certain company due to a scandal, or when a company faces legal charges due to some societal or environmental damage that has taken place. The economy can be restricted by the labor force necessary for production or by consumer purchasing power. The biggest of the concentric circles is the environmental sphere, the planet, which constrains society in its growth. Unless we consider space colonization a viable option, the biological carrying capacity of the Earth is the final boundary for human population growth and economic growth alike.

Based on this graph, two further ways of describing the three dimensions of sustainable development are also shown in Figure 3.1. In the center, the famous pillar model conceptualizes how development can only be sustainable when balancing all three dimensions, co-creating and protecting social, environmental, and economic capital. On the right, a Venn diagram describes the different outcomes of unbalanced development. For instance, a strong focus on joint economic and social development, as has been observed in the People's Republic of China (with a stronger focus on the economic dimension), is equitable. It is an economic development whose fruits are shared with people. Nevertheless, such a development pattern is not viable in the intersection between economy and environment. Environment is a necessary production input. Natural resources-based economic inputs, such as steel and energy, cannot keep pace with economic

Figure 3.1: Main graphic concepts of sustainable development

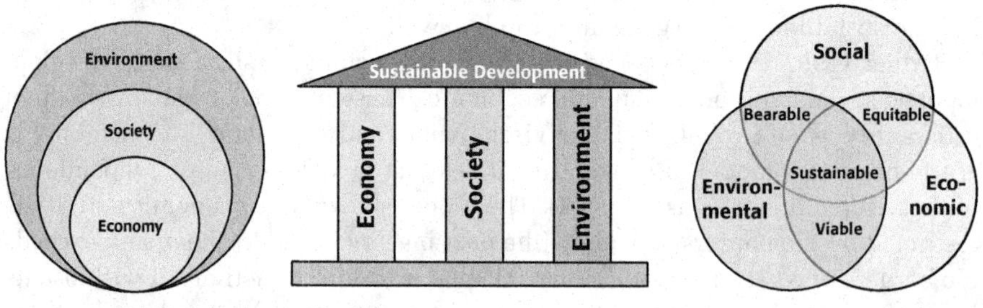

Source: United Nations (2005), Barbier (1987)

development. Such development is also not bearable in the relationship between society and environment. The air quality of China's cities, for instance, is among the world's worst. People in cities largely suffer from pulmonary diseases; the outcomes of development are socially unbearable.

Elkington (1998) coined the term "triple bottom line," which translates the lofty sustainability concept into a practical application. According to Elkington, in order to be sustainable, any activity has to produce a well-balanced triple bottom line among its social, environmental, and economic capital. While the financial bottom line is a universal business concept, the triple-bottom-line framework has recently become widely accepted as a tool for sustainable individual and governmental behavior. The basic assumption of the triple bottom line is that the three kinds of capital (social, environmental, and economic) must all be protected, or even renewed, in order for an activity to be called sustainable. In the frame of this book, we will describe the three main types of capital as follows:

1. **Social capital** is any capital directly embodied in human beings. Social capital on the one hand comprises individual—so-called human—capital including, such as knowledge, skills, values, and even physical health and personal wellbeing. On the other hand, social capital also comprises capital collectively created by interaction inside groups of human beings, such as joint values, culture, and collective welfare.

2. **Natural (environmental) capital** comprises both renewable and nonrenewable natural resources. Resources here should not be narrowly misunderstood as material production inputs, but also as nonmaterial services provided by the natural environment such as recreational value, or flower pollination by bees.

3. **Economic capital** can be expressed in monetary terms. It comprises tangible assets (often called man-made capital), such as machines or production facilities; intangible assets, such as customer loyalty or brand value; and financial resources, such as cash flows or a certain revenue margin. Economic capital can be attributed to an individual company or to the economic system as a whole.

Sustainable development and sustainability as goals for business, society, and government have to fulfill two basic characteristics. A truly sustainable activity has to be characterized by balancing and sustaining all three types of capital (Fig. 3.2). Horizontal sustainability creates harmony between the social, environmental, and economic components of the activity. Vertical sustainability aims to sustain, either by protecting or even increasing, the social, environmental, and economic capital involved for the future.

One might apply these two basic characteristics of analyzing sustainability for many types of activity. A law about to be passed by the government might be analyzed according to its social, environmental, and economic consequences. Likewise a certain consumption choice by a private individual might be analyzed. Two examples show the importance of both vertical and horizontal sustainability in the business sector:

Figure 3.2: Characteristics necessary to achieve sustainability

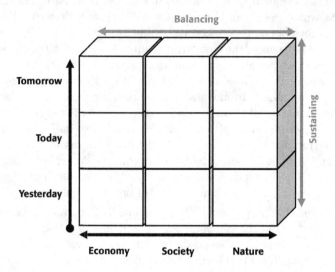

1. **Donations are economically unsustainable.** Should one consider a company that spends considerable amounts of money on donations for various good social and environmental causes a sustainable business? Most likely this company is creating social and/or environmental capital through its economic capital donations. Thus, the company is balancing two out of the three dimensions of horizontal sustainability. Then again, the company is not sustaining, and is possibly even decreasing, the economic capital involved in the activity: spending money. Once the money is all spent, the donation campaign will cease to exist (the vertical dimension). It has not been sustained economically and, therefore, cannot sustain the creation of social and environmental capital in the future.

2. **Unsustainability of short-term profit maximization.** Consider a typical short-term, profit-maximizing company that exploits natural resources and workers. While this company seems to be economically sustainable, it is not harmonized, or balanced, with the environmental and social dimensions. Using up the environmental and social capital will ultimately have negative repercussions on what had previously seemed to be economically sustainable. Workers might go on strike or leave the company completely. The environmental capital used for production might be exhausted. In the long run, this business activity is not vertically sustainable in any of the three dimensions of sustainable development.

From unsustainable behavior to global crisis

The 2007 subprime mortgage crisis, with devastating effects on the global economy, was based on unsustainable behavior. The root of the crisis, selling mortgages to people who were unlikely to pay them back, was in itself economically unsustainable and morally wrong. In the aftermath, the crisis also proved socially unsustainable. It resulted in massive job losses, mostly in the rather vulnerable employee groups of youth, immigrants, low-skilled, and older workers, and employees with short-term contracts (OECD, 2009).

The final goal of sustainable development has to be to live harmoniously within the Earth's carrying capacity. In order to reach this goal, there has to be a paradigm shift. Achieving harmony among people, nature, and the economy, is contradictory to a continued quantitative growth of economic activity and population size. Even sustaining the current situation will not lead to the declared goal of sustainable development. In order to reach sustainability on a planetary level, the most promising path is degrowth in combination with a qualitative development of economy and society. In setting this goal, one truly sees how big the task is. The current social and business paradigms are based on growth: managers are trained to increase market share, to grow the market size, to create additional wants, and to increase revenues. Workers in the private sector typically aim to earn more, spend more, and own more. Limitless abundance is the object of desire. Unless we are able to change these most basic behavior patterns, we will not achieve sustainable development, and humanity will become a highly endangered species.

An atypical business attitude

A region in northern Argentina, famous for its impressive scenery, lends its name to the outdoor clothing company Patagonia. This company shares a very special vision of how abundance may be just the right recipe for degrowth. The company's owner Yvonne Chouinard explains:

> At Patagonia we choose to call them "economies of abundance". In an economy of abundance, there is enough. Not too much. Not too little. Enough. Most importantly, there is enough time for the things that matter: relationships, delicious food, art, games and the rest. ... At Patagonia, we are dedicated to abundance. We don't want to grow larger, but want to remain lean and quick. We want to make the best clothes and make them so they will last a long, long time. Our idea is to make the best product so you can consume less and consume better. (Chouinard and Gallagher, 2004)

Customers at Patagonia shops reported that cashiers even asked them: "Do you really need to buy this item?" (Wise, 2011).

Sectoral contributions to sustainable development

In 2015, the United Nations proposed a series of Sustainable Development Goals for achieving global sustainable development, comprising 17 goals, and six central enablers for achieving these goals as illustrated in Table 3.1. The SDGs replaced the Millennium Development Goals that had expired in 2014. As we can grasp from the picture, no single societal sector, business, industry, civil society, or government will be able to reach these goals alone.

Figure 3.3 shows how the different societal sectors of business, civil society, and government can contribute to sustainable development. In order to reach the ultimate goal of sustainable development, the three main sectors of society must reach a state of sustainability socially, environmentally, and economically. The

Table 3.1: UN Sustainable Development Goals 2015

1. End poverty in all its forms everywhere
2. End hunger, achieve food security and improved nutrition, and promote sustainable agriculture
3. Ensure healthy lives and promote wellbeing for all at all ages
4. Ensure inclusive and equitable quality education and promote lifelong learning opportunities for all
5. Achieve gender equality and empower all women and girls
6. Ensure availability and sustainable management of water and sanitation for all
7. Ensure access to affordable, reliable, sustainable and modern energy for all
8. Promote sustained, inclusive and sustainable economic growth, full and productive employment and decent work for all
9. Build resilient infrastructure, promote inclusive and sustainable industrialization and foster innovation
10. Reduce inequality within and among countries
11. Make cities and human settlements inclusive, safe, resilient and sustainable
12. Ensure sustainable consumption and production patterns
13. Take urgent action to combat climate change and its impacts
14. Conserve and sustainably use the oceans, seas and marine resources for sustainable development
15. Protect, restore and promote sustainable use of terrestrial ecosystems, sustainably manage forests, combat desertification, halt and reverse land degradation and halt biodiversity loss
16. Promote peaceful and inclusive societies for sustainable development, provide access to justice for all and build effective, accountable and inclusive institutions at all levels
17. Strengthen the means of implementation and revitalize the global partnership for sustainable development

Source: United Nations, 2016.

desired outcome is sustainable business for the business sector, sustainable living for civil society, and sustainable governance for the governmental sector.

Designing multisector solutions

In 2007, the city of Toronto, Canada, launched the "Live Green Toronto" program in response to the "Climate Change, Clean Air, and Sustainable Energy" action plan. Large and small businesses and hundreds of consumers use an electronic card system to receive benefits from the purchase of eco-friendly products. Live Green Toronto includes all three sectors to jointly move toward sustainable regional development. The program has spread into many activities, including an app and an annual festival. A current focus is on creating a strategy for 2050 to "reduce emissions by 80 per cent by 2050 while creating a more healthy, equitable and prosperous Toronto" (City of Toronto, 2016).

In order to reach the desired state of sustainable development, each sector must implement a responsible practice focused on sustainability. Here, responsibility is defined as a responsibility toward the ultimate goal of sustainable development. Responsible business is the practice of activities leading to the desired outcome of being sustainable. The responsible practice for each sector is highly enhanced when based on sound ethical decision-making. This is why every sector uses a specialized ethical framework, such as business ethics, personal ethics, or governance ethics.

Figure 3.3: Sectoral contributions to sustainable development

Sustainable governance

In the process of achieving sustainable governance, the governmental sector has important contributions to make. The governmental sector's most powerful contribution consists of the making and implementation of laws and public policy measures for sustainable development. This governmental stage-setting function broadly influences both civil society and business sectors. Thus, government fulfills a support function in providing the legal infrastructure for both sustainable business and sustainable living. The quality of public policies implemented to achieve responsible business have been divided into first-generation (rudimentary implementation of responsible business activities), second-generation (focus on priority sectors), and third-generation (integration and mainstreaming) policies (Bertelsmann Stiftung and GTZ, 2007).

The government and broad public sectors are also important economic players. Public spending and public enterprises are main drivers in many industries, such as construction, energy, and transportation. The public sector can be a role model for private businesses, showcasing responsible management in its own organization. Many governments have done so, starting to focus on renewable energies, implementing sustainable sourcing policies, or defining energy efficiency standards for public housing. The sustainability of governments is monitored in the Sustainable Governance Index (SGI), which covers main governmental performance indicators related to the social (e.g., welfare, social inclusion), environmental (environment) and economic (e.g., economy, budgets, enterprises) dimensions of sustainability (SGI Network, 2015). The topic of good governance refers to the process of governance, i.e., public administration. Issues of special concern are governance ethics, especially human rights and corruption-related factors (UN ESCAP, 2011).

While the governmental sector does have strong national power in creating legal and physical infrastructure, it also experiences major constraints in its potential to achieve sustainable development. One inhibiting factor is the speed of decision-making, which includes implementation of changes that have already been decided on. Due to mostly democratic and highly hierarchical structures, urgent developments might not be implemented at the desired and necessary pace. Especially in countries with a weak governmental structure, corruption and lack of knowledge are potential factors leading to suboptimal outcomes. Governments have also been accused of being highly vulnerable to the lobbying activities of companies and industries opposed to sustainable development. Governments, while involved in diplomatic and supranational activities related to sustainable development, nevertheless exert the most significant influence on their own national territory. While most issues related to sustainable development transcend borders and have a global impact, this narrow sphere of influence by governments makes an effective contribution more difficult. The final section of Chapter 19 provides additional insights into what governments can do to contribute to sustainable development.

Sustainable living

Sustainable (or unsustainable) living is one of the most powerful forces for or against sustainable development. Lifestyles influence consumption choices, which in turn define the demand for certain products and services. The saying, "every time you spend money, you're casting a vote for the kind of world you want," perfectly captures the essence of how consumption influences social and economic structures (Lappé and Lappé, 2002). The legal voting power of citizens can also exert an enormous influence over the public policies implemented for sustainable development. Sustainable living is not only about how to spend, but also how to earn the money spent. Sustainable living includes promoting sustainability throughout any job practiced by an individual and to "vote with your feet" if the employing organization is not conducive to improving its social and environmental footprint.

What are you owned by?

After its release in 1999, the movie *Fight Club* became a cult classic showing the protagonist's way of dealing with his nonconformity with society and consumerism. A famous quotation from the movie is, "the things you own end up owning you" (Fincher, 1999).

Sustainable living refers to living in a way that does not exceed the Earth's carrying capacity and involves (and actively promotes) change toward sustainability among the individuals and organizations with whom one is in contact. In order to not exceed one's personal footprint on the world's natural resources, sustainable living needs to be based on a certain change in behavior patterns: individuals of middle and high economic purchasing power usually far exceed their environmental footprint. The movement of simple living, for instance, promotes a lifestyle of voluntarily focusing on the basic needs, while aiming to reduce personal dependence on superficial wants. Such simpler lives often lead to highly altered consumption patterns: "Freegans" are individuals who try to totally avoid consumerism by living off society's leftovers; and people living Lifestyles of Health and Sustainability (LOHAS) aim to change their consumption patterns to more sustainable ways. There are many living and consumption styles related to sustainable living; understanding these patterns is crucial for marketing sustainable products and will be further explained in Chapters 14 and 15.

Activist, or civic, behavior is another facet of sustainable living whereby a person promotes sustainability in their personal sphere of influence. Employing oneself as a change agent for sustainability can happen in an individual pattern, as previously described, or can be carried out in some type of civil society organization. Civil society organizations, or nongovernmental organizations (NGOs), address many different social, environmental, political, or economic causes. A weakness of civil society sector initiatives for sustainable development is the alleged lack of institutionalization, professionalization, and efficiency. Chapter 17 illustrates the necessary changes to reach a sustainable living situation.

Sustainable business

Sustainable business is still a utopia. To be truly sustainable, a business would need to have a sustainable (neutral or even positive) impact throughout the social, environmental, and economic dimensions. A responsible business is a business that has made a commitment to reach this goal. On the way to this ultimate goal, responsible business conduct can very effectively contribute to sustainable development. A salient advantage of the business sector is its speed of decision-making, based on an efficient organizational structure. This means that businesses have the ability to tackle social, environmental, and economic issues quickly—if they wish to. Also, businesses are less constrained by national borders. Policies for sustainable development can be implemented simultaneously and on a global scale throughout business facilities in the most diverse locations. The business sector also has the financial means to put extensive policies in place. Even more importantly, if business is able to make social and environmental responsibility a profitable part of its core business, the financial resources to contribute to sustainable development become self-renewing and abundant.

A natural incentive

Imagine a business that develops a product such as solar heaters in order to tap into a LOHAS market segment. This business is likely to discover that this market segment is not only creating value for the goal of environmental sustainability, but is also highly attractive and profitable. A natural reaction would be to invest even more resources in this venture. Automatically the business's contribution to sustainable development would grow in parallel with increased profit.

One of the most ambitious business-sector initiatives for sustainable development is the World Business Council for Sustainable Development's (WBCSD) *Vision 2050*, which proposes that 9 billion people will be able to "live well and within the limits of the planet" by the year 2050 (WBCSD, 2010). The WBCSD "Actions 2020" strategy translates this vision into tangible direct actions in nine impact areas (e.g., climate change, ecosystems, sustainable lifestyles) and five characteristics for business solutions (e.g., beyond business as usual, scalable, impactful). But is following general principles enough? How do we know we have achieved the goal of sustainable business? There is a strong argument that a company can only claim to have become sustainable based on an understanding of how its own performance relates to the planetary boundaries described in Chapter 1 (Whiteman *et al.*, 2013). Only if we can see the business in the context of local and planetary environmental systems can we reach an appreciation of the business's sustainability.

Disadvantageous characteristics of the business sector, when it comes to achieving sustainable businesses, are the inherent short-term profit maximization and the search for quick growth. One thing is certain: however committed a business is to its ultimate responsibility for sustainable development, if its sole goal is the quest for constant quantitative growth (as opposed to qualitative improvement), in the long run, it will not and cannot be sustainable. As identified in the previous section, businesses and the economy must to some extent stop growing in order to serve the needs of society that can be efficiently and sustainably met.

Exercises

A. Know

Use the multiple choice questions below to test your knowledge. Each answer may be wrong or right and there may be zero to four right or wrong answers per question:

1. Sustainable development ...

    a. ... in one of its primary concepts refers to the "three dimensions" of world development, state development, and individual development.
    b. ... has been defined as a development that "satisfies all wants of present generations, while also enabling a luxurious life for future generations."
    c. ... in one of its main graphical representations defines joint economic and environmental development without social development as viable, while it is neither bearable, nor equitable, and also not sustainable.
    d. ... does have a vertical and a horizontal dimension with the first describing persistence in time and the second describing the balance between social, environmental, and economic development.

2. Sustainable governance ...

    a. ... is the contribution to sustainable development made by governmental and the public sector.
    b. ... comprises as one of its main functions the development and implementation of laws for sustainable development.
    c. ... also has an economic component, related to public enterprises.
    d. ... can have an immense influence by lawmaking and enforcement. Nevertheless, its effectiveness in contributing to sustainable development is often mitigated by—compared with the business sector—slow decision-making and influence over a rather restricted territory.

3. Sustainable business ...

    a. ... is the contribution of the business sector to sustainable development.
    b. ... when contributing to sustainable development displays the main advantages: first, multinational businesses in particular have the capacity to make an impact in many countries at once; second, a business's natural incentive for degrowth helps to reduce its negative impact.
    c. ... can use its own profit-seeking nature to co-create socio-environmental and business value.
    d. ... connects to sustainable living for instance through the LOHAS market.

4. Sustainable living ...

    a. ... is the contribution of the public sector to sustainable development.
    b. ... among other things aims to enable consumers to "vote with their wallets."

c.   … comprises "voting with one's feet," which in the context of this book is defined as quitting work at a company that does not pay the highest wage in the market.

d.   … is easy as only those people living very luxuriously are likely to have an unsustainable footprint on the planet's systems.

B. Think

Think about one sustainability issue, such as water scarcity or poverty, to understand how the civic, private, and public sectors may contribute to solving it. Make sure you appreciate how the three sectors relate instead of describing their contributions in isolation.

C. Do

Think about one concrete action that you could take to reduce negative environmental impact, or even to create a positive environmental impact. Repeat this action at least five times.

D. Relate

Convince one person to change a concrete practice (e.g., printing, use of packaging, energy usage) to more sustainable ways.

E. Be

What does the topic of climate change mean to you? Then compare this appreciation with what it means to A) a Kenyan fisherman, and B) the Brazilian head of state.

Feedback

A. Know

Question 1

a.   Wrong: society, environment, and economy are typically called the three dimensions of sustainable development.

b.   Wrong: the main definition of sustainable development given by the Brundtland report defines a development that "meets the needs of the present without comprising the ability of future generations." By no means is it a development that aims to satisfy neither today's nor future superficial wants, broadly exceeding people's basic needs to live a decent life.

c.   Right: the Venn diagram model, first used by Barbier in 1987, represents the described fact. Sustainable development can only be a joint social, environmental, and economic development. Only if the three go together can development be environmentally and socially bearable, economically and environmentally viable, and economically and socially equitable.

d.   Right: the vertical and horizontal dimensions of sustainable development are its two basic defining characteristics.

Question 2

a.   Right: sustainable governance together with sustainable living and sustainable business is one of the three main necessary sectoral contributions to sustainable development.

b.   Right: the the governmental sector's most important contribution to sustainable development is related to creating a legal infrastructure.

c.   Right: public enterprises are important economic players which, being significantly controlled by governments, form part of the governmental sector.

d.   Right: while businesses are often characterized by a fast decision-making and implementation as well as a multinational influence, governments often work at a slower pace and only on national territory.

Question 3

a.   Right: sustainable business together with sustainable governance and sustainable business is one of the three main necessary sectoral contributions to sustainable development.

b.   Wrong: businesses are naturally geared to growth. In fact, degrowth, while being highly advantageous to reach sustainable development, is not supported by the contemporary economic structure.

c.   Right: the solar heater example illustrates a situation where the creation of environmental value is linked to profit-seeking activity.

d.   Right: the Lifestyles of Health and Sustainability (LOHAS) market connects to sustainable living by proposing sustainable lifestyles, while

LOHAS connects to sustainable business as a market segment prone to improve its socio-environmental impact.

Question 4

a. Wrong: the contribution to sustainable development of the public sector is called sustainable governance. Sustainable living is the contribution by civil society.

b. Right: a popular Lappé quotation is, "Every time you spend money, you're casting a vote for the kind of world you want." Consumption choices automatically enforce or weaken companies and their respective impact on society and environment. Buying from sustainable businesses therefore gives power to the sustainable business movement, fostering sustainable development.

c. Wrong: "voting with one's feet" in the context of this book means to base the decision about which company to work with on its social and environmental impact and/or improvements.

d. Wrong: most people of middle-class socioeconomic segments by far exceed what would be a sustainable footprint.

B. Think

Level	Multilevel analysis competence	Notes
+	Solid description of each sector's distinct contribution and of the connection between the sectors	
=	Solid description of each sector's distinct contribution	
–	Little description of each sector's distinct contribution to the issue	

C. Do

Level	Taking and sustaining action	Notes
+	Action was taken and repeated at least five times	
=	Action was taken	
–	Action was either not identified or was identified but not taken	

D. Relate

Level	Persuasion competence	Notes
+	Adoption of new practice after application of persuasion	
=	Adoption of practice in spite of little persuasive skill, or good persuasive skill, but no adoption of practice	
−	Little evidence of persuasive skill and no adoption of more sustainable practice	

E. Be

Level	Ability to take different perspectives	Notes
+	Profound level of insight into multiple perspectives displayed	
=	Multiple perspectives evident in description	
−	Evidence of singular perspective on climate change	

4
Responsibility

When approaching and practicing social responsibility, the overarching objective for an organization is to maximize its contribution to sustainable development.

(ISO, 2010, p. 10)

Having extensively discussed sustainable development, the question is: "How does all this relate to responsible business?" ISO 26000, which is expected to be the future standard for responsible business, defines the achievement of sustainable development as the ultimate responsibility of a responsible business. This is just one of a wide variety of terms and related frameworks used to describe responsible business.

One of the main terms used for responsible business is corporate social responsibility (CSR). When forecasting coming developments in corporate social responsibility at the start of the millennium, Windsor (2001) raised significant doubts about how CSR would develop in theory and practice. Nowadays, corporate social responsibility, or responsible business, in all its facets and varieties has become stronger than ever. Windsor was certainly right to predict that the traditional term and understanding of CSR would change. Today, terms such as responsible business, corporate responsibility, corporate citizenship, or business sustainability are used almost interchangeably, especially in business practice.

In spite of the often confusing use of vocabulary, business practitioners and scholars agree on one point: social and environmental business performance is a mainstream business megatrend, whether it is called responsible business, CSR, corporate citizenship, philanthropy, or business sustainability. The following quotations illustrate the scale and scope of the responsible business megatrend.

The responsibility imperative and revolution

- *Harvard Business Review*: "Most executives know that how they respond to the challenge of sustainability will profoundly affect the competitiveness—and perhaps even the survival—of their organizations" (Lubin and Esty, 2010, p. 2).

- Accenture and Global Compact CEO study: "Ninety-three percent of CEOs are convinced that sustainability will be critical for the future success of their business. Ninety-six percent believe it should be deeply integrated into companies' strategy and operations" (Lacey *et al.*, 2010).

- *Academy of Management Executive* (now called *Academy of Management Perspectives*): "A wide range of stakeholders is pushing companies to respond in a more responsible way" (Waddock *et al.*, 2002, p. 132).

- *The Responsibility Revolution*: "The voices of business establishment have come to recognize eight key drivers ... that make responsible corporate behavior an imperative. Not only are they persistent, they are predominant, and they will endure for decades to come" (Hollender and Breen, 2010, p. 7).

- *The Sustainability Revolution*: "A revolution of interconnections. The sustainability revolution provides a vital new approach to tackling the issues confronting the world today" (Edwards, 2005, p. 9).

From responsible business and management to sustainable business and development

What is meant by responsible and sustainable business? How are they different? In the context of this book, sustainable business has the intended goal of shaping a business that strongly contributes to sustainable development, a business with an at least neutral socio-environmental impact or, even better, a positive one. Responsible business, instead describes businesses that have made a commitment and implemented activities to reach the goal of sustainable business. Responsibility here means a commitment to achieving the status of a sustainable business and the ultimate responsibility of (collaboratively with the contributions of the governmental and civil society sectors) achieving sustainable development. Responsible management refers to the management processes, tools, and activities necessary to achieve the goal of sustainable business (Fig. 4.1).

This conceptualization of responsible and sustainable business, at first glance, might sound different than the traditionally established definitions. Nevertheless, on closer examination, it is a highly open and inclusive view which embraces the majority of the historical and contemporary understanding of the relationship between business, society, and environment. The final responsibility of achieving sustainable development can be seen as a categorical imperative (not to be

Figure 4.1: Dynamics and definitions of responsible business, responsible management, sustainable business, and sustainable development

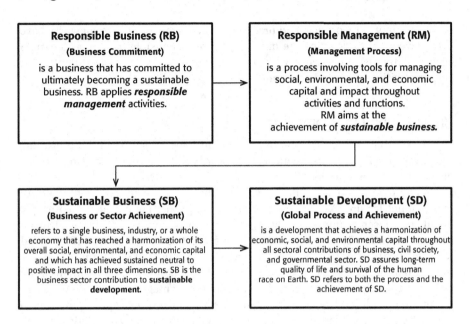

confused with Kant's categorical imperative) for evaluating each and every action a business takes. If aligning all business activity can become the main maxim of decision-making in business, it will automatically lead to fulfilling responsibilities to various stakeholders. This creates value for society, environment, and the economy alike. However, it has to be noted that this very narrow instrumental (responsibility as instrument for sustainability) working definition of responsible business and management may be complemented by a wider understanding. The wider understanding sees responsible management as a management embracing principles of sustainability, responsibility, and ethics (Laasch and Conaway, 2015).

Fruits on a sustainable business mission

Innocent is a British fruit smoothie company whose responsible business commitment reads like a textbook definition:

> We take responsibility for the impact of our business on society and the environment, aiming to move these impacts from negative to neutral or (better still) positive. It's part of our quest to become a truly sustainable business where we have a net positive effect on the wonderful world around us. (Innocent Drinks, 2012)

Background frameworks of responsible business

A wide variety of theoretical and practice-oriented management frameworks have been developed to describe the management of responsible business. The main academically discussed frameworks include the topics of business philanthropy, corporate citizenship, and corporate social responsibility.

Business philanthropy: altruist giving

Business philanthropy was one of the first and, for a long time, the prevailing framework for responsible business. The word "philanthropy" has Greek roots, meaning "love for mankind."

This basic altruism, or selfless giving for the good of mankind, is philanthropy's distinct feature. As we will see, many things that are called philanthropic might, on closer examination, be shown not to be motivated by an altruistic love for mankind. Topical variations, such as strategic philanthropy (Porter and Kramer, 2002), are not to be included under the umbrella of philanthropic activities. By definition, there is no such thing as strategic philanthropy. Philanthropy performed for the achievement of competitive advantage is not altruistic, and, therefore, not philanthropic. Also, venture philanthropy, or capital provided to power ventures with social value added, cannot be completely altruistic, as there is an intended return on the capital invested.

> ### Philanthropy, the divine fire
>
> It was the ancient Greeks and their saga of the god Prometheus sharing Zeus's divine fire with mortals that gave birth to the concept of "philanthropia" (Grosby, 2010).

It will later be shown how actions that seem to be altruistically, or philanthropically, motivated are actually egoistic. It is important to note that this lack of altruistic motivation does not necessarily have to be negatively interpreted. In fact, later it will be argued that a philanthropic motivation may lead to suboptimal results in responsible business.

"The age of philanthropy," as Visser (2010) puts it, is as old as civilized mankind. Ever since the term was coined in ancient Greece around 2500 BC, affluent individuals and institutions have been involved in charitable giving. Many religions expect their followers to share wealth in a selfless manner. Even today many charitable activities are religiously motivated. Industrial philanthropists, such as Microsoft's Bill Gates and CNN's Ted Turner, have made the headlines by donating billions of dollars of their private property to good causes (Visser, 2010). Individual philanthropic giving, as described here, is one form of philanthropic activity in the business field. Another type is institutional giving, which is usually done by corporate foundations.

Corporate citizenship: the company as political actor and part of the community

Corporate citizenship has become something of a buzzword. Crane and Matten (2010a) explain three different ways of understanding corporate citizenship:

1. **Limited view:** corporate citizenship = corporate philanthropy
2. **Equivalent view:** corporate citizenship= corporate social responsibility
3. **Extended view:** corporate citizenship recognizes the extended political role of the corporation in society

An extended view of corporate citizenship reveals its distinct features. A company is considered another civic actor in a specific community, i.e., it is a citizen. How community is defined in a specific case constitutes the scale of the respective citizenship activities. A company could be defined as a citizen of the local community in which its facilities are located, the national community, or even the global community. Citizenship brings about rights and responsibilities. Governments often are not able to completely fulfill all the responsibilities toward their citizens, so companies in many areas may support governmental functions if they accept and assume their political role in society by strengthening the three basic rights of citizens (Marshall, 1977):

1. **Social rights:** create social welfare for other citizens of the community. A company could establish community centers to provide education, invest in physical infrastructure, and provide volunteering opportunities.
2. **Civil rights:** assure the protection of unalienable entitlements. Companies can make a commitment to respect human rights throughout all their interactions with any kind of stakeholder.
3. **Political rights:** support political activism. Companies can support the political activity of their stakeholders by, for instance, giving employees leave time for political engagement.

Honing skills and doing even more good

Supporting employees to make an impact in the community is at the heart of corporate citizenship. The trend today is skills-based volunteering, in which employees base their contributions on personal strengths and skills (Hands On Network, 2011). Volunteering can also give skill training that is important to job performance: 83% of volunteers state that their volunteering improved their leadership skills, 78% communication skills, 62% problem-solving, 57% organization and multitasking, and 52% marketing skills (Women's Way, 2006).

Among the three types of citizen entitlement, companies are probably the most strongly engaged in the promotion of social welfare and the protection of human rights. The connection with responsible business is very obvious when corporate citizenship is defined as the "aspirational metaphor for business to be part of developing a better world" (McIntosh, 2010, p. 89).

This understanding of corporate citizenship as business activities for an improved world community is in accordance with the previously applied definition of responsible business being activities with the ultimate responsibility of achieving the sustainable development of the world.

Corporate (social) responsibility: fulfilling stakeholder responsibilities

The focus of study within corporate social responsibility is business conduct that acts on the various social responsibilities of a business toward its stakeholders. The most complete and inclusive definition of corporate social responsibility (CSR) stems from the European Union's development of a regional focus, a pole of excellence on CSR (Commission of the European Communities, 2006):

> Corporate social responsibility (CSR) is a concept whereby companies **integrate** social and environmental concerns in their business operations and in their interaction with their stakeholders on a **voluntary basis**. It is about enterprises deciding to go beyond minimum legal requirements and obligations stemming from collective agreements in order to address societal needs. Through CSR, **enterprises of all sizes**, in cooperation with their stakeholders, can help to reconcile **economic, social and environmental** ambitions. [our emphasis]

This definition includes the most salient points of the concept, as highlighted in the quotation. "Responsibility to whom?" might one ask. The answer is that business responsibility is defined by the different "stakeholders" that a company is connected with. The responsibilities toward these stakeholders might be of an "economic, social, or environmental" nature. Organizational responsibility is not only a topic for big corporations. "Enterprises of all sizes" can "integrate" responsible business practices into their operations. It is important to highlight the "voluntary basis" of such responsibilities. If a company is coerced by legal or societal pressure to adopt desirable practices, this cannot be considered a responsibility that the company accepted voluntarily.

One established framework for the description is the CSR pyramid developed by Carroll (1991). The pyramid proposes a sequence of levels of responsibility as follows:

- **Economic responsibilities:** the company does what is necessary to survive economically
- **Legal responsibilities:** the company does what is required by the law

- **Ethical responsibilities:** the company does what is considered moral behavior by stakeholders and broader society
- **Philanthropic/discretionary responsibilities:** the company exceeds basic expectations and chooses freely to engage with additional responsibilities

Carroll's stages of responsibility illustrate how corporate social responsibility is intertwined with other background theories presented throughout this chapter. Philanthropy and business ethics are presented as two subtopics under the broad umbrella of corporate social responsibility. Law is also presented as a subtopic, although this position contradicts the European Union definition, which defined corporate social responsibility as a responsibility above the sphere of legal requirements. This inclusiveness of corporate social responsibility toward related topics has served to define it as an umbrella term for responsible business management frameworks (Matten and Moon, 2004).

During the years of academic refinement of the term "corporate social responsibility" (CSR1), researchers have developed many similar terms, which in practice are often used interchangeably. Knowing these terms and their differences provides access to a rich field of research. Clarkson (1995) has provided an excellent framework for understanding the finer differences. Corporate social responsiveness (CSR2) refers to the characteristic posture and reaction toward social issues. The level of a company's responsiveness can be categorized in one of the following four stages:

1. **Defensive:** deny responsibility—doing less than required
2. **Reactive:** admit responsibility, but fight it—doing the least that is required
3. **Accommodative:** accept responsibility—doing all that is required
4. **Proactive:** anticipates responsibility—doing more than is required

Clarkson also describes corporate social performance (CSP), which refers to a company's performance in the direct relationship with one, several, or all of its stakeholder groups. This is why CSP has also been described as stakeholder

Wiggling responsiveness

It is fascinating how one company's corporate responsiveness can vary over time and different responsibility areas within the same business. Walmart, for instance, has implemented an extensively praised supplier code and assessment, considerably improving its sustainability throughout the company's massive supply chain. This progressive activity has all the characteristics of a highly advanced proactive activity (Walmart, 2009). Only a few years before, in 2005, Walmart had been criticized for questionable business practices involving its competitors and employees, when attacked by the filmmaker Robert Greenwald in the movie *Wal-Mart: The High Cost of Low Price*. Because of Walmart's denial of these responsibilities, this particular behavior would be characterized as defensive (Greenwald, 2005).

performance. Corporate social performance is less well defined than corporate social responsiveness. Carroll describes CSP as a cube bringing together the four types of responsibility covered in Carroll's pyramid, the four different levels of responsiveness, and several different stakeholder types. According to Carroll, such a combination of tools to describe a company's responsible behavior is best able to categorize a business's overall social performance (Carroll, 1979).

The term "corporate social responsibility" has many flaws. As summarized by Laasch and Flores (2010), the word "corporation" excludes businesses of other legal forms and sizes. The word "social" neglects the environmental and economic responsibilities of the business. By using the term "responsibility" the business is automatically guided into a mode of compliance (with responsibilities), which fails to reflect the immense opportunities related to responsible business. In recent years, have been made amendments to such semantic inconsistencies. For instance, Grayson and Hodges (2004) introduced the term "corporate social opportunity." The contemporary use of "corporate responsibility," which many practitioners have come to use, avoids the exclusion of environmental and economic responsibilities by referring to responsibility in general. The ISO 26000 standard uses the term "organizational responsibilities," instead of referring to mere "corporate responsibilities." This broadens the concept to include businesses of all types and sizes (ISO, 2010). The term "responsible business" does the same thing. Nevertheless, these adjustments remain incomplete. In Chapter 6, three-dimensional management will be proposed as an alternative, completely avoiding such semantic flaws.

"This is only for big corporations"

Due to the "corporate" focus, small and medium enterprises (SMEs) may be expected to have an intuitive barrier to embracing the concept and implementing corporate responsibility activities. However, in 2002, a survey in five European countries revealed that 48% of very small, 65% of small, and even 75% of medium-sized businesses had been involved in social causes. Business cases highlighted included a wide variety of SMEs, from a Polish construction company to an Austrian chocolate manufacturer (Mandl, 2005).

Exercises

A. Know

Use the multiple choice questions below to test your knowledge. Each answer may be wrong or right and there may be zero to four right or wrong answers per question:

1. Responsible business ...
   a. ... includes sustainable development as one of the background management frameworks.
   b. ... includes philanthropy as one of the background management frameworks. Philanthropy includes both organizational and individual giving.
   c. ... includes main practice frameworks for its management such as the Global Compact, ISO 26000 and the SGI.
   d. ... as one main element aims to manage stakeholder relationships.

2. Corporate citizenship ...
   a. ... in its equivalent view equals corporate philanthropy.
   b. ... as one of the central ideas sees companies as political actors with responsibility for improving their respective communities.
   c. ... defines community as strictly the community (in the sense of a settlement) that the company operates in locally.
   d. ... aims at the company promoting and supporting the three main rights of citizens.

3. Corporate social responsibility (CSR) ...
   a. ... has been defined by Archie B. Carroll in a pyramid model.
   b. ... in its definition by the European Union and others, defines corporate social responsibility as interaction with stakeholders. Corporate social responsibility in this definition primarily targets compliance with local and international laws.
   c. ... is related to the topic of corporate social performance. It is defined as high corporate social performance when a company proactively reacts even before stakeholders claim the company has engaged in a particular activity.
   d. ... is a flawless description of an organization's social, environmental, and economic responsibilities.

4. Imagine a company refuses to talk to the members of the local community who have gathered at the gate of one of their factories after a chemical spill. This is an example of ...
   a. ... philanthropic responsibility
   b. ... of an accommodative response

    c.   ... high corporate social responsiveness
    d.   ... a defensive response

B. Think

Inform yourself about the British Petroleum oil spill in the Gulf of Mexico and make a list of the main stakeholders affected by the disaster. Think about how each of them was affected by the oil spill and rank them based on the level of negative consequences they had to suffer.

C. Do

Find a company's corporate responsibility report online and review it. Write a short brief which explains what concrete actions you would take to improve the company's corporate social performance.

D. Relate

Find a company's social network presence (e.g., on Facebook, LinkedIn, Twitter, or YouTube; some companies have independent social networks or blogs), and ask them a question in an ongoing conversation there. If necessary try it several times until you receive an answer and are able to reply to it. Try to draw others into the conversation.

E. Be

Think about someone in your sphere of influence (anyone there is a stakeholder by definition) who might benefit most from something you could do. Then do it and reflect on how it made you feel.

Feedback

A. Know

Question 1

a. Wrong: sustainable development is the intended outcome to which sustainable business aims to contribute.
b. Right: both forms of giving fall into the broad category of philanthropy.
c. Wrong: the Sustainable Governance Index (SGI) is a norm primarily applied to the field of responsible governance.
d. Right: one of the main activities in responsible business is stakeholder management.

Question 2

a. Wrong: the limited view describes CC as corporate philanthropy. In the equivalent view, it equals corporate social responsibility.
b. Right: community thinking and seeing the company as a political entity are central elements of CC.
c. Wrong: the understanding of community in CC varies largely from small local communities to even the world community.
d. Right: companies being good citizens should protect and promote the social, civil, and political rights of their stakeholders.

Question 3

a. Right: the four steps of the pyramid of corporate social responsibility are: 1) economic, 2) legal, 3) ethical, and 4) discretionary/philanthropic.
b. Wrong: the European Union definition aims to fulfill voluntary responsibilities, which exceed the basic legal requirements and expectations of society.
c. Wrong: proactive reactions are part of the corporate social responsiveness framework, which describes a company's mode of reaction to stakeholder claims.
d. Wrong: the term "CSR" in all three of its words is flawed. "Corporate" excludes other business and organization forms, "social" does not include environmental and economic responsibilities, and "responsibility" excludes opportunity.

Question 4

a. Wrong: if this was a philanthropic responsibility the company would do something good for their stakeholders without anyone asking them to do so.
b. Wrong: an accommodative response is when a company "does all that is required." Here a minimum requirement would be to listen to and speak to the stakeholders.

   c.   Wrong: high corporate social responsiveness would be if the company responds either in an accommodative or even in a proactive fashion. In this case their response is defensive.

   d.   Right: by not speaking to stakeholders the company denies their responsibility, which is a defensive response.

B. Think

Level	Analyzing social consequences	Notes
+	Wide appreciation of stakeholders affected and well-reasoned, sensible appreciation of the different degrees of impact.	
=	Wide appreciation of the stakeholders affected.	
−	Narrow or no appreciation of the breadth of stakeholders affected.	

C. Do

Level	Improvement and adaptation skills	Notes
+	Feasible and well-thought-through actions to increase corporate social performance, based on a deep understanding of the company status quo as outlined in the corporate responsibility report.	
=	Either a good appreciation of the company status quo or concrete actions to improve its corporate social performance.	
−	Little appreciation of the company status quo and no concrete actions to improve its corporate social performance.	

D. Relate

Level	Initiating and sustaining multilateral dialogue	Notes
+	Ongoing conversation with multiple partners.	
=	Bilateral dialogue with company.	
−	No communication established.	

E. Be

Level	Caring attitude	Notes
+	Someone has been cared for and the reflection shows a deeper inclination toward caring.	
=	Someone has been positively affected.	
–	No evidence someone has been cared for.	

5
Ethics

If you build that foundation, both the moral and the ethical foundation, as well as the business foundation, and the experience foundation, then the building won't crumble.

Henry Kravis, venture capitalist (2010)

What is business ethics?

Business ethics is the study of morally right or wrong decisions in a managerial context. Why are such decisions so fundamentally important for business conduct in general? Why is business ethics the very basis for responsible business? According to Crane and Matten (2010b, p. 46), "business ethics can be seen as the analytical tool that managers and others can use to understand, conceptualize and legitimize the moral status of corporate policies, strategies and programmes." Business ethics supports a concise reflection of what the business is doing, what it should or should not do, and, therefore, builds the foundation for any subsequent business activity, from mainstream management to the implementation of responsible business policies.

The terms "ethics" and "morality" are often used interchangeably, which, from a conceptual perspective, is wrong. Understanding the difference between ethics and morality supports a clearer understanding of concrete issues in practice. Ethics and morality are two mutually affecting components of the same reasoning and decision-making process. The philosophical foundation of ethics provides the tools for determining right from wrong in an ethical dilemma. Ethics is based on often philosophical decision-making schemes, while morality is the application of these schemes to concrete situations. One could also say that ethics is the tool for developing morality, while morality is the outcome of the ethical decision-making process. The moral outcome of ethical decisions can take many forms, such as a group's values, a written code of ethics, or a certain culture of "dos and don'ts" within a specific group of people.

Codes of morality?

In 2007, 85% of the first 100 companies listed in the London-based FTSE stock index had codes of ethics. While the term "codes of ethics" might suggest that such a code provides ethical reasoning mechanisms, the contents instead illustrate a pre-fixed set of moral rules, or "dos and don'ts," for certain situations. Strictly speaking, these documents should rather be called codes of morality (Webley, 2007).

Morality without ethics is a static product of rules, which may become out of date. This is why ethical reasoning should not only create a certain morality, but should also constantly be applied in order to reevaluate whether that morality still reflects the ethical reasoning on which it was originally based. Also, ethics without morality does not live up to the full potential of ethical reasoning, as it lacks application. A philosophical ethical debate, which is not translated into a practical application (morality), has, at best, theoretical value.

Figure 5.1 illustrates how business ethics can be divided into three main domains (Crane and Matten, 2010a). The first and most commonly considered domain is normative business ethics, which aims to provide guidance to determine right or wrong for an ethical decision in a business context. Normative ethics is often erroneously equated with the entire business ethics field, disregarding the second domain, descriptive business ethics, and the third, ethics management. Descriptive business ethics focuses on understanding and describing the "why" of an ethical decision, scrutinizing individual and situational factors important to understanding it. Ethics management is concerned with the institutional implementation of tools that assure "good ethics" and avoid ethical misconduct.

Figure 5.1: Domains of business ethics

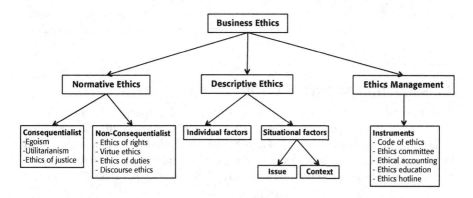

Examples of such tools include codes of ethics, ethics officers, and ethics hotlines. This chapter focuses on the first domain, normative business ethics, while Chapter 6 provides deeper insight into the management implications of descriptive ethics and ethics management.

Not all decisions have an ethical component. Crane and Matten (2010a) define three main characteristics of ethical decisions. One can talk of an ethical decision only if it is:

- Ethically relevant
- Has potential effect on others
- Involves a choice to be made

Normative business ethics: making right decisions

What is the right decision? What should not be done? Normative business ethics, as framed in this book, does *not* provide a definite answer to these questions. Instead, it provides a set of reasoning mechanisms which lead to a diverse set of potential answers. Such an approach is called ethical moral pluralism, as opposed to moral absolutism, which postulates that there can only be one absolutely right solution to an ethical dilemma. The pluralist line-up of different ethical solutions to a specific problem should not lead to a moral ambiguity in the sense of "anything goes," but instead should enable managers to evaluate a solid basis of different ethical alternatives, which is a very "pragmatic perspective," as proposed by Crane and Matten (2010a). In communicating responsible business, understanding these alternatives also helps to understand the different types of reasoning applied by a company's stakeholders and helps to shape adequate answers.

The main streams of ethical reasoning can be divided into consequentialist (outcome oriented) and non-consequentialist (non-outcome oriented) ethics. In the academic tradition, these two categories have often been used very narrowly, applying only a few streams of ethical reasoning. In the context of this book, the literal understanding of the term will be applied in order to provide a practical categorization of important streams of thought in either consequentialist or non-consequentialist ethics.

Consequentialist ethics: judging by the outcome

Consequentialist ethics judge the right or wrong of a specific situation by its outcomes, or its consequences. The main concepts in consequentialist ethics are egoism and utilitarianism. Ethics of rights is here included under consequentialist ethics. As framed here, it judges ethical right or wrong by analyzing whether the outcomes of a decision respect the unalienable rights of all involved.

First, egoist ethics focuses on the self-interest of the ethical decision-maker. This interest might, on the one hand, be short-term, desire-based egoism, or "doing what one wants." Self-interest might also be interpreted as long-term self-interest. Thus, egoism does not necessarily contradict responsible business. If, for instance, the business owner decides to donate a certain amount of money because it makes him feel better, this superficially philanthropic activity is motivated by egoist ethics. The more obvious it becomes that responsible business activities can be very advantageous, or that responsible business has a "business case," the more value for society and environment will be created from egoist motivations. Egoism does not always mean that the decisions being made are to the disadvantage of others. This would only be true if the pursuit of individual self-interest leads to harm for others, which is not always the case. In order to understand egoism, it is important to see it from a neutral perspective. Yes, egoist decision-making does involve a certain danger that it might lead to negative consequences for others. Nevertheless, it can become a powerful tool for doing good when there is a win–win situation, a situation where the pursuit of self-interest also creates value for others.

Egoists, genetically altruistic

The Selfish Gene, a book published in 1975 by the British evolutionary biologist Richard Dawkins, argues that altruistic behavior is in the genes. From an evolutionary perspective, it makes sense to be good to others as this behavior increases the likelihood of reproduction and genetic survival in the long run. Thus, egoism, or selfishness, even on a genetic level of interpretation, may lead to a behavior perceived as altruistic (Dawkins, 1976).

Second, utilitarianism aims to create maximum utility, or welfare, for all groups and individuals affected by a decision. In contrast to egoism, the right decision is not the one making the decision-maker "maximum happy," but the one creating the greatest happiness for all involved (Mills, 2008). This so-called "greatest happiness principle" has found very modern applications in responsible business. The responsible business management tool of stakeholder management facilitates a consideration of all effects that a certain business activity has on the various groups that it "can affect or are affected" (Freeman, 2010, p. 25). The discussion about maximizing stakeholders' value instead of maximizing shareholders' value is one of utilitarian versus egoist ethics arguments.

Third, ethics of rights considers a decision right when its outcome does not harm the unalienable rights and entitlements of the groups and individuals involved. The most common theory of ethics of rights is in the field of citizen and human rights. The Universal Declaration of Human Rights is the most recent document defining human rights (United Nations, 2011b). Ethics of rights has recently been extended to include special fields, such as the rights of future and unborn generations, animal rights, and the right of nature as a whole.

Non-consequentialist ethics: judging by intrinsic qualities

Non-consequentialist streams of normative ethical thinking can be based on various factors not being the outcome of the action or decision. Ethical right and wrong is based on the intrinsic qualities of the decision, such as motivation (ethics of duties), the virtuous characteristics of the actor (virtue ethics), or the fairness of an action (ethics of justice).

First, ethics of justice follows the principle of fairness. Fairness is comprised of the two domains of fair outcomes and fair procedures leading to these outcomes (Crane and Matten, 2010a; Rawls, 1999). Thus, ethics of justice has components of both consequentialist and non-consequentialist ethics. Consequentialist outcome-oriented justice aims at "everybody getting what he deserves." Non-consequentialist procedural justice, instead, assures what a fair outcome is and implements the adequate process leading to this outcome.

Fairness in executive remuneration?

A controversial topic in the fairness debate is the topic of executive payment. Is it fair that, among the Standard & Poor's 500 companies, a CEO in 2015, on average, earned US$13.5 million? This sum equaled the annual wage of 373 average U.S. workers (AFL-CIO, 2015).

Second, virtue ethics defines a right decision by the virtuous character of the actor or decision-maker. Good decisions are ones that are made by a person of virtuous character. When focusing on virtue ethics, character education increases in importance in order to foster good ethical decisions. While the other streams of ethical thought can be learned and understood on an intellectual level, virtue ethics requires character building. A conceptual flaw of virtue ethics is that there is hardly a generally accepted set of virtues one should possess. The underlying question is: "What is a virtuous character?"

Third, ethics of duties means the duty or responsibility to adhere to higher rules and principles. Such rules are not given: human beings should be able to derive these rules themselves. Kant's set of three maxims is the most commonly known framework for developing such higher principles for any given situation. According to Kant, in order to be considered right and good every action has to comply with the following three points (Kant et al., 2002):

1. Would you want your action to become universally lawgiving? Would you wish everybody else to act the same way?

2. Do you treat human beings as a means or as an end? It is not desirable to use human beings for a certain purpose, but instead to align your action for the good of humanity.

3. Act as if, by your action, what you do would automatically become a natural law.

Applying normative ethics

While the previously mentioned streams of normative ethical thought are not complete, they provide a powerful toolset for ethical decision-making. See the box below for an example.

News of the world, freshly hacked

The 168-year-old traditional British newspaper *News of the World* (NoW) was shut down in 2011. It was revealed that thousands of phones had allegedly been hacked, including those of politicians, celebrities, and even a kidnapped girl, and it had been going on for several years. Sean Hoare, a former NoW reporter, was quoted as saying "Everyone knew. The office cat knew." Imagine you are a newly hired mid-level manager of the *News of the World* and happen to find out about the phone-hacking activity. Due to your strong values and your past congruent application of ethics in your private and professional life, this situation poses a serious dilemma. What would be the right thing to do? (CBC News, 2011; Sabbagh, 2011; New Statesman, 2010)

Table 5.1 sums up the likely recommendations given by the streams of ethical reasoning described above. Imagining you were a NoW employee who had found out about the questionable phone-hacking practices. What might be the typical considerations stemming from the different types of ethical reasoning?

Table 5.1: Applying pluralistic ethical decision-making to the NoW case

Reasoning	Core question	Typical considerations
Egoism	Which decision is in my best interest?	Will I be fired for whistle-blowing?
		Will other companies want to hire me if I am perceived as a "traitor?"
		Will my colleagues be mad at me and give me a hard time?
		Will the general public see me as a hero?
Utilitarianism	What is the best decision for all involved?	Is the overall effect among all people affected by the hacking, positive or negative?
		Is the harm done to the victims of the hacking smaller or bigger than the suffering of the people losing their jobs when the NoW collapses?
Ethics of rights	How do I avoid harming human rights?	How can I best prevent the NoW from continuing to violate the right of privacy?
		How are the NoW's freedom of press and its readers' right to information involved?
Ethics of justice	What is the fairest solution?	Is it fair that the NoW is making business by harming the hacking victims?
Virtue ethics	Does the actor have a virtuous character?	Is the NoW generally a good ("virtuous") newspaper?
		Is the hacking done out of good or bad intentions?
Ethics of duties	Does the action comply with the requirements of being universally lawgiving and considering human beings involved as ends?	Would I want all newspapers to start hacking mailboxes?
		Does the NoW use people or does it intend to help people through its hacking activities?
		What would I want others in my situation to do?
		By which decision do I involve people as ends and not as means for my own benefit?

Exercises

A. Know

Use the multiple choice questions below to test your knowledge. Each answer may be wrong or right and there may be zero to four right or wrong answers per question:

1. Business ethics ...

    a.   ... is a synonym for business morality.
    b.   ... comprises the three main domains of normative and descriptive ethics and ethics management.
    c.   ... in its subdomain normative business ethics primarily aims to understand why people make bad or good decisions in ethical dilemma situations.
    d.   ... is just a synonym for ethics management.

2. Normative ethical theories ...

    a.   ... in this book has been divided into consequentialist and non-consequentialist ethical theories.
    b.   ... include ethics of duties mainly based on the thinking of John Stuart Mills.
    c.   ... include virtue ethics, which is rooted in ancient Greek philosophy. Virtue ethics is a typical consequentialist theory.
    d.   ... includes egoism, the opposite of altruism. In egoist ethics, the intended outcome is one's own good. Somebody motivated by egoist thinking would, for instance, never donate money to a good cause.

3. Imagine if, in the retail corporation where you work, it has become a common practice that buyers ask suppliers to forfeit money in exchange for the renewal of their supplier contract. Which of the following sentences describing the situation would express a descriptive ethics perspective?

    a.   I think the reason why the buyers act this way is that they have high pressures to keep a high margin. Paying the money the suppliers are owed would reduce their margin.
    b.   This practice is wrong as it is not fair that suppliers are not paid what they are owed.
    c.   I think we need a buyer code of conduct that explicitly states that such behavior is forbidden.
    d.   Business is as it is. It is perfectly legitimate to drive a hard bargain!

B. Think

Imagine you work in a company's HR department and have found out that it is a common practice to systematically pay less than is contractually agreed to some employees in order to save the company money. Whenever single employees find out, it is justified as "accounting mistake" and the difference is paid. Apparently, the practice is widely known in the senior management team, and is approved by them, as the company is currently in a difficult economic situation. It is apparent that any major issue or scandal impacting in further loss of customer confidence might lead to bankruptcy. What would you do?

C. Do

Look up one company's code of ethics and inform yourself about the typical ethical issues in the company's industry, past ethical issues encountered by the company (e.g., through news coverage), and potential ethical issues.

D. Relate

Think about one situation where you thought you knew what the ethically right thing to do was, but you did not speak up so people ended up doing the wrong thing. Get in touch with the people involved, tell them what you think would have been the right thing, and why you did not tell them back then.

E. Be

Reflect on how you make your ethical decisions. Think about several occasions where you had to make a morally difficult decision. What were the main thoughts and arguments leading to the decision you finally took? Can you recognize any of the above normative theories or decision-making principles as dominant in the way you made these decisions?

Feedback

A. Know

Question 1

a.   Wrong: business ethics as ethics in general refers to the mechanism of making right or wrong decisions, while morality rather focuses on values of specific individuals, groups, and situations, which are the outcomes of the ethical decision-making process.

b.   Right: the three main domains of business ethics mentioned in the question are illustrated in Figure 5.1.

c.   Wrong: this description refers to descriptive ethics, while normative ethics aims to provide reasoning mechanisms that aim to normatively define right or wrong or any given situation.

d.   Wrong: ethics management is a subdomain of business ethics, which deals with the management instruments necessary to achieve "good ethics" in an organization.

Question 2

a.   Right: mainstream philosophy aims at more complex subdivisions of normative ethics. For the pragmatic, management-focused purpose of this book the distinction has been made between outcome-based (consequentialist) and not-outcome-based (non-consequentialist) ethics.

b.   Wrong: ethics of duties is mainly based on the thinking of Kant. John Stuart Mills is the grandfather of utilitarianism.

c.   Wrong: virtue ethics as basing the reasoning for right or wrong on the actors' virtuous, good character is non-consequentialist theory.

d.   Wrong: egoist ethics explicitly predicates that someone acts out of self-interest, but nevertheless creates positive outcome for others. Someone donating money might for instance do so for the egoist motivation of the desire to feel like a good person.

Question 3

a.   Right: this statements aims to describe the reasons underlying the (unethical) behavior.

b.   Wrong: the question about right or wrong is made from a normative ethics position, not from a descriptive ethics stance.

c.   Wrong: this statement describes a management instrument (a code of ethics) to manage behavior in a way that leads to the buyers doing the right thing, which is typical for the domain of ethics management.

d.   Wrong: no assumption about the reasons for the unethical behavior is made. The statement legitimizes the behavior.

B. Think

Level	Moral reasoning	Notes
+	Decision based on higher principles such as justice, fairness, or the categorical imperative, possibly going beyond established societal norms with such typical statements as "I don't care what people think—it is the right thing to do" or "I cannot do it, as it is against a fundamental human rights principle"	
=	Decision based on arguments and motivations related to social conformity, with such typical statements as "I will do it if it is legal" or "what will people think?"	
−	Decision based on arguments and motivations related to avoiding punishment, and achieving direct reward, with such typical statements as "what's in for me?" and "I do it if I am certain not to be caught"	

C. Do

Level	Using ethics management tools	Notes
+	Code has been corroborated or adapted, based on a demonstrated deep understanding of ethical issues encountered in company and industry	
=	Code has been corroborated or adapted	
−	Code has been neither corroborated nor adapted	

D. Relate

Level	Asserting one's moral concerns	Notes
+	Moral concern has been voiced, and learning about how to make sure to voice concerns in similar future situations has been realized	
=	People have been contacted and the moral concern has been voiced	
−	Situation has not been identified and/or people have not been contacted	

E. Be

Level	Reflecting on own decision-making	Notes
+	Deep introspection into own ethical decision-making patterns and a link to underlying ethical theories or values	
=	Basic introspection into own ethical decision-making patterns	
–	Reflection has not happened or not led to introspection	

C.
MANAGING

6
Responsible management process

The triple bottom line (TBL) concept underscores the fact that companies and other organizations create value in multiple dimensions. ... A linked phrase, People, Planet, Profit ... is based on the same concept.

(Elkington, 2010, p. 406)

[T]he economic, environmental and social bottom lines.

(Elkington, 1998, p. 73)

Three-dimensional management for the triple bottom line

How does one manage a responsible business? As previously defined, the ultimate goal of responsible business must be to contribute to sustainable development. The three dimensions of sustainable development are social, environmental, and economic. Therefore, any management activity in a responsible business has to create value in all three dimensions, achieving performance and the creation of all three kinds of capital. Elkington (1998) described this intended management outcome as the triple bottom line, in contrast to traditional business's single bottom line of financial value. Three-dimensional management (3D management) is the integrated management process aimed at the creation of a sound triple bottom line (Fig. 6.1). From this point on, responsible management and 3D management will be used synonymously.

Figure 6.1: Three-dimensional management and the triple bottom line

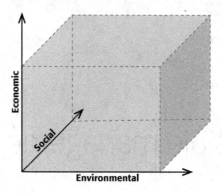

Social, environmental, and economic capital can be impacted inside and outside the company. Social value outside the company could be social welfare created by a donation to a local school, while internal social value could be increased job satisfaction of employees. Outside environmental value could be reflected by the reduction of environmental impacts of a zero-waste facility, while internal environmental value might be the improvement of an office's internal environment by the use of sustainable architecture. External economic value of a business activity could be the economic benefit created for the supplier of a company, while a typical internal economic value could be the profit created from a particular business activity. Value here should not to be confused with a person's or a group's values, referring to a set of moral standards. Value instead refers to the positive or negative effect of an action along the lines of external and internal effects as they are used in welfare and environmental economics. Value refers to an effect in social, environmental, and economic capital.

Managing blended value

John Elkington, the creator of the term "triple bottom line" (TBL), describes sustainable business as a "multidimensional challenge," defined by the basic task to manage social, financial, and environmental (3D) value simultaneously (Elkington, 2011). This task, which could also be called the management of "blended value" (Emerson, 2003), is the very basis of 3D management. The difference between the two terms is that the TBL describes the desired outcome, while 3D (or responsible management) describes the management process.

Value creation is a highly interlinked process. Often one type of value automatically leads to another. A wage increase for workers (positive economic value) leads to an increase in the welfare of families (positive social value). The workers might be able to take their families on vacation, which in turn might lead

Table 6.1: Classifying value creation into internal, external, social, environmental, and economic

	Internal	External
Social	(+) Employee satisfaction (–) Number of accidents (+) Diversity indicators (+) Direct employment	(+) Customer satisfaction (+) Healthiness of products (+) Community wellbeing (+) Indirect employment
Environmental	(+) Lighting and air quality (+) Biodiversity in facility (+) Gardening (–) Land use	(–) CO_2 emissions (–) Water discharged (–) Waste disposed (–) Biodiversity loss
Economic	(+) Revenue (+) Profit (+) Wages paid (+) Stock value	(–) Competitor destruction (+) Supplier economies (+) Regional economic development (+) Innovation spillovers

to an additional amount of CO_2 emissions in the form of transportation used to reach the holiday destination (negative environmental value). Also the external and internal creations of value are highly connected. The activity leading to the creation of a certain value does not have to be realized in the same location as the value created. Porter and Kramer (2006) describe how company-internal factors create value outside the company (inside-out linkages) and external factors lead to value creation inside the company (outside-in linkages). Value creation can also be understood in light of the three different types (social, environmental, economic) of capital as illustrated in Chapter 3. A positive value reflects an increase, a negative value a reduction in the respective capital. Table 6.1 provides an overview of different types of positive and negative value that might be created in typical business conduct.

"Value creation:" why talk about responsible business in such a lifeless and technical way? Is not responsible business all about exciting topics such as saving the planet, combating poverty, and being a good person and moral manager? Yes it is. Still, in order to reach these goals management is in urgent need of a meta-perspective, which allows for understanding, measurement, and management of the effect of the responsible management process as described in the following section.

Immediate versus intergenerational responsibilities

As mentioned previously, sustainable development, a development that allows for the survival of the human race on Planet Earth, is the ultimate goal of every responsible business. Do the working conditions in a third-world factory affect humanity's survival on Earth? Does it really matter if another species, for instance the polar bear, becomes extinct? On a more cynical note, wouldn't it be good for the survival of humanity to keep the majority of the world population in poverty, given that poor people have the smallest average environmental footprint?

What does this ultimate responsibility to sustainable development mean? What responsibilities should or shouldn't a business assume? To answer these questions, it helps to review the Brundtland definition (United Nations, 1987) of sustainable development mentioned in Chapter 3. The definition refers to the goal of fulfilling the present generation's needs and to create a situation in which future generations can also fulfill their own needs. Thus, for a responsible business, making this ultimate commitment to contribute to sustainable development means assuming two kinds of responsibility: immediate and intergenerational.

Responsible business and responsible management require both kinds of responsibility to be addressed, balancing the fulfillment of current needs with the fulfillment of future needs:

- Immediate responsibilities focus on fulfilling the needs of stakeholders by maximizing stakeholder welfare. This would include the poor's right to improve their standard of living. It would also include fair, healthy, and safe working conditions. Immediate responsibilities should also include responsibilities not necessarily basic to human wellbeing. A company needs to go beyond the question of "What do people need?" and include the rights of other beings, beyond their value to people. Even if the survival of polar bears might not be instrumental to human wellbeing, neither today, nor in the future, responsible businesses should assume the responsibility to protect natural entities beyond their instrumental value.

- Intergenerational responsibilities focus on assuring humanity's survival on Earth and maintaining and restoring today's resources for future generations. Intergenerational responsibilities pragmatically follow the question: "What do we need for the future?"

The responsible management process

The responsible management process, aimed at the management of social and environmental business performance—3D management—requires three main elements of the responsible management process, and one management instrument, as depicted in Figure 6.2. These four components are always present in any responsible management activity. The three elements could be called the trinity of responsible management:

1. The **actor**, or agent, of a 3D management activity executes 3D management. An actor might be a corporation, an entrepreneur, an NGO, or a government agency.

2. The **impacts** to be made on social, environmental, or economic issues involved in the management process are manifold and may require substantial and diverse specialist knowledge. Issues might, for instance, be CO_2 emissions, demographic diversity, or global warming.

3. **Stakeholders** are the groups that "can affect or are affected" (Freeman, 2010, p. 25) by the business in general and more specifically by the 3D management activity at hand.

The responsible **management instrument** is the specific administrative tool applied to a responsible management activity.

To manage responsible business, it makes sense to split a company's overall activity into individual manageable activities. Once such a list of individual activities is established, it is crucial to deeply understand the three main elements and the management instrument applied to each activity. Imagine the three different responsible management activities below:

Figure 6.2: The responsible management process trinity

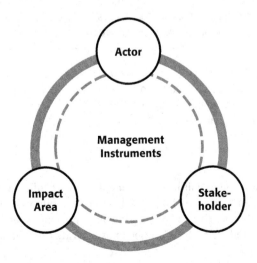

Green packaging technology

The Mexican bakery and pastry products manufacturer Bimbo is a leader in the biodegradable plastic packaging movement. In 2008, Bimbo was one of the first companies in Latin America to introduce a biodegradable polyethylene wrapping for bread products. In 2010, the company implemented the first biodegradable metalized packaging for many pastry products (Ortiz, 2008). Recently, Bimbo has teamed up with Terracycle to increase the recycling of plastic bags from not only their own, but also competitors' products (Terracycle, 2016).

Responsible consumption

The Danish brewing multinational Heineken aims to promote the responsible consumption of alcohol. As part of this activity, Heineken lobbies against drunk driving in South Korea, which has experienced a strong cultural bias toward such behavior. The campaign has lead to more than 2,000 people directly pledging not to drink and drive, and more than 3 million people learning about the campaign via news media. Heineken also promoted similar activities among its local competitors and lobbied the South Korean government (Heineken, 2010). Since 2013 Heineken has promote moderate alcohol consumption through the global "Dance More, Drink Slow" campaign with DJ Armin van Buuren (Heineken, 2016).

Employee workplace inclusion

The U.S. company Hewlett-Packard is highly involved in the promotion of diversity and inclusive labor practices among its employees. The company has implemented a broad set of related practices, such as an extensive nondiscrimination policy, flexible working hours, and the creation of employee networking activities for often marginalized groups (HP, 2016).

Table 6.2 provides an overview analysis of the key elements of the 3D management activities introduced. It shows how different the basic parameters are and how management must adapt. The table also includes the principal management instruments applied in each activity.

Actors

Actors in a specific responsible management activity might be either a single manager or an organization in charge of that activity. When management is seen in its simplest understanding of "organizing and applying given resources for the achievement of a predefined goal," it becomes clear that the management process

Table 6.2: Elements and management instruments of typical responsible management activities

Activity	Actor	Stakeholder(s)	Impact area	Management instrument
Biodegradable packaging	Bimbo	Natural environment	Waste reduction	Sustainable innovation
Promotion of responsible alcohol consumption	Heineken	Consumers, competitors, government, civil society	Drunk driving	Social marketing
Promotion of diversity and inclusion	Hewlett-Packard	Employees	Workplace inclusion	Sustainable human resources management

does not exclusively apply to a business environment (McNamara, 2011). There are also management activities in civil society organizations, governments, and other organizational actors. Within our topic of responsible business, the clear focus is on management in a business context. Nevertheless, it is important to learn how organizational parameters change when responsible management is executed by other organizational actors outside the realm of business.

As illustrated in Table 6.3, there are three main types of organization, and individuals affiliated with these organizations, who typically administer responsible management activities. It is important to appreciate the main differences between actors from the three sectors (business, government, and civil society), in order to successfully manage collaborations for a common cause among them. The potential for conflict is as big as the structural differences. For instance, businesses sometimes refrain from teaming up with civil society organizations (CSOs) due to the low level of CSO professionalism. Often collaborators, especially in smaller CSOs, join the organization due to an idealistic motivation to help the cause, but do not necessarily have a professional background in the field covered by the organization. Very often CSOs are run by volunteers, whose main job comes first in terms of commitment and available time. CSOs, on the other hand, may see a conflict in a company's drive for profit, which is not always in accordance with promoting a CSO's cause. Also, if profit is the main priority of an organization, the attention it can pay to topics not directly affecting the financial bottom line may be limited. In the relationship between businesses and governmental institutions, businesses often perceive governmental institutions as reacting sluggishly in the management process.

In spite of such differences, collaboration among these three different actor groups is absolutely necessary to achieve the goal of sustainable development.

Table 6.3: Types of organizational actor and their main characteristics

Organizational actor type	Primary motivation	Management characteristics	Resources and strengths for sustainable development
Business	Economic (profit)	Quick reaction to trends and opportunities High effectiveness and efficiency Pragmatism Often little professionalization in the social and environmental field	Financial resources Frequent international outreach Quick response capacity
Civil society organization (CSO)	Social, environmental, economic (depends on specific CSO focus)	High motivation for achievement of stated social and environmental goals Strong idealism Often little professionalization	High cause knowledge High cause motivation Cost-effective contribution
Governmental sector	Social (welfare)	Hierarchical and often sluggish reaction to external developments	Legislative power Institutional mandate to improve social and environmental causes

Only with the three actors' complementary contributions can the ultimate goal of sustainable development be reached.

Even though the focus has so far been on organizational actors for sustainable development, one should not underestimate the potential power for change that individual actors, so-called change agents, can have. Chapter 17 extensively covers the role of individual actors as change agents for a more sustainable society in all three sectors: business, government, and civil society.

Stakeholders

Stakeholders are all groups, individuals, or even nonhuman entities (such as animals and plants) that "can affect or are affected" (Freeman, 2010, p. 25; Buchholtz and Carroll, 2008). Stakeholders may be affected by any activity of any actors previously characterized, which means all such activities have stakeholders.

Business stakeholders typically are employees, customers, communities, civil society organizations, governments, suppliers, shareholders, and competitors. Competitors are the most frequently forgotten stakeholders. Probably due to the antagonistic relationship with competitors, companies tend not to consider competitors as stakeholders. Nevertheless, a company and its competitors do have a strong mutual relationship. Many activities in responsible business do strongly affect competitors. On the one hand, responsible business is a strong differentiation factor among competitors, and on the other hand, many industry-wide movements toward responsible business require considerable intra-industry collaboration among competitors.

Stakeholders, let's play

Gamification is the newest trend in engaging stakeholders. Sustainable development actors increasingly use games to foster awareness and sustainable behavior. One example is the collaborative simulation "World Without Oil" (Peters, 2011). Jane McGonigal claims that the state of mind attained while gaming can solve most of the world's problems by achieving "epic wins", thereby changing people's behavior toward more sustainability (McGonigal, 2010).

For a better understanding of the basic characteristics of stakeholders, and how to manage the stakeholder relationship, Table 6.4 describes some important stakeholder groups. It is obvious that the list of typical stakeholders includes governments, civil society organizations (CSOs), and companies, which were previously described as actors in 3D management. Depending on the responsible management activity at hand, any of these organization types might either be an actor or a stakeholder of a responsible management activity. Imagine, for instance, a company's donation campaign to a CSO, such as Médecins Sans Frontières. If one takes the perspective of the person managing the campaign from inside a for-profit business, the actor would be the company and the stakeholder would be the CSO. If one takes the perspective of a manager in charge of fundraising at Médecins Sans Frontières, the actor is the CSO and the company becomes a stakeholder of this fundraising activity.

Impact area

Responsible business jargon often includes the terms "issues," "causes," and "crises." What do these terms mean exactly? How can one characterize their internal relationship? An issue describes a social, environmental, or economic factor, which if ignored has the latent potential to cause problems, or even result in a crisis. A cause is an issue that a company has started to mitigate or solve. Issues a company faces can, for instance, be the environmental impact of its operations, the job satisfaction created among its employees, customer protection, and supply chain sustainability. The difference between an issue and a cause

Table 6.4: Typical stakeholders and their characteristics

Stakeholder	Mutual interests	Typical issues/causes
Customers	**Customers:** high-quality products, satisfaction of consumption wants and needs **Business:** maximum willingness to pay, brand loyalty	Product security Sustainable consumption Consumer boycotts Sales and lending practices
Employees	**Employees:** good work, high wage, professional fulfillment **Business:** motivation, productivity, loyalty, human capital	Work–life balance Labor conditions and fair wage Workplace inclusiveness Labor union association Ethical misconduct of employees
Owners	**Owners:** return on investment, investment security, influence over company **Business:** funding, liberty in use of funds	Corporate governance Accounting practices Socially responsible investment Transparency
Civil society organizations (CSOs)	**CSO:** influence on a business's behavior, cooperation for funding **Business:** minimum CSO influence, cooperation for issue know-how, association for credibility	Variable issues, depending on CSO's focus Contributions to society (citizenship) Community involvement
Competitors	**Competitors:** gain competitive advantage, collaborate to share the burden of sustainability **Business:** gain competitive advantage, collaborate to share the burden of sustainability	Industry sustainability initiatives Sustainable innovation products Collusion/oligopolies Fair competition
Suppliers	**Suppliers:** Long-term relationships, high sales volume, high price, independence **Business:** long-term relationships, high sales volume, low price, high-quality relationship	Labor conditions Exploitative contracting Supply-chain inclusiveness Responsible sourcing
Governments	**Governments:** regulation and taxation, the contribution of business to society, business support of governmental institutional interests **Business:** minimum taxation and regulation, governmental support for own interest	Legal compliance Corruption/lobbying Privatization Monopolies Relationship between governmental legislation and business policies

is simple, but very significant for communication and motivational purposes. A cause is an issue a company is positively involved in; an issue on the way to mitigation or even solution. This difference is highly important when it comes to communicating an organization's responsible business activity. In order to create a positive picture of a business, it makes sense to, whenever justified by good socio-environmental performance, talk about the solutions (causes) and not just about the problems (issues) the company is facing. There might even be responsible management activities that address a cause that has never been an issue (problem) to the company. For instance, Deutsche Bank is very active in the promotion of arts and culture (cause). The topic never constituted a problem (issue) for the company and, if ignored, definitely would not have resulted in negative consequences, much less in a crisis. So we can unify the topics of issues and causes under the umbrella of impact areas, certain themes under which we can make a certain type of impact, be it positive or negative.

The business case for high-level inclusion

The issue of discrimination based on ethnicity, race, religion, physical abilities, gender, and sexual preferences is a widespread problem in many businesses. This issue has become a common cause when companies make an effort to counteract discriminatory behaviors and structures. Nondiscrimination policies have become a mainstream business topic best known under the term "inclusion." A diversity topic that has received special attention is gender diversity. Although 72% of corporate leaders believe that gender diversity increases financial performance, the share of women in C-level leadership positions (15%) is far below an equal 50:50 distribution (McKinsey, 2010).

In order to identify how important a certain issue is to stakeholders and to an actor of responsible management, the concept of materiality is applied. The Global Reporting Initiative (GRI) defines materiality by how important an issue is to the inside of a company and how important it is to the outside. Internal factors include, for instance, the actual financial impact and risk posed by the issue, or how much the issue is aligned with the business's values, goals, and core competences. External factors may comprise the degree of stakeholder interest in the issue or future challenges faced by industry and the planet (GRI, 2016). To analyze how much an issue matters, companies frequently use a graph split into the two axes of external and internal importance, as proposed by the GRI. However, the international NGO AccountAbility proposes a set of five tests to detect the materiality of a certain issue—the tests are in accordance with the GRI framework, but give more detailed advice (Zadeck and Merme, 2003).

A survey of CEOs of Global Compact member companies revealed that the social and environmental issues viewed as most material by companies are education, climate change, and poverty, followed by diversity, access to clean water and sanitation, and food security (Lacey *et al.*, 2010). Interestingly, when comparing those issues most important to company executives with the threatening global issues as described earlier in this book, one discovers that CEOs are very aware of the importance of these topics. Seeing them as material means an implicit commitment by the companies to become active in making them their causes and solving them. For a hands-on materiality assessment, see the materiality assessment section of Chapter 9.

Picking the right responsible management instrument

Responsible management instruments for the management of integrated social, environmental, and economic performance—3D management instruments—fall into two broad categories. First, specialized responsible management instruments have been developed for the creation of social and environmental business performance. These instruments, comprising stakeholder, life-cycle, and ethics management, are new to mainstream business management. Specialized 3D management instruments are fundamental to managing responsible business. As illustrated in Figure 6.3, each of the three specialized responsible management instruments corresponds to one of the three main elements of the responsible management trinity. In most 3D management activities, all three specialized responsible management instruments are applied.

The second category is mainstream responsible management instruments, and these are applied in more specific ways. They are well-known business management instruments, such as accounting, marketing, or innovation, that have been reinterpreted in order to add to economic performance, increase social and environmental performance, or create value. Some examples of such instruments are sustainable innovation, cause-related marketing, or socio-environmental accounting. While each specialized responsible management instrument corresponds to one of the three main elements of the responsible management process, and is, therefore, present in any responsible management activity, the mainstream management instruments change depending on the specific functional area of the company in which the activity is located. The mainstream management process can be divided into three main subprocesses in which many different responsible management instruments are used:

1. **Planning:** the main goal of the first process of planning is to design responsible management activities that are neatly aligned with the organization's strategic infrastructure, such as vision and mission statements, the strategy development process, and the implemented corporate, business unit, and function strategies. The strategic management process functions as the brain and guiding light of an organization and all its activities. This is why the strategic management process has a lead role in achieving sustainable business.

Figure 6.3: Specialized responsible management instruments

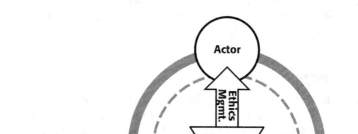

2. **Implementation:** the second process is the realization or implementation of responsible business practice throughout all business functions and hierarchical levels. The implementation process includes not only the main business functions (e.g., logistics, production) involved in the resource transformation process, but also the support functions (e.g., human resources, innovation) which enable this process.

3. **Communication:** the last process fulfills the function of communicating the results of the responsible management process to the various stakeholder groups, but also forms an important part of the previous planning and implementation processes. Communication instruments are, for instance, social and cause-related marketing, sustainability reporting, and codes of ethics.

The sequencing of the three phases of the responsible business management process is of crucial importance. Planning often has to be the first step. Many companies have tried to do "some philanthropy" in a manner that is rather disconnected from the core business and without a long-term strategy. The result has often been unsatisfactory for both stakeholders and the business. Such strategically unaligned activities not only lack high-level management support, but also are seen as an extra that can be downsized whenever resources have to be reassigned for "more strategic" activities. Sound implementation of responsible management practices has to come before the communication of social and environmental topics. "Social" and "eco" claims, when unsubstantiated by organizational practice, are quickly perceived as "greenwashing," a situation where a business focuses more on "talking responsibility," than actually "walking it"— greenwashing obviously has the potential to cause considerable reputational havoc.

The next section will cover the specialized responsible management instruments—stakeholder management, life-cycle impact management, and ethics management—in greater detail, while mainstream responsible management tools will be discussed extensively in later chapters.

Stakeholder management

Stakeholder relationships exert significant influence on both the business and the stakeholders. The role of stakeholder management is to optimize this influence. Do governments oppose or support your business? Do activist groups boycott or endorse? Are employees motivated or frustrated? Does the media idolize or bash what you are doing? All these opposing stakeholder behaviors are factors that can make or break a business. Stakeholder management is the management tool which aims to manage stakeholder relationships for the benefit of both the business and stakeholders. It sounds overly simplistic, but how stakeholders affect the business very much depends on how the business affects stakeholders. "You get what you give." This is why the very purpose of stakeholder management is to create value for a business's stakeholders and enable them in turn to create value for the business.

How is such mutual value creation achieved? The stakeholder management process consists of two phases, each comprising two main activities for successful stakeholder management. Phase A is the stakeholder analysis and consists of 1) identifying and 2) categorizing the groups a company affects or is affected by. Phase B, the stakeholder engagement, consists of 3) communication with stakeholders and 4) implementing actions based on the outcomes of steps 1–3 (Fig. 6.4).

Figure 6.4: The stakeholder management process

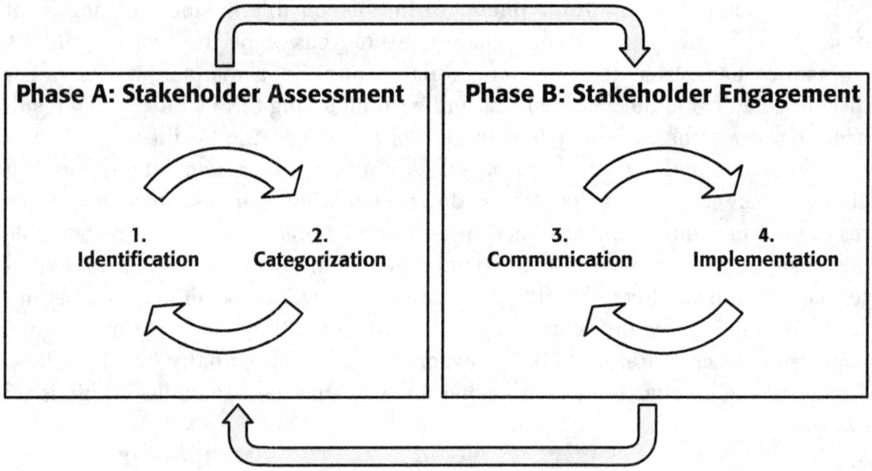

Figure 6.5: Typical stakeholder map of a taco restaurant

The first step of the stakeholder assessment phase consists of identifying the stakeholders of an organization. Usually, this is done by creating a stakeholder map. Stakeholder maps can be very general or highly specific, from merely showing the direct obvious connections to covering various levels of stakeholder involvement. At this stage of the analysis, it also makes sense to define the mutual relationship between each respective stakeholder and the company. Figure 6.5 illustrates the fictional case of a Mexican taco business which will be discussed in more detail in Chapter 9.

The second step is to categorize stakeholders in order to better understand their position and importance to the organization. Many different stakeholder categorization schemes have been developed, each providing a different means of understanding stakeholders, their impact, and their relationship to the organization; Table 6.5 provides an overview of the most commonly used approaches. A

Should stakeholders rule the (world) business?

Stakeholder theory is a field that criticizes the very foundations of typical capitalist enterprises. For instance, the concept of stakeholder democracy proposes that stakeholders should have a say in activities and the very survival of businesses, not shareholders or owners (Matten and Crane, 2005). Another revolutionary approach is to change from shareholder value-based management, a central instrument in financial management, to stakeholder value-based management. Interestingly, there is evidence that a focus on stakeholder value can also be instrumental in creating shareholder value.

Table 6.5: Stakeholder categories

Definition/stakeholder characteristic	Examples	Analysis criteria
1. Internal: stakeholder located inside the company 2. External: stakeholders located outside the company	1. Employees; shareholders 2. Government; competitors	Physical location of stakeholder and proximity to company structure and mainstream business activities (Freeman, 2010, pp. 8-13, 216; ISO, 2010, p. 15; Buchholtz and Carroll, 2008, p. 27)
1. Primary: stakeholders directly involved in transactions with the company 2. Secondary: stakeholder with an indirect relationship with the company	1. An employee of a company; the natural environment affected by operations 2. The family of a company's employee; an environmental interest group	Proximity of relationship (Clarkson, 1995)
1. Social: an individual or group of human beings currently alive 2. Nonsocial: nonhuman entities and individuals and groups not living in the present	1. Today's society; an environmental activist group 2. Future generations; the natural environment	Stakeholder (Buchholtz and Carroll, 2008, pp. 86-88; Fitch, 1976, p. 39)
1. Powerful: stakeholders having the potential to "impose their will" on the company 2. Legitimate: stakeholders with a legitimate claim 3. Urgent: stakeholders issuing an urgent claim	1. A CEO, a major single client, a critical supplier 2. An employee asking for legal wage and benefits; a community member being negatively affected by the company's operations 3. An ecosystem whose existence is imminently threatened by the company's operations; customers to be negatively affected by a product's manufacturing error	Importance (salience) of stakeholder: The most important stakeholder is the one that combines most of the three stakeholder characteristics. No characteristic: non-stakeholder One characteristic: Latent stakeholder Two characteristics: Expectant stakeholder Three characteristics: Definite stakeholder (Mitchel *et al.*, 1997, pp. 874-875)

Definition/stakeholder characteristic	Examples	Analysis criteria
1. Core: stakeholders without which the company is not able to survive 2. Strategic: stakeholders crucial for success of the company 3. Environmental: stakeholders neither important for survival nor for success of the company	1. A key employee 2. A strong competitor 3. An activist group unrelated to business and its impacts	Significance of impact on company (Clarkson, 1995 as cited in Buchholtz and Carroll, 2008)
1. Potential for threat: stakeholder has a high potential to harm the company 2. Potential for cooperation: stakeholder has a high potential to cooperate with the company	1. Competitor introducing a sustainable innovation product that will gain immense market share 2. A NGO with an excellent reputation, willing to support a company's responsible management efforts	Potential impact of stakeholder: impacts might be positive or negative (Freeman, 2010, p. 143; Savage et al., 1991)

Note: Definitions given here have been slightly altered from the original sources in order to create a coherent stakeholder classification framework.

2010 study showed that, as perceived by companies, the stakeholders exerting the highest influence are consumers, followed by employees, and then governments. Interestingly, investors scored only seventh (Lacey *et al.*, 2010). Such a general prioritization of stakeholder importance based on managers' intuitive perception is a good starting point. Stakeholder categorization tools can then be applied for a more detailed picture. After stakeholders have been identified and categorized, an organization should be clear about which stakeholder to engage (or not engage) with, and for which goal.

Phase B of the stakeholder management process is stakeholder engagement, which consists of two additional steps. Step 3, communicating with stakeholders, fulfills important functions, such as gathering information on stakeholder claims, attitudes, ideas, propensity to collaboration, etc. Stakeholder communication can refine the results achieved from the stakeholder assessment phase and serve as a basis for the subsequent step. In the fourth and last step, companies implement activities to satisfy stakeholder needs. Steps 3 and 4 should be repeated in an interlinked fashion in order to gather feedback from stakeholders on the process of implementation and on the quality of the outcome. Chapters 11 and 12 will provide extensive guidance on the implementation step, while Chapters 14 and 15 can be seen as a manual for successful stakeholder communication.

Life-cycle impact management

The physical product life-cycle model depicts all stages of a product, from the extraction of the first raw material through the various stages of production, through use, and finally to the end of the product's useful lifetime (Fig. 6.6). The life-cycle impact management instrument aims to simultaneously optimize the impact throughout all of these stages. The first stage of application is life-cycle assessment, analyzing and depicting the overall social, environmental and economic performance from "cradle to grave." If the product can be recycled, the circle closes and the life-cycle management process could even be described as ranging from "cradle to cradle" (McDonough and Braungart, 2002).

Life-cycle management is most related to the issue element of the 3D management process. This is due to the life-cycle's capacity to capture any kind of social, environmental, and economic value creation throughout all issues at any stage of a product's life-cycle. Thus, the life-cycle model has the capacity to holistically describe and manage any beneficial or adverse effect on any social, environmental, or economic issue. One might wonder why the life-cycle instrument shifts the focus from a complete responsible business to the mere product. The idea is that if one can assess the individual impact of all products of a company throughout all life-cycle stages, this assessment can reflect the overall impact of the company as a whole. The main advantage is that life-cycle assessment does not stop at the company gate or consider only the production process. Instead, the tool delivers a holistic picture of the impact created directly or indirectly by the product created upstream (in its sourcing activities) or downstream (in its use).

The physical product life-cycle consists of three major phases, as described in Figure 6.6. The first phase, the production stage, can be divided into two parts: the production external to the company throughout its supply chain and the production process within the company. The usage stage describes employment of the

Figure 6.6: The physical product life-cycle

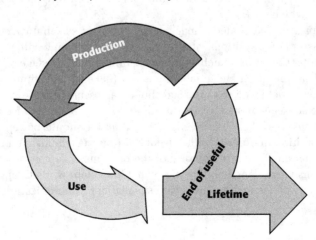

LCA for THC?

Life-cycle assessment (LCA) can be a tool for unusual, or even illegal, products. The cannabis legalization debate is implicitly conducting a life-cycle assessment of the plant's impact on society. Proponents and opponents of the drug's legalization discuss impacts of mainly two life-cycle stages. Concerning the "usage" stage, pro- and anti-legalization groups debate the health and addiction impacts of the drug and the supposed medical effects of its active substance, THC. During the "production and sourcing" phase, the main negative impacts are the severe results of criminal activity, such as over 40,000 deaths in the Mexican fight against drug cartels from 2005 to 2011 (Messerli, 2011; BBC, 2014).

product until the end of its useful lifetime. At the end of useful lifetime (the third phase), a product can either be disposed of or recycled to another useful lifetime. This last step is called revalorization, or giving the product back a certain value. Revalorization does not always mean to return to the raw material. Alternatives are to repair, refurbish, disassemble, or reuse the same product. Table 6.6 provides a typical list of positive and negative impacts made throughout the life-cycle stages.

The life-cycle management process consists of three main stages. First, during the life-cycle mapping stage, a company lists all social, environmental, and economic impacts created at every stage of the life-cycle as shown in Table 6.6. During the second stage, the stage of impact evaluation, each impact is analyzed to evaluate how positive or negative it is. In the same step, the impacts that should be altered are identified. In the third and final stage, called impact improvement, concrete changes for the improvement of the overall life-cycle impact are planned and implemented. Such changes could relate to any impact at any life-cycle stage. Examples might be to improve working conditions throughout the supply chain, improve the eco-efficiency of the in-house production process, design a product that consumes less energy during its usage, or to assure that the product can be fully recycled at the end of its useful life. Life-cycle management might even lead to the complete replacement of a very negative impact product type by another one with an improved 3D performance.

Ethics management

Ethics management is the managerial application of business ethics and focuses on increasing a company's right or desirable ethical decisions on both an individual employee level as well as on the overall organizational level. Thus, ethics management aims to create both moral employees and a moral organization. Ethics management is the management instrument focusing on the ethical decision-making of actors of responsible business. The ethics management process consists of four main steps:

Table 6.6: Typical impacts throughout the life-cycle

Life-cycle stage			Examples of positive (+) and negative (–) impacts		
			Social	Environmental	Economic
Production	External sourcing		(–) Supply-chain labor conditions (+) Poverty reduction by inclusive supply chains	(–) Exploitation of natural resources (+) Environmental impact exceeding local standards	(–) Destruction of local industries (+) Support of developing countries
	Internal production		(–) Factory labor conditions (+) Socioeconomic welfare effects	(–) Waste produced (+) Energy surplus production (e.g., internal wind energy plant)	(–) Net-value destruction by unsustainable behavior (+) Economic spillover effects on local clusters and business environment
	Use		(–) Harmful or insecure products (+) Satisfaction of customer needs (and wants)	(–) Energy, water, gas usage (–) Planned redundancy	(–) Running expenses (+) Service and repair
End of useful life	Disposal		(–) Waste as health risk (+) Ease of "throwing away"	(–) Packaging waste (–) Product/component toxicity	(–) Destruction of residual value by ultimate disposal (+) The waste business
	Revalorization		(–) Complexity and effort of revalorization (e.g., waste separation) (+) Reusage as cost saving as factor for poor people	(–) Reuse, refurbishment, recycling (+) Lower energy intensity of recycling compared with production from virgin materials	(–) Cost of reverse logistics for product recovery (+) Income from selling recycling materials

1. **Dilemma mapping:** first, the typical ethical dilemmas of an organization's activities and impacts throughout the whole product life-cycle have to be identified and analyzed.

2. **Identifying good choices:** second, one should decide on the desired "most ethical" decision for every dilemma encountered. In order to define the ethical "best choice" one should systematically analyze the dilemma, drawing on the normative ethical theories described in Chapter 5.

3. **Understanding behaviors:** the third step is to apply descriptive business ethics to every dilemma situation in order to fully understand why a certain actor does or does not make desirable decisions in practice. Factors influencing ethical behavior in practice might either be individual (directly related to the actor) or situational (related to factors external to the actor).

4. **Applying management tools:** the fourth and final step is to apply ethics management tools in order to make desired ethical decisions. Typical ethics management tools are ethics education, codes of ethics, ethics officers, and hotlines. A more seldom applied but highly effective tool is social marketing, which is defined as marketing for behavioral change. The deployment of ethics management tools must attach to the individual and situational factors identified as crucial in Step 3 of the ethics management process.

The power of the CECO

The highest job function in ethics management is the chief ethics and compliance officer (CECO). CECOs cover far-reaching responsibilities. Based on a working knowledge of their company's strategy, processes, policies, and risks, a CECO develops standards and monitors good ethical conduct throughout the whole company. Among U.S.-based companies, 87% of the CECOs regularly report on the state of ethics and compliance to the company's chief executive officers (CEOs) (ECOA and ERC, 2011).

Exercises

A. Know

Use the multiple choice questions below to test your knowledge. Each answer may be wrong or right and there may be zero to four right or wrong answers per question:

1. 3D value creation ...
   a. ... in a responsible business happens internally and externally, leading to social, environmental, and economic value.
   b. ... as an economic value internal to the business might include, for instance, increased sales income from sales of a more sustainable product.
   c. ... is related to inside-out, outside-in linkages. Porter and Kramer describe an outside-in linkage as the effect a company's business activity has on its surrounding environment.
   d. ... provides a meta-perspective as an important analytical basis throughout the responsible management process.

2. The responsible management process ...
   a. ... consists of three main elements and at least one management instrument.
   b. ... centrally involves at least one responsible management instrument such as social marketing, or stakeholder management.
   c. ... with its constituent elements might be relevant to some responsible management situations, but not to others.
   d. ... primarily aims to manage the overall social, environmental, and economic performance of an organization simultaneously for all activities of the organization.

3. Actors ...
   a. ... may for instance be a company, a government agency, or a civil society organization.
   b. ... from different sectors should not collaborate, as their primary motivations and management characteristics are inherently incompatible.
   c. ... include businesses, which are well equipped to contribute to sustainable development, among other things, due to their quick response capacity and international outreach.
   d. ... as mentioned in this chapter include so-called CSOs, chief security officers.

4. Stakeholders ...
   a. ... of an organization can be fully identified by thinking about who are the groups and individuals that affect the company.
   b. ... do not include competitors, as they are the "enemies" of the business.

    c.   ... include future generations as so-called social stakeholders.

    d.   A CSO can be either actor or stakeholder in a certain responsible management activity.

5.   Issues ...

    a.   ... are latent problems, which might turn into crises if unattended.

    b.   ... once they are addressed become a cause.

    c.   ... help to understand an impact area, which makes them one of the basic elements of the responsible management process.

    d.   ... may be addressed by the life-cycle impact management instrument.

6.   Responsible management instruments ...

    a.   ... may be specialized or mainstream management instruments.

    b.   ... may also be called 3D management instruments.

    c.   ... include corporate citizenship and sustainable development.

    d.   ... include sustainable innovation, a management instrument that the Bimbo bakery business used in its packaging technology.

B. Think

Imagine you are a company fleet manager of a large logistics company. You have been tasked to make a decision whether to adopt alternative fuels for your vehicles. Think through the topic of biodiesel usage for your company, based on extensive research of the sustainability, responsibility, and ethics aspects of its use. Make a decision about adoption.

C. Do

Conduct a life-cycle assessment for a product of your choice. Make sure you are able to access information on the product's impacts. Localizing information on different stages and impact types from multiple websites will most likely be necessary.

D. Relate

Talk with someone you know well about a typical ethical issue encountered in their work environment. Ask about ethics management tools in place in this job and discuss what other ethics management tools could possibly help to manage the situation.

E. Be

Think about one situation where you had to manage (this could be either in a private or a professional role). How do you think you did? How would others describe what you did well and/or where you didn't? What could have been done better? Do you think your management activity would be described as "responsible" management? Why, or why not?

Feedback

A. Know

Question 1

a. Right: value creation in a responsible business includes both external and internal value throughout all three dimensions.

b. Right: increased sales from a sustainable innovation product is an internal economic business value.

c. Wrong: outside-in linkages are effects inside the company, caused by developments in the company's environment.

d. Right: 3D value creation generates a value-neutral analytical basis or meta-perspective.

Question 2

a. Right: the three main elements of the responsible management process are actor, impact, and stakeholder. Management instruments might be specialized responsible management and/or mainstream management instruments.

b. Right: without such an instrument, it would not be a management process. The responsible management process might involve one or many specialized or mainstream responsible management instruments.

c. Wrong: the three constituent elements are called the "trinity" of responsible management, as they can be found in any responsible management activity.

d. Wrong: the purpose of 3D or responsible management is to create sustainable management results for single activities involving social, environmental, and economic capital.

Question 3

a. Right: actors in responsible management do not necessarily have to be only companies. It could be any type of organization, or an individual.

b. Wrong: while different sectoral actors show different characteristics that might make collaboration difficult, they also have valuable complementary resources and strengths which make collaboration for sustainable development promising and necessary.

c. Right: the two strengths mentioned are correct. Another strength mentioned is the financial endowment of businesses.

d. Wrong: CSO stands for civil society organization.

Question 4

a. Wrong: in order to fully identify all stakeholders of an organization, one has to think about both types of group and individual, those that affect the organization and even more importantly those who might not affect the organization, but are affected by it.

b. Wrong: competitors strongly affect the business and are strongly affected by it. They are stakeholders.
c. Wrong: future generations are classified as nonsocial stakeholders, as they are not currently living human beings.
d. Right: a manager inside a civil society organization would see the CSO as an actor, while the CSO is seen as a stakeholder if the responsible management activity is controlled from a business, which involves the CSO in its activities.

Question 5

a. Right: not attending to an issue such as discrimination might lead to a crisis if, for instance, consumers start boycotting (crisis) a company for misconduct (issue).
b. Right: an issue is a mere problem, while a cause is a problem addressed for mitigation or solution.
c. Right: the other two elements are actors/agents and stakeholders.
d. Right: life-cycle impact management is the management instrument managing the impacts of an organization throughout its various issues.

Question 6

a. Right: the two different groups of instruments are specialized responsible management instruments (stakeholder, life-cycle, and ethics management) and mainstream management instruments (e.g., sustainable innovation, social marketing) that have been reinterpreted to also manage social and environmental impacts.
b. Right: responsible management and 3D management (the management of the social, environmental, and economic dimension) are used synonymously.
c. Wrong: both are background theories of responsible business. Responsible management instruments are, for instance, stakeholder management, cause-related marketing, and social accounting.
d. Right: Bimbo used sustainable innovation to become a pioneer in the biodegradable packaging business.

B. Think

Level	Dealing with complexity	Notes
+	Decision is well grounded in an appreciation of the complexity of the topic	
=	Decision has been made, but based on an incomplete grasp of the complexities and competing issues	
−	Little capture of the complexities and competing issues around biofuels	

C. Do

Level	Using (LCA) management tools	Notes
+	Complete representation of all major life-cycle impacts across all life-cycle stages	
=	Sensible, but incomplete representation of major product life-cycle impacts across all stages	
−	Incomplete life-cycle assessment, not covering all three stages of the life-cycle	

D. Relate

Level	Orienting others	Notes
+	Successful orientation of the other toward additional ethics management tools and options	
=	Appreciation of issue and context, but no guidance given	
−	No appreciation of the ethical issue and its context	

E. Be

Level	Awareness of own performance and limitations	Notes
+	Well-evidenced account of awareness of own performance and limitations	
=	Convincing account of either performance or limitations	
−	No convincing account of either performance or limitations in this situation	

7
Practice norms

It has been a challenge to narrow down the field from the thousands of codes and standards into 34 key tools. ... Another challenge has been to describe a constantly moving target, as each of the initiatives described herein are evolving.

(Leipziger, 2010, p. 16)

The norms and frameworks guiding responsible business conduct are many. Some of the most recognized and prominently applied norms will now be presented in order to provide an overview and point of departure for further study and application. Leipziger lists differing terms which can be included under the umbrella term of "norm." Norms are codes, standards, principles, values, guidelines, and framework agreements. They may differ considerably in scope and scale, stakeholders, issues, industry foci, and in methods of development (Leipziger, 2010, p. 37). In day-to-day management practice it does not make a big difference, though, in what category a specific norm falls: the important value lies in understanding a norm's contribution to responsible management practice. The function of norms differs considerably. They can be categorized by their coverage of different issues and stakeholders (broad or narrow) or their focus on either an intended outcome or the implementation process. Figure 7.1 summarizes some of the most important norms using the two categories mentioned: process vs. outcome focus and broad vs. narrow coverage.

Norms for responsible business can also be classified in a wide variety of additional ways. Industry and sector initiatives focus on a specific type of business, instead of providing advice for businesses in general. Cause-focused norms, such as the Forest Stewardship Council for the protection of forests, focus on single

Figure 7.1: Classifying responsible business norms

Outcome orientation	**Process orientation**
Broad coverage	• Global Compact (GC) • World Business Council for Sustainable Development (WBCSD) • Millennium Development Goals (MDG) • Dow Jones Sustainability Index (DJSI) • Guidelines for Multinational Enterprises • Empresa Socialmente Responsable (ESR)	• AA1000 Series • ISO 26000 • ISO 14000 • Natural Step Framework • Global Reporting Initiative (GRI) Guidelines
Narrow coverage	• Leadership in Energy and Environmental Design (LEED) • FSC certified forest products • Fairtrade Standards and Label • Energy Star	• ILO Declaration on Fundamental Principles and Rights at Work • Rio Declaration on Environment and Development • Universal Declaration of Human Rights • CERES Principles • SA8000 • Business Principles for Countering Bribery • Equator Principles (EPs) • Carbon Disclosure Project (CDP) • Principles for Responsible Management Education (PRME)

or narrow sets of causes. Initiatives might be global, such as the Global Compact, or local, such as the Empresa Socialmente Responsable organization in Latin America. Some norms might provide a certification or label, such as ISO 14000, or even provide benchmarking or rankings, such as the Dow Jones Sustainability Index. Background norms, such as the Universal Declaration of Human Rights, offer a very basic framework for responsible business behavior, while guidance norms, such as ISO 26000, aim to provide concise hands-on advice. Networking initiatives, such as the Principles for Responsible Management Education, provide strong connections and interactions between members. Table 7.1 in the appendix to this chapter illustrates the characteristics of some of the most important norms in responsible business. The remainder of this chapter focuses on four of the most frequently applied norms: the Global Compact, the Global Reporting Initiative, ISO 14000, and ISO 26000.

United Nations norms

The United Nations' (UN) background in the promotion of human rights and its engagement in social, environmental, and economic causes for the good of the world community has led to the UN taking a strong interest in responsible business. Two of the most influential UN norms are the ten Global Compact principles and the Global Reporting Initiative guidelines for establishing sustainability reports, both of which were developed in collaboration with the Ceres organization.

A norm against war?

The Extractive Industries Transparency Initiative (EITI) has developed the EITI Principles and Criteria, which foster transparency in the amount of natural resources extracted from a country and usage of the revenues generated (EITI, 2009). One of the initiative's candidate countries is the Democratic Republic of Congo (DRC), which experienced the second Congo War at the beginning of the 21st century, also called the "Coltan War." As a direct result of this war, 5.4 million people perished (EITI, 2011), making it the most deadly conflict since World War II. The war was largely financed by the extraction of natural resources, mainly coltan, a mineral crucial for the production of many consumer electronics from computers to MP3 players. DRC holds 80% of the world's coltan resources, meaning that most of the cell phones used by consumers around the world indirectly financed the tragedy in the Congo (Hogg, 2011; Bavier, 2008; cellular-news, 2011; Dizolele, 2006). The conflict has also been called the "PlayStation War" after the console's producer, Sony, became entangled in it (Lasker, 2008). Could a norm such as the EITI Principles really mitigate or even solve such a conflict-laden situation?

Global Compact

The ten Global Compact (GC) principles cover a broad range of issues. In 2016, more than 8,000 companies and 4,000 other organizations pledged to adhere to the Global Compact principles. Among them are many of the world's most influential multinational enterprises, such as BMW, PepsiCo, and Microsoft. The ten principles are listed in the box overleaf.

Companies adhering to these ten principles are supposed to make considerable contributions to some of the world's most pressing social and environmental problems by improving their own social and environmental performance. GC subscriber organizations are encouraged to "share information on progress" periodically. In spite of these positive points, the Global Compact has been criticized on a handful of issues. Critics commonly state that the GC is not binding enough. Commitment to the principles is on a voluntary basis and, therefore, can hardly be enforced. A related criticism is that of "bluewashing," referring to the blue color of the United Nations flag. The GC is accused of being used as an easy tool for a company to appear socially and environmentally responsible on the outside, but not necessarily implementing such behavior on the inside (Bandi, 2007). The flexible structure of the GC must not necessarily be seen as a weakness. Proponents of the GC state that the norm has to be very general and non-enforcing in order to be able to provide a broadly applicable and worldwide platform for responsible business practice (Leipziger, 2010, p. 37).

The GC is highly interrelated to various other UN-powered initiatives (further illustrated in Table 7.1). The GC is also seen as the business counterpart of the Sustainable Development Goals (SDGs). In fact, compliance with the GC principles is likely to support the achievement of the SDGs.

Human rights

- Principle 1: Businesses should support and respect the protection of internationally proclaimed human rights; and
- Principle 2: make sure that they are not complicit in human rights abuses.

Labor

- Principle 3: Businesses should uphold the freedom of association and the effective recognition of the right to collective bargaining;
- Principle 4: the elimination of all forms of forced and compulsory labour;
- Principle 5: the effective abolition of child labour; and
- Principle 6: the elimination of discrimination in respect of employment and occupation.

Environment

- Principle 7: Businesses should support a precautionary approach to environmental challenges;
- Principle 8: undertake initiatives to promote greater environmental responsibility; and
- Principle 9: encourage the development and diffusion of environmentally friendly technologies.

Anti-corruption

- Principle 10: Businesses should work against corruption in all its forms, including extortion and bribery.

(UNGC, 2011a)

Global Reporting Initiative

The Global Compact and the Global Reporting Initiative (GRI) are highly complementary norms. On a continuum from broad guidance to specific advice, the GC and the GRI lie at opposite extremes. The GRI delivers a concise set of guidelines on how to establish reports that are comparable, consistent, and of high utility (Leipziger, 2010, p. 490). Many companies of all sizes, industries, and regions have established periodic GRI reports covering social and environmental business performance, and the length of such reports ranges from approximately 60 to 100 pages. Report quality can be rated by independent organizations following the GRI standard. Investigating GRI-based responsibility reports can be an endless source of highly consistent information and inspiration so, in order to maximize the learning from such reading, an understanding of the GRI guidelines is crucial.

The GRI reporting standards can be broadly divided into two main topic areas (Fig. 7.2). The first area of "Reporting Principles" defines criteria for identifying report contents and quality assessment. Defining report content is based on a materiality assessment. The decision as to what contents are included should be based on the principles defined in the following (GRI, 2015, pp. 16-17):

- **Materiality principle:** "The information in a report should cover topics and indicators that reflect the organization's significant economic, environmental, and social impacts, or that would substantively influence the assessments and decisions of stakeholders."

- **Stakeholder inclusiveness principle:** "The reporting organization should identify its stakeholders and explain in the report how it has responded to their reasonable expectations and interests."

- **Sustainability context:** "The report should present the organization's performance in the wider context of sustainability."

- **Completeness:** "The report should include coverage of material Aspects and their Boundaries, sufficient to reflect significant economic, environmental and social impacts, and to enable stakeholders to assess the organization's performance in the reporting period."

Figure 7.2: Main components of the GRI guidelines

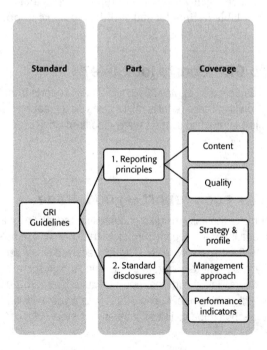

Integrated reporting

The reporting trend promotes integration: 10% of sustainability reports in 2015 were integrated reports, which jointly covered social, environmental, and mainstream financial performance. Such triple-bottom-line reports reflect the overall trend of an increasing convergence and integration of responsible and mainstream management (KPMG, 2016). Leading countries in the percentage of integrated reports are South Africa (91%), Netherland and Spain (27% each) and Japan (21%).

To define the quality of a report, organizations are invited to follow these guidelines (GRI, 2015, pp. 17-18):

- **Balance principle:** "The report should reflect positive and negative aspects of the organization's performance to enable a reasoned assessment of overall performance."

- **Comparability principle:** "The organization should select, compile and report information consistently. The reported information should be presented in a manner that enables stakeholders to analyze changes in the organization's performance over time, and that could support analysis relative to other organizations."

- **Accuracy:** "The reported information should be sufficiently accurate and detailed for stakeholders to assess the reporting organization's performance."

- **Timeliness:** "The organization should report on a regular schedule and information is available in time for stakeholders to make informed decisions."

So what do GRI reports look like?

The GRI reports database as of May 2016 held 23,381 reports from 9,101 organizations. Browsing these reports might give you a great idea about what GRI reporting looks like in practice (https://www.globalreporting.org).

Bad impact + good report = good grade

One should not make the easy mistake of confusing the quality of a GRI report with the quality of a company's impact. An excellent example is British Petroleum's 2010 "sustainability review," which received a self-declared grade of A+. It is crucially important to understand that such a high score is merely based on the degree of compliance with the reporting guidelines (GRI, 2006b). Due to the massive oil spill in the gulf of Mexico, 2010 was a year with one of the highest negative environmental impacts in the company's history (BP, 2011).

While the first area of the guiding principles provides guidance on different options for reporting, the second area ("standard disclosures") informs about the required topic areas to be covered. "General standard disclosures" include, for instance, the organizational profile and strategy, an explanation of the materiality of issues, the boundaries of the report, and topics of ethics, as well as governance. Specialized disclosures are the organization's management approach and reporting indicators (GRI, 2015, p. 45):

1. **Management approach:** The disclosure on management approach is intended to give the organization an opportunity to explain how the economic, environmental, and social impacts related to material aspects are managed.

2. **Performance indicators:** "Indicators that elicit comparable information on the economic, environmental, and social performance of the organization."

The Global Reporting Initiative guidelines might be perceived as extensive and complex. Nevertheless, being able to read, understand, evaluate, and communicate an organizations' social, environmental, and economic performance is an invaluable step toward successful and responsible management.

Sustainability reporting is a quickly developing topic. There is a strong trend toward **integrated reporting**, which refers to reports that combine the financial annual report and the sustainability report in a single document. The idea is that integrated reporting will also reflect integrated thinking and ultimately lead to both financial stability and social, environmental, and economic sustainability (IIRC, 2013). While we strongly support this aspiration behind integrated reports, we also see a danger of a loss in depth of sustainability reporting, if the integrated report is seen as a substitute for the GRI report. The typically 5–20 pages explicitly dedicated to sustainability or corporate responsibility in integrated reports provide a much more shallow picture than that provided by the 60–100 pages of a GRI report.

International Organization for Standardization (ISO) guidelines

The International Organization for Standardization (ISO) is widely accepted for its standards in the most diverse fields. Since it was launched in 1996, the ISO 14000 series on environmental management systems has become the most applied norm internationally for managing a business's environmental performance. The ISO 26000 standard on social responsibility is a recent product of the responsible business boom. After its publication in 2010, it quickly gained both recognition and extensive criticism. Both norms, while issued by the same institution, differ widely in outreach, coverage, and structure. While management systems developed using the ISO 14000 standard can be audited and certified, ISO 26000 does not target direct certification, instead aiming to provide guidance on the vocabulary and basic structure of social responsibility. The standard also defines the very concept of social responsibility.

> ## Where did ISO 26000 come from?
> The ISO 26000 standard on social responsibility was developed through the collaboration of the main stakeholder groups, including industry, government, labor, consumers, nongovernmental organizations, service, support, and research. A geographical and gender-based balance of participants was assured to avoid biases. The process was led by experts from ISO members (national standards bodies) and from liaison organizations, associations representing business, consumers, labor, and intergovernmental or nongovernmental organizations. The ISO working group on Social Responsibility had 450 participating experts and 210 observers from 99 ISO member countries and 42 liaison organizations (ISO, 2012b).

ISO 26000

The ISO 26000 standard on social responsibility, often abbreviated as ISO SR, is divided into seven clauses, each covering different aspects of social responsibility (ISO, 2010).

1. **Scope.** Interestingly, the norm applies to any kind of organization and, therefore, avoids the narrow understanding of social responsibility as only applying to businesses.

2. **Terms and definitions.** The definitions used for the ISO SR have been both hailed and criticized. On the one hand, the definition of "social responsibility" provides a highly inclusive and integrated understanding of responsible business subjects, such as ethics and transparency. The definition also defines sustainable development as the intended outcome of social responsibility in line with the understanding assumed in this book. Further positive features are: that the document defines the stakeholder relationship as a core piece of the responsible management process; the alignment with norms, law, and international frameworks; and the focus on "mainstreamed" integration of responsible business into the organization's main activities. The document also avoids the European Union definition's narrow focus on voluntary initiatives by including compulsory legal aspects as part of the responsibilities. The overall evaluation of this definition is definitely positive. Unfortunately, other concepts such as "stakeholders" have been unnecessarily altered. Defining a stakeholder as the "interest" taken in the organization lacks the reciprocal relationship of "affects or is affected" from the commonly accepted definition by Freeman (2010, p. 25). Definitions of terms related to social responsibility range from "a" as in "accountability" to "v" as in "vulnerable groups."

3. **Understanding.** This clause describes a "colorful bunch" of interesting—but loosely structured—pieces of background knowledge, such as the historical development, actual external conditions, and the relationships between social responsibility and sustainable development.

4. **Principles of social responsibility.** The ISO SR defines seven principles of social responsibility as universal to a responsible organization, while admitting that these seven principles cannot be a definite and ultimate list. The text also mentions subject-related (issue-related) additional principles. The first three subject-comprehensive principles are accountability, transparency, and ethical behavior. Principles 4–7 refer to respecting stakeholder interests, laws, international norms of behavior, and human rights. While these principles can be central to a responsible organization, it remains unclear why human rights is mentioned twice, once as an overarching principle of social responsibility and then again in Clause 6 as a subject area.

5. **Fundamental practices.** The ISO SR defines two fundamental practices for social responsibility. First, recognizing the concrete characteristics of a specific organization's responsibilities and, second, identifying and engaging stakeholders. While these two practices are fundamentally important, one can easily identify other fundamentally important practices such as impact and life-cycle management.

6. **Core subjects.** Core subjects are supposed to "cover the most likely economic, social, and environmental impacts" (ISO, 2010, p. 15). The core subjects proposed are organizational governance, human rights, labor practices, the environment, fair operating practices, consumer issues, and community involvement and development. What is questionable about these core subjects is their supposed exhaustiveness. It remains subject to a detailed check of the coverage of typical organizational impacts to verify the exhaustiveness of the core subjects. The homogeneity of the subjects identified is not given. While, for example, the subject of human rights is an "across-stakeholder" subject, other subjects, such as consumer issues and labor practices, refer to specific stakeholders (consumers and employees). The ISO SR has confused a stakeholder categorization with the identification of issues. As described in the three elements of responsible management, stakeholders might be related to various issues and issues are likely to relate to many stakeholders.

7. **Integrating social responsibility.** Integrating social responsibility as proposed by the norm is characterized by a loosely connected set of "good practices," such as voluntary initiatives, which include organizational characteristics and communicating social responsibility. By improving the integration of these good practices, they may become an important source of advice for the "how" of implementing social responsibility in an integrated manner and not just as an unconnected addition.

ISO SR solves many common problems of definition and has created a fairly sound basis for the future development of a common language in the field of social responsibility. The main problems still to be addressed in order for ISO SR to reach its potential are to resolve definitional and structural inconsistencies in the framework, such as the double coverage of human rights, the definition of a stakeholder being inconsistent with the long-established understanding, and the intuitively inconsistent subordination of environmental issues under a social responsibility construct.

From converging norms to legislation?

Norms for responsible business are increasingly complementary instead of competing. For instance, the ISO SR and the GRI work well together as seen in the following statement: "GRI provides the most suitable guidelines to support organizations interested in reporting on the topics covered by ISO 26000" (GRI, 2010, p. 4). Sustainability reporting has become mandatory for a large number of companies through the requirements of stock exchanges and country legislations (Ernst & Young, 2014). Companies have reacted to these requirements in a variety of ways, including the adoption of new standards or changing practices toward more sustainable ways (Ioannou and Serafeim, 2014).

ISO 14000

While ISO 26000 primarily focuses on social topics, the ISO 14000 standard for the development of environmental management systems extensively covers the environmental responsibility of a company's operations. ISO 14000's methodology is arranged in the six steps for the implementation of an environmental management system:

1. Environmental policy
2. Planning
3. Implementation and operation
4. Checking a corrective action
5. Management review
6. Continual improvement

The rigorous methodology allows for audit and certification of the implementation of environmental management systems. Some strongly criticize that the norm and certification do not include benchmarks for what should be considered a "good" environmental impact, as the certification merely refers to the installation of the environmental management system. This could create a misleading impression that all ISO 14000 certified organizations are automatically "clean enterprises." While in reality the certification means that such an organization does have a management system in place which might improve its environmental impact, it does not necessarily mean the organization would be considered environmentally friendly in and of itself.

Exercises

A. Know

Use the multiple choice questions below to test your knowledge. Each answer may be wrong or right and there may be zero to four right or wrong answers per question:

1. Practice norms ...
   a. ... include corporate citizenship and sustainable development.
   b. ... include the Global Reporting Initiative (GRI), a set of ten standards aiming to improve collaboration by multinationals on topics such as human rights and good environmental performance.
   c. ... include ISO 14000, which aims to improve an organization's social responsibility.
   d. ... include the GRI which also covers the balance principle, which recommends that companies report not only positive, but also negative aspects of their performance.

2. Someone is complaining that a company's corporate responsibility report did not cover the company's involvement in a major environmental scandal during the year, and which is of highest interest to the stakeholders. The person is implicitly complaining that the company had not applied the ...
   a. ... materiality principle.
   b. ... completeness principle.
   c. ... balance principle.
   d. ... timeliness principle.

3. You hear from a colleague that your company has adopted this new standard which has a strong focus on human rights and labor practices, but which also covers anticorruption. Which standard is most likely being talking about?
   a. Global Compact principles
   b. ILO standard
   c. Universal Declaration of Human Rights
   d. ISO 14000

B. Think

Imagine you are the managing director of a small enterprise and you would like to formalize your responsible business agenda by adopting a norm. Evaluate the value of several distinct norms for your company, based on a set of criteria you chose.

C. Do

Review the points on the Universal Declaration of Human Rights and identify one reality that interferes with one of these rights, in your environment. Often human rights abuses can be quite small things of daily life, either in the private or professional context. Write an action plan outlining what would need to happen to change this situation, including one step you can take in mitigation. Take that step!

D. Relate

Look up a company's Global Compact (GC) report and compare it with news coverage about the company. Find one point where the company has apparently acted against one of the ten GC principles. Get in touch with the company to let them know that you have studied their efforts to abide by the GC principles, but that you would like to understand better why they acted against them in this specific case.

E. Be

Write your personal professional norm. It could include principles such as "I will never be involved in corruption" or "I will always treat all work colleagues with friendliness and respect." Make sure your personal professional norm reflects both your values and elements related to work culture and profession.

Feedback

A. Know

Question 1

a. Wrong: both are background theories of responsible business. Practice norms include, for instance, ISO 26000 or the Extractive Industries Transparency Initiative.

b. Wrong: the description given fits the Global Compact. The GRI provides guidelines for the reporting of social, environmental, and economic business performance.

c. Wrong: ISO 14000 targets environmental performance, while ISO 26000 focuses on organizational social responsibility.

d. Right: the balance principle is one of four defining the quality of sustainability reports.

Question 2

a. Right: the issue appears to be of high materiality to the stakeholders which is why it would have to be included.

b. Right: the completeness principle says that all material issues have to be covered.

c. Wrong: the balance principle says that both positive and negative topics have to be covered in a balanced manner. To make a statement about balance the person would have had to look at all topics covered.

d. Wrong: no statement about the regularity and timely provision of the report has been made.

Question 3

a. Right: the description perfectly fits the ten Global Compact principles, while not mentioning the environment part.

b. Wrong: the International Labour Organization (ILO) standard focuses exclusively on labor-related topics.

c. Wrong: the Universal Declaration exclusively focuses on human rights. Some of the other topics might be covered indirectly.

d. Wrong: ISO 14000 is a series of norms on environmental management.

B. Think

Level	Multi-criteria analysis	Notes
+	Decision was made and explained well, based on an adequate set of criteria	
=	Decision was made, but criteria do not appear adequate for the situation	
−	Decision was not made, or only single norms and single criteria were considered	

C. Do

Level	Actioning change skills	Notes
+	Own action taken as part of a feasible larger action plan	
=	Feasible action plan, based on a fair understanding of the observed human rights issue	
−	No action plan or no fair appreciation of a human rights issue	

D. Relate

Level	Appreciative feedback skill	Notes
+	Feedback given on fair appreciation of Global Compact performance, both in general and in relation to the news story	
=	Feedback given on fair appreciation of Global Compact performance, either in general or in relation to the news story	
−	No feedback based on appreciation of Global Compact performance, either in general or in relation to the news story	

E. Be

Level	Responsible professional identity	Notes
+	Personal values and professional factors deeply reflected in personal norm	
=	Personal values or professional factors well reflected in personal norm	
−	Norm reflects neither personal values nor professional considerations	

Appendix

Table 7.1: Overview of responsible business norms

Norm	Organization	Type	Description
1. Broad coverage + outcome orientation			
Global Compact (GC) principles	United Nations Global Compact	Global + network norm	Network of businesses and stakeholder institutions, self-committing to the ten Global Compact principles.
Content areas	Human and labor rights, environment, corruption		
World Business Council for Sustainable Development (WBCSD)	WBCSD	Network	WBCSD is a CEO-led business initiative with joint agenda for sustainable business, focusing on the business case for sustainable development (WBCSD, 2011).
Content areas	Work program includes focus areas (e.g., ecosystems, development, climate), sector projects (e.g., buildings, energy, water), systems solutions, and capacity building for sustainable development		
Sustainable Development Goals (SDGs)	United Nations	Global + guidance	The SDGs define 17 goals, each featuring comprehensive tangible indicators for sustainable development (United Nations, 2016). Commitments to the SDGs have been made by the governmental sector. Also many businesses use the SDGs as reference points for their responsible business activities.
Content areas	1. Poverty; 2. Hunger and food security; 3. Health; 4. Education; 5. Gender equality and women's empowerment; 6. Water and sanitation; 7. Energy; 8. Economic growth; 9. Infrastructure, industrialization; 10. Inequality; 11. Cities; 12. Sustainable consumption and production; 13. Climate change; 14. Oceans; 15. Biodiversity, forests, deforestation; 16. Peace and justice; 17. Partnerships		

Norm	Organization	Type	Description
Dow Jones Sustainability Indexes (DJSI)	Dow Jones Indexes / Sustainable Asset Management (SAM)	Global + benchmarking	Rigorous and highly selective ("best-in-class approach") assessment based on extensive catalog of hard indicators, which have to be improved constantly. DJSI is mostly used as a responsible investment benchmarking system (DJSI, 2011). A norm with similar approach and importance is the London-based FTSE4Good index.
Content areas			1. Economic dimension: corporate governance, risk and crisis management, codes of conduct, compliance, bribery, customer relationship management, brand management, privacy protection, environmental reporting 2. Environmental dimension: environmental policy/management system, operational eco-efficiency 3. Social dimension: social reporting, labor practices, human capital development, talent attraction and retention, corporate citizenship and philanthropy, standards for suppliers, stakeholder engagement (SAM Research AG, 2010)
Guidelines for Multinational Enterprises	Organisation for Economic Co-operation and Development (OECD)	Global + guidance	Extensive set of responsible business recommendations for multinational enterprises unequaled in its broad coverage of social, environmental, and ethical issues (OECD, 2011).
Content areas			The guidelines cover concepts and principles, general policies, disclosure, human rights, employment and industrial relations, environment, combating bribery, bribe solicitation and extortion, consumer interests, science and technology, competition, and taxation.
Empresa Socialmente Responsible (ESR)	Centro Mexicano para la Filantropía (CEMEFI)	Distinction, local standard, label	First implemented in Mexico, ESR has evolved as a widely applied responsible business label throughout Latin America. Based on an evidence-based self-evaluation, businesses of all sizes may be awarded the ESR distinction on a yearly basis. The ESR label is widely recognized among consumers (CEMEFI, 2011). ESR in the context of this overview represents many local norms that have gained importance throughout the world by responding to local issues, and specific responsible business culture.
Content areas			Quality of life inside the business; business ethics; community involvement; relationship with the natural environment; ethics, communication and promotion of sustainable consumption

Norm	Organization	Type	Description
2. Broad coverage + process orientation			
AA1000 series	AccountAbility	Guidance, certification	AA1000 is a series of three standards describing basic tasks of responsible management. The accountability principles standard (APS) describes the basic principles of accountability (materiality, responsiveness, completeness, and inclusivity). The assurance standard (AS) describes the process of externally assuring a company's information on responsible business. The stakeholder engagement standard (SES) provides detailed guidance on the stakeholder engagement process (AccountAbility, 2011).
Content areas	Accountability, assurance, stakeholder engagement		
ISO 26000	International Organization for Standardization (ISO)	Guidance	ISO 26000 aims to provide guidance on the social responsibilities of organizations, its elements, concepts and vocabulary.
Content areas	Clause 1 (Scope): any kind of organization independent of size, legal form, etc. Clause 2 (Terms, definitions, abbreviations): attempt to standardize language used Clause 3 (Understanding): background knowledge Clause 4 (Principles of SR): seven principles of social responsibility, universal to a responsible organization Clause 5 (Fundamental practices): acceptance of the social responsibility of business; identifying and engaging with stakeholders Clause 6 (Core subjects): organizational governance, human rights, labor practices, the environment, fair operating practices, consumer issues, and community involvement and development Clause 7 (Integrating SR): "good practices"		

Norm	Organization	Type	Description
ISO 14000	International Organization for Standardization (ISO)	Guidance + certification	ISO 14000 provides an easy-to-apply and certifiable methodology for establishing environmental management systems (ISO, 2012a). A comparable standard is the European Environmental Management and Accounting Scheme (EMAS).
Content areas	Six steps for implementing an environmental management system: environmental policy; planning; implementation and operation; checking a corrective action; management review; continual improvement		
Natural Step Framework	The Natural Step	Guidance	The Natural Step Framework takes a systemic approach to guiding organizations, governments, and individuals toward sustainable behavior, based on four system conditions that have to be met to reach sustainable development and create a sustainable society (Natural Step, 2011).
Content areas	Problems to be solved: concentrations of substances extracted from the Earth's crust; concentrations of substances produced by society; degradation by physical means; people are not subject to conditions that systemically undermine their capacity to meet their needs		
Global Reporting Initiative (GRI) Guidelines	Ceres, United Nations	Guidance, ranking	The GRI guidelines provide a standardized framework for the establishment of a business's high-quality sustainability reports (GRI, 2016). Report quality is assessed through the application of different application levels (from A to C) for reports.
Content areas	Guidance for: defining report content; report boundary setting		
	Principles for: defining report content; report quality		
	Standard disclosures are: profile; management approach; performance indicators		

Norm	Organization	Type	Description
3. Narrow coverage + outcome orientation			
Leadership in Energy and Environmental Design (LEED)	U.S. Green Building Council	Guidance, certification, ranking, label	LEED provides a ranking system to assess a building's environmental and health performance. Ranking levels are certified, silver, gold, and platinum (U.S. Green Building Council, 2011).
Content areas	Impacts of buildings in design, construction, and operations		
FSC certified forest products	Forest Stewardship Council (FSC)	Label	FSC certified forest products comply with ten principles assuring an above-average social and environmental impact of such products in forestry activities during product sourcing and elaboration (Forest Stewardship Council, 2011). The marine stewardship council (MSC) certification is a similar approach for seafood products.
Content areas	Compliance; land tenure and use; indigenous peoples' rights; wellbeing of forest workers and local communities; equitable sharing of benefits; environmental impact of logging; forest management plan; monitoring and assessment of social and environmental impacts; high conservation value forests; restoration and conservation of natural forests		
Fair-trade standards and label	Fairtrade International	Global, cause-focused, label	Fair-trade certifications form a generic standard that must be met by all fair-trade producers and traders (Fairtrade International, 2011).
Content areas	Fair-trade principles: pay a price to producer that aims to cover the costs of sustainable production (the Fairtrade minimum price); pay an additional sum that producers can invest in development (the Fairtrade Premium); partially pay in advance, when producers ask for it; sign contracts that allow for long-term planning and sustainable production practices		

Norm	Organization	Type	Description
Energy Star	U.S. Environmental Protection Agency and the U.S. Department of Energy	Label	The Energy Star initiative consists of several programs from building certification to industrial process improvement and its flagship program, the electronic product certification initiative. All programs aim to save "money and protect the environment through energy-efficient products and practices" (U.S. Environmental Protection Agency, 2011).
Content areas			Guiding principles for product label: significant energy savings; complies with features and performance demanded by consumers; price increase (if exists) is compensated by financial savings in reasonable time; applied technology also generally available to competitors; energy performance can be measured and verified; label when applied differentiates the product and is visible for consumers

4. Narrow coverage + process orientation

Norm	Organization	Type	Description
ILO Declaration on Fundamental Principles and Rights at Work	International Labour Organization (ILO)	Global, cause-focused, background document	ILO is a "tripartite" United Nations agency that brings together representatives of governments, employers and workers to jointly shape policies and programmes promoting decent work for all (ILO, 2012).
Content areas			Fundamental principles and rights at work: freedom of association and the effective recognition of the right to collective bargaining; the elimination of all forms of forced or compulsory labor; the effective abolition of child labor; the elimination of discrimination in respect of employment and occupation

Norm	Organization	Type	Description
Rio Declaration on Environment and Development	United Nations Environment Programme (UNEP)	Background document	The Rio Declaration is a landmark document, addressing a broad variety of declarations and practices all aiming to achieve sustainable social and environmental world development (UNEP, 2012).
Content areas	The 27 Rio principles: 1. Role of humans 2. Sovereignty of states 3. Right to development 4. Environmental protection and development 5. Poverty eradication 6. Least developed are priority 7. State cooperation for ecosystem protection 8. Unsustainable production and consumption	9. Sustainable development capacities 10. Public participation 11. National environmental legislation 12. Economic system 13. Compensation for victims 14. Prevent environmental dumping 15. Precautionary principle 16. International environmental costs 17. Environmental impacts assessment 18. Disaster notification	19. Notification practice 20. Vital role of women 21. Youth mobilization 22. Vital role of indigenous people 23. Oppressed people 24. Warfare 25. Peace, development, environmental protection 26. Environmental disputes 27. Cooperation between state and people

Norm	Organization	Type	Description
Universal Declaration of Human Rights	United Nations	Background document, global	The Universal Declaration of Human Rights is the most widely accepted list of rights to which all human beings are universally entitled. The last three of the declaration's 30 articles are not rights, but duties (United Nations, 2012b).
Content areas			The contents of the 30 articles of the Universal Declaration of Human Rights can be summarized as follows (Amnesty International, 2013):

1. Everyone is free and we should all be treated in the same way.
2. Everyone is equal despite differences in skin color, sex, religion, or language, for example.
3. Everyone has the right to life and to live in freedom and safety.
4. No one has the right to treat you as a slave nor should you make anyone your slave.
5. No one has the right to hurt you or to torture you.
6. Everyone has the right to be treated equally by the law.
7. The law is the same for everyone, it should be applied in the same way to all.
8. Everyone has the right to ask for legal help when their rights are not respected.
9. No one has the right to imprison you unjustly or expel you from your own country.
10. Everyone has the right to a fair and public trial.
11. Everyone should be considered innocent until guilt is proved.
12. Everyone has the right to ask for help if someone tries to harm you, but no one can enter your home, open your letters or harass you or your family without a good reason.

13. Everyone has the right to travel as they wish.
14. Everyone has the right to go to another country and ask for protection if they are being persecuted or are in danger of being persecuted.
15. Everyone has the right to belong to a country. No one has the right to prevent you from belonging to another country if you wish to.
16. Everyone has the right to marry and have a family.
17. Everyone has the right to own property and possessions.
18. Everyone has the right to practice and observe all aspects of their own religion and change their religion if they want to.
19. Everyone has the right to say what they think and to give and receive information.
20. Everyone has the right to take part in meetings and to join associations in a peaceful way.
21. Everyone has the right to help choose and take part in the government of their country.
22. Everyone has the right to social security and to opportunities to develop their skills.
23. Everyone has the right to work for a fair wage in a safe environment and to join a trade union.
24. Everyone has the right to rest and leisure.

Norm	Organization	Type	Description
Content areas (cont)			25. Everyone has the right to an adequate standard of living and medical help if they are ill. 26. Everyone has the right to go to school. 27. Everyone has the right to share in their community's cultural life. 28. Everyone must respect the "social order" that is necessary for all these rights to be available. 29. Everyone must respect the rights of others, the community, and public property. 30. No one has the right to take away any of the rights in this declaration.
Ceres principles	Coalition for Environmentally Responsible Economies (Ceres)	International, background standard	Triggered by the Exxon Valdez oil spill of 1989, Ceres launched these principles to promote environmentally responsible business behavior, which served as a basis for many subsequent norms. In 2010 the Ceres principles were transformed and updated through the document *The 21st Century Corporation: The Ceres Roadmap for Sustainability* (Ceres, 2012).
Content areas			The Ceres principles: protection of the biosphere; sustainable use of natural resources; reduction and disposal of wastes; energy conservation; risk reduction; safe products and services; environmental restoration; informing the public; management commitment; audits and reports
SA8000	Social Accountability International (SAI)	International standard, certification	SA8000 is a widely applied standard for responsible labor practices that can be integrated into existing management systems. SA8000 provides an extensive section defining terms central to the workplace responsibilities of both direct and indirect employees (SAI, 2008).
Content areas			Definitions: company, personnel, worker, supplier/subcontractor, sub-supplier, corrective and preventive action, interested party, child, young worker, child labor, forced and compulsory labor, human trafficking, remediation of children, homeworker, SA8000 worker representative, management representative, worker organization, collective bargaining Requirement topics: child labor; forced and compulsory labor; health and safety; freedom of association and right to collective bargaining; discrimination; disciplinary practices; working hours; remuneration; management systems

Norm	Organization	Type	Description
Business Principles for Countering Bribery	Transparency International	Global, cause-focused	The Business Principles for Countering Bribery provide an action plan to combat bribery as one of the most widespread forms of corruption in business. Participating businesses make a board-level commitment to the values of integrity, transparency, and accountability, to prohibit bribery in any form, and to implement a formal program to counter bribery (Transparency International, 2009).
			Cause-wise, related norms are the United Nations Convention against Corruption and the OECD Anti-Bribery Convention.
Content areas	Program topics: bribes; political contributions; charitable contributions and sponsorships; facilitation payments; gifts; hospitality and expenses		
Equator Principles (EPs)	Equator Principles Association (EPA)	Global, industry initiative	The EPs are an initiative of the financial sector that "are a credit risk management framework for determining, assessing and managing environmental and social risk in project finance transactions "(EPA, 2012).
			The EPs in the context of this summary are introduced as an example of an industry-focused norm. Other popular examples include the Extractive Industries Transparency Initiative (EITI), the Retail Environmental Sustainability Code, and the Responsible Care Initiative by the International Council of Chemical Associations.
Content areas	Principles to be applied by Equator Principles Financial Institutions (EPFIs): review and categorization; social and environmental assessment; applicable social and environmental standards; action plan and management system; consultation and disclosure; grievance mechanism; independent review; covenants; independent monitoring and reporting; EPFI reporting		

Norm	Organization	Type	Description
Carbon Disclosure Project (CDP)	Carbon Disclosure Project	Global network, reporting	The CDP is an investor-centered organization, promoting the disclosure of carbon and water impacts through five independent programs, of which the Carbon Action Program and the Supply Chain Program (Carbon Disclosure Project, 2012) are highlighted below.
Content areas			Carbon Action Program: "A vanguard group of 35 investors with US$7.6 trillion assets under management are asking the world's largest companies to demonstrate that they are managing carbon effectively."
			Supply Chain Initiative: "Global corporations aim to understand the impacts of climate change across the supply chain, harnessing their collective purchasing power to encourage suppliers to measure and disclose climate change information."
Principles for Responsible Management Education (PRME)	United Nations Global Compact	Global network, cause-focused	The PRME is an open international network of business schools that have made a self-commitment to six principles with the joint purpose of promoting responsible management education (PRME, 2011).
Content areas			1. Purpose: to develop the capabilities of students to be future generators of sustainable value for business and society at large and to work for an inclusive and sustainable global economy
			2. Values: to incorporate into academic activities and curricula the values of global social responsibility as portrayed in international initiatives such as the United Nations Global Compact
			3. Method: to create educational frameworks, materials, processes, and environments that enable effective learning experiences for responsible leadership
			4. Research: to engage in conceptual and empirical research that advances our understanding about the role, dynamics, and impact of corporations in the creation of sustainable social, environmental and economic value
			5. Partnership: to interact with managers of business corporations to extend our knowledge of their challenges in meeting social and environmental responsibilities and to explore jointly effective approaches to meeting these challenges
			6. Dialogue: to facilitate and support dialog and debate among educators, students, business, government, consumers, media, civil society organizations, and other interested groups and stakeholders on critical issues related to global social responsibility and sustainability

D.
STRATEGIZING

8
Envisioning responsible business

The story of the frog placed in cold water that is heated so gradually it fails to notice and eventually dies. Companies that have succeeded in marrying environmental, health, and social issues with business strategy have done so using increasingly outdated strategy processes and management concepts. ... Companies that fail to notice are, like the frog in the story, putting their future at risk.

(Laszlo and Zhexembayeva, 2011, p. 2)

Effective moves toward responsible business have to be bold. Established management wisdom in many cases has to be altered significantly, if not abandoned completely, in order to keep pace with the rapid degradation of our habitat. To make tangible strides toward becoming a truly responsible business and achieving the ultimate goal of becoming a sustainable business, there is no place for superficial and unaligned management moves. Questions have to be asked, putting the very foundations, procedures, values, and wisdoms to the test—a sustainability test. The two most fundamental questions are:

1. What is the business's primary motivation and objective? Profit or non-profit (e.g., furthering a particular cause, being a virtuous business)?

2. What is the responsible business's development strategy? Growth or nongrowth (e.g., maintenance of actual business or even degrowth)?

There is a responsible business strategy for every company. Even the aggressively economic growth-seeking and profit-maximizing type will find a responsible business strategy within these basic drivers. However, they might also be well advised to rethink these basic characteristics in the long term, as neither primary motivation nor development strategy are fixed and thus may change through time. A purely profit-maximizing company might, for instance, with a change in organizational culture, become a company that instead begins to focus on its virtuous characteristics. It must be noted that the conceptualization of primary motivation and development strategy is one that we find particularly helpful in the context of responsible business for sustainable development. However, there may be many other valuable ways of envisioning responsible business, especially in different contexts.

Primary motivations for becoming a responsible business

As depicted in Figure 8.1, a business's primary motivations for responsible business can be divided into two types: profit motivation and non-profit motivation. It must be stressed that these two types of motivation are not mutually exclusive. A motivation here means primary motivation, which leaves ample room for subsequent secondary motivations. A business might, for instance, primarily be motivated by increasing profitability, but achieves it by furthering social and environmental performance, a typical non-profit motivation. A social enterprise may only reduce poverty by being economically viable and profitable.

Figure 8.1: Primary motivation for responsible business

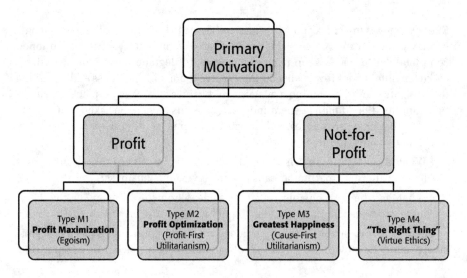

The business case

The central question for the validity of profit motivation for responsible business is: "Is responsible business actually profitable?" The inevitable answer is: "It depends." Research into the quantitative links between socio-environmental business performance and financial performance has provided positive, negative, and neutral results. The majority of research rather suggests a positive relationship between responsibility and profits (Griffin and Mahoon, 1997; Orlitzky et al., 2003; Roman et al., 1999).

While academia still searches for the proverbial philosopher's stone, practice seems to be fairly convinced that being a responsible business pays off. The Corporate Responsibility Officers Association asked if the respondents' companies could prove that they increased profits by being responsible: 68.5% confirmed that responsible business has proven profitable, while 31.2% stated they could not measure it. Only 0.3% found responsible business activities to be unprofitable (Corporate Responsibility Magazine, 2010). As early as 2002, the World Business Council for Sustainable Development (WBCSD, 2002) had stated that:

> pursuing a mission of sustainable development can make our firms more competitive, more resilient to shocks, nimbler in a fast-changing world, more unified in purpose, more likely to attract and hold customers and the best employees, and more at ease with regulators, banks, insurers and the financial market.

A wide variety of recent executive surveys has shown the breadth and magnitude of the different advantages businesses hope to reap from responsible management activities. During a survey of 250 business executives worldwide, the IBM Institute for Business Value found that not only did over half (54%) of participants believe that their companies' corporate social responsibility (CSR) activities gave them a competitive advantage over their competitors, but also that more than two-thirds (68%) focused on CSR activities to create new revenues (Pohle and Hittner, 2008). Two worldwide studies, one of 766 CEOs and the other of 1,200 consulting executives, found very similar results when asking for the most important benefits expected from a business's involvement in sustainability activities. Respondents expected many different types of benefit, such as stronger reputation, accessing new markets, revenue growth, cost reduction, shareholder value improvement, risk reduction, attraction, motivation and retention of employees, as well as improved relations with regulators (Pohle and Hittner, 2008; Lacey et al., 2010). These different mechanisms for becoming responsible are summarized as the "business case" for responsible business.

Irresponsible profit maximization in practice

Germany's leading chicken brand, Wiesenhof, which translates as "meadow farm," had made the slogan "Responsibility for people, animals and the environment" its public credo (PHW, 2011). In 2011, *The Wiesenhof System*, a documentary by German public television, presented a rather different picture. Starting with the words, "Pictures which are not directed at the general public; pictures that provide insight into a system with profit as the first priority," the documentary claimed that the only and ultimate priority of the company was profit and in evidence presented cost-reducing but barbaric farming practices, cost-efficient but inhumane working conditions, and depletion of local groundwater resources (Anthes and Verheyen, 2011).

Profit motivation

A profit motivation for responsible business is firmly based on the achievement of a sound business case for responsible business and can be divided into two categories, profit maximization and profit optimization.

A business motivated by profit maximization follows egoist ethical decision-making and will only engage in responsible business practices if there is no other activity or investment opportunity more profitable than making a commitment to responsible business activities (Thielemann and Wettstein, 2008). Such a profit-maximizing business may also be tempted to behave irresponsibly when an irresponsible business activity promises higher profits (Vogel, 2005). Carr (1968) even claims that the business context is characterized by a generally lower morale than the private context and that profit maximization has to lead to irresponsible behavior.

Fortunately nowadays, the business context has become very favorable to responsible business being the highest profit alternative. The reasons for believing that responsibility will pay off are manifold and there is sound evidence for a profit-maximizing business to believe that business responsibility makes maximum money sense.

Responsible profit maximization in practice

An interesting example of how profit maximization can lead to an exemplary responsible business activity is the story of the birth of the Toyota Prius, the world's first mass-produced alternative engine-powered car. The primary motivation of Toyota to venture into the Prius was a concern about the future profitability of the auto industry because of rising oil prices and environmental damage, a typical profit maximization rationale (Taylor, 2006). In hindsight, the move toward the Prius was one of the cornerstones of Toyota's position as market leader in the worldwide auto industry (Laasch and Flores, 2010).

In contrast to a business striving for maximum profit, one striving for profit optimization will not have maximum profit as its only goal. A profit-optimizing business will target maximum profit while at the same time paying attention to the parallel condition of acting responsibly. As long as it is acting responsibly, such a profit-optimizing business will make the most profitable choice. One could also call profit optimization "profit-first utilitarianism," as the company will always try to create as much social, environmental, and economic value as possible (the "greatest happiness principle") while favoring economic value creation first.

Profit optimization in practice

An impressive example of a profit-optimizing responsible business is Procter & Gamble's (P&G) approach to social and environmental business performance. Instead of talking about responsibilities, P&G refers to opportunities in sustainable behavior. In 2007, P&G drastically increased the percentage of sustainable innovation products in its portfolio (Laasch and Flores, 2010). P&G saw a shared opportunity between society, environment, and the company's profit in sustainable innovation products with an improved social and/or environmental impact. The advantage for society and environment lay in the immense environmental impact that the packaged consumer goods company creates through the use of its products, such as detergents, diapers, and grooming products. The business opportunity for P&G lay in seizing the immense market opportunity (roughly 75% of the overall market) in the "sustainable mainstream customers" segment (P&G, 2016).

Non-profit motivation

Businesses primarily motivated by non-profit objectives can be divided into those focusing on creating the greatest happiness among all their stakeholders and those aiming to achieve virtuousness and doing "the right thing." One might be tempted to say that these two types of motivation do not sound much like traditional business motivation. In fact, these motivational patterns can indeed be found among social or environmental entrepreneurial ventures, not traditional businesses.

Businesses operating based on the greatest happiness motivation usually start with the urgent drive to mitigate or solve a pressing social or environmental issue, which is why they make this issue their cause and the very core of all business activity. Such cause-driven businesses are often quick-growth, high-revenue ventures in order to make the greatest impact on the cause—to achieve greatest happiness—and so this is inseparably married to the success of such a business. One could therefore call this business motivation for responsible management "cause-first utilitarianism."

Greatest happiness in practice

TOMS Shoes started with the greatest happiness principle as its initial motivation. The company's founder, Blake Mycoskie, was searching for a business solution to giving shoes to poor children in Argentina and, later, all over the world. He describes the initial thought for founding the company as:

> What if I started a shoe company and every time I sold a pair of shoes, I gave a pair away? And that way, as long as I keep selling shoes, those kids will have shoes for the rest of their life. ... this was when I decided, I am going to build this into the most successful, profitable and charitable shoe company in the world. (TOMS Shoes, 2016a)

While a business aimed at creating greatest happiness measures fulfillment externally—by how much good it has done—a business motivated primarily by improving its virtuousness is focused on its internal acts and how to live up to the values for which the business stands. Such a business might rather focus on the qualitative rather than the quantitative aspects of its responsible business activities.

Virtuousness in practice

The U.K.-based smoothie business, Innocent, carries virtuousness in its name. The whole brand image is based on virtuous "innocent" products and operations. Smoothies are made of "pure crushed fruits and juices. No added sugar. No concentrates" (Design Council, 2010; Innocent Drinks, 2016). This value of purity is complemented by the additional virtues of a "non-corporate attitude, a sincere commitment to the cause and creative thinking" (CSA, 2011). When Innocent sold a minor stake to the Coca-Cola Company to finance its European growth activities in 2009, a central point in the agreement was that the Innocent values and existing labor structures would remain untouched (Sweney, 2009).

Development strategies for becoming a responsible business

Being responsible can be pursued in two drastically different underlying business strategies, permeating any subsequent business decision. Figure 8.2 illustrates the main development strategies for responsible business divided into growth and nongrowth strategies. A growth-oriented responsible business strategy will quantitatively increase the business in the economic dimension: market share, profit, and revenue. Growth might be pursued at all cost, or also at the cost of

Figure 8.2: Development strategy for responsible business

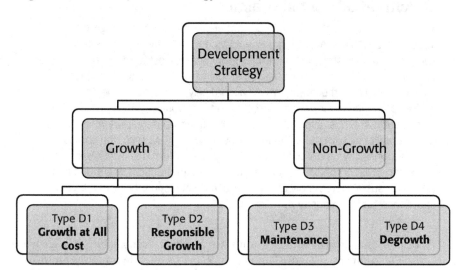

responsibility. Nongrowth strategies focus on qualitative development of the business, which could lead to maintenance of the company's economic status quo or even to a degrowth situation, a shrinking of the business's economic size. A voluntarily degrowing business sounds counterintuitive in a traditional capitalist competitive economy. In fact, an arduous discussion questioning the compat- ibility of degrowth and capitalism is in full swing (Joutsenvirta, 2016; Hornborg, 2016). Nevertheless, degrowth of consumption patterns and economic activity has been identified as a necessary prerequisite for a sustainable world develop- ment. Chapter 19 will further illustrate the enablers, inhibitors, and scenarios of a degrowing world economy.

A business pursuing a "growth-at-all-cost" strategy will only apply responsible management if it provides the most attractive growth opportunity. Many traditional businesses, from mining to alcohol, weapons to junk food, may be categorized as displaying growth-at-all-cost strategies. An expansion of these businesses due to their negative footprint always has negative effects on society and/or the environ- ment, leading to the destruction of social, environmental, and economic capital. Often such companies have overproportionately active responsible management activities, are superficially "doing good things," and are media-attractive, but are unconcerned about the overwhelming negative effects of the company's core business. Such behavior can be explained by the license to operate: businesses being perceived as largely irresponsible might experience serious resistance to their growth efforts or even to their very existence. Figuratively speaking, society might withdraw their social license to operate (Gunningham *et al.*, 2002).

Growth at all cost in practice

Marketing among children is an important element of McDonald's growth strategy. A 2011 campaign to "fire Ronald McDonald" may be interpreted as social uproar against the irresponsible "growth-at-all-cost" strategy of marketing unhealthy junk food to those most vulnerable to such marketing activities: children. A letter to the company was accordingly signed by 550 health professionals and organizations (Jargon, 2011). McDonald's, on the other hand, carries out numerous responsible management activities in areas which largely do not conflicting with the company's growth strategy. As such, the company's 2010 responsibility report claimed what McDonald's "is made of," presenting an extensive list of topical responsible management practices: "Nutrition and wellbeing, sustainable supply chain, environmental responsibility, employee experience, and community" (McDonald's, 2011).

A responsible growth strategy aims to combine responsible management activity and company growth. The match seems to provide a highly promising mechanism. Responsible management activities have an outstanding potential to be market openers and to create new revenues and innovation. Nevertheless, a growth strategy can only lead to a sustainable business if it is based on a sound positive social, environmental, and economic impact of the business activity which is being increased.

Responsible growth in practice

Entrepreneur Blake Mycoskie reveals his company's impressive basic development strategy, which achieves growth based on a positive social and economic business impact:

> By creating the one-for-one model with TOMS, we have created a never going away benefactor and that is the reason why I spend as much time hiring great people in the fashion and shoe world and that is why we have to charge a premium price.

TOMS Shoes' giving report displays how the company's positive growth was matched by its positive impact. In 2010, only four years after its foundation, TOMS had given away more than a million pairs of shoes. By 2016, the figure had climbed to over 60 million (TOMS Shoes, 2016b). "Giving is what fuels us" (TOMS Shoes, 2011). TOMS since has ventured in the eyewear industry and various other markets with the same one-for-one business development philosophy.

Scaling credit for the poor

The Bangladesh-based Grameen Bank was created with the clear development objective of reducing poverty on a large scale. The bank was so successful that in 2009, just a few years after its founders first jumped into micro-banking, it had almost 8 million customers (Grameen Bank, 2011). The average income of a Grameen customer compared with a control group has been estimated to be 50% higher, very likely a result of these businesses being founded with credit from Grameen Bank (Grameen Bank, 2010).

Maintenance strategies for responsible business are slowly becoming a visible phenomenon. Businesses continuing to put economic growth first have usually accepted their negative impact on society and the environment in respect of that relentless growth. Maintenance often sees qualitative improvements as an alternative to total economic growth. Sustainability thinking makes increased profitability without changing size an ever more attractive option.

Maintenance strategy in practice

Patagonia, a world-leading outdoor clothing company, displays a somewhat different perspective on its development strategy toward responsible business:

> We don't want to grow larger, but want to remain lean and quick. We want to make the best clothes and make them so they will last a long, long time. Our idea is to make the best product so you can consume less and consume better. Every decision we make must include its impact on the environment. We want to zero in on quality. (Chouinard and Gallagher, 2004)

The company desires to become a truly virtuous responsible business, transforming its basic processes and culture toward more sustainable ways. Patagonia's "Footprint Chronicles" show the extensive effort being made to transparently transform the business from the inside, beginning with its products. Patagonia's development strategy comes from the insight "that everything we do as a business ... leaves its mark on the environment. There is still no such thing as sustainable business" (Patagonia, 2011).

Probably the least common strategy for a typical market economy business is responsible degrowth. A business might realize that the only way to become a sustainable business in the long term is to reduce its scale. Degrowth is perhaps the most complex strategic approach to responsible business development. Companies reducing size usually need to reduce the number of staff, a move with potentially severe social consequences. Degrowth often goes against the most basic incentives of a competitive market system. The business that shrinks appears not to be competitive. Reducing market share, reducing revenues, reducing business units, reducing the product line, or even actively decreasing the market goes against the very basis of the free market: competition.

> ## Baby steps toward degrowth in practice
>
> While Unilever does not aim to degrow the economic business volume, the company at least focuses on decoupling its economic growth from its negative environmental impact. The company's sustainability plan reads as follows: "We will decouple our growth from our environmental impact, achieving absolute reductions across the product life-cycle. Our goal is to halve the environmental footprint of the making and use of our products". If these commitments contribute to an overall degrowth of the company's environmental impact, one would need to determine if this halving of impact refers to the relative impact per product or the total impact of all the company's products as a whole. Unilever claims to have achieved both a reduction in environmental impact and above-average economic growth (Unilever, 2015).

We increasingly see degrowth efforts by companies. For instance, "responsible consumption" has become a common cause for many alcohol companies. Telling your customers to consume responsibly and avoid addictive consumption patterns implicitly means recommending that they drink less. Energy companies start investing, for instance, in "smart meters" that help their customers reduce the consumption of the company's own product. Nevertheless, such efforts only display partial degrowth, which does not assure the overall degrowth of the company as a whole.

Making responsible business commitments

The first step toward making a commitment to responsible business has to be a conscious decision about the basic parameters of that step. What should be the primary motivation: profit or not? How should we develop the business: growth or not? These basic questions, which define the conditions of responsible business conduct, are of crucial importance. The answers drastically change how responsible business activities will be implemented. It sounds drastic, but there is a strong case for drastic decisions. If a company is not able to become a sustainable business while growing, a growth strategy coupled with whatever good deeds occur along the way cannot reflect truly responsible business practice. Figure 8.3 illustrates the different types of business emerging from combining the basic parameters of responsible business described in the preceding section. For instance, a business primarily motivated by profit and growth is "business as usual," while a company with the primary motivation of creating the "greatest happiness" and the pursuit of responsible growth is a "responsibility superstar," due to its often stellar rise. A

Figure 8.3: Responsible business categories

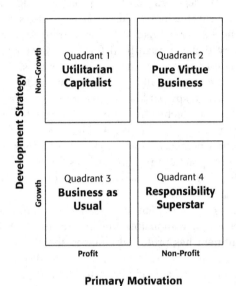

Figure 8.4: Responsible business self-assessment

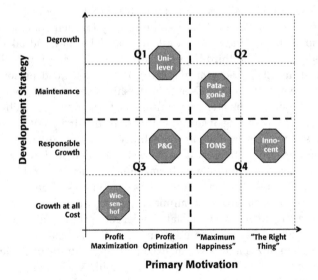

business desiring maintenance and profit optimization is called a "utilitarian capi-talist," while a company degrowing and motivated by being a virtuous business is described as a "pure virtue business." Figure 8.4 is a self-assessment tool to catego-rize the basic parameters of responsible business strategy.

Only the company that has identified the basic parameters of its long-term perspective can credibly commit to responsible business. Anything else would be unsubstantiated and hollow talk. The two most fundamental components of a formal commitment to responsible business are its primary motivation and its development strategy. The technicalities of committing to responsible business, what communication instruments to use, and how to design such a commitment from a communication perspective are covered in Chapters 14 and 15. At this point, two crucial best practices in making a responsible business commitment need to be highlighted. Without these two points, commitments tend to be paper tigers without effecting real change inside the company.

The first practice is to show high-level leadership and make living up to the commitment a priority. If responsible business is taken seriously, a company making this commitment has profound changes ahead. Only if the responsible business is directed from the very top of the organization are such changes possible. A large-scale survey among responsibility officers revealed that 77% of companies had made commitments to ethical-responsible values by their lead-ership team, while only 63% regularly communicated this commitment. It also showed that only 61% of the C-level leaders took personal action based on these values and only half of the leaders would turn down a business offer that contra-dicted the responsible business commitment (Corporate Responsibility Magazine, 2010). Interestingly, 42% of CEOs cared personally for their companies' commit-ment to responsible business. When asked about why they had taken action on responsible business, the third-biggest driver of such activity was the personal motivation of the CEO (Lacey et al., 2010). With such broad personal commit-ment, doors are open to get the C-level leadership team on board when planning and making responsible business commitments. Corporate responsibility officers perceived strategic planning of sustainability to be the first point on their respon-sible business agenda (Corporate Responsibility Magazine, 2010).

The second practice is to broadly involve stakeholders in drafting the commit-ment and achieve co-commitments. If stakeholder consultation is important for the management of responsible business, it is even more so when setting the most basic parameters and making a commitment. Coordinating a business's motivation and development perspective with stakeholder interest prevents future problems if its main stakeholders are not in agreement with the business's commitment. Drafting the commitment is also an excellent opportunity to achieve upfront co-commitments from the most important stakeholders. Such joint commitments are especially efficient among industry peers to improve an initiative by a whole industry or sector. For instance, automotive companies increasingly collaborate in the development of new environmentally friendly technologies. Co-commitments may also help important allies permanently support the business becoming a sustainable business.

Exercises

A. Know

Use the multiple choice questions below to test your knowledge. Each answer may be wrong or right and there may be zero to four right or wrong answers per question:

1. Primary motivations of business ...
    a. ... may be divided into profit and non-profit motivations.
    b. ... may include a profit motivation. In order for a profit motivation for responsible business to make sense, there must be a so-called business case for responsible business.
    c. ... may include profit optimization, which describes a situation where the only goal of a business is to generate maximum profit.
    d. ... may include a motivation to create the "greatest happiness" and to "be virtuous." Both motivations are mostly found among traditional businesses.

2. Development strategies for responsible business ...
    a. ... may be divided into profit and non-profit approaches.
    b. ... include, for instance, degrowth strategies.
    c. ... include, for instance, growth-at-all-cost strategies.
    d. ... includes Patagonia as an example of a growth-at-all-cost strategy.

3. The four responsible business categories ...
    a. ... include the "responsibility superstar," a business that combines a non-profit motivation with a nongrowth development strategy.
    b. ... include the "pure utilitarian" business.
    c. ... are the result of combining different business motivations and development strategies.
    d. ... may be used to better understand a business's basic motivation and development perspective toward responsible business.

B. Think

Imagine you are working in an electronic goods company such as Samsung or Philips and your boss, the head of sourcing, asks you to recommend whether or not to accept a batch of minerals, used for mobile phone screens, of which the origin is unknown. How do you deal with the incomplete information you have and what is your advice?

C. Do

Imagine you are working in an investment company and one of your main clients wants to invest in a company that is mainly motivated by "doing the right thing." The investor is highly sensitive to "greenwashers" and wants to make sure the motivation of the company identified is "pure." A good starting point for identifying such a company are the databases of networks of sustainable, responsible, and ethical companies, such as B Lab, UNGC, or the WBCSD. Develop a tool to make your assessment decision explainable to your investor.

D. Relate

Write a short description of a responsible business practice that has inspired you and publish it through a social network. Try to formulate the message in a way that inspires others to take similar actions.

E. Be

Analyze one occasion that you considered as a personal success. What do you think was your primary motivation? Was it to get the most out of it for yourself? To get the most for yourself while also thinking about others? To make all involved as happy as possible? To do "the right thing," based on some higher principles? Something else?

Feedback

A. Know

Question 1

a. Right: profit motivations can be further divided into profit maximization and optimization, while a non-profit motivation may be divided into "greatest happiness" and doing "the right thing."

b. Right: if there was no business case for responsible business, a profit motivation would not make sense as there would not be any profit to be made from responsible business.

c. Wrong: profit maximization targets maximum profit, while profit-optimizing businesses aim to maximize profit only if this behavior does not lead to irresponsible behavior.

d. Wrong: these motivational patterns are more typical for social and environmental entrepreneurial ventures than they are for traditional businesses.

Question 2

a. Wrong: development strategies are either growth or nongrowth-based.

b. Right: degrowth is one of the nongrowth strategies.

c. Right: a growth-at-all-cost strategy will only apply to responsible business if it provides the most attractive growth alternative.

d. Wrong: Patagonia was used as an example of a maintenance development strategy.

Question 3

a. Wrong: a "responsibility superstar" business has a strong growth development strategy.

b. Wrong: such a business is not mentioned.

c. Right: the four categories are "business as usual," "responsibility superstar," "utilitarian capitalist," and "pure virtue business."

d. Right: as outlined in this chapter, this is the purpose of the four responsible business types.

B. Think

Level	Dealing with incomplete information	Notes
+	Judgment made after successfully applying strategies for dealing with incomplete information	
=	Reasonable judgment based on incomplete information given in text	
−	No judgment made, due to insecurity about how to deal with incomplete information	

C. Do

Level	Developing tools	Notes
+	Company has been identified based on a rigorous and transparent process based on the developed tool	
=	Company has been identified applying a reasonable argument	
−	No company has been identified	

D. Relate

Level	Inspiring others	Notes
+	Message has the strong potential to inspire others to take similar action	
=	Message gives a fair account of what is special about the responsible business practice	
−	Message does not allow others to understand what is special about the practice	

E. Be

Level	Developing critical distance to own actions	Notes
+	Impartial evaluation identifying deeper behavioral and motivational structures	
=	Impartial evaluation of the situation similar to an outside observer	
–	Description appears entangled with self-justification and a "clouded view" of oneself	

9
Strategic management

Many companies have already done much to improve the social and environmental consequences of their activities, yet those efforts have not been nearly as productive as they could be—for two reasons ... First, they pit business against society, when clearly the two are interdependent. Second, they pressure companies to think of corporate social responsibility in generic ways instead of in the way most appropriate to each firm's strategy.

(Porter and Kramer, 2006, p. 78)

Analyzing the status quo

The precondition for crafting effective strategies, and the first part of the strategic management process, is to develop a sound appreciation of the status quo. Only if we know where we are, are we able to find the path that leads us to where we want to be—the strategy. In this section we will look at tools invaluable to understanding the status quo: SWOT analysis, materiality assessment, and portfolios of responsible business activities.

Responsible business SWOT analysis

After making a basic commitment to responsible business, the next step is to investigate sources of different strategic alternatives. This analysis can be divided into two basic spheres. First, in the business-internal sphere the analytical focus is on internal factors, such as processes, culture, and capabilities. Second, the external sphere can be divided into the business's industry environment, which includes suppliers, customers, industry competition, substitutes, and new entrants (Porter, 1980). The external macro environment includes the factors surrounding and permeating industries such as technologies, norms and legislation, culture, natural environment, and demographics. The most commonly used integrative tool for responsible business is the "SWOT analysis." The first two letters "S" and "W" refer to analyzing the internal business dimensions of strengths and weaknesses, while "O" and "T" refer to opportunities and threats within the external dimension. Figure 9.1 illustrates typical helpful and harmful factors related to responsible business throughout the external and internal business environment.

Analyzing the internal business environment first, typical strengths helpful for implementing responsible business activities include a strong internal business culture fostering social and environmental business performance. Procter & Gamble began to improve its socio-environmental business performance as early as 1992 (P&G, 2006). As a result, the company was internally well prepared to take on the goal of producing US$50 billion in revenues from sustainable innovation products from 2007 to 2012 (Laasch and Flores, 2010). Also, mainstream business resources may be capitalized for responsible management. For instance, Walmart's highly efficient logistics and warehousing system allows for a concise

Figure 9.1: Responsible business SWOT analysis

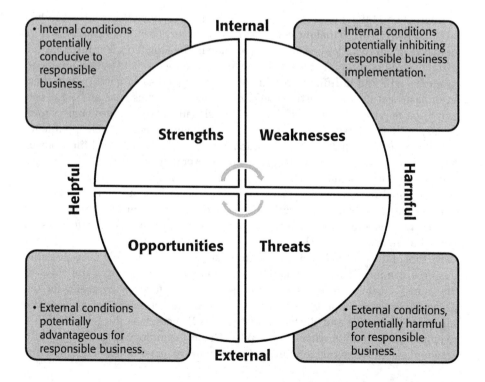

estimation and handling of food products that do not fulfill Walmart's quality standards. It is only through the logistics of this system that Walmart was able to donate US$2 billion in cash and kind by 2015. Most of the food Walmart donates would otherwise have ended up in the trash (Walmart, 2011). The Company has recently committed to donate another US$4 billion by 2020 (Walmart, 2016). Other internally positive conditions might be a management system standard (such as for quality, safety, or environment) that can be adapted to integrate responsible management. The personal conviction of individual leaders may also be a condition highly conducive to drafting a viable and scalable strategy for implementing responsible business conduct.

Mountain guide for climbing "Mount Sustainability"

One of the most powerful internal strengths for successfully implementing responsible business is high-level visionary leadership and commitment. One of the most impressive leaders for responsible business was InterfaceFLOR's late CEO Ray Anderson. He had been inspired by Hawken's book *The Ecology of Commerce* (1993) and from this point on had pushed his company to ever new heights of responsible business. The self-declared medium-term goal was to rise to the top of "Mount Sustainability." InterfaceFLOR has committed to becoming a truly sustainable business with zero negative impact by 2020 (Anderson, 2012).

Internal conditions with the potential to inhibit responsible business conduct (weaknesses) might be that the core business, in its very basic characteristics, does not leave much room for becoming sustainable in the long term. For instance, the extractive industry, or any business involved in the life-cycle of petroleum-based products, will find it difficult to achieve environmental sustainability over time. In order to get there, a drastic change of the very core business and processes would be required. British Petroleum's (BP) slogan "Beyond Petroleum" superficially indicates a shift away from the imminently unsustainable petroleum core business, but whether this aspiration has been followed by real-life changes has largely been questioned (Walker, 2010). Another internal inhibitor typically encountered is the human tendency to resist change, however virtuous the intended goal may be. Truly changing a business to become more responsible requires major shifts in structure, processes, work patterns, and attitudes. Change is usually work-intensive: Chapter 18 provides an extensive toolset for change toward more responsible behavior.

Factors of the external business environment play a crucial role in responsible business conduct. The sustainability megatrend rapidly "changes the rules of the game," creates threats for the unprepared, and offers opportunities for the prepared. External opportunities are many. New markets open up, such as the Lifestyles of Health and Sustainability (LOHAS) market or the bottom-of-the-pyramid market which caters to the poor. Green technology is another rapidly growing market. External opportunities also lie in governmental support for sustainable business, be it grants or know-how, and the search of investors for socially responsible investment opportunities.

Typical external threats related to business responsibility include restricting legislation about ethics, society, or environment. There is always a threat of losing customers, employees, and investors due to their search for more responsible business alternatives. Broad environmental and societal issues may also develop into a tangible business threat. The Coca-Cola Company, for example, ventured into a US$17 million water protection program in collaboration with the World Wildlife Fund. Water scarcity is an imminent threat to Coca-Cola's water-intensive production process as well as to production of sugar cane, one of its crucial ingredients.

Materiality assessment

In Chapter 6, the three most salient specialized responsible management instruments were defined. It is these three instruments (stakeholder management, life-cycle impact management, and ethics management) that deliver the basic insight necessary to understand a company's stakeholders, impacts, and ethical risks. As

Figure 9.2: Materiality assessment for a taco business

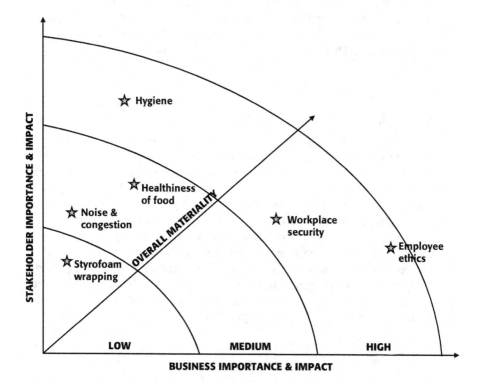

was illustrated, these three assessments enable a company to define the "materiality," or the importance of engaging in a certain responsible management activity.

Materiality consists of both a business and a stakeholder dimension. The business dimension comprises both importance and impact of a certain issue to the business, while the stakeholder dimension does the same thing jointly for all stakeholder groups. The fictional case of a typical Mexican taco restaurant, Tacos de la Esquinita, as illustrated in Figure 9.2, will be used to further illustrate how a materiality analysis might be conducted in practice. It may be helpful to review the taco restaurant's stakeholder map in Figure 6.5.

Issues at the Tacos

The owner of Tacos de la Esquinita, Luis Gómez, was concerned about various latent problems with his business. Among other things, he wanted to deal with the noise and congestion from the intensive customer traffic, and the environmental impact of Styrofoam packaging had recently caught his attention. To find out which issue he should take care of first, Luis talked to the main stakeholders of his business, his employees, customers, and neighbors. The most important issues identified were hygienic aspects, the safety of his cooks (a lot of heat and sharp instruments), and the bad ethics of several employees which had resulted in upset customers and financial losses when waiters had stolen considerable amounts of money charged to customers. In spite of its low immediate materiality, Luis also decided to act on the Styrofoam packaging issue, wanting to be proactive with pending legislation about to ban Styrofoam in general throughout Mexico.

Responsible business portfolio

A basic prerequisite for planning the responsible management process is to have a clear picture and continuous assessment of issues related to the business. A responsible business portfolio establishes such an inventory (similar to a risk portfolio). It supports the ongoing responsible management and planning process by providing information on every issue's materiality, interrelatedness, potential, or actions taken, as well as the business's performance in every issue. Table 9.1 provides an excerpt of the taco business's responsible business portfolio.

A responsible business portfolio summarizes an initial mapping of issues and the involved stakeholders, then analyzes the entities mapped, and finally provides potential responsible business alternatives and outcomes. This scheme, rather than claiming exhaustiveness, provides a basic framework that can be adjusted according to a business's situation and practice.

Table 9.1: Excerpt from Tacos de la Esquinita's responsible business portfolio

	A. Mapping	B. Analysis			C. Outcomes	
Issue	Main stakeholders	Materiality level	Main related SWOT factor	Responsible management actions		Indicators
Styrofoam	Customers Environment	Low	(T)hreat: impending legislation to ban Styrofoam	Implement alternative packaging technologies Use Styrofoam only for take-out meals.		Percentage of overall servings in Styrofoam Total amount of Styrofoam used
Congestion and noise	Neighbors Customers	Intermediate	(T)hreat: neighbors obstructing business	Offer home service		Monthly number of "angry neighbor incidents"
Employee ethics	Employees Customers	High	(W)eakness: low work satisfaction.	Decrease stress level by hiring additional waiters Improve control mechanisms		Monthly number of employee immorality incidents

Strategic management processes

Figure 9.3 illustrates how Step 1 (defining the basic prerequisites) and Step 2 (understanding the status quo) interrelate with every business's components of classic strategic management. The ultimate goal of the strategic management process for a responsible business is to shape a customized sustainability strategy to become a sustainable business. A sustainability strategy must be deeply integrated with the organization's mainstream strategy—ideally, they should be identical. Thus, vision, mission, and value have to be formed by responsible business planning, which includes social, environmental, and economic factors. The same applies to the strategy development process and the control and evaluation tools. The three main components of strategic management will now be described, with a particular focus on how they relate to responsible business.

Figure 9.3: Dynamics of responsible business planning and mainstream strategic management components

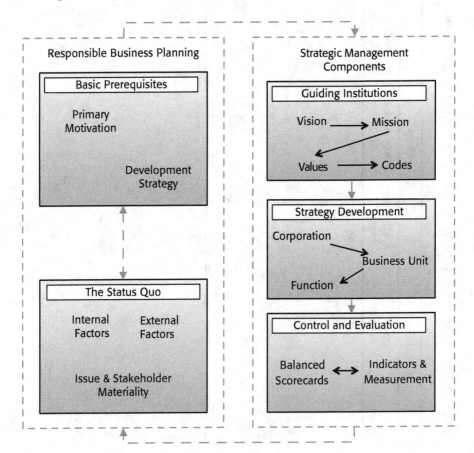

Vision, mission, and value statements of business are the strategic guidance statements, or lighthouses, of business conduct. Thus, a responsible business strategy of ultimately becoming a truly sustainable business has to begin with fine-tuning these guidance statements. Vision statements describe what a company ultimately wants to become. The company's vision statement, therefore, should contain the goal of becoming a sustainable business. A company's mission statement, instead, describes what the company is and does, its practices, typical customers, products, and processes.

Guiding light or just creative writing?

The company, Enron, finally threw in the towel after probably the largest accounting scandal in world history. But Enron had a very well-developed mission statement. The text was centered on the four key values of respect, integrity, communication, and excellence (Business Library, 2002). In fact, the scandal showed a reality that was contradictory to the values intended. Responsible business statements have to strongly reflect a true commitment to a desired and achievable business reality.

Mission statements provide an excellent opportunity to outline how responsible business practices should be implemented. Company value statements are a natural extension of the mission statement, describing "how to do business" by providing the underlying values, principles, and cultural and ethical guidance. It is not recommended to separate the mainstream business/financial guiding instruments from the responsible business ones. Some companies have drafted impressive plans covering social and environmental business elements, which are presented on beautiful responsible business homepages. Unfortunately these documents are often isolated from the respective mainstream financial/economic instruments. As extensively described in Chapter 3, a sustainable business is the one that balances and integrates social, environmental, and economic business performance. Thus, such integration has to begin with the guiding instruments themselves.

Business strategies should follow a company's guiding instruments (Table 9.2). The main reference document to be followed in strategy development should be the mission statement. Strategies are usually developed at three different levels. At the broadest level, corporate strategies manage and integrate several business units operating in distinct markets. Business unit strategies focus on achieving competitive advantages in single markets by strategically positioning the company's products and brands. The narrowest level, called functional strategies, coordinates single business functions, such as marketing, accounting, and human resources, to support the higher level strategies.

Responsible business strongly influences strategy development at all three levels. At the corporate level, many companies achieve responsible diversification of their business portfolio by acquiring or developing new units with

Table 9.2: Integrating mainstream and responsible business across the strategic guidance instruments

Strategic guidance instrument	Responsible business function	Typical contents
Vision statement	Describing a vision of what the sustainable business should look like	Achievement through growth, maintenance or degrowth Main motivation is profit (financial value creation) or non-profit (maximum happiness, virtue)
Mission statement	Describes the actual responsible business conduct to be implemented in the day-to-day business and necessary to achieve the vision	Main causes and stakeholders addressed Management focus on growth or nongrowth; profit or non-profit Main activity areas necessary to implement responsible business
Values statement	Is an important benchmark document for drafting intended business culture and describes the values that company employees should use to guide their actions	Values conducive to responsible management conduct: transparency, ethical behavior, respect, accountability, responsibility, etc.
Codes of conduct and ethics	Defines intended behaviors for the business at large or in areas of key importance	Definition of intended processes and behaviors in areas crucial to becoming a responsible business for each respective business Examples include general codes of ethics, supplier codes, sourcing codes, sales ethics, finance, accounting, etc.

above-average social and environmental performance. The Coca-Cola Company, for example, tried to buy the German eco-lemonade producer Bionade and invested in shares of the British natural smoothie producer, Innocent (Local, 2009; Sweney, 2009). Clorox developed the Green Works environmentally friendly cleansers business unit (Green Works, 2011). L'Oreal bought the organic cosmetics pioneer, The Body Shop (Bones, 2006). At the business unit strategy level, companies want to improve their strategic positioning, based on either low cost or differentiation (Porter, 1985). For instance, eco-efficiency measures, such as reducing packaging and energy usage, may facilitate a substantial reduction in product prices. Responsible business may also differentiate among product offers. Car manufacturers increasingly differentiate their products with "eco-features," and "hybrids," "hydrogens," "electrics," and "fuel-efficient" have become common marketing terms for auto-makers. Each functional level strategy contributes differently to the overall strategy of a business. For example, PepsiCo strongly focuses on inclusiveness and diversity in its human resources function and claims that this policy strongly enhances its innovative potential, which in turn contributes to the company's overall strategy (PepsiCo, 2016).

Racing to the top?

Many main industry incumbents have begun to increasingly compete on sustainability. Prominent examples are UPS and Fedex, P&G and Unilever, and Coca-Cola and Pepsi (Gallisa, 2011). For instance, the Coca-Cola Company announced a 30% plant-based PET bottle in 2009; in 2012 Pepsi raised the bar with its 100% plant-based bottles; Coca-Cola responded with entirely recyclable plant-bottles in 2015. Car manufacturers are outgunning each other in the fight for the alternative engine standard of the future. Construction companies overbid each other in the most sustainable housing, targeting a zero-sum emission construction. Such "races to the top" are important drivers of innovation toward more responsible industries and maybe even toward a sustainable economic system.

Traditional strategic management creates competitive advantage with the ultimate goal of achieving above-average returns (Hitt *et al.*, 2007). For responsible business, such above-average returns, or profit, can only be one of several intended outcomes in the strategic management process. To become a sustainable business, the strategic management goal structure is multi-dimensional. It consists of above-average social, environmental, and, of course, economic business performance (profit versus non-profit motivations), as well as the type of development to be achieved (growth versus nongrowth). This is why strategy evaluation and control mechanisms have to reflect these multiple dimensions.

Controlling and evaluating strategy is usually conducted through the development of performance indicators reflecting the outcomes to be achieved by the strategies implemented. Performance indicators for responsible business are social, environmental, and economic (financial). Examples of financial indicators are total revenues, profit margins, and shareholder value creation. Environmental performance indicators may be related to environmental resource efficiency, such as water usage, CO_2 emissions, and toxicity. Often environmental indicators are expressed as footprints such as "trees per tonne of paper" and "liters of water per cup of coffee produced." Social indicators largely depend on the main social causes the company targets. For a company desiring to improve primary education, a social indicator might be the literacy rate of local communities. For a business wanting to improve employee wellbeing, organizational climate surveys may measure changes in job satisfaction.

A common practice is to measure activity (e.g., volunteering hours, money donated, responsibility budget) for social and environmental causes instead of the actual outcome of these activities. Whenever possible it is preferable to measure realized outcomes instead of activities which have real-life repercussions that are hard to estimate.

Indicators for responsible impact?

Unilever's "Sustainable Living Plan" has changed lofty slogans into tangible indicators. For instance, the ideal of "enhancing livelihoods" translates into the tangible goal of sourcing 100% of agricultural materials sustainably, which in turn integrates at least 500,000 smallholder farmers into the company's supply chain by 2020. This is only one example of the 50 indicators that aim to achieve concrete goals for society and the environment (Unilever, 2016).

Sustainability balanced scorecards strategically plan social, environmental, and economic business performance. They provide a management system that integrates not only profit and non-profit goals, but also long-term and short-term thinking (Figge *et al.*, 2002). The original balanced scorecard model was invented by Kaplan and Norton (1996) to get away from short-term profit thinking. They believed it was an inadequate indicator for business performance, so they directed attention to long-term profit drivers. Figure 9.4 combines the classic four scorecard perspectives:

1. Financial performance
2. Customers
3. Internal processes
4. Growth and learning

with two additional sustainability perspectives of environmental and social performance. The model is then used to analyze the effect of Unilever's (2010) sustainable living plan on the company's balanced scorecard and, subsequently, on its strategy. The plan's three main activity areas can be neatly divided under the three scorecard indicators. The customer perspective is influenced by the goal of using Unilever products to improve their health and wellbeing. The ambitious goal to halve the company's environmental impact mainly refers to the impact of internal operations. The goal of sourcing 100% of agricultural materials sustainably falls under the category of organizational learning and growth, as its main goals are to train small farmers and micro-entrepreneurs to form a crucial part of the company's upstream and downstream supply chain. All goals are to be fulfilled by 2020, ten years after the plan was established in 2010. The sustainability balanced scorecard model has been adjusted extensively to many different settings, of which Figure 9.4 represents just one design that works for the Unilever case (Hansen and Schaltegger, 2016). Every company is well advised to design a balanced scorecard that best fits their settings.

In Chapters 10–13, we will see how a business might translate balanced scorecard objectives into real-life practice across its internal functions, and even to its supply chain outside the company.

Figure 9.4: Sustainability scorecards applied to Unilever's sustainable living plan

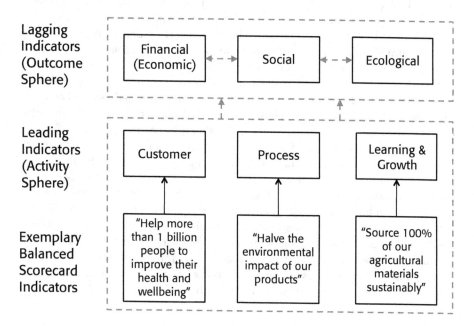

Business models

The concept of a business model is used to reflect a company's realized strategy (Casadesus-Masanell and Ricart, 2010). A business model describes the essence of a business, the basic logic of everything it does. So if we are to know if a responsible business strategy has truly become a business reality we have to see if it is reflected in the business model. The most dominant understanding of the elements of a business model is one that divides the business model into the following four main functions (Osterwalder, 2004; Osterwalder and Pigneur, 2010):

1. **Value proposition** describes what value the company offers
2. **Value creation** describes the structures, processes, and actors involved in creating the value offered
3. **Value delivery** describes the different customer segments, the relationship to them, and the channels applied to offer the value to them
4. **Value capture** describes how the company retains a certain amount of economic value (the profit), based on the costs and revenues realized

The above points demonstrate the dominance of for-profit thinking as main motivation—and customers as main stakeholders—in the mainstream business model concept. In a responsible business, where sustainability, responsibility, and ethics are also dominant themes, a business model structure as outlined above cannot provide a full appreciation of the logic of a responsible business. Mainstream, for-profit business, and responsible business elements have to be combined which often leads to so-called "hybrid" business organization, following a profit and a not-for-profit logic in parallel (Battilana *et al.*, 2012; Haigh and Hoffman, 2012). If we are to build such hybrid organizations, business model thinking has to reflect the nonmainstream business factors of sustainability, responsibility, and ethics. This results in a number of changes in business model thinking. For instance, instead of thinking about a mainly economic value proposition for only customers, a more holistic idea of value has to be adopted. In responsible business the value to be considered also includes value for other stakeholders, such as the work satisfaction of employees in a company that is a great place to work, the community contribution of a locally involved business, or possibly a positive environmental value for the local ecosystem, for instance in the case of a recycling business. It is shared value between multiple stakeholders and blended social, environmental, and economic value. This then translates into the three other business model functions of creation, delivery, and capture. Figure 9.5 further illustrates the questions to be asked for integrating mainstream and responsible business in a business model. As the business models of responsible businesses are strongly influenced by specific environmental factors, Figure 9.5 also includes three sections aimed at the appreciation of the moral, stakeholder, and triple equity systems in which the company is embedded.

Figure 9.5: Questions to be asked when designing business models for responsible business

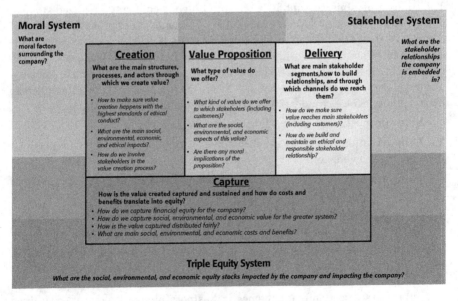

Source: Loosely based on Osterwalder and Pigneur, 2010.

Figure 9.7 in the appendix of this chapter includes a "blank canvas" version of this business model for you to draw on and to design a vision of your responsible business. It is immensely helpful as simple model of the business as it may be used to communicate to the many different business stakeholders (Baden-Fuller and Morgan, 2010; Doganovaa and Eyquem-Renault, 2009). However, we are rarely presented with such a blank sheet of paper, unless we are trying to design a business venture that is not yet in existence. Existing business models are often complex activity systems with multiple connections and feedback loops among these activities (Casadesus-Masanell and Ricart, 2010; Zott and Amit, 2010). The reality is therefore much messier than the neat business model of the "blank canvas." Accordingly, if we want to consider both an idealized perfect business model and its current status quo, we need an additional tool geared toward showing this messy reality.

Imagine, for instance, an existing business like TOMS, the innovative shoe company we introduced Chapter 8. TOMS' unique quick growth from having a disruptive business idea to becoming a global player in the fashion industry is often attributed to its business model. Figure 9.6 provides a basic impression of the activity system that has led to this success. While the figure does not put the different functions of the business model into boxes as neatly as the canvas model, the four main business model functions are still visible. We see, for instance, that TOMS achieves both an economic value capture for the business in the form of a

Figure 9.6: Feedback loops in the TOMS business model activity system

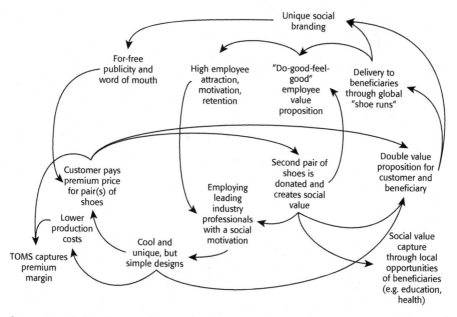

Source: Loosely based on Casadesus-Masanell and Ricart (2010)

premium margin, and a social value capture as the shoes donated have variable lasting social impacts. For instance, they improve the health of beneficiaries, and they enable kids to go to school, for which shoes are often an entry requirement in developing countries. We may also appreciate the delivery mechanism of "shoe runs" and a multiple-value proposition to three main stakeholders. The customer value proposition consists of a stylish pair of shoes and the warm feeling of having done good by buying them. The beneficiaries, mostly kids, benefit from receiving a pair of shoes which may improve their health of give them access to social opportunities, such as attending school. The third value proposition is toward employees who, working in TOMS, may get a chance to do good through their job, which might not be possible in many other companies in the fashion industry.

Business models are higher level descriptions of all of the activities realized in the different company functions, all of which will be described in greater detail in Chapters 10–13.

Exercises

A. Know

Use the multiple choice questions below to test your knowledge. Each answer may be wrong or right and there may be zero to four right or wrong answers per question:

1. A responsible business SWOT analysis ...

    a. ... abbreviates the words "Sustainability–Weakness–Organizational–Tactics."
    b. ... may include a CEO opposing responsible business as a harmful internal factor.
    c. ... helps to analyze an organization's external and internal conditions.
    d. ... supports subsequent strategy development.

2. Materiality ...

    a. ... helps to define how important a certain issue should be.
    b. ... has been illustrated by the example of a taco business. In this example, workplace security was one of the "most material" issues.
    c. ... combines business importance and impact with stakeholder importance and impact.
    d. ... may be one component reflected in a responsible business portfolio.

3. Strategy development ...

    a. ... is usually conducted on three different levels: the sustainability level, the corporate level, and the responsible business level.
    b. ... on the corporate level includes the Coca-Cola Company's attempt to buy Bionade.
    c. ... includes functional level strategy development. The goal is to have functional strategies contributing to the higher hierarchical levels of strategy development.
    d. ... should be informed by the preceding responsible business SWOT analysis, the business's primary motivation and development strategy.

4. Indicators for the strategic management of responsible business ...

    a. ... include social indicators. One social indicator might be "the percentage of workers unionized."
    b. ... may be included in a balanced scorecard.
    c. ... should be social, environmental, and economic. These dimensions reflect the triple bottom line.
    d. ... are different for every business, depending on the specific causes it focuses on.

5. The balanced scorecard ...
    a. ... was originally developed to avoid short-term profit thinking as the primary driver of business.
    b. ... integrating responsible business indicators has been illustrated by Unilever's sustainable living plan.
    c. ... reflects outcomes and activities in its indicators.
    d. ... is an instrument for strategy control and evaluation.

6. Business models ...
    a. ... typically have the five elements of value proposition, value offer, value creation, value delivery, and value capture.
    b. ... are best described through the business model "blank canvas" if we want to fully appreciate the "messy reality" of an existing business.
    c. ... are reflections of a company's realized strategy.
    d. ... for responsible business are typically hybrids between "mainstream" and responsible business activities.

B. Think

Imagine two competitors are secretly conspiring to fix their product prices. What moral implications can you think of? Explain why you think the points you mention are morally relevant.

C. Do

Think about your own idea for a responsible business and use the business model "blank canvas" (Fig. 9.7 in the appendix of this chapter) to describe the big picture of your idea.

D. Relate

Imagine you are in charge of rewriting a big tobacco company's vision statement so that it sets the company on a responsible business path. Meet with three other people to jointly come up with a statement that serves this purpose.

E. Be

Use the SWOT tool analysis to develop a personal action plan for you to become a responsible manager.

Feedback

A. Know

Question 1

a. Wrong: SWOT stands for "Strength–Weaknesses–Opportunities–Threats."
b. Right: such a CEO would be an organizational weakness for responsible business conduct.
c. Right: internal conditions are strengths and weaknesses, while external conditions are threats and opportunities.
d. Right: the appreciation of relevant internal and external environments is a necessary precondition for crafting viable strategies.

Question 2

a. Right: a materiality analysis does so by estimating an issue's importance to the business and stakeholders.
b. Right: workplace security, employee ethics, and hygiene were in the highest materiality category.
c. Right: both categories are used to define the materiality of a certain issue.
d. Right: including materiality in a responsible business portfolio helps to categorize the various issues and causes of a business.

Question 3

a. Wrong: the three levels of strategy development are corporate level, business unit (or market) level, and functional level.
b. Right: the buying attempt is an example of how companies try to achieve a responsible diversification at the corporate level.
c. Right: the functional level strategy should contribute to the business unit level strategy by either contributing to a product differentiation or a low-cost strategy.
d. Right: as shown in Figure 9.3, responsible business planning and mainstream strategic management are highly interconnected.

Question 4

a. Right: membership of labor unions might be an indicator in the social topic area of work and labor rights.
b. Right: the traditional balanced scorecard model categorizes indicators in four perspectives, potentially covering many social and environmental indicators.
c. Right: in spite of the triple bottom line not being mentioned explicitly, these three performance dimensions perfectly reflect the triple-bottom-line concept.
d. Right: indicators are different for each cause.

Question 5

a. Right: developing long-term indicators for business success was Kaplan and Norton's goal when devising the balanced scorecard model.
b. Right: the sustainable living plan's three main macro indicators may each be categorized in one of the three nonfinancial scorecard perspectives.
c. Right: as shown in Figure 9.4, it has an outcome and an activity sphere.
d. Right: the balanced scorecard fulfills both functions, to identify if the strategy is working and to evaluate if it is the right strategy to reach set goals.

Question 6

a. Wrong: value offer and value proposition is the same thing.
b. Wrong: the business model "blank canvas" is a tool that primarily creates an idealized business model of a company that doesn't yet exist.
c. Right: the closer the business model is to the company's strategy, the more it may be called a "realized strategy."
d. Right: the mix of mainstream and responsible business elements leads to hybrid organizations.

B. Think

Level	Moral imagination	Notes
+	Description of complex moral implications that have been described convincingly and in depth	
=	Description of less obvious moral implications	
−	Description of the obvious moral implications, i.e., those which are "in plain view"	

C. Do

Level	Using specialized tools	Notes
+	Tool has been used to its full potential	
=	Tool has been used correctly, but might have been put to more effective use	
−	Tool has been used incorrectly, leading to a minimal helpful outcome	

D. Relate

Level	Co-design competence	Notes
+	An adequate vision statement has been designed and shows that it has been co-designed by integrating multiple distinct perspectives on the company	
=	A vision statement has been designed that appears adequate for providing direction toward becoming a responsible company	
−	No feasible vision statement has been designed	

E. Be

Level	Fortitude (matching actions and capability)	Notes
+	Planned actions are congruent with well-developed appreciation of capacity understood through the SWOT analysis	
=	Planned actions and capability (SWOT) are both well described, but appear incongruent	
−	Unrealistic, nontransparent, or incomplete picture through SWOT analysis	

Appendix

Figure 9.7: Responsible business model blank canvas

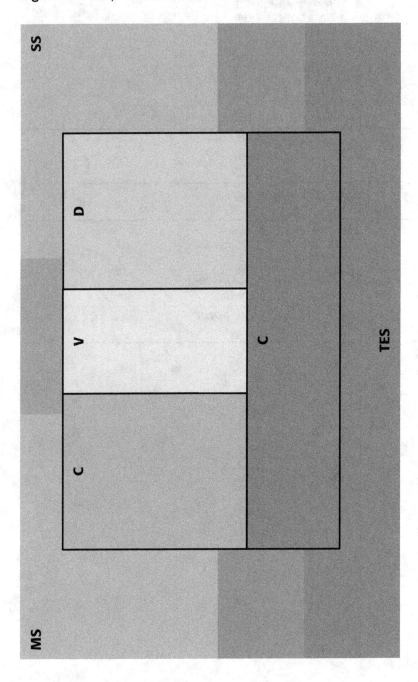

E.
IMPLEMENTING

10

Implementation basics

It is a decade that, CEOs believe, could usher in a new
era where sustainability issues are fully integrated into all
elements of business and market forces are truly aligned
with sustainability outcomes.

Georg Kell, Executive Director, UN Global
Compact (Lacey *et al.*, 2010, p. 2)

Good implementation practices

There has been much advice on how to become a responsible business and to
implement responsible management activities, with not only qualitative "step-
by-step approaches" but also quantitatively supported best-practice reports. The
often extensive, and in the worst case confusingly rich, body of knowledge on
best practices in implementing responsible management, can be boiled down to
a rather narrow set of principles. These three principles are considered the most
crucial for truly moving a business toward becoming sustainable.

Transformative and aligned

If a business truly desires to become sustainable, which means having zero or
even positive impact, the implementation of responsible business has to be transformative. Profound change for most businesses is inevitable. Most likely, "sacred
cows" will have to be slaughtered. If the criteria of "planet sense" are applied
jointly with the conventional "money sense" rationale, long-established evaluations may change drastically. It might be necessary to change or abandon a highly
profitable, but unsustainable core process. A long-serving high-level executive's

profit-first mind-set might make a replacement necessary. One of the company's cash cow products might, while being a financial pillar, be unacceptable.

To overprotect disadvantageous elements of a company's status quo is one commonly made mistake and obstacle to successful responsible business conduct. The opposite extreme is to implement responsible business activities which are completely unaligned with the strategy of the company. Responsible business has immense potential to strengthen strategy and core business. Thus, a deep integration of responsible management activities throughout an organization's strategic infrastructure is an indispensable must. Embedded, measured and controlled.

A typical mistake made by many businesses first implementing responsible management activities is to perceive them as nice add-ons, and separate them from core business. Responsible management should be deeply embedded, not merely "bolted on" (Laszlo and Zhexembayeva, 2011, p. 100). If merely bolted on, responsible business activities are often costly, not very credible, and, as a result, mostly short-lived. Only when embedded in existing business functions does responsible management make a tangible contribution to the business structure.

Another typical problem resulting from responsible management implemented just as an add-on is that it often is not treated with the same rigorous management practices as any other business activity, so that the result is often unsatisfactory. The results of responsible management, as is the case with any other management activity, need to be measured, controlled, and related to success. The sustainability scorecard model presented in Chapter 9 and the section on accounting in Chapter 12 provide rich insight into how to implement an indicator and control system for responsible management.

Scoring climate performance

The Climate Counts scorecard is a tool, customized for multisectoral companies, that makes performance for or against climate change tangible, visible, and manageable. Additionally, companies can submit their scorecard results, which will then be made public. Companies within the same sector are able to benchmark their climate performance against their peers. Let the climate-competition begin! (Climate Counts, 2012).

Systemic and collaborative

Silo mentality is one of the most commonly experienced pitfalls in responsible management. Responsible management has to take the overall system of social, environmental, and economic factors into consideration. Collaboration with the many different stakeholder groups inside and outside the company is indispensable. Of special operational importance is the need to connect all of a company's functional departments in a coherent responsible management system. Such systemic and collaborative management systems take different shapes and forms and need to be aware of each respective company's specific conditions. There are many helpful resources for developing such a management system for companies:

- The ISO 26000 norm on social responsibility (ISO, 2010) provides a background framework for developing more specific company management systems

- Blackburn (2007) proposes sustainability operating systems (SOS), which integrate social, environmental, and economic factors

- Laszlo and Zhexembayeva (2011) recommend a sustainability management system that is embedded in all business functions and highly aligned with the company's strategy

- Waddock and Bodwell (2007) propose **total responsibility management** based on quality management thinking

- Morsing and Oswald (2009) illustrate how to use **mainstream management systems** for responsible business

How can you plan a responsibility management system that connects all the different functional departments of a company to the best of business, society, and environment? An initial step is to map a specific responsible management activity, including all responsible management instruments throughout the involved functional departments, and the management outputs expected by each function. Such a responsible management map is an excellent first step in planning the organizational architecture of a company's responsible management system, defining processes, responsibilities, and intended outcomes

"Aids is your business"

This is the title of a 2003 article in *Harvard Business Review*, which begins with the words, "If you've got global operations, you've got an HIV-infected workforce. Doing something about it will save lives—as well as money" (Rosen *et al.*, 2003, p. 80). In fact, the cost of HIV/Aids cases inside South African companies was surveyed to be 0.5–3.6 times the annual salary of a worker. Costs included in the calculations were "sick leave; productivity loss; supervisory time; retirement, death, disability, and medical benefits; and recruitment and training of replacement workers" (Rosen *et al.*, 2004, p. 317). With such a well-documented case for doing well by doing good, it is not surprising that many multinational companies such as the beer brewer Heineken have become active in fighting HIV/Aids for the good of both their employees and their families (Van der Borght *et al.*, 2006).

The example of implementing an HIV/Aids program on-site will be used to show the system of different functions collaborating as a coherent system of functional mainstream management instruments (see Figure 10.1). The starting point has to be the activity of providing an HIV/Aids prevention, screening,

Figure 10.1: Mapping a responsible management subsystem

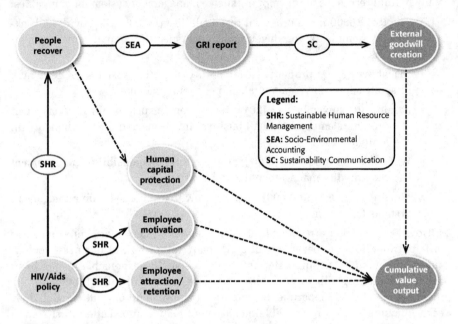

and treatment program. This is a typical activity for the responsible management instrument of sustainable human resources management. The intended outcomes of this activity are to achieve a lower infection rate, and recovery from the disease's symptoms for already infected employees. Other major outcomes are protection of the company's human resources, motivation of employees, and improved employee attraction and retention rates. The management instrument of social accounting keeps track of resources used and outcomes achieved, which then are used as feedback for the management process and are covered in a sustainability report. The tool of sustainability communication then uses the data raised to create goodwill among strategic stakeholders of the company. Of course, this description, while providing a first systemic approach, is strongly reduced in complexity. In the following section, functional mainstream management instruments, such as those used in this example, will be illustrated in further detail to provide an extensive toolset for successfully managing the responsible business in all its systemic interconnectedness.

Mainstream responsible management instruments and business functions

Implementing responsible management activities throughout all functions and departments of a business is a highly complex task. Successful implementation requires a profound understanding of both the mainstream management function and the responsible management instruments that might be deployed in each function. Functions can be divided into primary activities (also called primary or line functions) and support functions. Primary functions are directly involved in the process of handling inputs, transforming them into a product or service, marketing and selling it to customers, and providing after-sales service. Support functions, also called staffing functions, support the primary functions process. Typical support functions are human resources, finance, accounting, etc. Figure 10.2 describes the main functions of a business as they are developed in this book.

It is important to bear in mind that responsible management instruments can be divided into two groups as described in Chapter 6. The first group is mainstream responsible management instruments which have been developed by adapting mainstream management functions for social and environmental value creation. The second group is specialized instruments, which have been developed based on pure responsible management tasks (specialized responsible management instruments). Specialized responsible management instruments, as explained previously, are highly important to inform decisions being made

Figure 10.2: Mainstream management functions in a company's value chain

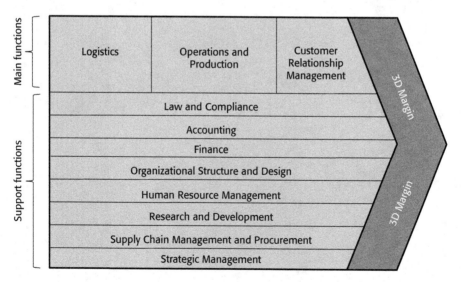

Source: Adapted from Porter (1985)

inside the functional departments of a business. These three specialized instruments (ethics management, stakeholder management, life-cycle management) provide the bigger context of sustainable business. Nevertheless, the main practical work of moving a company toward becoming a sustainable business is with mainstream responsible management instruments that can neatly be incorporated into existing functional departments within businesses. At least as important as the management tools deployed inside business functions are the typical social, environmental, and ethical issues found in the functions. Table 10.1 covers both management instruments and typical issues.

Who is managing responsible business activities in a company?

Which functions should be involved? The answer is simple: ALL! For instance, consider the sustainability report of the Indian Tata Motors Company. Tata's development and marketing teams created the Tata Nano, the first US$2,000 car, which was a milestone for customers of cost-effective transportation. The human resources, procurement, and finance departments were instrumental in fulfilling Tata's stakeholder mission "to create an organization that people enjoy working for, doing business with and investing in." In this simple example of the company's responsible business activities, five departments were involved (Tata Motors, 2010).

Table 10.1: Responsible management instruments used in a company's functions in order of appearance in this book

Department	Function	Main responsible management instruments by function	Typical issues
Strategic management	Setting the company's strategic direction and parameters	Strategic responsible management	Monopoly power Aggressive strategies
Logistics	Making inputs available to the production process and delivering products and services to customers	Sustainable logistics; green logistics	Environmental impact of packaging (waste) and transportation (emissions) Accidents in road transportation Congestion, noise, infrastructure deterioration
Operations	Transforming inputs into products and services	Eco-efficient operations; green information technology	Natural resource usage (raw materials, energy, water, etc.) Waste Labor conditions
Customer relationship management (marketing, sales, service)	Managing contact with business clients and end-consumers	Cause-related marketing; social marketing; cause branding	Promotion of consumerism Marketing to "vulnerable groups" (e.g., children) Product service and security
Organizational structure, control, governance	Establishing the organization's infrastructure	Responsible management institutions; corporate governance	Power abuse Transparency in information flow and decision-making

Department	Function	Main responsible management instruments by function	Typical issues
Finance and accounting	Providing financial resources; planning and documenting resource usage and resulting outputs	Socially responsible investment; sustainability accounting; inclusive pricing and costing; sustainability reporting	Accounting fraud and corruption Measurement of social-environmental performance
Human resources management	Managing employee relations	Responsible human resources management; employee volunteering; sustainability training and empowerment	Work and contractual issues Work–life balance
Research and development	Innovating products and processes	Sustainable innovation; bottom-of-the-pyramid products; sustainable process innovation	Product safety Planned redundancy
Legal and compliance department	Complying with norms and legislation	Environmental and social norms and compliance	Legal compliance Fair contracts
Procurement	Procuring inputs necessary for production	Sustainable procurement; inclusive and sustainable supply chain management; fair trade	Ethical procurement Fair trade Corruption
Communication	Communicating activities and outcomes	Stakeholder communication; codes of conduct; sustainability training; sustainability vision/mission statements; issues and crisis communication; social marketing; cause-related marketing	Truthfulness Transparency

Exercises

A. Know

Use the multiple choice questions below to test your knowledge. Each answer may be wrong or right and there may be zero to four right or wrong answers per question:

1. Good practices in implementing responsible business ...

   a.   ... include, for instance, that implementation should be transformative. Transformative means that the company has to transform business practices to become a responsible business. These changes should never affect established institutions or generation of profit.

   b.   ... include, for instance, that implementation should be embedded (part of the main business structure) and controlled (applying rigorous management practices).

   c.   ... include a systemic implementation. An important tool for this good practice is the establishment of a responsible management system.

   d.   ... include the mapping of management instruments deployed and the outcomes created by them.

2. Implementing responsible management throughout company functions and departments ...

   a.   ... usually involves so-called mainstream responsible management instruments such as ethics management.

   b.   ... involves both the implementation of support functions (e.g., operations and logistics) and main functions (e.g., human resources and finance).

   c.   ... for instance in the research and development department, involves both implementing the responsible management instrument of sustainable innovation and ensuring product safety as one of the typical issues encountered in this department.

   d.   ... involves knowledge of both the main responsible management instruments of the respective function and the issues typically encountered in the function.

3. The Mexican cinema chain Cinépolis has integrated responsible business key performance indicators across the four areas of its balanced scorecard through which the company and its executives evaluate their success. This is a direct example of ...

   a.   ... a systemic and collaborative approach to responsible business implementation.

   b.   ... transformative and aligned responsible business implementation.

   c.   ... embedded and controlled responsible business implementation.

   d.   ... an organizational control mechanism.

B. Think

Identify one responsible business activity from a case study (e.g., from the OIKOS case collection, among many other sources) and translate what you find into a map similar to Figure 10.1 describing the HIV/Aids initiative at Heineken.

C. Do

Download a company's corporate social responsibility or corporate sustainability report and try to identify at least one company activity located in each of the functions of the value chain model illustrated above and describe how they fit together in the big picture of responsible business.

D. Relate

Your professional background or goals will probably make you particularly interested in a specific function (e.g., human resources, strategy, accounting) of a company. Search online and possibly offline for a group of people that best reflects your interest (e.g., through groups on social networks such as Facebook and LinkedIn; through professional associations such as the "responsible sourcing network" or the "sustainable banking network;" or through student associations for responsible business such as NetImpact or OIKOS). Get in touch with the group and become part of their network.

E. Be

A good practice for responsibility and sustainability measures is to embed and control them. Think about one thing you could do to lead a more responsible and/or sustainable life. Design a control mechanism to ensure you do it correctly and repeatedly for a predefined period of time. Then do it!

Feedback

A. Know

Question 1

a. Wrong: transformation toward responsible business often requires managers to question practices.
b. Right: as illustrated at the beginning of this chapter, embeddedness is a basis of good practice in responsible business and management.
c. Right: as illustrated at the beginning of this chapter, systemic implementation, such as through an integrated management system, is a basis of good practice in responsible business and management.
d. Right: such mapping is a basic precondition for the good practice of both systemic and embedded activities.

Question 2

a. Wrong: ethics management is not a mainstream responsible management instrument, but a specialized responsible management instrument.
b. Wrong: the concrete functions mentioned do not correspond to the type of function they are used to exemplify. For instance, logistics is not an example of a support function, but of a main function.
c. Right: this point is reflected in depth in Table 10.1.
d. Right: this point is reflected in depth in Table 10.1.

Question 3

a. Right: the balanced scorecard connects different functions of the business which makes it collaborative and systemic.
b. Right: as the balanced scorecard is a strategic instrument that applies to the whole business, anything that is on it is automatically aligned with the overall business strategy.
c. Right: the balanced scorecard is a control instrument and, as it applies to all kinds of department in the business, anything that is on it is embedded in the company.
d. Right: the balanced scorecard and the key performance indicators on it are organizational and managerial control mechanisms.

B. Think

Level	Reducing complexity through structuring	Notes
+	Case has been described and its understanding enhanced in comparison to written text	
=	Case has been described adequately and accessibly through map	
−	Case has not been captured adequately in map	

C. Do

Level	Holistic activity analysis	Notes
+	All of the value chain functions have been matched and they have been described interdependently	
=	Most value chain functions have been independently matched with at least one activity mentioned in the report	
−	No or few activities and value chain functions have been matched convincingly	

D. Relate

Level	Participating in community	Notes
+	Evidence of participation in the community	
=	Community identified, but no contact has been made	
−	Community has not been identified	

E. Be

Level	Self-direction competence	Notes
+	Activity and control mechanism are in place and there is evidence of their functioning in action	
=	Feasible activity and control mechanism are in place	
−	Activity and control mechanism are either not feasible or not in place	

11
Main business functions

49% of CEOs cite complexity of implementation across functions as the most significant barrier to implementing an integrated, company-wide approach to sustainability.

(Lacey *et al.*, 2010, p. 12)

Logistics

Logistics include both inbound and outbound logistics. Inbound logistics are concerned with delivering inputs to the production process, while outbound logistics deliver finished products and services to the customer. On the one hand, logistics are often outsourced, which suggests that the topic should rather be covered under supply chain management. On the other hand, in a responsible management context, logistics is so intimately linked with a business's main functions that it makes sense to cover both in an interlinked fashion. Logistics are also a crucial part of the management of worldwide supply chains, as will be described in Chapter 13.

Bring your own mug!

Since 1985, Starbucks has been encouraging customers to have their beverage served in their own reusable mug. The company even rewards this effort with a 10% discount on any beverage bought. This example of outbound logistics shows how simple it can be to reduce your logistics impact, in this case the paper used and waste made (Sustainable Brands, 2010).

Depending on the product and production process, logistics can be very intensive in natural resources and harmful for the environment. Typical environmental issues are noise, air pollution, traffic congestion, land consumption (the land occupied by roads, railways, airports), and mostly excessive packaging. Typical negative social impacts of logistics activity are road accidents and pulmonary diseases. The logistics network of most products is worldwide and involves extensive and complex transportation activities. In order to move logistics activities toward sustainability, it is helpful to understand the typical conflicts of interest between efficient logistics and sustainable development. The following list includes some of the most salient paradoxes of "green logistics," as they have been described by Rodrigue *et al.* (2001):

- **Minimizing costs:** a crucial competitive factor of logistics is the ability to provide transportation at the lowest cost possible. This is contrasted with the urgent need to internalize the external environmental costs mentioned above. Internalization of these expenses would increase costs of the logistics activity immensely.

- **Speed, flexibility, reliability:** speed, flexibility, and reliability are basic requirements for logistics networks. Unfortunately, the means of transportation fulfilling these requirements (such as planes and trucks) also do more harm to the environment than the less desirable alternatives (such as ships and trains).

- **Hub and spoke:** the usage of centralized hub and spoke logistical networks creates highly concentrated negative impact at the center of logistics networks.

- **Warehousing and just-in-time logistics:** the just-in-time movement has drastically reduced the amount of goods stored. A result is that much of the storage has been transferred "to the streets," increasing the overall amount of goods in movement and their negative environmental impact.

- **E-commerce:** small, individual shipments are required by the logistical structures of the rapidly increasing e-commerce sector. Such methods highly decrease the efficiency of logistics due to increased packaging and the need for customized transportation efforts.

What's so bad about a left turn?

The vehicle motor is idling using gasoline while you wait for the oncoming traffic to pass. Right turns (on systems where traffic drives on the right-hand side of the road) are just more eco-efficient and prevent unnecessary emissions. The logistics enterprise UPS took notice and implemented a formal program to minimize the number of left turns made by their delivery drivers. Considering this single effort by the 95,000 delivery trucks in the company's fleet, the environmental and economic impact is enormous (Lovell, 2007).

Actions to mitigate the negative impact of logistics take many forms, and can be divided into two basic approaches:

1. Reducing the impact of logistics activities, while maintaining or growing the volume

2. Reducing the logistics volume

Listed below are some typical practices which may result in one of the approaches mentioned or in some cases both:

- **Transport impact transparency:** the social and environmental impact of transportation is often hidden. While many products are labeled with the country of origin, this only provides a superficial impression of the overall transport activities necessary. Some industries and individual companies have started to increase the transparency of their impact. Food miles, which describe the distance traveled by food products, are a good example.

- **Eco-efficient logistics:** eco-efficiency improves the ratio between economic output and required input of natural resources. For the logistics sector this ratio is highly important. Eco-efficient logistics aim to reduce the environmental impact of a given logistics activity. The weakness of the methodology is that it does not aim to reduce the overall amount of harmful activity, but rather maintain (or even increase) economic activity, while making each logistics output unit (such as kilometers traveled, items transported, etc.) more eco-efficient. The cumulative negative impact might not be reduced at all.

- **Reverse logistics:** recycling only works if products at the end of their useful life-cycle are transported back to be reintegrated into the production process. This is the main task of reverse logistics, which makes it a crucial part of a circular and sustainable economy. Reverse logistics may also have ecological downsides, such as in the case of returns management. Many companies provide convenient financial and logistics take-back schemes for unsold goods. Such returns management systems create an incentive to order more goods than are actually used.

- **E-commerce (retailing) logistics:** traditional logistics activities are increasingly altered and frequently replaced by new business models. E-commerce has often been described as more environmental friendly due to the reduction of resource-intensive bricks-and-mortar store networks. Also, research suggests that the home-delivery services connected to e-commerce are less polluting than customers picking up the purchase in store themselves (Edwards *et al.*, 2010).

- **Servitization logistics:** complementing or replacing products with services often reduces the necessity to transport a physical product. Examples of servitization models are "repair instead of replace" and "rent instead of own." The customer relationship management section below will cover servitization in greater depth.

- **Local production and consumption networks:** increasingly, local production and consumption networks replace the need for extensive global logistics networks and activities. This is not necessarily always more sustainable. Focusing only on environmental impact, local production is in some cases actually less sustainable than foreign production plus importation. In food products, for instance, the reason may lie in local differences in productivity and refrigeration efforts (AEA Technology, 2008).

Local production vs. global logistics

The central Mexican city of San Luis Potosí has been ranked as the third most promising global free trade zone in the world, just behind Shanghai and Dubai, with one of the main reasons being its great logistics infrastructure and location (Financial Times, 2010).

However, the city also sees an opposite trend, with local production and consumption on the spotlight. The "Puro Potosino" initiative, which roughly translates to "purely from San Luis Potosí," has energized local production : several hundred enterprises of all sizes, all located within the city, have created a local network of businesses rendering many international logistics efforts pointless. A broad variety of products is mainly sourced, produced, and sold locally (H. Ayuntamiento San Luis Potosí, 2013). There is also an industrial park of over 100 businesses, mainly from the food sector, moving even closer together to create a unique local production network (Código San Luís, 2012). Positive effects are not only reducing the environmental impact of logistics, but also strengthening local economic development by creating jobs and welfare.

Operations and production

The terms "operations" and "production management" are often used interchangeably. Here, operations management will be used to refer to the activities of managing the operational level of a business, in contrast with the nonoperational (strategic or planning) activities. Operations management achieves strategic objectives through operational efficiency (minimum resource usage) and effectiveness (maximum value creation for customers) across all business functions. Production management, by contrast, takes a rather narrow view of the core manufacturing process (see Table 11.1). This section covers operations management and production management given that, in terms of responsible management, they share similar characteristics. Often operations management includes supply chain management (SCM) and the management of innovation and technology (R&D); because of the special importance of these two topics, they will be covered separately in Chapters 12 and 13.

Table 11.1: Comparing strategic, operations, and production management

Management level	Strategic management	Operations management	Production management
Description	Planning, strategic infrastructure and goal-setting for the company as a whole	Managing intra-departmental and interdepartmental efficiency and effectiveness	Managing core manufacturing processes from raw material to finished product, often on a local scope and from a floor-level perspective
Intended goal	Strategic competitiveness	Quality of business processes	Manufacturing process efficiency
Departments	Supra-department, organizational level	All	Mainly production and logistics
Typical job positions*	Staff functions such as sustainability officer, vice president for sustainability	Line functions such as sustainability manager	Environment health and safety (EHS) manager/supervisor
Typical tools	Sustainability balanced scorecards and key performance indicators (KPI)	Sustainability operating systems (SOS); total responsibility management	Eco-efficiency; environmental health and safety frameworks

* Job titles may differ widely depending on organizational structure, history and size

While the social and environmental impact of operations can be immensely negative (depleting resources, dangerous for workers, polluting, etc.), the most basic goals of operations management and the goals of a responsible business seem to be highly compatible on a managerial level. Some responsible business managers even go so far to say that "sustainability and operational excellence" are "one goal, not two;" that one cannot be reached without the other due to considerable synergies (Hutchins, 2010, p. 1; Kleindorfer *et al.*, 2005). Thus, it is not surprising that many of the approaches to responsible operations are derived from well-known and long-established approaches in operations management. Operational efficiency becomes reinterpreted as eco-efficiency; total quality management becomes total responsibility management; and general management systems serve as a blueprint for sustainable operating and environmental management systems.

Some of the most common approaches to sustainable operations management are summarized below. Most of them have been adapted from well-known operations management tools, which function under the parameters of a business's established processes and structures. In the "Innovating" section of this book, tools for the proactive change of existing structures are discussed. The approaches summarized below are a valuable tool set for improving a business's social and environmental performance at the operational level (see Table 11.2).

- **Compliance with EHS management:** probably the most extensive implementation of responsible business in operations is the one legally required in most regions. If not required by local law, certain behaviors toward the environment and employee safety have become a fixed element of business operations; usually such activities are incorporated under the term "compliance." At the local level, compliance often translates into the job position of environmental health and safety (EHS) managers or supervisors. The main goal of EHS management is to avoid events with high negative impacts (such as accidents, chemical spills, or toxic emissions). EHS management is a well-established part of the operational risk management process.

- **Operational efficiency to eco-efficiency:** a main focus of operational management is to achieve operational efficiency, i.e., to assure the minimum required resource usage for a given output. Efficiency is achieved when the amount of waste (waste = unused resources) is minimized. Minimizing (natural) resource usage and avoiding waste (pollution) sound rather like environmentalist jargon and, in fact, operational efficiency is highly aligned with improving environmental business performance. The responsible management tool of eco-efficiency locates and attacks areas of improvement for both better environmental performance and economic cost reduction (WBCSD, 1999). Eco-efficiency methodologies can often be integrated into existing management practices, such as lean manufacturing and management.

- **Total quality management to total responsibility management:** while efficiency has a process focus, quality management instead strives for customer satisfaction as its ultimate purpose. In fact, in an operational management context, quality is commonly understood as anything that contributes to satisfaction and value. Total quality management (TQM), the Six Sigma framework, the ISO 9000 series, and Kaizen are common management tools used to meet or exceed customer expectations. In responsible management, the customer satisfaction focus has been broadened to a general stakeholder satisfaction focus. The way to achieving stakeholder satisfaction is fulfilling the responsibilities toward stakeholders, giving birth to the term "total responsibility management" (TRM). The goal of TRM is to achieve maximum quality in responsible management within all operations of an organization (Waddock et al., 2002; Waddock and Bodwell, 2004). A quality management-based approach to environmental performance is environmental Kaizen, which establishes a continuous improvement process toward better environmental performance (Széll, 2004).

Table 11.2: Operations approaches to responsible management

Approach	Responsible management instruments	Goal	Actors and stakeholders	Typical advantages achieved
Compliance and damage reduction	EHS management; cleaner production	Comply with normative requirements	Employees, government, normative organizations	Reduction in accidents or environmental damage leads to a reduction in operational risk and law suits
Operational efficiency	Eco-efficiency	Efficiency	Employees, the environment	Reduction in resource consumption leads to a reduction in cost
Quality management	Total responsibility management; environmental Kaizen	Quality/ customer satisfaction	Employees, customers	Increase in product quality leads to increase in customer satisfaction
Management systems	ISO 14000; ISO 26000; EMAS	Process integration and control	Managers, employees	Increase in capacity to manage the approaches listed above
Metrics and benchmarking	E.g., GRI indicators	Ensure measurability and manageability	Managers, independent research institutions	Increase in capability of goal-based responsible management

In order for these operational management instruments to work well, companies need to use them with two additional basic tools. The establishment of hard, tangible metrics, measuring social, environmental, and economic business performance, is a must for any subsequent management activity. Operations must also be embedded in the company's overall management system in order to work in a truly integrated, efficient, and effective manner:

- **Metrics and benchmarking:** a common misconception is that social and environmental performance is not measurable. This is not true. In Chapter 12 the field of sustainability accounting will be highlighted to show how to develop sustainability metrics. Many companies use social and environmental metrics to measure various areas, such as employee satisfaction in an employee welfare program, water usage per product for water protection programs, or male/female employee ratios to measure the progress of gender diversity initiatives. After the development of metrics, these measurements can be used in many ways adding value to responsible management in operations. One of the most important applications after controlling success is the establishment of benchmarks, either internally between different company facilities or externally with industry peers. An excellent benchmarking tool is the (often quantifiable) required disclosures system of the Global Reporting Initiative, which can easily be accessed through company sustainability reports.

- **Operations management system connecting company departments through procedures, coordination and information channels:** social and environmental factors for the management of business responsibility can often be integrated into existing management systems. Practices to do so vary, as do terms used for such systems. The oldest are environmental management systems, such as the ISO 14000 standards and the European Environmental Management and Auditing Standard (EMAS). While ISO 26000 on social responsibility officially does not establish a management system standard, it nevertheless is often treated as one. Blackburn (2007) integrates social and environmental topics by proposing a "sustainability operating system (SOS)."

How can there ever be zero waste?

Isn't it amazing that many companies announce zero waste to landfill goals for their factories? How can these companies measure the achievement of this goal? The GreenBiz website provides an interesting insight into seven companies and their "journey to zero waste." Successful practices include recycling, reusage, the inverse logistics of giving packaging to suppliers, and, of course, the redesign of processes to avoid creating waste in the first place (Lehrer, 2011).

Customer relationship management: marketing, sales, service

The departments of a company in direct contact with customers are marketing, sales, and service. These three departments are typically called customer relationship management (CRM). They are crucial in maintaining a good relationship with clients as one of the most influential stakeholders. In order to responsibly manage the customer relationship, a both preventive and proactive perspective is needed.

Preventively, harm that could possibly be done by CRM needs to be avoided. The list of potential negative effects is long. Most prominently, marketing tends to reinforce consumerism and unnecessary overconsumption, which in turn creates adverse effects on the natural environment. Marketing may also be subject to many ethical conflicts. Marketing fast food to children, promoting unhealthy beauty ideals, and untruthful claims about products are only a few of the many potential areas of ethical conflicts with responsible management. Sales staff have often been accused of maximizing their own benefits instead of considering the best interest of their customers. Bad after-sales service, resulting in faulty products and decreased product lifetimes, not only decreases consumer satisfaction but also speeds up the product turnover rate, boosting the negative environmental impacts from production and disposal.

Creating the wrong wants

The negative health effects of smoking are well known and, as a result, tobacco marketing has long been aggressively restricted. However, there are many other side effects among tobacco customers. For instance, in Mexico, the poorest households spend more money on tobacco than on healthcare, demonstrating that marketing does have the power and responsibility to promote viable and healthy consumption patterns (Miera-Juárez et al., 2011).

In spite of the often extensive criticism of the marketing, sales, and service functions, these departments have at least as much potential to do good as doing bad. The field of social marketing, for instance, uses marketing methods to achieve a behavior change for the good of society and environment. They encourage people to quit smoking, to stop using their cars, or to save water. Social marketing does not sell a product, but it sells behavior change. This approach is very different than cause-related marketing, which connects a product's sale to a good cause: TOMS Shoes donates a pair of shoes every time consumers buy a pair; Danone in Mexico donates a percentage of product sales revenue to a child cancer foundation; the Product RED initiative allows multiple brands to associate with its cause of fighting HIV/Aids in Africa if these brands commit to donating a portion of sales revenue to Product RED. Chapters 14 and 15 will provide deeper insight into the practical aspects of both marketing tools. Servitization is another promising tool applied to responsible management within customer relations. Servitization substitutes products with services in order to reduce negative environmental as well as economic and social impacts. Ownership of a car, for example, can be replaced with carpooling, which significantly decreases the environmental impact and ownership costs.

Many consumer tendencies and markets have been associated with responsible business. The worldwide Lifestyles of Health and Sustainability (LOHAS)

Figure 11.1: Applying the "four Ps" to LOHAS and BoP markets

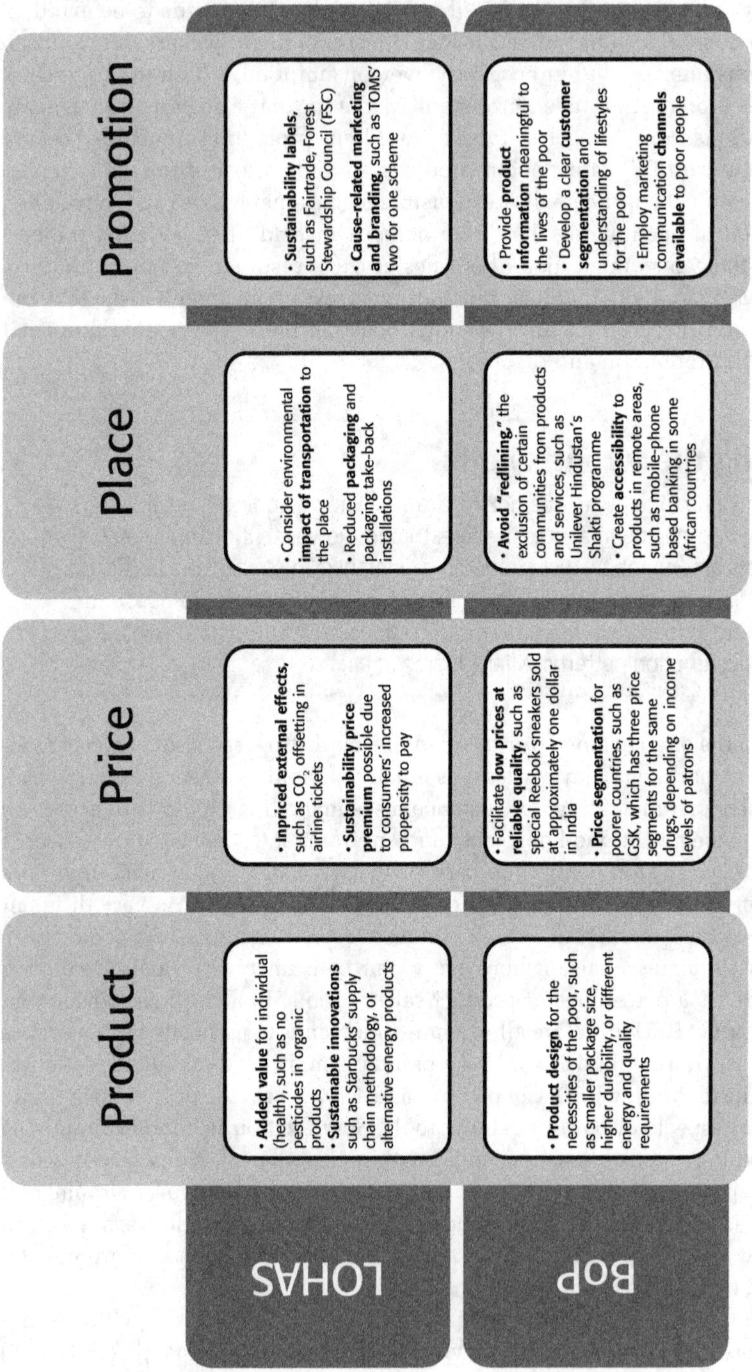

	Product	Price	Place	Promotion
LOHAS	• **Added value** for individual (health), such as no pesticides in organic products • **Sustainable innovations** such as Starbucks' supply chain methodology, or alternative energy products	• **Inpriced external effects,** such as CO_2 offsetting in airline tickets • **Sustainability price premium** possible due to consumers' increased propensity to pay	• Consider environmental **impact of transportation** to the place • Reduced **packaging** and packaging take-back installations	• **Sustainability labels,** such as Fairtrade, Forest Stewardship Council (FSC) • **Cause-related marketing and branding,** such as TOMS' two for one scheme
BoP	• **Product design** for the necessities of the poor, such as smaller package size, higher durability, or different energy and quality requirements	• Facilitate **low prices at reliable quality,** such as special Reebok sneakers sold at approximately one dollar in India • **Price segmentation** for poorer countries, such as GSK, which has three price segments for the same drugs, depending on income levels of patrons	• **Avoid "redlining,"** the exclusion of certain communities from products and services, such as Unilever Hindustan's Shakti programme • Create **accessibility** to products in remote areas, such as mobile-phone based banking in some African countries	• Provide **product information** meaningful to the lives of the poor • Develop a clear **customer segmentation** and understanding of lifestyles for the poor • Employ marketing communication **channels available** to poor people

market covers a wide variety of market segments which are associated with the improved social and environmental performance of the products being sold: ecotourism, alternative energy, sustainable mobility, and socially responsible investment are just a few of the market segments included in the overall LOHAS market (LOHAS Magazine, 2010). The bottom-of-the-pyramid (BoP) market is another global phenomenon seeking responsible marketing attention. Whereas marketing has traditionally focused on medium- to high-income groups, BoP instead calls for marketing to the poor, a largely unattended market. Marketing to low-income households is not only an important task to alleviate poverty, but also provides an attractive and fresh market, for over 4 billion people worldwide live below the poverty line (Prahalad, 2010). In order to access these markets, the marketing management strategy needs to be adjusted, often drastically. The well-known "four Ps" of the marketing management process (product, price, place, promotion) provide a helpful framework for analyzing the necessary adjustments to be made in order to assess new markets responsibly. Figure 11.1 shows how the "four Ps" have been applied by companies in order to shape solutions to the LOHAS and BoP markets. Analyzing the "four Ps" of a company's existing product portfolio with an eye on the products' social and environmental performance may bring drastic improvements in the products' social, environmental, and economic performance.

Exercises

A. Know

Use the multiple choice questions below to test your knowledge. Each answer may be wrong or right and there may be zero to four right or wrong answers per question:

1. Responsible management in logistics and operations …
   a. … involves conflicts of interest between efficient logistics and sustainable development. One example is that logistics aims to offer transportation at the lowest cost possible, while sustainable development requires internalizing external costs.
   b. … among the actions to mitigate the negative impact of logistics, involves so-called reverse logistics, which follows the primary goal of creating a local production and consumption network.
   c. … among the actions to improve the social and environmental impact on the operational level, includes moving from mainstream operational efficiency to eco-efficiency.
   d. … would require establishing indicators to measure social, environmental, and economic business performance alike. Unfortunately, social and environmental performance cannot be measured quantitatively.

2. The marketing, service, and sales function of responsible management …
   a. … involves the deployment of social marketing, a tool which aims to increase product sales by connecting them to a good cause.
   b. … may attach marketing activities to social and environmental consumer movements such as the LOHAS sector.
   c. … may attach marketing activities to the "BOP" (Basic Organic Products) market.
   d. … involves manifold responsibilities toward customers stemming from the function's close relationship with customers.

3. Car2Go, a subsidiary of Daimler AG (the producer of car brands such as SMART, Maybach, and Mercedes-Benz), has established a carpooling network in European and North American cities. This is an example of …
   a. … a BoP market.
   b. … servitization.
   c. … approaching a LOHAS market.
   d. … a local production and consumption network.

B. Think

Total responsibility management is based on the idea that companies should optimize the quality of their product or service for all stakeholders. Think of one situation where two company stakeholders would have very distinct ideas about the quality of a product. Then come up with changes to the product or services which reconcile these distinct requirements.

C. Do

The EMAS environmental management framework is based on the Plan–Do–Check–Act (PDCA) cycle to improve environmental performance. Run through the process in one area of activity, either in your private or professional life.

D. Relate

Visit a business's environment (e.g., the area around a factory, or a shop) in person and try to discover how the business relates to its social, environmental, and economic local environment.

E. Be

Imagine you are the hygiene manager of a food poultry processing factory. Any time you have a doubt about a potential hygiene risk the production stops, which causes your colleagues pressure to keep up with their goals. How would that make you feel, and how would you cope with the situation?

Feedback

A. Know

Question 1

    a.   Right: this is an excellent example of typical conflicts experienced.

    b.   Wrong: reverse logistics and local production and consumption networks are two distinct activities to mitigate the negative impact of logistics.

    c.   Right: moving from mainstream operational efficiency to eco-efficiency includes environmental impacts in efficiency thinking, which in turn supports the environmental dimension of responsible business and management.

    d.   Wrong: the text provides many examples of excellent quantitative metrics.

Question 2

    a.   Wrong: social marketing uses marketing to change individuals' behavior for the good of society.

    b.   Right: both the BoP and the LOHAS market segments are presented in this chapter as relevant new markets.

    c.   Wrong: "BOP" stands for "bottom-of-the-pyramid" market and refers to consumers of low income at the bottom of the income pyramid.

    d.   Right: this is correct. However, while being customer-focused, the customer relationship function could also be reinterpreted as a stakeholder relationship function, if we consider the value proposition to our main stakeholders to be our product.

Question 3

    a.   Wrong: there is no indication that users of the carpooling scheme are located at the bottom of the economic wealth pyramid.

    b.   Right: Daimler moves from producing and selling a product (a car), to providing the service of having a car available (carpooling).

    c.   Right: while carpooling is not necessarily a health topic, the more eco-efficient usage of cars when shared is often related to a more sustainable lifestyle.

    d.   Wrong: the cars are still produced somewhere else and shipped to the location. So production and consumption are not in the same place.

B. Think

Level	Reconcile divergent perspectives	Notes
+	Identification and reconciliation	
=	Identification of divergent perspectives, but no reconciliation	
–	Divergent perspectives have not been identified	

C. Do

Level	Application of management tools	Notes
+	Cycle has been applied correctly and environmental performance has been improved	
=	Cycle has been applied correctly	
–	Cycle has not been applied correctly	

D. Relate

Level	Ability to learn about local needs and impacts	Notes
+	Deep appreciation of multiple relationships of the business to its locality	
=	Basic ("obvious") appreciation of the relationship of the business to its locality	
–	No visible relationship between business and its locality	

E. Be

Level	Moral agency	Notes
+	Answer expresses a commitment to involve in moral agency no matter what	
=	Answer expresses a commitment to balance moral agency and environmental pressures	
–	Answer expresses an avoidance of moral agency when faced with potential opposition	

12

Business support functions

The value chain depicts all the activities a company engages in while doing business. It can be used as a framework to identify the positive and negative social impact of those activities.

(Porter and Kramer, 2006, p. 85)

The previous chapter was focused on responsible business and management in the main functions of a company that directly relate to the production and delivery of products and services. This chapter will describe how to integrate responsible business and management into the functions of a company that support this process, such as law and compliance, finance, and human resources.

Law and compliance

Compliance is not one of the business functions usually considered central, but most definitions of responsible business and its subfields of social and environmental responsibilities take the topic beyond mere legal compliance. Why should one then think of the law and compliance department when managing responsible business? The answer becomes obvious when responsible management is understood as management of the triple bottom line, of performance in the three dimensions of society, environment, and economy. Responsible management is largely influenced by a variety of compulsory regulations and laws (often called hard law) and voluntary norms and standards (also called soft law) with which to comply. Environmental and labor legislation, antitrust law, human rights, and international norms and standards are just some examples of how norms set the baseline for social and environmental business performance (Sobczak, 2006). This also agrees with Carroll's (1991) popular pyramid model of business responsibilities, which describes legal responsibilities as a part of the responsible business concept.

Legislation that will transform business

"Obeying the law" sounds easy at first, but becomes very complex when put into practice. Just understanding which laws apply to your job position, your function, your business, your industry, the locations of your company, including all branches, your suppliers, and your customers is a highly complex task. Before assuming any voluntary responsibility with stakeholders in responsible business, a company must first determine whether legal responsibilities have been fulfilled. An important part of this law-mapping task is to keep up with new legislation in responsible business. The following trends are two worldwide movements in legislation that will transform your business. In 2011, the Australian clean energy act, which forces the country's 500 worst polluting companies to pay a tax on carbon emissions, was widely reported (BBC, 2011). In fact, carbon taxes have long been an element of legislation in many countries from the European Union to India to South Africa. Another strong trend is the increase in a company's sustainability reporting duties, which is an important external driver for responsible business (Ioannou and Serafeim, 2014), which moves toward mandatory sustainability reporting (UNEP and KPMG, 2006). The Global Reporting Initiative has announced the commitment that "all large and medium size companies in OECD countries and large emerging economies should be required to report on their Environmental, Social and Governance (ESG) performance and, if they do not do so, to explain why" (GRI, 2016, p. 1).

The job description of the compliance officer probably best describes how responsible business and law intersect. Compliance officers assure conformity of the company's actions with both compulsory law and voluntary norms. Knowing hard and soft law is important for compliance job functions, and obeying the law becomes the baseline for responsible managers throughout all job functions. For instance, production managers will need to comply with environmental legislation in terms of waste treatment or emissions. Human resources professionals need to know and apply labor regulations. Anticorruption, especially anti-bribery, legislation is an important factor for procurement managers. Consumer protection and product safety norms are basic parameters for activities research and development, marketing, and sales. Figure 12.1 describes some of the most salient areas of hard law as it applies to responsible management practice. For important soft law applications, please review the list of norms in Chapter 7.

Companies are not only obeying, but also making norms and "laws" applying to employees and other stakeholders, such as suppliers, shareholders, or even consumers. The manifestation of such norms can take various forms, from soft

Figure 12.1: Classifications of hard law relevant to responsible management

By stakeholder
E.g. consumer protection, employee rights, corporate governance (shareholders), procument legisation (suppliers)

By function	By dimensions
E.g. regulation for the management of dangerous substances (logistics), Sarbanes–Oxley Act (accounting), emissions requirements (production)	Social, environmental, economic legislation

By industry	By issue	By scope
E.g. anti-money laundering (banking), extractives industry act (mining)	E.g. antitrust law (competition), climate & water protection, anti-corruption	Global, regional, national, local legislation

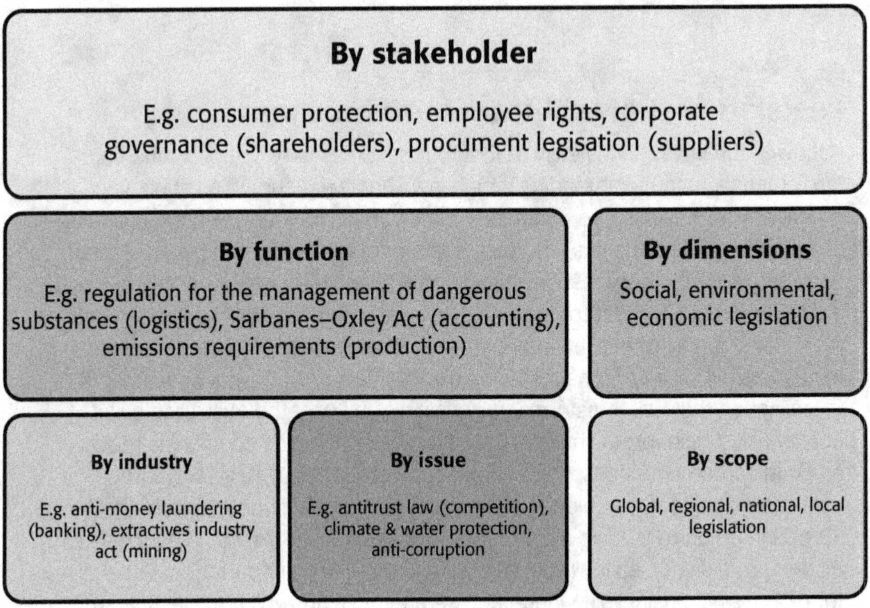

procedures to codes of conduct or firm contractual agreements. Such norms need to be constantly checked for consistency with external norms and with their ethical viability. The two basic approaches for establishing these norms are either to base them on values or on compliance. Values-based programs support the development of values and employee ethics to prevent misconduct, while compliance-based programs consistently monitor and enforce concise rules. Both approaches show results in reducing misconduct, while there is evidence that values-based programs achieved better results (Weaver and Treviño, 1999).

Accounting

Accounting is typically done for two main purposes: either to provide numbers for the internal managerial process or to report externally. First, managerial accounting (often also called controlling) follows the philosophy of "What cannot be measured cannot be managed." Measuring and documenting social and environmental factors is an indispensable basis for successfully managing the responsible business. This is not exclusively true for financial accounting. The second purpose of accounting is to create documentation for required external reporting and tax purposes. This purpose is also transferable to responsible management.

"Should trees have standing?"

This is the controversial title of a much-cited scientific paper from 1972. The author promotes the idea that natural objects should have rights, which then can be translated to concrete legislation (Stone, 1972). Obviously, that has not happened in the four decades since. The question is, why? What would happen if there was a "Universal Declaration of Nature's Rights" as inviolable as human rights? What would happen if animals, plants, rivers, mountains, oceans, and whole ecosystems had the same rights for existence and integrity as human beings? The ecology movement has long postulated such rights and their implementation, considering the protection of the environment as an end in itself rather than a necessary precondition for human wellbeing and survival (Naess, 1973). What companies can do, in spite of lacking legislation, is at least provide nonhuman nature with the same stakeholder attention as human beings (Starik, 1995).

Companies are increasingly required to report their social and environmental performance, just as they are in terms of their economic performance (GRI, 2016). Accounting for responsible management has to be an integrated social, environmental, and economic (three-dimensional) process, also called sustainability accounting (Bent and Richardson, 2003). The Global Reporting Initiative, described in Chapter 7, has made its goal to establish required reporting for medium and big companies of OECD countries. Many local legislators have begun to require social and environmental reporting by companies falling under their area of responsibility.

Figure 12.2 illustrates main elements of the accounting process. Activities and performance (outcomes) are first measured and then documented. The documentation then usually triggers a feedback by both managers and general stakeholders, which in turn influences the activities of the company and ultimately the social, environmental, and economic performance achieved. A central role throughout the accounting process is played by sustainability indicators, which are well-defined social, environmental, and economic entities that can be observed, measured, and managed (Keeble et al., 2003). The number of accidents happening in a company might, for instance, be a social indicator reflecting workplace security, which in turn is highly important in assuming responsibilities for employee stakeholders. An environmental indicator frequently used is the amount of CO_2 produced by production activities. An economic indicator could be the return on investment. Indicators are valuable to both main purposes of accounting, as they help to adjust management activities, are the basis for sustainability scorecards, and can be used to evaluate and give incentives to managers, projects, business functions, and even triple-bottom-line performance. Indicators also provide tangible units to report and evaluate reported data. The following points provide a quick checklist highlighting critical considerations to be made in developing powerful indicators:

Figure 12.2: Basic elements of the sustainability accounting process

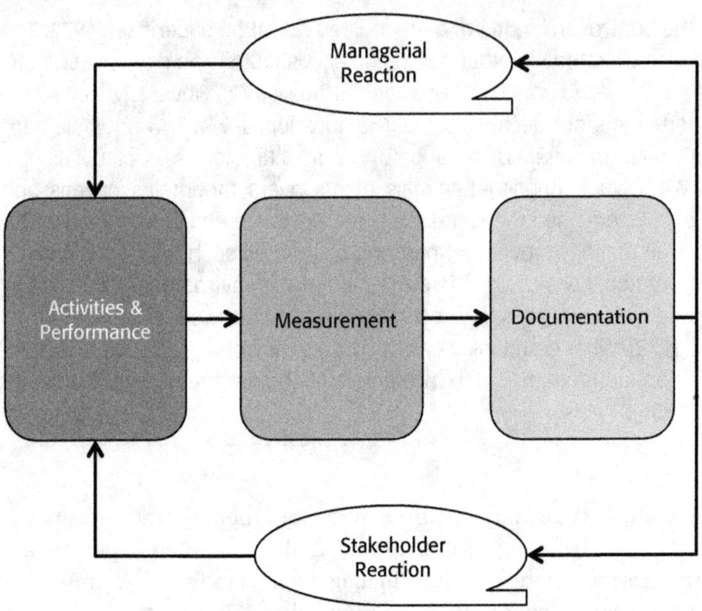

- **Activity and performance:** is it more important to develop indicators reflecting three-dimensional activities or performance? Both are valuable in different ways. While accounting activities provide an insight into the commitment of a company, accounting performance gives an important insight into the effectiveness of the company in achieving desired outcomes. Accounting is most powerful when it provides insight into both activity and performance. Merely knowing that a company has planted 10,000 trees (activity), without the information that only two of these trees survived the first two months (performance), provides a very distorted picture.

- **Internal and external:** external effects are outcomes of an activity that are not incurred by the actor. Internal effects, instead, are incurred by the actor. These effects might be positive or negative. A negative environmental externality might be the pollution of a river with waste-water from a company's production activities. A positive social externality is the standard of living and satisfaction experienced by the family of a company employee because of the wage level. A positive internal economic effect of a company's overall activity is the profit that remains in the company. Sustainability accounting has the critical task of including both internal and external effects caused by a business's activity in the indicators applied.

- **Influence and materiality:** it is greatly discussed to what degree companies should be held accountable for the impacts they create and how far-reaching their sphere of influence is. Typical questions for defining sphere

Sustainability accounting grows with time and with responsible business

Going from purely financial accounting to the integration of social, environmental, and economic indicators is quite a process. For example, the Argentine natural gas business, Gas Natural Fenosa, describes itself as an evolution. The company published its first responsible business report in 2005 and has since then evolved from a C ranking, to a B, and finally to an A+ ranking in 2009 and 2010. The company stresses that each of the over 100 indicators covered in the reports should not be seen as mere figures, but as a whole management process, a team, and extensive policies (Ambito.com, 2011; Gas Natural Fenosa, 2011). This statement reflects very well another important aspect of sustainability accounting: as in financial accounting, sustainability accounting done well is a mirror image of company practices and results, either good or bad. Since 2014, Fenosa has published not only a responsible business report, but also an integrated annual report that includes economic, social, and environmental performance (Gas Natural Fenosa, 2016).

of influence might be "Are we able to improve the sustainability performance of our suppliers?" and "Are we able to influence the health of the ecosystems close to our production facilities?" The sphere of influence is defined as the potential influence a company has. Materiality (see Chapter 9) refers to the process of assessing how important single issues are to a certain business. Effective sustainability accounting must include indicators for all material issues of a business within a sphere of influence as broadly as possible. Even if a company finally decides not to assume accountability (responsibility) for indicators in its sphere of influence, it is important for managerial decisions to monitor factors that can potentially be influenced.

- **Measurability and monetarization:** it is a common misconception to think that environmental and social topics are "soft factors" that cannot be measured. However, there are more than 80 sustainability performance indicators, all of them quantitatively measurable (GRI, 2006a). One suggestion has been to translate social and environmental indicators into monetary units, a process called monetarization. The main advantages of monetarization are the creation of a common unit for measurement and comparison of different impacts and the creation of a basis for integrating social and environmental factors in the financial management of a company. Critics highlight the potential inaccuracies in transforming nonmonetary indicators into monetary terms.

Sustainability accounting cannot be an end in itself. It should be used as a necessary condition to monitor and improve a company's activities and performance in order to move it toward becoming a truly sustainable business. To fulfill this function, outcomes of the accounting process must be made accessible to both managers and a broad set of external stakeholders. Chapter 7 provided deeper insight into how to establish GRI reports covering the outcomes of the accounting process, and Chapters 14 and 15 will illustrate how to generally communicate outcomes. For both, it is of crucial importance to run these outcomes through an external verification and review process, an assurance, which assesses the quality of the accounting process conducted and its outcomes.

Finance

The goal of financial management is to maximize financial business performance indicators, such as stock and shareholder value and profits. As already discussed, there has been an ongoing debate on the relationship between social and financial business performance (see "The business case" box in Chapter 8). Interestingly, some prominent financial management scholars have adopted the view that there is not even a conflict between financial value and social value creation: a leading financial management textbook even argues that maximizing "stock value also benefits society" (Erhardt and Brigham, 2010, p. 11). In business ethics, maximizing financial performance is often seen as the main "root of evil" leading to unethical business conduct (Thielemann and Wettstein, 2008). Whichever argument one tends to support, one fact remains clear: financial functions and financial management are central target areas for responsible management. Responsible management in finance can be divided into three main areas of interest. First, financial management, which primarily deals with money, is the lifeblood of every business and needs to be transformed toward more responsible behavior if the company as a whole is to be made first responsible and ultimately sustainable. Second, there are responsible finance tools, such as socially responsible investment and microfinance, that have the potential to strengthen the finance function while creating value for society and environment. Third, it is important to evaluate and transform the structure of financial institutions in order to assure the social, environmental, and economic sustainability of the financial industry as a whole. The focus here will be on activity areas one and two, while area three will be covered in Chapter 19.

The processes and parameters given by financial management largely define how decisions in business are made. Inquiries such as, "Is this profitable?," "How risky is this?," "Do we have budget for this?," and "How much does it cost us?" are the important questions that influence decision-making in companies. Often these questions cannot be answered satisfactorily for responsible management advocates. The reason is that the crucial social and environmental components of responsible management are partially new to the field of finance. Thus, transforming financial management to align it with social and environmental value creation is key to getting responsible management right. The following list provides an initial overview of important required action areas to establish responsible financial management:

- **Inclusion:** including social and environmental, external and internal indicators in the financial management process is a crucial task for achieving well-informed and responsible outcomes. Effective sustainability accounting, as illustrated in the previous section, is a necessary condition for the integration of socio-environmental factors with economic factors inside and outside the company. Inclusion can be reached if the company conducts an extensive impact assessment of all its activities and then monetarizes these impacts so that they can be included in the calculation of financial key indicators. For example, the project to build a road through the Peruvian Amazon might seem a financially viable alternative, if contrasting the rather small cost of road construction with the great economic opportunities provided by the project. The outcome of such an assessment might change drastically when taking into consideration the destruction of valuable ecosystems and the damage done to native communities losing their basis for subsistence.

- **Integration:** social and environmental factors need to be integrated into the vocabulary and frameworks used in financial management. For instance, in addition to an economic value added, there is a need also to analyze the social and environmental value added. The term "shareholder value" might partially be replaced by stakeholder value. There could be a social and an environmental return on investment (ROI) in addition to the normally used financial ROI.

- **Harmonization:** maximization of financial indicators is usually conducted in a short-term fashion. Sustainability is about maximizing the economic, social, and environmental value in the long term, and about sustaining value in the long term. This is why responsible finance must find a balance between short-, medium-, and long-term indicators when evaluating performance.

In a simplistic description, the financial management process can be divided into the three phases described in Figure 12.3, throughout which many responsible business topics find application. During the money-raising stage, paying attention to responsible business topics can lead to tangible advantages, as fundraising becomes easier because of good social and environmental performance. Sustainability indices such as the Dow Jones Sustainability Index, the FTSE4Good or the Mexican IPC Sustentable provide information on companies' sustainability performance; based on these and other sources of sustainability information, socially responsible investors will choose whether to finance responsible companies' operations.

A special type of investor is the "angel investor," an affluent individual who financially supports start-ups. Increasingly, angel investors focus on entrepreneurial ventures with added social and environmental value. For established companies with social, environmental, or ethical issues, activist investors are another important topic. Activist investors usually buy a minority share in a company in order to have a speaking right in stockholder meetings, and then use this right to influence other shareholders and company leadership. Often

Figure 12.3: Responsible management topics throughout the financial management process

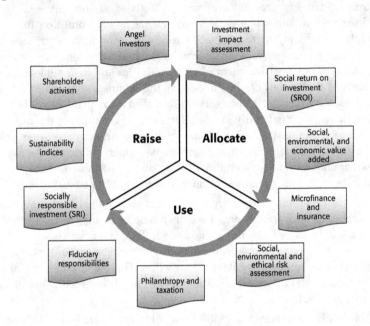

shareholder activism is used to aggressively lobby for changes toward better social, environmental, and ethical business performance.

When companies allocate money to business activities, they usually align their allocation priorities with the company's strategy and the potential economic value added by each activity. To allocate money to the right project leading to a responsible business, the selection criteria need to include additional factors. Projects need to go through a rigorous assessment of their social and environmental impacts and ethical risks, and helpful concepts for such an assessment are the social and economic value added frameworks (Bent and Richardson, 2003). Such an assessment allows consideration of the triple bottom line of single company activities and the assignment of budgets, instead of the single financial bottom line considered traditionally. Attractive areas of activity are micro-banking and micro-insurance programs. Companies from both financial and nonfinancial sectors have increasingly used these frameworks to add value to their operations and at the same time reduce poverty.

When companies use money earned from business operations, the basic options are either to disburse it to owners or to reinvest. In the case of disbursement, owners might decide to spend the money or reinvest. Responsible ventures and businesses might be attractive investment opportunities. When companies reinvest, they might do so internally, or invest by acquiring other companies as part of the business's diversification strategy. Major mainstream corporations have done this very thing. For instance, the cleaning products giant CLOROX bought

Redefining return on investment

One of the most important financial indicators is the return on investment (ROI). Traditionally the ROI is understood as the profit made from a certain amount of money invested (e.g., 30% of annual profit on an investment in the stock market). Two variants of ROI are especially important for responsible business. The ROI on social and environmental projects is an important indicator to understand. If you actually have a business case for your responsible business activity, then the results often can be monetarized (e.g., an increase in profit from sales of 40% through a cause-related marketing campaign). You could call this percentage a "return on responsible business." Such numbers will go a long way in explaining to stakeholders who think in financial terms (e.g., investors, owners, managers) why you act responsibly. For stakeholders focusing on the social and environmental impacts made by businesses (e.g., NGOs and governments), it is important to be able to provide an environmental or social return on investment. Such an E-ROI or S-ROI can take various forms, depending on the respective social (S-) and environmental (E-) activity. A reforestation campaign, for instance, could use trees planted per dollar spent as E-ROI. The S-ROI of a gender diversity campaign could calculate the number of women hired per dollar spent on the campaign.

Burt's Bees, a natural cosmetics producer, L'Oreal bought The Body Shop, and the Coca-Cola Company invested in shares of the smoothie producer, Innocent. Generally, such investments are likely to yield high return as well as low risk. The high return can be explained by the operations of these businesses in the rapidly growing markets related to social and environmental topics. Low risk stems from their focus on doing good business socially, environmentally, and ethically. Many risks are social, environmental, and ethical (SEE) risks, which are reduced when explicitly focusing on SEE topics. Some companies, such as CLOROX, also justify such acquisitions by the need to learn from the acquired businesses how to become a responsible business.

Organizational structure and design

Organizational structure and design are management tasks very central to responsible business. Companies wanting to ultimately become sustainable businesses often require substantial change in their organizational structure to reach this goal. Central questions are, "Which job functions, departments, and institutions should be empowered to lead the change toward more responsibility?," "What is the role of individuals in a responsible company?," "What role, responsibilities, and power does the organization provide stakeholders?," and "What processes

Figure 12.4: Elements of organizational structure

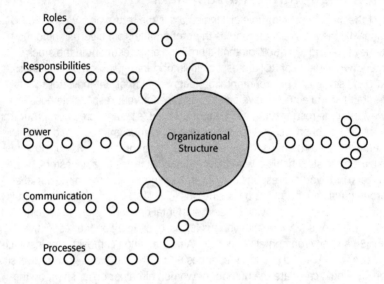

need to be changed to become a responsible business?" As reflected in many of the preceding questions, the management task of organizational structure and design is to determine roles, power, responsibilities, information flows, and processes inside a company (see Fig. 12.4).

From the basic task description, it becomes clear that organizational design and structure has the power to question and change the basic structure of the firm. It can either be an inhibitor, preventing or considerably slowing down the development of a responsible business, or a strong catalyst, creating an internal business structure conducive to assuming stakeholder responsibilities. Below is a checklist for organizational structure change toward responsible business which provides basic starting points for facilitating responsible business through organizational structure:

- Has your organization established and empowered institutions promoting responsible business? Examples for such institutions range from codes of conduct and ethics, responsibility budgets, corporate foundations, responsibility hotlines, and whistle-blowing mechanisms, to whole departments in charge of responsible business. It is of critical importance not only to establish such institutions, but also to provide them with the necessary power to exert a significant influence. Empowerment features consist of a salient position in organizational hierarchy, a big budget, and support of and proximity to high-level leaders.

- Has your organization created high-impact job positions with responsible business as a main part of their job description? The titles "Global Sustainability Director," "Vice President for Responsible Business," and "Chief

> ## Spotting responsible business throughout the organizational institutions and structure
>
> Do businesses really consider responsible business in their organizational institutions? Among the world's biggest corporations, 96% have a formal corporate responsibility (CR) function. The number increases with organization size. Among the businesses without such a function, 66% mention that CR integrated with other functions as the reason for the absence of a stand-alone function. Company boards increasingly (41%) include designated members for CR topics (Corporate Responsibility Magazine, 2010). The C-level leaders in charge of such departments widely vary in names. Examples are the well-known chief compliance officer and the chief sustainability and responsibility officer. Other versions include the chief reputation and sustainability officer and the chief visionary officer (Vives, 2011).

Responsibility Officer" all reflect an increasing trend to place C-level individuals in charge of developing responsible businesses.

- Has your organization redefined the role and power of main stakeholders throughout the organizational structure? A responsible business must have stakeholders at its core. How does your company institutionalize stakeholder engagement and equip stakeholders with the power to take part in shaping and managing the organization? Examples providing stakeholders with central roles are boards of directors representing primary internal and external stakeholders, inclusion of stakeholders in core processes, and the creation of channels for exchange with stakeholder groups.

- Does your organization facilitate criticism, innovation, and disruptive change? Hierarchies and power structures can be a serious impediment to change toward becoming a responsible business. Whistle-blowing and proposal mechanisms for employees help to create a critical culture inside the company that brings problematic areas to the attention of decision-makers. Transformation to responsible business is only possible if innovation is furthered and structures are flexible enough to facilitate disruptive change instead of inhibiting it. Chapter 18 provides a deeper insight into how to achieve such change by illustrating the tool of change management.

Human resources management

Human resources (HR) and responsible business are interlinked in a symbiotic relationship. HR needs responsible business as much as responsible business needs HR. Responsible business activities throughout many surveys has been shown to support and enrich the work of HR management (Fig. 12.5).

Corporate governance

The term "corporate governance" refers to the rules, mechanisms, and institutions that regulate and control businesses. The main difference between organizational structure and corporate governance lies in the governance focus on managing the principal–agent relationship that exists between managers and owners of a company. In the traditional understanding of corporate governance, the aim is to assure that managers in companies act in the best interest of owners. A main conflict is that owners usually want to maximize profits, while managers prefer to maximize their personal wellbeing. Managers might prefer less risky investments in order to protect their own jobs, prefer higher compensation than is justified, and strive for personal power against the best interest of maximizing profits.

A progressive understanding of corporate governance is based not on a narrow owner perspective, but on assuring that managers act in the best interest of a broader set of stakeholders. The principal–agent relationship between managers and society as a whole needs to be managed. Such a progressive understanding is rather aligned with the business's overall responsibilities instead of the narrow set of responsibilities toward owners (Freeman and Reed, 1983). The contemporary understanding of corporate governance, as illustrated in the OECD Principles of Corporate Governance, is usually a mixture of traditional and progressive understanding (OECD, 2004).

Governance is about the way companies are controlled externally and internally. External control in the traditional understanding stems from mechanisms of the financial market. If management is not able to assure above-average returns on the

How does responsible business support HR? Responsible business covers many causes related to company employee responsibilities, which are also foundational to the activity of the HR department. Responsible business means improvement of workplace health and security, increased work satisfaction and human development, assurance of a healthy work–life balance, promotion of diversity, equal opportunities, and fair wages. Key performance indicators of HR management may be positively influenced by employee perception of working for a responsible company. One positively influenced indicator is typically the motivation of existing employees. Also, the attraction of prospective employees by a company's reputation of providing a responsible "great place to work" is a factor positively affecting the work of the HR department. The employee retention rate is usually increased and the turnover rate reduced by becoming a responsible business. Low turnover rates and higher work motivation normally result in tangible cost savings throughout the employee life-cycle. As a result, companies managing the responsible human resources process correctly have the potential to, at the same time, increase employee welfare, improve the quality of their human resources, and reduce costs (SHRM, 2007).

owners' investment in the company, two regulation mechanisms take place. Either owners will replace the existing management or the company will be bought by new owners that have detected that it is under-performing. Also new owners would replace the old management. External control, in the progressive understanding, consists of increasing stakeholder opposition to the activities in which the company is not acting in the stakeholders' best interest. Stakeholders would thereby revoke the company's social license to operate.

Companies' main internal control mechanisms can be divided into three main topics (Hitt *et al.*, 2007). The ownership structure of companies might be characterized by individual, family, or conglomerate ownership, or by large institutional owners such as banks or governmental institutions. This structure largely influences the power and preferences of owners. The board of directors might consist of a mixture of internal and external individuals to balance interests. Also, the fact that many CEOs simultaneously serve as chairman of the board has been criticized as a "fox guarding the henhouse" situation, compromising the board's control function. Executive compensation is considered an important tool to align manager interest and stockholder interest. High performance-based compensation packages are a typical practice which is often questioned because of a lack of fairness. The high manager wages resulting from good performance have often brought about aggressive criticism from employees and civil society in general. Control mechanisms for good corporate governance operate in a constant stress field between narrow shareholder responsibilities and the broader responsibility to other stakeholders and society as a whole.

How does HR support responsible business? "CSRHR=PR" (SHRM, 2011) is a formula used by the Society for Human Resources Management to describe the importance of HR management to implementing responsible business. The message is that if HR is not involved in responsible business activities, it can only result in superficial, weakly integrated public relations talk. Such public relations work definitely fulfills an important function in responsible business, but can easily result in greenwashing accusations if not based on sound implementation through the human resources activities. In fact, the HR department is crucially instrumental in implementing successful responsible business activities. Why? HR does broad things, such as hiring employees with the right attitudes, values, and skill sets, as well as specific things such as conducting volunteering programs. HR is also crucially important when it comes to credibly communicating business responsibility internally. Last, but not least, employees are the critical entity in creating a responsible corporate culture, a situation which is often called "embedding responsible business into the DNA of the company."

Companies successfully implementing a responsible human resources culture do so throughout all stages of the employee life-cycle, as described in Figure 12.6.

Figure 12.5: Symbiosis of human resources and responsible business

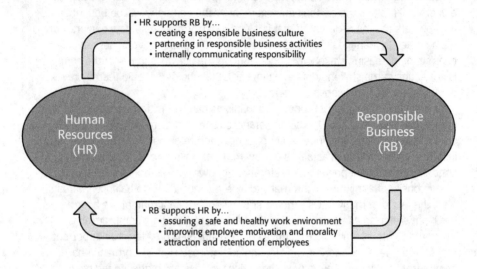

The hiring stage begins even before there is a concrete job offer. Employer branding, a measure of promoting the company's responsible image among potential employees, aims at generally attracting employees to the company. Some companies heavily invest in external education programs at public schools and universities in order to actively qualify future employees who otherwise would not have a possibility of being hired. The creation of job profiles focusing on responsible business may additionally attract the right employees for the company's shift toward responsible and sustainable business. It goes without saying that transparency and fairness in the hiring process and the provision of adequate wages and benefits are baseline requirements for a responsible business.

Figure 12.6: Simplified employee life-cycle

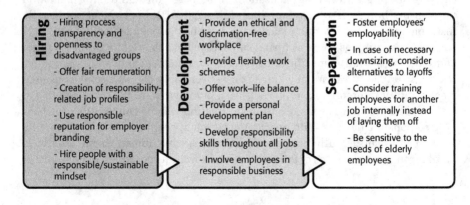

The employee development stage describes the time of productive engagement between employees and the company. The underlying goal during this time is to simultaneously increase employee welfare and increase the value of the overall human capital involved in the company. Activities to reach these goals are to provide an ethical and discrimination-free workplace, to provide flexible work schemes such as telework or flexible work hours, to provide an attractive personnel development plan including feedback opportunities, and to offer the right prerequisites to develop a healthy work–life balance. In order to develop responsibility skills throughout the company, it is also important to empower employees to contribute to and participate in responsible business. Active development of sustainability job skills is also an important contribution of HR management to the development of responsible business.

Work–life balance, good for employee and employer

Should it be of any concern to a business whether employees are able to live a life that is balanced between professional and private life? According to the British *HR Magazine*, it pays off for businesses to support such a balance, as a work–life imbalance is the number one reason for workplace absence. A healthy work–life balance contributes to motivation and increases productivity. Thus, it is not surprising that as much as 38% of employers participating in a U.K. survey mentioned improving their employees' work–life balance as a top priority (HR Magazine, 2012).

The separation stage deals with the situation in which employees leave the company for whatever reason. In the case of downsizing, responsible companies might consider options other than laying people off. Alternatives might be part-time employment and temporal leaves. Separation due to a redundancy of employees' skills can be avoided by training employees in other skills required. An irresponsible practice in some companies is to fire employees before the old-age benefits to be paid by the company grow too big. To avoid such irresponsible practices is the minimum baseline of responsible business during the separation phase. Companies may offer active outplacement support, which prepares employees to succeed in the labor market. Even before people are outplaced, responsible business should take care to build up employees' employability and their ability to succeed in the labor market, long before they need to change jobs.

Research, development and innovation

Research and development (R&D), technology, and innovation are important building blocks in the development of responsible and sustainable processes and products. The process of innovating for better social, environmental, and economic performance is called sustainable innovation. Examples might include changes from integrating a material produced by a poor community into the production process to fully powering production facilities with renewable energies. Other examples are changing the formula of a beverage product to not use industry sugar or switching from producing a product to supplying a less resource-intensive service. As with any other innovation process, sustainable innovation follows the basic steps of the innovation business life-cycle. The life-cycle runs from product development, to pilot-testing it, to its launch and use, until the product is redundant, which will typically lead to the development of a new product or service running through the same stages.

What usually comes to mind when thinking of research and development is development, which is only the first step of the overall R&D process. It is an important step, however. The basic question to be asked for sustainable innovation is: "How can we change processes and products in order to improve the social, environmental, and economic performance and sustainability of companies' activities?" During the development process, it is crucially important to thoroughly assess the social, environmental, and economic impacts of the innovation to be implemented throughout the product's physical life-cycle and to involve stakeholders in the development process. Social and environmental issues have proven to inspire business innovations and to open new markets. Sustainable innovation supports marketing through the products and helps to shape them with improved social and environmental impact while simultaneously accessing new markets, such as the LOHAS and BoP sectors. The testing stage might use "the social sector as beta site" (Kanter, 1999), a place where prototypes can be honed to perfection. A win–win practice is to give a product or process to communities that usually would not be able to afford to buy them and in return ask for feedback. The testing stage is also where products can be scrutinized for sustainability in real-life situations.

The launch stage is critical for positioning the product in the market segment where it truly adds sustainable value and to make sure that its use is truly sustainable. It needs to be assured that consumers (product innovations) and employees (process innovations) use the product in an adequate way to realize its potential to make a positive impact. The interconnection with marketing again plays an important role. However, as sustainable as a product might be, if it is marketed to be overconsumed its potential positive impact is limited through the negative environmental impact of that overconsumption.

The last stage in the business life-cycle of innovations is the redundancy of the product or process. Redundancy in mainstream business occurs when a product has lost its market potential or when a process can be replaced by something more efficient. For sustainable innovation, two additional questions have to be added to assess redundancy. Is the product or process still environmentally viable or should it be abandoned? Is there a more responsible and sustainable alternative to the product or process?

The above description is focused on product and process innovation as part of a company's R&D efforts. However, this is not always the dominant setting. For instance, a distinct subject of innovation efforts, apart from product and process, is a form of organizational innovation known as business model innovation. As this is typically not part of the activities of support functions such as R&D, we will not discuss business model innovation further here; indeed, business model innovation as outlined in Chapters 9 and 16 implies a much more exhaustive change. Suffice to say, though, that business models are the underlying logic and the very essence of what a business is and does. Thus, business model innovation has to be a company-embracing process which "changes everything," and so products and processes may also be changed as part of that process.

Exercises

A. Know

Use the multiple choice questions below to test your knowledge. Each answer may be wrong or right and there may be zero to four right or wrong answers per question:

1. Responsible management in the law and compliance and in the accounting functions …

    a. … involves compliance with soft law. Soft law refers to formal legislation that only applies to a small, specific set of companies.
    b. … involves areas of hard law, such as environmental legislation, consumer protection, and labor rights.
    c. … in the sustainability accounting process involves measurement and documentation of social, environmental, and economic activities and performance.
    d. … involves the development of indicators to measure social, environmental, and economic performance and activity. In order to reduce complexity, such indicators should exclusively focus on company-internal business activity, the so-called sphere of influence.

2. Responsible management in finance, organizational structure, and governance …

    a. … involves three activity areas for responsible management in finance: transforming financial management in businesses, implementing responsible finance tools such as microfinance, and transforming financial institutions.
    b. … involves establishing a responsible financial management framework. An important point to be noted in such a framework is integration, which here refers to the necessity to integrate finance and accounting.
    c. … includes structural change toward responsible business, such as creating institutions and assuring that the business structure allows for criticism, innovation, and even disruptive change.
    d. … includes the topic of corporate governance, which describes the rules, mechanisms, and institutions that regulate and control businesses. Corporate governance fulfills the one and only function to ensure that the organization is governed in the best interests of shareholders.

3. Responsible management in human resources …

    a. … can be seen as a one-sided relationship for the unique benefit of human resources.
    b. … often leads to a situation where responsible business supports human resources management by, for instance, improving employee motivation and morale and by supporting the attraction and retention of employees.

c.   ... involves implementing a culture of responsibility in human resources, which in turn may influence the whole employee life-cycle.

d.   ... builds on the assumption that the responsibility for employees ends at the time when it is clear when the employee will leave the business.

4. Research and development in responsible business ...

a.   ... involves sustainable innovation as the process of innovating with the goal of better social, environmental, and economic performance of products and processes.

b.   ... involves adjustments throughout the business life-cycle of innovations, integrating sustainable innovation into this life-cycle.

c.   ... involves eco-innovation, which always refers to the application of green technologies in businesses.

d.   ... involves the social innovation approach, which aims to create processes and products with an improved social impact.

B. Think

Rethink one of the following concepts by asking how it relates to responsible business, and how it would need to be reconceptualized to fit well into a responsible business world: 1) shareholder value maximization, 2) human resource, and 3) bottom line.

C. Do

Design and implement a small-scale sustainability accounting process for something you do.

D. Relate

Think about one organization you know well, or identify one that has much information publicly available. Who would you need to speak to in this organization to change it toward more sustainability? What motivations and interests might people have to join your cause or oppose it? Who might become your allies and opponents in the process? What would your game plan look like?

E. Be

In human resources assessment situations you might find questions like the following. Answer the one that best reflects your attitude to moral goals at work (Spurgin, 2004):

a.   It is important for me to use prudential judgment in making decisions at work

b.   When engaged in action, I do not typically consider how virtuous my motives are as I move to accomplish objectives

c.   I think about my motives when achieving the mission, to ensure they are based on moral ends

Feedback

A. Know

Question 1

a. Wrong: soft law refers to voluntary norms and standards, such as the ISO norms.
b. Right: these areas of hard law are exemplified in Figure 12.1.
c. Right: these are central elements of the sustainability accounting process as illustrated Figure 12.2.
d. Wrong: the sphere of influence to be included in indicator development usually involves much more than only company-internal activity.

Question 2

a. Right: all three are illustrated in the section on responsible management in the finance function.
b. Wrong: integration refers to integrating social and environmental factors into the frameworks used in financial management.
c. Right: these elements have been described as part of the organizational structuring process for responsible business and management.
d. Wrong: corporate governance may also be understood as managing in the best interests of a broad set of stakeholders, not only shareholders (see the "Corporate governance" box).

Question 3

a. Wrong: responsible management and human resources co-exist in a mutually beneficial symbiotic relationship.
b. Right: right, responsible management practices supporting the goals of HR management are part of the symbiotic relationship between both topics.
c. Right: responsibility may become a cultural aspect of a company that leads to a set of responsible practices in all different parts of the employee life-cycle.
d. Wrong: responsible human resources management includes responsibility in the so-called separation phase, after it is clear when the employee will leave the business.

Question 4

a. Right: improved triple-bottom-line performance is the unifying goal for sustainable innovation.
b. Right: sustainable innovation may impact the business life-cycle of a product or process innovation at several stages.
c. Wrong: the green technology movement is only one possible approach to reducing negative environmental impact through innovation.
d. Right: the improvement of social impact is the desired outcome of social innovation.

B. Think

Level	Rethinking business concepts and principles	Notes
+	Appreciation of conceptual issues when applied in a responsible business world and convincing proposals for reconceptualization	
=	Appreciation of the issues of the concept in a responsible business world	
−	No appreciation of the need for the concept to change in a responsible business world	

C. Do

Level	Implementation skills	Notes
+	Designed and implemented	
=	Feasible sustainability accounting process has been designed	
−	No sustainability accounting process	

D. Relate

Level	Political skills	Notes
+	Promising game plan for change based on convincing understanding of the inner workings of the organization	
=	Insight into political structures, but no feasible game plan	
−	Little insight into the political structures of the organization	

E. Be

Level	Enacting moral goals	Notes
+	c) I think about my motives when achieving the mission, to ensure they are based on moral ends	
=	a) It is important for me to use prudential judgment in making decisions at work	
−	b) When engaged in action, I do not typically consider how virtuous my motives are as I move to accomplish objectives	

13
Supply chain management

> Our research finds a significant performance gap between those CEOs who agree that sustainability should be embedded throughout their subsidiaries (91 percent) and supply chain (88 percent), and those who report their company is already doing so (59 percent and 54 percent, respectively)
>
> (Lacey *et al.*, 2010, p. 12)

While the preceding chapters have illustrated how to conduct responsible business throughout a business's internal functions, the focus will now shift to how to disseminate responsible business throughout a company's external supply chain relations. The application is complex and the sustainable supply chain management process is much more than simply duplicating responsible business practices. Supply chain management today often confronts two main issues: the complexity of globalization and numerous ethical issues that are encountered in global supply chains (Svensson, 2009).

What is supply chain management and what is not? Supply chain management manages and integrates a series of companies into a supply chain that jointly delivers a value proposition through a product or service to customers. To understand supply chain management in responsible business and in general, it is crucial to consider the following three points:

1. **External supply chain versus internal value chain:** supply chain management deals with managing intercompany relationships along the supply chain, while value chain management optimizes the value creation intra-company, from the inside of a business through its value chain.

Dangerous supply chain

The list of costly supply chain scandals is long. One of the most prominent examples is the struggle between Nike and activists about working conditions in the sports shoes giant's factories. Another scandal that ruined a reputation was suffered by Mattel, when the company had to recall millions of toys that had been painted by Chinese manufacturers using highly toxic lead paint (Barboza, 2007b). In 2011, a contractor of the fashion retailer Zara was accused of employing slave labor in the production process (Pereira and Alerigi, 2011). In the same year, Apple faced the existence of fake Apple stores in China that even the local employees thought were real (Lee, 2011b). A *Guardian* headline from 2016 reads "Nestlé admits slavery in Thailand while fighting child labour lawsuit in Ivory Coast." As we can see, dangers in the supply chain can take many forms. Supply chain issues are a continuously evolving concern (Kelly, 2016).

2. **Beyond procurement:** supply chain management should not be mistaken for merely a task of the procurement or purchasing department. While these departments play a crucial role in establishing a contract-based relationship with suppliers, true engagement throughout the supply chain goes much further than an economic exchange of goods for money.

3. **NOT merely about suppliers:** managing a company's suppliers is only the upstream part of supply chain management. The often forgotten downstream part consists of managing the relationships from direct clients to the final end-consumer.

Figure 13.1 illustrates the basic components of a supply chain integrating sustainability features. Supply chains consist of a series of companies that are

A life-or-death matter

Increasingly, supply chain issues are a matter of life or death. Consider just three out of many more examples. Six children were killed and almost 300,000 became sick from poisoned milk powder tainted with Melanin manufactured by the Sanlu company in China. The factory supervisor responsible for the disaster was sentenced to death by Chinese authorities (Branigan, 2009). The factory of Apple's provider Foxconn was the scene of the suicides of seven young Chinese workers in the midst of the Apple iPad boom (Chamberlain, 2011). Even more bizarre, the company is reported to have installed nets and to have forced workers to sign "non-suicide pledges" to keep them from killing themselves (A. Lee, 2011). The boss of a Mattel provider, responsible for the company's scandal of lead-poisoned toys, hanged himself in the warehouse of his company, Lee Der Industrial (Barboza, 2007a).

Figure 13.1: Sustainable supply chain management model

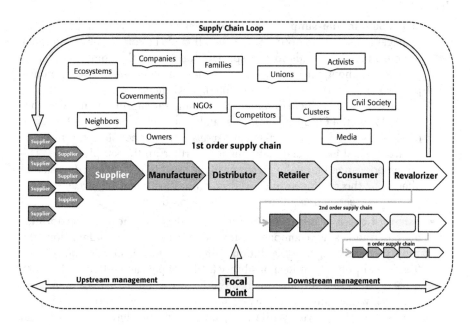

jointly involved in producing a product or service. Depending on the stage of the supply chain they are involved in, companies are traditionally classified as suppliers, manufacturers, distributors, and retailers. Between these different businesses, a constant flow of inputs, products, money, and information creates a connectedness which has to be managed by supply chain management. A business might have vertically integrated more than one supply chain stage into its structure. A dairy product business might, for instance, own all stages from dairy farming (supplier) to stores (retailers), or merely focus on the production and branding of dairy products (manufacturing) and leave the other stages to independent companies. Considerations about supply chain stage and degree of integration of a company are important in defining the focal point for subsequent value chain management activities. The focal point helps to define upstream supply chain management activities, which target the company's suppliers, and downstream activities, which focus on the company's clients.

Defining sustainable supply chains

How is a specific supply chain made sustainable? The ultimate goal of sustainable supply chain management is to ensure that the respective supply chain contributes to sustainable development in the long term. To do so, the overall supply chain has to integrate measures to assume the responsibility to reach this ultimate goal. Below is a list of central characteristics needed to create a sustainable supply chain (SSC):

- **Triple-bottom-line supply chain management:** sustainable supply chain management needs to optimize the overall triple bottom line from supplier to consumer, and needs to pay special attention to the complex interdependences among the supply chain's social, environmental, and economic performance (Carter and Rogers, 2008). SSC management also needs to identify and solve ethical dilemmas throughout the supply chain (Svensson, 2009). When the European Union set ambitious goals to increase the usage of biofuels, the decision-makers apparently did not consider the negative environmental and social consequences further up the supply chain. The increased demand for palm oil as one of the top biofuels created devastating effects for the rainforest and local communities when big areas became cleared to create monocultures for palm oil production.

- **Extended chain of responsibility:** this term describes how responsibilities migrate from a single company's stakeholders to all stakeholders along the supply chain, i.e., the "Evolution from Corporate Social Responsibility (CSR) to Supply Chain Responsibility (SCR)" (Spence and Bourlakis, 2009, p. 291). Two central questions need to be answered by management. The first, "How far into the supply chain do our responsibilities reach?," is a tricky one to answer. While companies might not have extended legal responsibilities for their supply chain, there often is a moral responsibility as general stakeholders may hold companies responsible for realities, often off the map of corporate managers' thinking. For instance, the issues Apple encountered at the legally independent Foxconn plant (including seven worker suicides) were perceived by the public as an Apple responsibility (Moore, 2010). The second central question, once the company has assumed supply chain responsibility, is about power: "How can we gain influence over the supply chain to make it sustainable?"

- **Circular, stretched, and restorative supply chain:** to become sustainable a supply chain must be circular, stretched, and restorative. Circular refers to a movement of goods and services not only from supplier to end-consumer, but also a movement back from the end of the supply chain to its beginning in a recycling fashion. Reverse logistics facilitate a reintegration of what usually would be considered waste into the supply chain. Stretched supply chains refers to second-order supply chains that consist of a higher share of renewable and recycled inputs and products in the same chain. For instance in Kenya, the supply chain for secondhand clothes is strong, as 80% of the population buys secondhand clothes, for reasons of both price and fashion (Svensson, 2007). Second-order supply chains are crucially important to extend the product and input lifetime, increase the value that can be extracted by consumers, and reduce the environmental impact per product or input. To become sustainable, supply chains need to be restorative. Social, environmental, and economic capital of the supply chain is worn off in the process of establishing a product or service. According to the law of entropy there will always be energy losses through processes, which will lead to the reduction of certain capital during its usage. This becomes clearer through three simple examples: 1) the amount of materials recyclable from a product will always be smaller than the inputs used to produce the product (environmental capital); 2) employees will become exhausted, if not living with a healthy work–life balance (social capital); and 3) production facilities, if not taken care of, will lose their value (economic capital).

An n-order downstream supply chain business model

The North American company Rent-A-Center (RAC) has successfully integrated several supply chains (n-tiered supply chains) into the same business model. If you enter a RAC branch, it first looks like a normal department store. Products range from furniture to TV sets. Not so familiar is the business model, which rents products instead of selling them. RAC customers may either rent a new (first-tier) product for a monthly fee, or do the same with a product that has been rented before (first-, second-, n-order supply chain). RAC customers may return the product at any time, without any final payment attached. The company also provides maintenance service throughout the useful life of a product (RAC, 2015). It can be assumed that the primary motivation for this business model is not sustainability. Nevertheless, the overall environmental impact of the product may be reduced drastically because of the characteristics of this business model. One of the major reasons is that customers have strong incentives to not rent two products at the same time. Another reason is that the same product is used by more people, which has the potential to drastically reduce the environmental footprint per person.

In order to integrate the three preceding characteristics, the sustainable supply chain model illustrated in Figure 13.1 includes numerous stakeholders throughout all stages of the supply chain and illustrates a supply chain loop to ensure circularity. The model also features a new supply chain function, which is to "revalorize." A revalorizing company adds value to products that traditionally would be considered worthless by either channeling them into recycling through the feedback loop or to second-order supply chains where such products can still be used. A revalorizer typically performs tasks such as recovering, repairing, reusing, refurbishing, recycling, or, in the most preferable case, upcycling (Pauli, 1999).

Stages of sustainable supply chain management

The actual practice of responsible supply chain management differs widely, depending on what stage of the supply chain a company operates in. This supply chain position has been called the focal point. Companies, depending on their supply chain position, can also be categorized into supply chain sustainability leaders or followers. For instance Walmart, as a company in the retail stage of its supply chain, requires preceding supply chain stages to comply with a basic supplier code of conduct. Hewlett-Packard does the same from a manufacturer supply chain position. Both can be called sustainability leaders in their respective supply chains. While sustainable supply chain leaders proactively facilitate change toward more sustainability, sustainable supply chain followers might react to pressure to become more responsible in many different modes of responsiveness. In the best cases, supply chain followers would react positively and become supply chain leaders themselves.

The following steps for developing responsible supply chain leaders are a recipe for progressively maximizing a single company's contribution to developing truly sustainable supply chains:

- **Be a responsible business:** for a company to credibly foster responsible business practices throughout its supply chain, it is of crucial importance to first make sure it excels internally in becoming a responsible business.

- **Implement codes and policies:** installing a sustainable procurement and purchasing program helps to communicate a company's stance in terms of upstream supplier ethics and sustainability (Roloff and Aßlander, 2010; Saini, 2010). While less common, companies might also draft policies for

Without a trace?

One of the big trends in sustainable supply chain management is traceability. Traceability refers to the ability to understand exactly the route taken by products throughout the complete production process, from extraction of the initial raw material to the final end-product. One example is the use of radio frequency identification (RFID) tags which store this information (Kelepouris *et al.*, 2007). A future scenario would be to go shopping with a reading device that is able to decipher all supply chain data, from miles traveled to information on companies involved. An excellent example is the New Zealand company Icebreaker, which has a "Baa Code." A baa code is a bar code for the company's sheep wool products which shows where the wool was produced for every product bought (TogBlog, 2008). Focusing on the transportation impact of a product, the Sourcemap tool provides extensive, hands-on information on a wide variety of products (Sourcemap, 2012).

downstream supply chain stages, determining the basic requirements that clients have to fulfill. A weapons producer, for example, might establish a strict code of ethics, defining to whom to sell.

- **Co-create and control:** most businesses do have well-drafted codes and policies, but these cannot assure compliance and much less sustainable supply chain excellence. Nevertheless, these documents are an excellent basis for assuming co-responsibility with supply chain partners and to co-create solutions to social, environmental, and ethical issues. These solutions have to be rechecked against policies established and effective control mechanisms have to be installed.

- **Extend and integrate:** once supply chain partners inside a company's direct sphere of influence have been influenced toward becoming responsible, it is time to extend the company's influence. Companies can influence deeper tiers of suppliers far upstream, clients of clients, and finally even second-tier supply chains downstream. The ultimate goal is to influence the complete supply chain until it becomes truly sustainable from initial raw material to the end-consumer.

Sustainable supply chain management tools

For companies wanting to improve supply chain performance, there is a variety of instruments available, most of which have been extensively tried and tested. Instruments for both upstream and downstream sustainable supply chain management are described below. Instruments for sustainable upstream supply chain management can be divided into sustainable supply chain standards, fair-trade and supply chain inclusiveness, and green supply chain management:

- Sustainable supply chain standards assure that social and environmental issues typically encountered in international supply chains are addressed in a responsible way. Such standards in the social dimension usually cover working conditions, safety and health, wages and benefits, and ethical issues, such as child labor and overtime. In the environmental dimension, good environmental management practices, such as emission and waste management, are key topics and often exceed standards given by local legislation (Reed, 2002). Such standards are a valuable tool in evaluating existing suppliers and identifying new ones (Ehrgott *et al.*, 2011).

- Fair-trade and inclusive supply chains both include poor suppliers in a company's supply chain. In practice, both approaches are closely connected, although there are minor differences in the underlying approaches for involvement. Fair trade focuses on providing distribution channels for "third-world" products in the "first world" under a characteristic value set of trust, fairness, and equity (Raynolds, 2002; Renard, 2003). Under fair-trade regimes, producers are usually paid a "fair" price, higher than the normal market price. Inclusive supply chain management has many characteristics of fair trade, but highlights the addressing of social exclusion through supply chain participation by means of an active involvement with small producers (Hall and Matos, 2010). This involvement exceeds a pure trade relationship, for supply chain inclusion often involves active collaboration and education to jointly improve small producers' production methods, quality standards, and often even their communities. The Oxfam stores, a global distribution channel for products solely from small communities in developing countries, is a classical fair-trade company, while the French retail giant Carrefour can be characterized as a highly inclusive business. Carrefour sells more than 400 products, produced in cooperation with small communities, with an overall sales volume of over €$70 million (Carrefour, 2013).

- Green supply chain management focuses on the environmental impact of supply chains in both production and transportation, and the environmental impact of transportation and the topic of responsible logistics have been covered extensively in Chapter 11. Improving the environmental impact of production activities throughout the supply chain is often described by the term "green and lean supply chains," and collaborating with suppliers to simultaneously increase their overall efficiency and eco-efficiency, by linking these efforts to supplier education in lean manufacturing, has proven to be successful (Simpson and Power, 2005; Mollenkopf et al., 2010). Indicators typically used to evaluate suppliers' environmental performance are the production of solid and hazardous waste, air and water pollution, and natural resource usage (Beamon, 1999). Many companies also require their suppliers to develop an ISO 14000 certified environmental management system.

Know your main impact!

Controlling upstream supply chains with all their different types of social and environmental impact is nearly an impossible task if a company wants to optimize all impacts simultaneously. Sustainable supply chain management can make the biggest difference where the company's supply chain has the biggest impact. For a furniture company, such as the Swedish IKEA, the main resource input is wood. The sourcing of wood may have immense negative environmental impacts on biodiversity, forests, and the communities living in them. As a consequence, IKEA has developed a highly sophisticated and effective four-stepped "staircase" model for the sourcing of the wood used in the company. The model improves the social and environmental performance of the company's suppliers until they reach the highest stage, which fulfills the most advanced standards of the Forest Stewardship Council (IKEA, 2003; Andersen and Skjoett-Larsen, 2009).

Sustainable downstream supply chain management tools are often related to the customer relationship management (CRM) function. As the main tools and techniques of responsible CRM have been illustrated in Chapter 11, just four specific points of engagement with the downstream supply will be highlighted here. In order to create demand for responsible products, companies, jointly with other market incumbents, might aim to actively change market demand toward such products. Online retailers such as Amazon and eBay, with their immense markets for secondhand products, have already done so. Educating consumers on how to use products and to recycle them is another field of action. Also, companies might start to create, scrutinize, or even manage markets in secondary supply chains, in order to increase the overall life of products and inputs. Finally, the creation of revalorization mechanisms in the downstream supply chain is a critically important task if the overall supply chain is to become sustainable.

Exercises

A. Know

Use the multiple choice questions below to test your knowledge. Each answer may be wrong or right and there may be zero to four right or wrong answers per question:

1. Sustainable supply chain management ...
    a.   ... has been defined in this chapter as the responsible management of company's supplier relationship.
    b.   ... involves the concept of an extended chain of responsibility, which means that companies should extend their responsibilities for suppliers beyond the contractually agreed responsibilities.
    c.   ... can be developed in stages, of which the first stage is for a company to become a responsible business, and the final step is to co-create solutions in collaboration with immediate supply chain partners.
    d.   ... involves the use of sustainable supply chain management tools, such as supply chain standards, fair trade, and green supply chain management.

2. A chocolate company pays their cocoa suppliers more than the market price. This is an example of ...
    a.   ... green supply chain management.
    b.   ... fair trade.
    c.   ... inclusive supply chains.
    d.   ... revalorization.

3. The German fashion chain store Humana exclusively sells secondhand clothing under the slogan "first class second hand." Most of the clothing sold is sourced through donations. This example involves elements of ...
    a.   ... fair trade.
    b.   ... reverse logistics.
    c.   ... an extended chain of responsibility.
    d.   ... a secondary supply chain.

B. Think

Imagine you are a sourcing manager in charge of assuring your company's global supply chain does not further any morally questionable practices. You have learned that one of your suppliers employs children, which in itself appears morally critical. Moreover, your company has just made a public commitment to not employ child labor. However, you learn that the same supplier gives these children access to education through their in-house secondary school, which they wouldn't have otherwise. Also, you personally speak to some of the children and learn that their family depends on their income to survive. What do you think you, as company representative, should decide to do?

C. Do

Pick a product of your choice. Identify and use a (probably web-based) tool to estimate the CO_2 emitted through its global supply chain.

D. Relate

Find a way to get in touch with someone who works in a factory in a developing country. Ask about this person's experience and try to understand how it relates to you. If this person wants to, help them to be heard by others.

E. Be

Think about one product or service you use. What social, environmental, economic, and moral impacts do you think are triggered by your use?

Feedback

A. Know

Question 1

a. Wrong: supply chain management involves managing both the suppliers (upstream supply chain) and clients (downstream supply chain) of a company.

b. Wrong: the term "extended chain of responsibility" refers to the ideal situation where companies take responsibility not only for their direct stakeholders, but for stakeholders along the whole supply chain of their product.

c. Wrong: the last step and highest level of responsible supply chain management is to extend the company's influence through the supply chain to co-create solutions with supplier and clients that could not be reached before.

d. Right: all the tools mentioned are typical examples of sustainable supply chain management tools.

Question 2

a. Wrong: there is no direct environmental impact visible in the description.

b. Right: paying higher-than-average market prices is the main element of fair trade.

c. Wrong: the example does not show any inclusion of marginalized suppliers or efforts to develop supply practices to make them eligible for inclusion into a greater supply chain.

d. Wrong: revalorization refers to recovering, repairing, reusing, refurbishing, and recycling activities that add value to a product after its use.

Question 3

a. Wrong: as far as we know from the description, no higher-than-average prices are paid to any marginalized group.

b. Right: reverse logistics is necessary to bring the products from an end-user back to the company.

c. Wrong: an extended chain of responsibility refers to an appreciation of responsibility that moves from a single company's stakeholders to all stakeholders along the supply chain.

d. Right: Humana is entirely built on a secondary supply chain, after the primary supply chain of newly produced clothing has been closed.

B. Think

Level	Dealing with moral complexity	Notes
+	A decision has been made considering all aspects of the moral setting	
=	A decision has been made, but parts of the information on the moral situation have not been dealt with in the decision-making process	
–	No reduction of complexity visible in the answer	

C. Do

Level	Green technology skills	Notes
+	Feasible estimation of CO_2 transport footprint has been conducted	
=	Tool and product have been identified, but the analysis was not conducted correctly	
–	Neither product nor tool has been identified	

D. Relate

Level	Facilitating voice for typically unheard groups	Notes
+	Factory worker's experience has been heard by others	
=	Personal account of the factory worker's experience	
–	No contact has been established	

E. Be

Level	Appreciating impacts of own actions	Notes
+	Wide and deep appreciation of impacts made throughout the product's or service's supply chain	
=	Only impacts very proximate to the individual and its action have been considered (e.g., the water used when using toothpaste)	
–	No appreciation of impacts	

F.
COMMUNICATING

14

Communication in responsible business

Messages about corporate ethical and socially responsible initiatives are likely to evoke strong and often positive reactions among stakeholders. Research has even pointed to the potential business benefits of the internal and external communication of corporate social responsibility.

(Morsing and Schultz, 2006, p. 323)

It has been a common public prejudice that companies who are conducting business responsibly are doing so as a public relations exercise. In other words, there is a lot of talk, but little "walk." However, the role given to communication in the context of this book rests on the different assumption that communication a vehicle that supports the implementation of responsible business and management throughout three phases of the implementation process. Only the final phase addresses public relations, or "talking the walk," whereas phases one and two address "walking the talk." To create a sound basis for communicating in responsible business, one needs to understand the role of stakeholders in communication and know basic communication formats that differentiate between external and internal communication. This chapter will prepare you for these important background topics.

Communicating with stakeholders

Responsible business implies various multifaceted responsibilities toward stakeholders, and communicating these responsibilities becomes crucial to managing the business. Each stakeholder has unique attitudes, interests, values, and needs, and communicating is a highly complex task. Before beginning the communication process, serious consideration must be given to understanding the stakeholder groups involved.

The AccountAbility stakeholder engagement standard organization provides one framework for communicating with stakeholders. The AA1000 standard (AccountAbility, 2011) lists the following set of basic questions to define why communication is desired:

- Is there a mutual dependence?
- Does the business have a responsibility toward the stakeholder?
- Is there tension because of a company-related issue that the stakeholder is involved in?
- Does the stakeholder have the power to influence the company?
- Does the stakeholder provide a diverse perspective?

Any of these communication motives is legitimate, and it is important to know what motivation exists with the stakeholder before beginning the communication process:

- Personal characteristics of stakeholders influence how they receive and assimilate messages, and how they respond. Personal characteristics may be as obvious as basic attitudes: perhaps the stakeholder generally has negative attitudes toward companies and wants to avoid contact. The profession of the stakeholder also matters: an engineer may be inclined to process information differently than a business major, a lawyer, or a philosophy major. Demographic factors of stakeholders such as age, income, gender, religion, and education are basic to understanding with whom the company is communicating.

- Potential communication barriers may prevent stakeholders from receiving, understanding, or answering the message sent. Barriers may include personal characteristics or physical or technical inhibitors, such as missing access to communication channels, including conflicting responsibilities or scheduling issues.

These communication criteria can be used to draft basic stakeholder segmentation, which in turn can help to plan and customize communication activities with these segments.

MTV, broadcasting about what, to whom, and why?

If you worked for a music and lifestyle broadcaster such as MTV and were charged with designing a campaign to spark civic action for the environment among your audience, what would you need to know? This is a stakeholder assessment question. Here are some answers: 41% of kids and teens worry about the environment and 34% worry specifically about animal extinction. When asked about what they believe the greatest issues are, 47% mention global warming and pollution, 45% environmental protection. You might also want to know that 94% say they are most motivated to take action because helping is fun and only 34% say they might be motivated by celebrities. The result was "MTV Switch," a fun-based campaign focused on climate change (von Walter, 2012).

Responsible communication formats

Is more frequent communication always better communication? A 2005 survey (Morsing and Schultz, 2006) found out that quality counts more than frequency. The survey conducted in Denmark, Sweden, and Norway asked how companies should communicate their responsible business. The results were challenging in several ways. First, 9% of the survey respondents were convinced that companies should not publicize their responsible business efforts at all. Just over half, 51%, stated that companies should focus on minimal releases only, such as reports and information on corporate websites, and merely 40% supported extended communication activities through the formats of corporate advertising and press releases. While these percentages may differ in other countries, there is still an important conclusion in this survey: communication frameworks and formats cannot follow a "the more the better" paradigm, but need to be closely tuned into stakeholders' expectations about the overall amount of communication activities and the means used. Successfully communicating responsible business requires a prudent deployment of communication formats aligned with each respective communicative situation, focused on the purpose of communication and the characteristics of primary stakeholders. Table 14.1 provides an overview of such communication formats applied in responsibility communication.

The table is only a rudimentary overview and toolset aimed at revealing a broad spectrum of formats for potential use. Later in this chapter we will provide a more extensive description on how to deploy these formats to address specific communication purposes. Each format represents a point of entry into a world of theoretical and practical information that can be recommended for deeper study. What are the important basics that need to be understood to put these communication formats to use? First, it is important to understand the basic processes involved. Stakeholder consultation and feedback, for instance, usually requires a complex social process of exchange and mutual sensemaking, while the process

Table 14.1: Overview of responsibility communication formats

Format	Process	Stage/purpose	Primary stakeholders
Stakeholder dialogue	Establish a constructive moderated dialogue with stakeholders involving extensive interaction and co-creation of messages and real-life impacts	Direction giving, sensemaking, consensus creation, inspiration (preparation, control)	Stakeholders involved vary depending on each respective consultation topic
Persuasion	Use of arguments to convince communication partners	Create approval and support for responsible business (preparation, implementation)	Management and general employees, internal and external key decision-makers
Vision, mission, values statements	Draft guidance documents for long-term strategy and short-term behavior	Provide guidance for decision-making and behavior (implementation)	Management, general employees
Training	Educate and train for knowledge, skills, and attitudes	Equip key stakeholders with the necessary prerequisites to support responsible business conduct (implementation)	Employees, suppliers, customers
Design	Design organizational structure, processes, and products that implicitly reflect responsible business conduct	Send an intrinsic message about how deeply implemented responsible business is (implementation)	Users of designs, such as customers, employees, or suppliers
By example and action	Be a role model through the responsible management conduct of exemplary individuals, leaders, groups, and the organization as a whole	Inspire, create trust and credibility of implementation (implementation)	Employees, general public
Social marketing	Use marketing as a tool to evoke individuals' behavior change with a positive effect on society and environment	Behavior change (implementation)	Customers, employees

Format	Process	Stage/purpose	Primary stakeholders
Lobbying	Influence the political decision-making process	Political decisions conducive to responsible business (implementation)	Governments, politicians
Policies, codes, handbooks	Create concise guidelines for operational decisions in processes critical for responsible business	Provide guidance for operational decisions and activities influencing responsible business (implementation)	Employees, specific departments, suppliers
PR (press releases)	Communicate responsible business activities and achievements	Raise awareness by highlighting responsible business activities (share)	Media, broader public
Endorsements	Achieve public endorsement by high credibility of individuals or organizations	Credibility catalyst effect (define, implement, share, control)	Any stakeholder targeted
Certification and labeling	Align your responsible business activities to compliance with responsible business labels and certifications for products, processes, or the complete organization	Credibility catalyst effect	End-consumers, business clients, government agencies
Reporting	Establish an extensive, factual, and neutral account of social, environmental, and economic business performance and activities	High-quality information provision (share, control)	Investors, employees, prospective employees, suppliers, industry analysts, competitors, general public
Newsletters	Publish a (usually company-internal) newsletter covering responsible business events and policies, highlighting individuals, or providing information on topical responsible business issues	Inform, motivate, and inspire for responsible business activities	Employees
Advertising	Start an advertising campaign, communicating responsible business activities and performance	Use marketing methods to inform and inspire people about your responsible business	Customers, general public

Format	Process	Stage/purpose	Primary stakeholders
Cause-related marketing and branding	Integrate a good cause into your marketing and branding activities	Increase product sales or brand positioning (implement, share)	Customers
Speeches and forewords	Use speeches to define the company's tone from the top, interpreting responsible business activities	Provide leadership interpretation and perspective (prepare, implement, share)	Depending on communication intention
Internet and social networks	Establish internet and intranet-based communication platforms, such as social networks, corporate blogs, microblogs, wikis, podcasts, or video blogs	Reach the broader internet public and capitalize on enhanced communication characteristics such as speed, low-cost, and interactiveness (prepare, implement, share)	Internet public, employees, activists, consumers
Issues and crisis communication	Protect and provide guidance and vision when faced with issues and crises threatening the business	Mitigate negative effects (e.g., negative publicity) of issues and crises (share)	Investors, employees, general public, activists
Hotlines and whistle-blowing mechanisms	Establish formal feedback channels	Create feedback for improvement (control)	Consumer, employee
Audits and assurance	Conduct internal or external audits, reviewing responsible business activities, outcomes, and reports	Create feedback for improvement (control)	Management, corporate headquarters, clients
Testimonials	Communicate the experience of stakeholders involved in or related to your responsible business conduct	Create credible and largely unfiltered insider information and perceptions	Employees, customers, etc.

of reporting consists of internal information-gathering and external one-way communication. Formats and their respective processes may also be combined, as a company might conduct stakeholder consultation in combination with using the internet or social network formats. Typically, a sustainability report would include a foreword and a printed letter.

Second, communicators need to understand the purpose and desired outcome of each format. A common mistake is to confuse social and cause-related marketing. While they are related in application, each respective purpose is distinct. Social marketing aims to create behavioral change in people for the good of society, while cause-related marketing aims to increase product sales.

A third essential characteristic of tools is to determine for which stakeholders they are intended. Lobbying usually targets the narrow and limited stakeholder group of politics and governmental institutions, while issues and crisis communication has a broader aim, consisting of shareholders, employees, customers, and the general public. A professional working in responsible business needs to understand and use all the different tools and the different solutions the tools provide. The following section will show how to reach an overall communication strategy by integrating all of these tools in a holistic and responsible communication plan that conveys an overall impression of consistency and integrity.

Integrated stakeholder communication

There is no such thing as purely internal or purely external communication. Messages cross the borders of companies freely, but the effect becomes even more distinct when scrutinizing communication processes in responsible business. Responsibility communication essentially is stakeholder communication when stakeholders cross borders, communicate with each other, and have roles inside and outside the company. Imagine a Google employee who learns from a supposedly "internal" newsletter about his company's algorithm to identify dissatisfied employees (Ballowe, 2009), a topic which becomes scandalous discussion at a party with his or her friends. Is that internal or external communication or a combination of both? Clearly, the effects of the communication transcended the company's borders. There is a growing overlap between the external and the internal sphere of communication, which is why in this book communication will be considered integrated external and internal processes, producing a consistent and congruent message outside and inside the company borders. Creating such a message requires that all communication tools and all organizational communicators become tuned in to the joint message. However, integrated communication here is understood even wider it means integration of:

- Internal and external communication
- All communication channels

- Explicit and implicit communication
- Customer and wider stakeholder communication

What does it mean to harmonize external and internal messages? For instance, the ice cream company Ben & Jerry's briefly renamed its "Chubby Hubby" flavor "Hubby Hubby" in support of marriage diversity (Wikipedia, 2016). Harmonization of messages would require that the company is also internally committing to diversity activities (Cohen, 2011). In theory, such a harmonization is a reasonable strategy to enhance the overall credibility of a responsible business. In practice, departmental responsibilities and borders often impede such efforts. Traditionally, external communication has been covered by the public relations or communications department and marketing, and internal messages have been handled by the human resources department. Who should be in charge of integrated stakeholder communication? Truly integrating business communication requires extensive coordination efforts beyond departmental borders. Many companies have separate communication departments for this task, but departments in charge of responsible business might be the most adequately equipped areas for sustainable communication, as they are usually connected to other departments in the company and to many stakeholders.

Integration at the movies

The "Del amor nace la vista" [Love Gives Birth to Eyesight] campaign by the Mexican movie chain Cinépolis relied on a broad set of communication channels and tools to integrate its communication efforts internally and externally. The social campaign aimed to improve the visual health of poor citizens, and the integrated campaign involved a diverse set of stakeholders. The theme was communicated to customers via trailers before the start of movies, and was addressed by staff at ticket and candy sales, and through transparent bathroom mirror stickers imitating the experience of cataract patients. Internally, Cinépolis communicated to employees through internal competitions ("Who saved the most eyes?") and the so-called eye-meter, which was used to keep count of fundraising and what it meant for beneficiaries (Laasch and Conaway, 2011). Since the first year of the program in 2005, the number of "eyes saved" per year has risen continuously. In 2015 there were 3,526 eye operations, 26 more than the goal of 3,500; the bar for 2016 was raised again to 4,000 operations (Cinépolis, 2016).

Communication purposes and the right formats

Why does a responsible business communicate? Is the primary communication goal to share the message of good deeds and responsible performance? It is, but communicating the outcomes of responsible business activities is just one of the four primary purposes of communication in responsible business. The first communication task consists of defining jointly with stakeholders the purpose, values, and basic characteristics of responsible business for a specific company. Second, the most intensive task is communication for implementation, to bring on board and enable stakeholders involved in the process for the joint endeavor of becoming a responsible business. Third, once responsible business conduct has reached a basic maturity and quality, the task of sharing the word helps to create goodwill among stakeholders. Fourth, the communication task that closes the stakeholder communication cycle consists of controlling the outcomes of communication. Has the message been shared and understood? Do stakeholders perceive the business as it was envisioned before? Most importantly: "Do we walk the talk?" The following sections provide insight into the distinct practice and use of the communication tools introduced above, for each of these four communication purposes.

Communication to prepare for responsible business

It is an easy and commonly made mistake to start by incrementally doing that "responsible business stuff" without truly understanding and defining what it should look like. The communication tool of stakeholder dialog can enrich all of the communication tasks in responsible business, but it is more powerful first to draft a picture of what a business should become. The goal is to reach a consensus between internal and external stakeholders and to develop responsible business based on this initial vision. How can a company reach this consensus? Interestingly, the two main approaches of stakeholder dialog and persuasion are often seen as opposing when trying to reach consensus and define a responsible business vision supported by all stakeholders of a company.

The stakeholder dialogue approach, as part of the stakeholder management process, aims to establish an exchange at eye level with a broad set of organizational stakeholders. Such a dialogue might be conducted in several ways, including meetings, broad stakeholder forums, surveys, or social-network-based interactions. Whatever form is chosen for the process needs to be designed so that it makes sense to the business. Sensemaking (Weick, 1995) refers to the process of jointly constructing consensus about responsible business and defining what the responsible business is supposed to be, do, and represent. It is important for the efficiency of a sensemaking process to establish an ideal speech situation (Bohman and Rehg, 2011; Habermas, 2005) and facilitate an optimum outcome of the communicative process. When applying the four basic conditions that establish the ideal, stakeholder dialog must include all stakeholder groups capable of making a relevant contribution. First, companies may make the mistake of only inviting the stakeholders that share their opinion, but the process is more likely to be fruitful if diverging opinions are represented. Second, it is also important to invite diverging stakeholder profiles and give them equal right to speak. Third, the process should facilitate a platform in which participants are able to provide an honest opinion, and fourth, to neither coerce to action nor be required to abstain from action. These general presuppositions provide a valuable framework for assessing the overall functionality of the process. In summary, the criteria for good stakeholder communication based on the "ideal speech situation" are:

- **Non-exclusion:** "No one capable of making a relevant contribution has been excluded" (inclusive stakeholder involvement)
- **Equal voice:** "Participants have equal voice" (equal contribution rights)
- **Honest opinion:** "Participants are internally free to speak their honest opinion without deception or self-deception" (honesty imperative)
- **No coercion:** "There are no sources of coercion built into the process and products of discourse" (coercion-free stakeholder dialog)

The AA1000 stakeholder engagement standard provides a practical shopping list that supports the implementation of stakeholder dialog in its operational aspects (AccountAbility, 2011, p. 45). It recommends the following quality criteria for good stakeholder dialog:

- Clearly define scope
- Have an agreed decision-making process
- Focus on issues material to the organization and/or its stakeholders
- Be integral to organizational governance
- Be transparent
- Have a process appropriate to the stakeholders engaged
- Be timely
- Be flexible and responsive

While stakeholder dialog aims to co-create consensus by a democratic process, the tool of persuasion aims to convince or influence the communication partner of a preestablished communication goal. Persuasion has been criticized for its forceful nature: it is a powerful tool that should be deployed with great care and only for a very specific set of situations where the communicator can be absolutely sure about the moral quality of the communication goal. Persuasion is important for creating support by those key individuals who implement the responsible business vision that was created through the stakeholder dialog process. Persuading or "selling" the idea of responsible business to high-level leadership might also be necessary to receive a green light for initiating the stakeholder dialog process. What should the persuader do if the CEO, vice presidents, heads of key departments, or other key individuals inside the company oppose the idea of becoming a responsible business? How can a persuader convince them of the necessity to support the transformation? Typically, three main issues in management support can be encountered and addressed by a persuasion-based communication strategy (O'Dwyer, 2003):

1. Managers restrict their activities for, and the understanding of, responsible business to a **shareholder wealth maximization rationale**. They can impede activities which are necessary to become a responsible business, but which are not easily identified as maximizing shareholder value.

2. Managers form "**pockets of resistance**" opposing the change toward responsible business.

3. Managers are not able to form a clear **understanding of responsible business**, due to conflicting definitions and usages of related terminologies.

Central to the persuasion process are arguments that relate to people's motivations. These arguments support the change in attitude intended by the communication purpose. It is helpful to group persuasive managerial arguments for the adoption of responsible business into three fundamental rationales (Aguilera *et al.*, 2007; Shiraishi *et al.*, 2009):

1. **Instrumental arguments** connect to individual self-interest. Managers need to understand what is in it for them or the organization. Typical arguments are the business case for responsible business or the congruence between performance indicators and responsible business.

2. **Relational arguments** connect with every individual's need for social belonging. These arguments refer to support by the manager's peers or highlight how an organization's internal community will thrive as a result of responsible business.

3. **Moral arguments** connect with individual needs for meaning and moral existence. Managers need to feel they can do good morally by supporting responsible business. Arguments may highlight the manager's potential contribution to a solution, for example, by presenting a pressing moral issue or by putting the manager in touch with people benefiting from responsible business conduct.

The persuasion framework proposed in this section has been illustrated by its application for managers, but it is just as instrumental for convincing any high-influence individual of the necessity to develop responsible business. This persuasive process is especially important for business transformation in more responsible ways.

Communication to implement responsible business

Many communication tools exist for supporting the implementation of responsible business. This section will highlight three high-impact communication instruments for the implementation phase:

1. **Policies, codes, and handbooks** provide a set of rules, decision mechanisms, and values with which the company must comply as a responsible business

2. **Social marketing** aims to change or create behaviors conducive to responsible business by using typical marketing mechanisms as a tool

3. **Sustainability education** aims to provide stakeholders with the necessary attitudes, skills, and knowledge to contribute to responsible business conduct

Policies, codes, and handbooks are characterized by many different formats, scope and scale, and tones. Broad policies help to formulate guidance, codes tend to be more concise, while handbooks meticulously provide operational details on how to behave in a responsible business. Codes related to responsible business can be divided into distinct groups. The broadest codes in scale and scope include general company-wide codes of conduct, separate codes of ethics, environmental policies, and responsible business policies. Codes which are narrow in scope cover specific issues, such as human rights or diversity, or specific departments such as purchasing or finance codes. There are also codes governing stakeholders' interaction within the company, such as supplier codes or shareholder policies (Preuss, 2010).

Codes of conduct: pleasure or pain?

When Walmart (2009) first published its supplier code of conduct for ethical sourcing, many stakeholders were overwhelmed by the social and environmental standards. What would happen if Walmart, the world's largest retailer, enforced codes with all its suppliers and, in this way, pushed them toward becoming responsible businesses? The power of codes of conduct can be enormous, but establishing a code requires due diligence. Walmart ran into problems in Germany when they were sued because the company's employee code of conduct aimed to regulate the love life of the employees and was judged to violate basic human rights of employees, particularly the personal freedoms guaranteed in Article 1 of the German constitution (Darsow, 2005).

The goal of social marketing is to create behavior change in people, and traditionally it has been used by public organizations to promote behavior changes, such as stopping smoking or reducing weight. Increasingly, social marketing is used by business actors, as implementing responsible business requires extensive behavior change of stakeholders inside and outside the business. Lines of action for social marketing among employees could be a green office program that requires employees to actively switch lights off and to reduce the amount of paper used for printing. A recycling business might be interested in social marketing to promote behavior change toward waste separation. Alcoholic beverage companies may market responsible consumption with marketing slogans such as "don't drink and drive."

Social marketing uses mainstream marketing tools, including the "four Ps" of marketing, to plan, conduct, and evaluate campaigns. Social marketing is often characterized as an awareness campaign, a perception that hinders the tool's full

Table 14.2: Stages of behavior change

Stage	Description	Marketing strategies	Exemplary message to facilitate change
1. Pre-contemplation	Denial or missing information about necessity for change	Inform and convince individuals about necessity to change	"The UN's Food and Agriculture Organization has estimated that meat production accounts for nearly a fifth of global greenhouse gas emissions. These are generated during the production of animal feeds, for example, while ruminants, particularly cows, emit methane, which is 23 times more effective as a global warming agent than carbon dioxide" (Jowit, 2008)
2. Contemplation	Considering change by weighing costs and benefits of change	Inform about the actions necessary for change and the full costs and benefits	"(…) health benefits of eating less meat. The average person in the U.K. eats 50 g of protein from meat a day, equivalent to a chicken breast or a lamb chop—a relatively low level for rich nations but 25–50% more than World Health Organization guidelines" (Jowit, 2008)
3. Preparation	Preparing a serious adoption of change by experimenting with small changes	Provide information and support for first experiences of success	"Give up meat for one day [a week] initially, and decrease it from there" (Jowit, 2008)
4. Adoption	Adoption of new behavior	Provide guidance on how to conduct the new behavior in all situations of life	"Going vegetarian has never been easier, and we have thousands of delicious recipes that are searchable by meal category and type of cuisine to help you get started. The following are some of our favorites: Breakfast and Brunch; Lunch; Dinner" (PETA, 2016b)
5. Maintenance	Maintaining new behaviors	Help to make the new behavior crisis-proven	"When going out to eat with family or friends, discuss ahead of time where you are going. Look up vegetarian-friendly restaurants in your area, and suggest some options. Calling a restaurant before you go is a great way to find out if the restaurant has good vegetarian options (or is willing to make them)" (PETA, 2016a)

potential as creating awareness is only the first of five steps of achieving and sustaining new behaviors (DiClemente and Prochaska, 1998). Companies must first assess the correct stage of behavior change for the target audience and then design social marketing campaigns based on this initial assessment. Table 14.2 summarizes the five stages of behavior change, typical stakeholder statements per stage, and a brief description of characteristics of marketing campaigns based on the respective stage.

A textbook example of social marketing

The animal protection NGO, PETA, offers advice on how to become a vegetarian. Its website (http://www.peta.org) follows the five steps of behavior change, starting with creating awareness (pre-contemplation), through a "Making the Transition" section (preparation), and tips to how not to quit the vegetarian lifestyle while traveling (maintenance).

Responsible business education aims to create responsible management competences among company stakeholders. Competences are usually developed among employees and can be classified into the three categories of attitudes, skills, and knowledge. Competences required for responsible business vary widely depending on the structure of a company's human capital, the company's approach to responsible business, and external factors such as the industry and the company's location of operations. Table 14.3 provides examples of each competence type and delivers insight into the educational means available to build these competences. Educational designs for responsible business education might be based externally or internally within company training and may involve formats such as mentoring, on-the-job training, computer-based training, single workshops, continuous programs, and even complete external degree programs, such as a master's degree program in responsible management.

Table 14.3: Competences for responsible business

Competence type	Exemplary competences	Educational means
Attitudes and values	Honesty, responsibility, environmental and social sensitivity, etc.	Moral dilemma training, social and environmental immersion, discussion and imaginative exercises, feedback circles, etc.
Skills	Stakeholder engagement skills, systemic thinking, change skills, etc.	Coaching, simulations, on-the-job training, etc.
Knowledge	Cross-functional knowledge, responsible management tools, etc.	Classroom education, e-learning-based programs, etc.

Additional communication tools used in implementing responsible business are business vision, mission, and value statements, or "light tower documents." These tools provide broad guidance and help with lobbying political stakeholders. Traditionally, designing communication and using examples has not been considered a communication instrument, but it is crucially important to design messages when conveying the seriousness of commitment to responsibility management.

Communication to share responsible business performance

Imagine a company that has completed considerable work toward becoming a responsible business. Let's assume it is at the forefront of responsible business in its market, its industry, and its region. The main communication task now is to cash in on the work done, as stakeholders are likely to reward responsible business with tangible benefits. To grasp the potential of such benefits, one only needs to scrutinize how the three most important stakeholder groups in companies' perceptions—consumers, employees, and owners—may reward responsible businesses (Lacey et al., 2010). Consumers may buy more products or services and pay higher prices. Employees might be attracted to work with a responsible business and become motivated to be more productive while working for the business. Shareholders may consider a responsible business an attractive investment for manifold reasons, including higher profit potential and lower investment risk. All three groups are likely to develop higher loyalty to the business because of the stronger perception of dealing with a "good business" (Bhattacharya and Sen, 2010; Du et al., 2007). The main tasks of the communication phase are to let stakeholders know about performance and to create goodwill. The goal of communication at this stage is "maximizing the returns" on responsible business (Bhattacharya and Sen, 2010, p. 8). In this section we will describe three main tools proven to be highly effective in sharing the word about responsible business:

1. **Cause-related marketing** connects product sales with a good cause and with the goal of achieving a higher percentage of a company's consumers

2. **Certification and labeling** signal compliance with external standards

3. **Reporting** provides extensive information to a broader set of stakeholders about social, environmental, and economic business performance and other activities

The first tool, cause-related marketing (CRM), connects the sales of a product to a good cause by associating the implementation of a responsible business activity (the donation) with spreading the word about the responsible business. Traditionally, CRM works by donating a certain percentage of sales revenue to a civil society organization, which further channels the money to the cause. The credit card business American Express is said to be the inventor of CRM in the early 1980s, when it donated money toward the renovation of the Statue of Liberty with every credit card issued and every payment made (Atkins, 1999). Today, different forms of CRM have been implemented in various ways, The most important ones are described in Table 14.4. In business, CRM is often perceived as an attractive

Table 14.4: Types of cause-related marketing

Type	Description	Example
Classic	A fraction of the sales revenue of a certain product is channeled to a civil society organization (CSO) that supports a good cause	As the pioneering classic cause-related marketing campaign, American Express still conducts cause-related marketing campaigns by donating lump sums for new credit cards issued and percentages for card usage to the World Monuments Fund and the National Trust for Historic Preservation (American Express, 2012).
In-kind donation	Based on the quantity of a products sold, a certain quantity of in-kind donation is realized	Following the one-for-one (buy one, donate one) movement, the toothbrush company Smile Squared donates a toothbrush for every one bought and even provides a "zero for two" option, where people buy both brushes to donate both.
Total process management	The company conducting the cause-related marketing campaign also manages the follow-up process of channeling the donation to the beneficiary instead of outsourcing it to a CSO	The Mexican movie theater chain Cinépolis manages every activity of their "Love Gives Birth to Eyesight" campaign, from fundraising to the cataract eye surgery, including fundraising and the collaboration with doctors, beneficiaries, and volunteers (Laasch and Conaway, 2011).
Cause-related branding	Instead of selling a specific product through a cause, cause-related branding connects a whole product line or brand to the cause	The Mexican pharmacy chain Farmacias del Ahorro [The Savings Pharmacy], through its corporate foundation, employs doctors in a small doctors' office next door to its branches. Doctors provide for-free medical consultations. The cause covered is health promotion and has a direct sales-increasing effect for the majority of products sold by the company (Farmacias del Ahorro, 2013).
Rotating causes	Causes rotate in a fixed period of time, while the general possibility of donating remains a constant offer	The restaurant chain TOCKS runs a "12 Months, 12 Causes" campaign, changing causes every month of the year.
Multi-company cause brands	The same cause is becomes a label that can be used by several companies	Product RED (cause = Aids) provides a branding opportunity that has been harnessed for cause-related marketing campaigns by many companies from Apple to Nike.

Type	Description	Example
Special cause editions	Companies offer a special edition of their product, which often has a visual connection with the cause	The Pink Ribbon International (cause = breast cancer) organization has teamed up with many companies such as Fiat, which issued a special edition of its 500 model, with a dark pink stripe and small ribbon as design feature. Every car sold generated a US$1,000 donation to breast cancer research (Tokic, 2011).
Virtual product	Companies provide a "decoy product," usually not bought, to raise awareness for a classic donation campaign	The Texas-based food chain Chili's invited customers to buy a coloring-book style Chili's logo for a minimum of US$1, 100% of which went to sponsoring medical research (Alden Keene, 2007).
Product as cause	There are products that further a cause just by being bought and used and do not involve an additional donation	The U.S. company Whole Foods Market has a complete product line branded as "locally grown." The consumption of these products achieves a number of positive effects such as biodiversity protection and reduction of CO_2 emissions (Whole Foods Market, 2016).

tool because of its direct and tangible financial benefits from increased product sales and ease of implementation. For the same reason, some stakeholders criticize CRM as being unconnected to the core activity of a business and as being purely profit-motivated. Chapter 15 provides further guidance on how to address such criticism.

To address these criticisms, certification and labeling provide a signal for stakeholders who search for easy-to-grasp information, and communicate compliance with responsible business principles. Labels are visual symbols placed on products or in company facilities, signaling compliance with a certification process, membership in a responsible business network, or support of a certain cause. Some labels such as the Latin American ESR label (Empresa Socialmente Responsible, Spanish for "socially responsible enterprise") cover the overall activity of a business, while others, such as the Great Place to Work or the Forest Stewardship Council (FSC) labels, focus on smaller sub-sections of the company and specific causes. Labels find wide use and come in a potentially confusing variety. Chapter 7 provides a good overview and more extensive description of some of the most common labels used.

While labeling aims to communicate with minimum depth of information, reporting has the different purpose of providing extensive, detailed, and highest-quality information for sophisticated stakeholders, who are keenly interested in the detail of a business's responsible management activities. The best-known reporting standard is the Global Reporting Initiative (GRI), which was illustrated in Chapters 6 and 7. Reports are not necessarily aimed at an external public or required to cover a company's overall activity: internal management reports and reports of individual responsible management activities are less frequent forms

"What is the message?"

This might be the question of someone who stumbled on the page on Google's website that extensively disclosed the search engine's energy usage. The intended message may have been: "We make the planet a little greener" (Google purports to have one of the best energy-efficient technical infrastructures). However, many stakeholders might have taken away a different message. To hear that the company's data center "only" used as much energy as 200,000 households (260 MW) might have been surprising to many. Google's senior vice president for technical infrastructure, Urs Hoelzle, offers the defense that a Google search uses less CO_2 than driving to the library to retrieve the same information there (Glanz, 2011; Google, 2011). Would we actually go to the library for the information we google? The lesson: if you want to spread a message, be concise about what you want to say and anticipate the reaction of your audience.

of reporting, but can be valuable communication instruments. Recent trends in reporting include annual reports that integrate economic, environmental, and social business activities and performance, and providing extensive information online.

Additional tools that are popular for sharing the message on responsible business are press releases, classical public relations work, advertising, web-based communication, external and internal newsletters, and testimonials. Issues and crisis communication is another, more specialized, tool that communicates topics related to difficult issues in times of crisis. Whereas the tools mentioned previously focus on sharing messages about a company's positive performance, issues and crisis communication carries negative messages that are critical of socio-environmental performance.

Communication to control responsible business

When the responsible business message has been shared, it is crucially important to receive and respond to feedback. Has the message been understood as intended? Does the responsible business meet stakeholder expectations? Do all parts of a business comply with the goals and standards set? The tool of stakeholder dialog, utilized when preparing for responsible business activities, is very fitting also for the response and control purpose.

Hotlines and ombudsmen provide institutional structures for feedback on specific issues, such as product quality for customers, and labor practices for employees. Employee hotlines facilitate the so-called whistle-blowing process, in which employees report misconduct related to any kind of social, environmental, or ethical issue from sexual harassment to corruption. Centrally important to good practices for establishing effective whistle-blowing mechanisms are personal protection mechanisms and institutional reactions mitigating criticisms.

Social network platforms such as Facebook and YouTube allow for group-based and dynamic opinion-building processes.

An external review of responsible business activities by trustworthy organizations and individuals fulfills a double purpose. On the one hand, such an external review may be used to enhance credibility throughout all other stages of the responsible business communication process. On the other hand, external opinions serve as valuable input to review and control responsible business according to the original vision of the business. Endorsement and assurance statements can both fulfill these functions, but each is different during the implementation and review process. The assurance process is a highly structured, standardized review of a company's responsible business activity by an external third party, and is used to identify the quality of reports. Endorsements typically are less rigorous in the review process and apply to the company's activity as a whole, and can also can apply to single departments or programs, or single documents such as a report. Endorsement contents are a short introduction by the endorser, information on the points reviewed, and a personal statement by the endorser. An endorsement by a person involved in a specific responsible business activity in practice is called a testimonial. Testimonials provide feedback on the experience of the person involved, which may help to continuously improve the process.

Exercises

A. Know

Use the multiple choice questions below to test your knowledge. Each answer may be wrong or right and there may be zero to four right or wrong answers per question:

1. Communicating with stakeholders ...

   a.   ... is a task of low complexity as most stakeholders are very alike when being communicated to.

   b.   ... can be based on an interest of the company to communicate with the stakeholder or of the stakeholder to communicate with the company.

   c.   ... might make it necessary to conduct a survey of stakeholders' access to different communication channels.

   d.   ... must pay attention to potential communication barriers, which impede the stakeholder communication process. A barrier might, for instance, be that the company has not established a feedback channel for stakeholders to respond to the company.

2. Responsible business communication tools ...

   a.   ... are diverse. In order to understand each, it is important to know first, the process involved in using the tool, second, the purpose and desired outcome of the tool, and third, the primary stakeholders to whom the tool is aimed.

   b.   ... include frameworks as diverse as lobbying, reporting, certifications, and labels.

   c.   ... should each be used alone. It does not make sense to combine these tools, as they are too diverse.

   d.   ... are each unique in terms of the primary stakeholder group to which they apply. For instance, lobbying is primarily applied to customer and employee stakeholders, while hotlines and whistle-blowing mechanisms primarily apply to governmental stakeholders.

3. Integrated communication ...

   a.   ... refers to integrating external and internal communication channels.

   b.   ... aims to better separate the communication to internal and external stakeholders.

   c.   ... aims to communicate a consistent message throughout all communication tools.

   d.   ... requires that each communicating department, such as public relations, marketing, and human resources management, communicate their own message separately.

4. Communication purposes in responsible business ...
   a. ... can be divided into two basic tasks. First, communication to increase sales, and second, communication to increase brand value.
   b. ... during the "define" task, include as the main goal to convince stakeholders about how "good" the company is in its responsible business activities and performance.
   c. ... during the "implementation" task, include as one of the main goals to achieve stakeholder contribution to responsible business activities.
   d. ... during the "control" task, include as the main goal to convince stakeholders about responsible business performance.

5. Communication to implement ...
   a. ... may involve social marketing, the main tool for selling green products to customers.
   b. ... typically involves hotlines as a central communication tool.
   c. ... may involve both social marketing and responsible business education. The difference is that social marketing aims at behavior change, while responsible business education aims to create competences for responsible business.
   d. ... responsible business education can aim to transmit a wide variety of different competences required for responsible business implementation by employees. An example might be the skills to manage a new recycling machine in a bottling plant.

6. Communication to control ...
   a. ... exclusively aims to ensure that stakeholders really do translate their good image of the company into tangible benefits.
   b. ... can involve feedback mechanisms, such as an ombudsman or an ethics hotline.
   c. ... can involve a whistle-blowing mechanism (helps stakeholders to give positive feedback on companies' excellent activities) and testimonials (stakeholders "testifying" about what the company is doing wrong).
   d. ... may involve assurance and endorsements, both of which involve external evaluations of the company's responsible business performance.

B. Think

Pick one company of your choice. Imagine you are in charge of developing a company slogan that captures what the company is, or wants to become, to its four main stakeholders.

C. Do

Identify one label or certification related to responsible business (e.g., Blauer Engel in Germany, ESR in Mexico, or the international Great Place to Work) and familiarize yourself with the criteria and steps to be taken for a company/product to be certified or labeled. Draft an action plan of the steps to be taken to achieve that goal.

D. Relate

Identify one company whose (ir)responsible business practices you consider questionable. Search for the company's social media presence and write a short message to the company, explaining convincingly why you do not approve of what they do/did.

E. Be

Think about one of your strongly held personal beliefs. How could you express this belief in one sentence? What do you think this sentence means to four of your personal stakeholders? How would they react to you saying this sentence to them? What would they think? How would they reply?

Feedback

A. Know

Question 1

a. Wrong: each stakeholder is provided with a unique set of attitudes, interests, values, and communication needs, which makes stakeholder communication a highly complex task.

b. Right: stakeholder communication is based on open bidirectional communication.

c. Right: access to different communication channels is a stakeholder characteristic, an important consideration for successful stakeholder communication.

d. Right: there are a number of communication barriers that might impede effective stakeholder communication.

Question 2

a. Right: the diversity of stakeholder communication tools makes appreciating their different characteristics crucial for their effective use.

b. Right: all the frameworks mentioned are tools for stakeholder communication.

c. Wrong: responsible business communication tools are frequently combined. A prominent example is sustainability reports, which are offered with interactive online navigation.

d. Wrong: the stakeholder groups mentioned are the wrong way round. Lobbying primarily applies to governmental actors and whistle-blowing to employees.

Question 3

a. Right: the integration of external and internal communication channels is the main characteristic of integrated communication.

b. Wrong: internal and external stakeholder communication cannot be separated. The goal is rather to send a consistent message that works as much for internal as it does for external stakeholders.

c. Right: shaping a consistent/integrated overall message is a main characteristic of integrated stakeholder communication.

d. Wrong: integrated stakeholder communication requires coordinating the messages of these departments in order to send a joint message.

Question 4

a. Wrong: increase in sales and brand value might both be motivations to communicate in responsible business. Nevertheless, in this chapter, we divided the communication purposes into four motivations (defining responsible business, implementation, sharing, control).

b.   Wrong: such behavior would endanger the "define" task's main goal of defining what the responsible business should be.

c.   Right: active contribution of stakeholders is a crucial input to the "implementation" task.

d.   Wrong: such behavior would conflict with the "control" task's main goal of checking on the communication outcomes.

Question 5

a.   Wrong: social marketing during the "implementation stage" supports necessary behavior changes among stakeholders in general. There might be behavior changes that might support sales, but this is not the main function of social marketing.

b.   Wrong: hotlines are typically applied as part of the communication "control" task.

c.   Right: social marketing focuses on behavior change, while education aims to create competences for responsible management.

d.   Right: skills such as that mentioned are part of the competences to be created for responsible management.

Question 6

a.   Wrong: the goal of the control task is much broader and involves checking the effectiveness of the communication process and ensuring congruence between communication and implementation of responsible business.

b.   Right: ombudsmen and ethics hotlines help to control as they provide feedback on where responsible management might have gone wrong.

c.   Wrong: the descriptions of both whistle-blowing and testimonials are incorrect.

d.   Right: assurance and endorsements are distinct external evaluation mechanisms.

B. Think

Level	Reconciling diverging perspectives	Notes
+	Slogan is directed at four main stakeholders and elegantly integrates their perspectives	
=	Slogan only integrates some of the four stakeholder relationships	
–	No slogan was established, or the main stakeholders were not identified	

C. Do

Level	Complying with standards	Notes
+	Feasible action plan, including areas to be improved before labeling has been established, based on a solid understanding of the criteria of the standard	
=	Criteria have been understood, but no feasible, or only a superficial, action plan has been established	
–	Label/certification standard has not been identified	

D. Relate

Level	Expression of difference	Notes
+	Clear argument convincingly and consistently expressing the critical position regarding the company practice(s)	
=	Argument has been made, but leaves room for improvement in terms of argument structure, tone, or similar aspects	
–	Company and/or their social media outlet have not been identified	

E. Be

Level	External orientation	Notes
+	Belief clearly captured in sentence and an in-depth appreciation of stakeholder reactions	
=	Belief expressed in sentence and basic appreciation of main stakeholders' reactions	
–	Major difficulties in describing belief, in translating it into a sentence, or in identifying personal stakeholders	

15
Communication challenges

Stakeholders' low awareness of and unfavorable attributions towards companies' CSR activities remain critical impediments (...) highlighting a need for companies to communicate CSR more effectively to stakeholders.

(Bhattacharya and Sen, 2010, p. 8)

Why are there cases where companies use a broad set of communication channels extensively and reach all important stakeholder groups, but still cannot create goodwill among them? One reason why the company cannot communicate credibly may be that it is not doing a good job being a responsible business. In this case the task is not to communicate better, but to review and improve actual responsible business performance. A second reason may be that there is nothing wrong with the responsible business conduct, but the communication is flawed (Bhattacharya and Sen, 2010; Du *et al.*, 2007). While Chapter 14 illustrated powerful communication tools, this chapter is aimed at enhancing the credibility of messages and addresses those stakeholder attitudes that might impede the creation of trust and goodwill.

Dealing with critical attitudes

Critical attitudes come in many forms and occur in many different types of stakeholder. Criticism in most cases does not come from the stereotypical, aggressive NGO or the activist consumer advocate group trying to harm the company. Table 15.1 describes commonly occurring negative attributions and communication strategies in each situation. First, the company must take all types of criticism

---

Dear Company, who are you really?

If the communication formats illustrated throughout Chapter 14 are not skillfully applied, they lead to many conflicting messages and impressions about a company. Stakeholders may get easily confused about how responsible a company is in reality. Are you one of these stakeholders? If so, you might fall into two negative, but typical, habits. You either believe companies are basically good or basically bad, without being able to justify such a bipolar stance. Each extreme is equally dangerous. To avoid these pitfalls, a good starting point for stakeholders is to start with a company's Global Reporting Initiative report, which provides the most complete, extensive, and well-rated information, and then to cross-check this report with other communication channels. If any final doubts still exist about a specific practice, send an email with a direct question to the company—most businesses are surprisingly diligent in answering such personalized requests.

---

seriously and see if there is factual necessity to change the point being criticized. If a factual necessity does not exist or after a change is made, the communication task becomes one of transforming negative attributions to positive ones.

There are many frameworks for achieving effective communication, but what follows is a simple but effective checklist. To avoid negative attributions and criticism, companies should always communicate responsible business in four categories—input, output, motives, and fit (Bhattacharya and Sen, 2010):

- Communicating both input and output, including the long-term results of responsible business conduct provides a factually substantiated complete picture and answers the questions "What does the business do?" and "What has the business achieved?" This type of communication helps to erase doubts about the real effort of the company and the impact and effectiveness of activities, all of which might lead to unfavorable stakeholder attitudes if left unattended.

- Communicating motives and fit answers stakeholder doubts about the company and its relationship to the respective responsible business communication. The question of fit between responsible business activities and the company's core business must be answered: it is intuitively reasonable that car companies reduce product emissions and paper companies use recycled paper; it is less understandable why an educational institution is involved in reforestation. Stakeholders need to know the motives leading to responsible business activities in order to understand the company's intentions.

Table 15.1: Negative attributions to responsible business conduct

Object of skepticism	Question posed	Communication strategy
Sincerity	Do they really mean it?	Communicate motivation of responsible business activities
Impact	Are they really making a difference?	Focus on communicating results of responsible business activity
Fittingness	What does it have to do with their core business?	Communicate relationship between responsible business activity and core business
Egoism	Are they only doing it for the money?	Communicate openly if the main motivation is or is not the money
Incongruence activity: company "character"	How is it consistent with their history and reputation?	Communicate either how responsible business is in line with the company's established "character" or how the character of the company will change to fit the responsible business activity
Incongruence between company and stakeholder	Is the company in line with my values and ideology?	Communicate communalities between stakeholder and company characteristics
Cause justification	Shouldn't they spend their money on more important things?	Communicate how the cause addressed is most important for the company, for stakeholders, and for society in general by comparing it to other causes that might be perceived as more important
Efficiency	Are they wasting money?	Communicate transparently about the usage of money and the results achieved by spending it
Cause quality	Is that a good cause?	Explain why the cause chosen should be addressed and what results can be achieved by addressing the cause
Capitalism and corporations	I am against whatever they do!	Educate to clarify prejudices and to show how responsible business conduct is having positive impacts independently from whatever system it is conducted in

Communicating about ... bloody chocolate

How about this: you bite into your favorite chocolate bar and blood splashes out! A horrifying idea! This was the plot of a Greenpeace video that went viral. It was aimed at preventing Nestlé from buying palm oil (one of the ingredients of the famous Kit Kat brand) from companies that destroyed the orangutan's habitat. Especially painful for the company was that the Greenpeace video resembled a popular TV advert and the long-established slogan, "Have a break, have a Kit Kat" (Greenpeace UK, 2012). The damage to the company and its brand is hard to estimate, but is likely to be considerable.

Greenwashing

Although "decoupling" is the academic term used to describe when an organization disconnects (decouples) its communication from its real activities, such as those mentioned in Table 15.1, the more common term used by stakeholders is "greenwashing." A play on the word "whitewash", this refers to a message that overstates the true environmental performance of a product, an initiative, a person, or a whole company.

However, the focus that "greenwashing" places on purely environmental performance can give a misleading impression: for instance, a company misrepresenting its *social* performance would not be called greenwashing. A responsible business must therefore not focus solely on avoiding greenwashing, but balance its communication efforts with actual performance or impact in all areas of activity.

As well as greenwashing, a number of other terms fall under the general umbrella of "decoupling":

- **Bluewashing, pinkwashing, and ethics-washing:** these are all variants of "greenwashing", used to refer to creating a misleading impression in other specific areas of activity. "Bluewashing" refers to the blue flag of the UN (companies that are irresponsible in spite of being part of the UN Global Compact), "pinkwashing" to using the pink color attributed to the breast cancer movement, and "ethics-washing" to companies pretending to be more ethical than they really are.
- **Green noise and green fatigue:** green noise describes the overwhelming and confusing amount of often contradictory or unclear messages related to environmental and social topics. A direct result is green fatigue, a stakeholder's state of exhaustion concerning these topics.
- **Astroturf:** alluding to the artificial grass found on sports fields, this refers to an activist movement that pretends to be grass-roots, but in reality is not.

How to avoid being accused of greenwashing and other decoupling? A very basic prerequisite to enable stakeholders to evaluate the congruence between

Figure 15.1: Stakeholder perceptions and subsequent outcomes

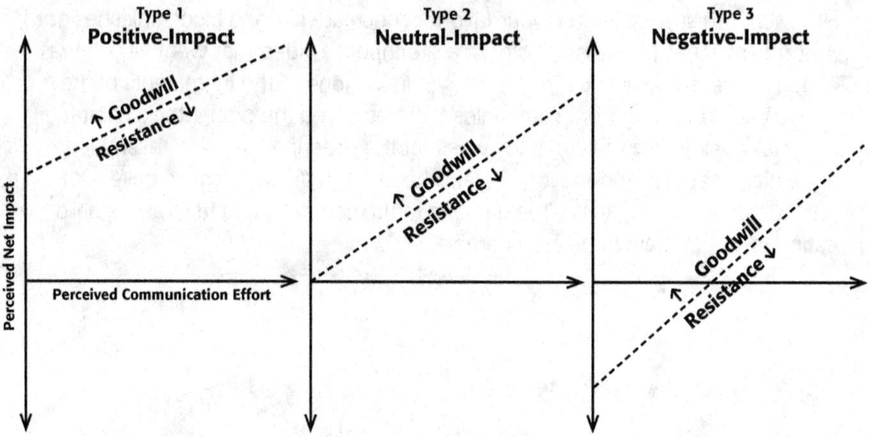

communication claim and actual responsible business performance is to communicate input and output transparently as proposed in the preceding section. This
way, the consumer can factually compare "walk" and "talk." Figure 15.1 shows
how companies should substantiate their communicative efforts by performance.

In each of the three scenarios, the "greenwash-risky" appears below the line
representing the perceived communication effort, and shows that stakeholders do
not apply the same criteria for greenwashing accusations to all organizations. For
instance, an organization known for its negative impact will require substantial
improvements in its socio-environmental performance before stakeholders will
perceive their messages as justified. At the opposite extreme, organizations that
are perceived to have a very positive impact, such as social enterprises, can be
much more daring in communicating responsible business without risking claims
of greenwashing.

Here is a checklist of typical communication errors that may lead to greenwashing accusations, compiled from a number of reports on greenwashing
(Horiuchi *et al.*, 2009; Terrachoice, 2007; Futerra, 2008):

- Lying. i.e., reporting factually untrue claims, such as "carbon-neutral" or
  "certified as great place to work," if these "facts" do not reflect reality.

- Giving unsubstantiated messages with no proof for claims about performance, such as claiming to be 100% environmental friendly without
  explaining what "environmental friendly" means or stating how to calculate
  this percentage, or claiming to be "the greenest in class" without explaining
  how this market leadership position can be justified.

- Communicating misleading associations by imagery, labels, and logos—
  such as trees, dolphins, happy children, and the color green—that are not
  backed up by performance.

- Participating in a hidden trade-off, such as actions that look responsible but have hidden side effects, e.g., energy-saving light bulbs that come with toxic mercury or fair-trade products that are less energy efficient than their non-fair-trade counterparts.
- Communicating "confusing 'less bad' with 'good'" messages, which happens when communicating incremental improvements with bad outcomes as a solution, such as organic cigarettes, "safe" weapons, or oil companies focusing on marginal efforts in renewable energies.
- Stating true but irrelevant claims that sound nice, but which in reality do not make any difference in terms of social and environmental performance, such as biodegradable tobacco (usually tobacco is smoked before it ends up in any landfill) or recyclable yogurt cartons in a country where household waste is neither separated nor recycled.

The Greenpeace greenwashing champion

In the early 2000s the petroleum business British Petroleum (BP) started a multimillion dollar public relations campaign to show how "green" the company supposedly was. In 2008 BP made 93% of its investment in oil, but merely 2.79% in bio-fuel and 1.39% in solar initiatives. The slogan "beyond" petroleum did not match the numbers and was therefore perceived as greenwashing. Additionally, the company's flowerlike logo and the catch phrases "from the earth to the sun and everything in between" and "the best way out of the energy fix is an energy mix" encountered strong critical reactions. In 2009 Greenpeace activists tried to award BP CEO Tony Hayward with a greenwashing award (a green paintbrush) for the company's overall campaign, which the company declined to accept (Walker, 2010).

Exercises

A. Know

Use the multiple choice questions below to test your knowledge. Each answer may be wrong or right and there may be zero to four right or wrong answers per question:

1. Critical attitudes ...

   a.   ... might lead to a situation where a company communicates its responsible business message well, but stakeholders still do not make a positive attribution to the business.

   b.   ... might for instance exist in employees who just cannot "believe" the company's external philanthropic attitude as they feel badly treated in their workplace.

   c.   ... might be avoided if a company communicates both inputs and outputs of responsible business conduct, thereby providing a factually substantiated and complete picture.

   d.   ... might be avoided if a company communicates both the motivation to be involved in responsible business and how the activities fit the company's core business.

2. Greenwashing ...

   a.   ... refers to offering "green products."

   b.   ... criteria for accusations are equally applied by stakeholders to all organizations.

   c.   ... should be avoided by increasing the quantity of communication.

   d.   ... can occur due to communication errors, such as lying, not communicating hidden trade-offs, and communicating that something is good for the environment or society, while it is just less harmful than other alternatives.

3. Bluewashing ...

   a.   ... refers to the misuse of a United Nations association.

   b.   ... is a form of greenwashing.

   c.   ... is a synonym for green noise.

   d.   ... is the opposite of greenwashing.

B. Think

Go to your local supermarket and identify three products you believe could be accused of greenwashing. Test your suspicion by locating more detailed information on the product and comparing your findings to the description of different types of greenwashing or possibly by communicating with the company.

C. Do

Write a brief text on a typical thinking and behavior pattern you think leads to greenwashing. Then provide a shopping list of three points someone in marketing and communication might adhere to in order to avoid falling into the green-washing trap.

D. Relate

Think about one product that you consider to be a clear example of greenwashing. Design an alternative communication strategy for the product that avoids green-washing and send it to the company. Be prepared to discuss your idea if they should answer back to you.

E. Be

Greenwashing is about "walking the talk." This is very similar to one aspect of personal integrity, where what we say should reflect our values, and what we do should reflect both values and our statements. Which of the following statements best reflects you? Briefly mention an example from your own life where you see the statement reflected:

  a. I have no difficulty communicating my values and most of the time I act on them
  b. Most of the time I feel I cannot translate my values into words or actions
  c. Generally I can clearly articulate my values, but often find it difficult to act on them

$$\overline{\qquad\qquad}$$

Feedback

A. Know

Question 1

a. Right: the attribution of responsible business to a company's communication also depends on the context, such as a preconceived negative attitude toward the company rather than only on the communication itself.

b. Right: this is a classic misleading imbalance between walk and talk.

c. Right: in this case the company would communicate a factually true picture reflecting the business reality. However, this truthfulness might not always be enough to avoid greenwashing accusations.

d. Right: communicating motivation and fit are good practices for avoiding greenwashing accusations.

Question 2

a. Wrong: offering "green products" is only greenwashing if the products are not as ecologically viable as their marketing and communication suggests.

b. Wrong: how sensitive stakeholders are to perceiving a company as greenwashing depends on stakeholders' often biased perception of the company's overall social and environmental performance, and the general attitude toward the business.

c. Wrong: even increasing the amount of communication, while not improving responsible business activities, will lead to stakeholders' perception of even stronger greenwashing.

d. Right: all of the communication errors mentioned are typically considered to be greenwashing.

Question 3

a. Right: "bluewashing" typically refers to a company that behaves irresponsibly in spite of being a member of the United Nations Global Compact initiative.

b. Right: bluewashing also falls under the definition of greenwashing as incongruence between responsible business reality and communication activity.

c. Wrong: "green noise" refers to the overwhelming and often confusing amount of messages related to environmental and social topics.

d. Wrong: it is a form of greenwashing specifically referring to the misleading perception created by a company that communicates its Global Compact membership, but that does not adhere to the ten Global Compact principles.

B. Think

Level	Critical discernment	Notes
+	Greenwashing suspicions have been refuted or corroborated, based on a sound investigation	
=	Greenwashing candidates have been identified based on concrete evidence and understanding of the characteristics of greenwashing	
−	No or weak identification of greenwashing candidates	

C. Do

Level	Breaking action patterns	Notes
+	Very feasible and pragmatic plan to break patterns leading to greenwashing behavior	
=	You are on to something: patterns have been identified, but the list does not seem effective in getting to the root of the behavior	
−	Thinking and behavior pattern could not be identified	

D. Relate

Level	Giving advice	Notes
+	Feasible alternative strategy has been communicated to the company; possibly, a dialogue has even been established	
=	Convincing non-greenwashing communication strategy has been designed and constitutes a feasible alternative	
−	No non-greenwashing communication strategy has been designed	

E. Be

Level	Personal integrity	Notes
+	I have no difficulty communicating my values and most of the time I act on them	
=	I can generally clearly articulate my values, but often find it difficult to act on them	
−	Most of the time I feel I cannot translate my values into words or actions	

G.
INNOVATING

16
Innovation for change

Smart companies now treat sustainability as innovation's new frontier.

(Nidumolu *et al.*, 2009, p. 60)

Thus far the chapters of this book have been aimed at providing a map of the known territory of responsible business and management. However, the magnitude of the social, environmental, and ethical challenges faced by businesses and humanity calls for solutions beyond what we know—off the map and out of the box. For tackling these challenges, "business as usual" and carrying on doing things as they have always been done will not create the necessary change. Or, as Albert Einstein famously stated, "We can't solve problems by using the same kind of thinking we used when we created them." Innovation is often used as a buzzword to describe ideas that lead to change.

Innovation describes "the successful exploitation of new ideas" (DTI, 2003, p. 8). Examining the idea of innovation more closely we find that there are two main elements to it: novelty (new ideas) and use (exploitation). Accordingly, a brilliant novel idea is no innovation if it is not used. Innovation begins with, but goes far beyond, the creativity which helps to generate ideas. However, there is a very practical component of putting these ideas to use, which constitutes innovation. Corporate sustainability, responsibility, and ethics represent immense opportunities for companies and managers to be innovative, with all of the potential advantages that go with it, such as access to new markets, cost savings, or competitive advantage (Nidumolu *et al.*, 2009). It has even been suggested that we are at the beginning of a wave of innovation with sustainability at its heart, a so-called "sixth wave of innovation" following previous waves including steam power, electricity, and information technology (see Figure 16.1), which for businesses appears to constitute as much of a game-changing megatrend as

Figure 16.1: The sixth wave of innovation

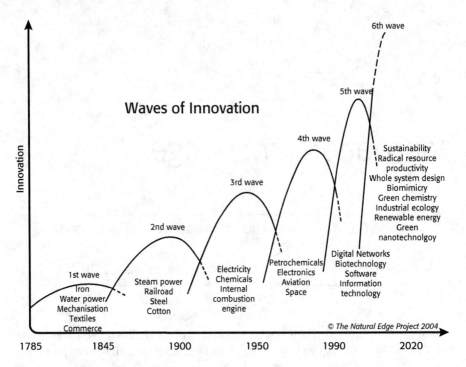

Source: Hargroves and Smith, 2005.

mass production and electrification before it (Lubin and Esty, 2010). However, this time of dramatic innovation does not necessarily only provide opportunities for businesses. It also may lead to the demise of those companies, possibly even whole industries, that cannot adopt to a swiftly changing business environment. A sustainable world might not be a place for unsustainable dinosaurs and this might lead to the "creative destruction of industries" or even to "corporate suicide" (Hart and Milstein, 1999; Kelso and Hetter, 1973).

In the context of innovation for sustainable development and corporate social responsibility, it is particularly important to distinguish divergent approaches to innovation and the related discussions:

- **Solow (restraint) versus Malthus (technology):** one ongoing discussion surrounds the different approaches to coping with environmental resource scarcity as the root cause of the current unsustainable situation (Martin and Kemper, 2012). On the one hand, the theories of Abraham Maslow (see Chapter 2) call for restraint in resource consumption and a curbing of population growth—a call for a strategy of austerity. Solow, on the other hand, advances the view that any resource can be replaced by some new technology and no resource is irreplaceable.

- **Disruptive versus incremental innovation:** a related, but different discussion lies in the distinction between incremental and disruptive innovation. Incremental innovation for resource consumption would, for instance, innovate to make existing "things" better—a good example is more eco-efficient production methods. Disruptive innovation, on the other hand, would lead to things radically different than what they used to be and replacing old things with new things (Christensen, 2013; Christensen *et al.*, 2006).

What is your innovation strategy? What do you think is the most promising strategy for achieving business sustainability, and ultimately global sustainable development? What are the arguments for and against the austerity and technology strategies? Do you think we need disruptive or incremental innovation?

This chapter features content related to both discussions, about restraint versus technology fix, and incremental versus disruptive innovation. The purpose of this chapter is to provide a mental map of the innovation concepts related to the areas of responsible business for sustainable development. As outlined in Figure 16.2, we will first provide an overview of "the things" to be innovated, the objects of innovation, then introduce different innovation frameworks aimed at distinct purposes, such as social innovation, or innovation for sustainability. We will then

Figure 16.2: Concepts of innovation covered in this chapter

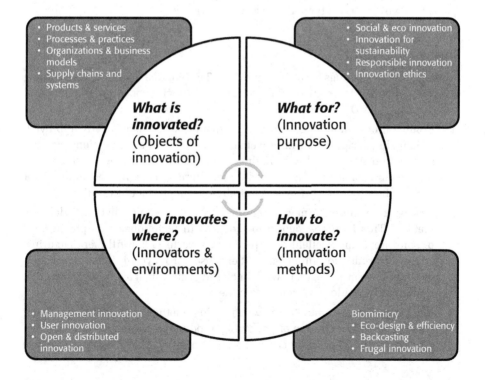

introduce innovation methods, such as frugal innovation or biomimicry, especially tailored for business responsibility for sustainable development. Finally, we will look frameworks that help us to better understand who innovates in what environment, such as management innovation or open innovation.

Objects and purposes of innovation

From our definition of innovation above we have learned that it is about both new ideas and their exploitation. In the context of responsible business, what kinds of idea are these, and what is their exploitation? We have to ask ourselves: "Innovating what and what for?" These two fundamental questions gain special importance in innovation for sustainability, responsibility, and ethics. All three topics have a strong normative orientation, as they are based on ideas of what *ought to* happen and be: we ought to ensure the survival of humanity on Planet Earth (sustainability); we ought to be responsible toward our stakeholders (responsibility); we ought to make sure we do the right thing and abstain from doing wrong (ethics). As you will discover, innovation approaches, such as innovation for sustainability or responsible innovation, are built on the purpose of fulfilling these oughts. In order to do so, an innovator may focus on a number of different objects of innovation. In order to achieve the normative purpose, do we best innovate products, business models, or maybe beliefs? The following section provides an overview of typical objects of innovation.

Innovating what?

So what are the "things" we can innovate? The popular OECD understanding outlines four objects or areas of innovation—product, process, marketing, and organization (OECD and EU, 2005):

1. **Product innovation:** "A good or service that is new or significantly improved. This includes significant improvements in technical specifications, components and materials, software in the product, user friendliness or other functional characteristics." The innovation of alternative engine technologies for cars, such as hybrid, hydrogen, or biodiesel, is a product innovation.

2. **Process innovation:** "A new or significantly improved production or delivery method. This includes significant changes in techniques, equipment and/ or software." An excellent example is zero waste to landfill manufacturing, where all production inputs are either reused or recycled. Some production facilities have even begun to work in closed cycles, such as reusing water that traditionally would have gone down the drain.

3. **Marketing innovation:** "A new marketing method involving significant changes in product design or packaging, product placement, product promotion or pricing." For instance, in the pharmaceutical industry, there used to

be the same (rather high) price for drugs all over the world. Some companies have innovated their pricing to provide drugs at lower prices, sometimes below production cost, in developing countries.

4. **Organizational innovation:** "A new organizational method in business practices, workplace organization or external relations." One example is the inclusion of small and/or marginalized suppliers as part of a fair-trade scheme.

While these objects of innovation cover many of the types of innovation typically found, there is a number of additional, partly overlapping areas of innovation that have become increasingly important, especially in the realm of responsible business:

- **Business model innovation:** the underlying logic of businesses may have to change to address responsible business challenges and to become sustainable. As outlined in Chapter 9, TOMS has invented a completely new business model for a shoe company which both sells and donates shoes at the same time.

- **Supply chain innovation:** this deserves to be highlighted, even though it it often included under organizational innovation. As illustrated in Chapter 13, a company can only claim to be sustainable if the whole supply chain impact is sustainable. Icebreaker's "Baa Code," which allows customers to trace where a sweater came from, right back to the original farm that produced the wool, is a supply chain innovation.

- **Systems innovation:** often single elements cannot change alone, but the whole system has to change. One attempt at such systems innovation are local currencies, such as the "Bristol Pound" in the U.K., which are typically intended to create independence from potential issues in the larger economic system, and to support the local economy (Grover, 2013).

- **Practice(s) innovation:** repeated meaningful actions, or practices, both in business and private life are of great relevance for business sustainability, responsibility, and ethics. For instance, the practice of always giving a plastic bag with any purchase has created a waste problem of global scale, and discriminatory employment practices create ethical and social problems.

- **Institutional innovation:** institutions as structures and mechanisms that create social order and govern behavior may both be helpful or harmful for achieving responsible business goals. The increasing social and legal acceptance of same-sex marriage is an institutional innovation, changing the institution of marriage.

Innovating what for?

A number of distinct innovation approaches have emerged, explicitly addressing goals related to responsible business. Innovations for sustainability can broadly be divided into two main innovation frameworks: social innovation, which aims to create social value, and eco-innovation, which reduces negative environmental impacts through innovation.

- **Social innovation** has been developed from the perspective of a non-profit organization and has often been related to social entrepreneurship. Nevertheless, social innovation has enormous potential to deliver scalable solutions to social issues when applied in long-established for-profit companies (Phills *et al.*, 2008). It is important not to confuse the understanding of social innovations as innovations with social value added (the understanding applied in this book) with the traditional definition which understands social innovations as big societal changes resulting from a shift in society.

- **Eco-innovation** has been approached from many angles. **Eco-efficiency**, for instance, aims at small, so-called **incremental innovations** throughout existing systems, while the **green technology** movement aims to invent new technological solutions to environmental issues, or **disruptive innovations**. The **design for environment (DfE)** framework provides a meta tool which combines both types of impact and establishes clear design principles to be followed for planned eco-innovation (Fiksel, 2010).

Table 16.1 illustrates examples of both social and eco-innovations in processes and products. It is important to mention that in practice a sustainability-oriented innovation has to be viable in the long term in all dimensions—socially, environmentally, and, of course, economically (Hansen *et al.*, 2009). Such sustainable innovation often serves as the basis for social or environmental entrepreneurship ventures, which will be described in more detail in Chapter 18.

While the above frameworks focus on the intended output of innovation, another line of thought is centered on predicting the unintended consequences of innovation, and the broader, potentially detrimental impact on society. Two examples of such frameworks are innovation ethics and responsible innovation. **Innovation ethics** concentrates on the multiple ethical issues that may arise during the innovation process, and as a result of a successful innovation. Such issues may be animal testing when developing a new drug, the ethical use of patents and other intellectual property rights, or the potential negative side effects of a new product. The list is endless and open, mostly related to direct ethical issues and consequences. **Responsible innovation**, by contrast, is more concerned about the larger ethical implications in a societal context. A typical question would be, "What are the societal dangers and potential side effects of innovations in nano-technology, or biofuels?" (Sutcliffe, 2014). While innovation ethics issues may be addressed one by one, responsible innovation aims to create the larger conditions that make sure an innovation is responsible, such as building responsible innovation capabilities, future-oriented learning, and institutional change (Randles *et al.*, 2015).

Table 16.1: Typical innovations combining distinct purposes and objects

Purpose	Object of innovation	
	Process	**Product**
Social	The international cement producer CEMEX has innovatively included low-income community members into its production process by establishing so-called "Blockeras," cement block-making machines in rural communities. Community members can use the machine and material for free. 50% of the blocks become the property of the community member, and 50% are sold (CEMEX, 2012).	Video game console producers increasingly replace traditional games with motion-controlled gaming (Steinberg, 2011).This innovation has the potential to transfer the negative health effects of excessive gaming into the positive effects associated with physical activity, very similar to sports, transforming console users from "couch potatoes" to superjocks.
Environmental	Supermarkets have found solar energy to be attractive and timely. In fact, supermarket energy usage peaks correspond to the highest productivity times for solar energy production, with refrigeration and air-conditioning (the main energy consumers) most needed when most sun is received. An excellent match!	Manufacturers of promotional items often mass-produce and distribute without due care and thus are usually not considered to be role models for responsible businesses. Earthimprints was the first company to focus on promotional products with environmental value added. How about a biodegradable pen with integrated seed? Take it out, put it into soil and with some watering you can grow a tree (Eco Imprints, 2016).

E-cigarettes, a socially responsible innovation?

E-cigarettes have become a worldwide phenomenon as a replacement for traditional cigarettes. Proponents argue that these cigarettes may be less hazardous to health than traditional cigarettes, but also admit that we know little about the long-term consequences (Reinberg, 2014). What do you think? Are e-cigarettes a responsible innovation?

Who innovates and how?

Now that we have considered what may be innovated for what purpose, there is a question about the "how" of innovation. Who innovates where, and what are innovation frameworks and methods that may be of value in the process?

Who innovates where?

Until recently, innovation was primarily considered an activity carried out by either "scientists" or "product developers" in companies' research and development departments, but the focus has now moved to innovators in other distinct environments. We will look at the two larger frameworks of open innovation and management innovation to develop an appreciation of who innovates where.

First coined by Henry Chesbrough (2003), the term "open innovation" refers to an approach where innovators both inside and outside the company work together in the same innovation process. Such an approach is particularly helpful in responsible business, where stakeholder groups inside and outside the company play an important role in defining what the company is and should become. Innovation processes and their actors are "distributed" inside and outside the company, and bring together the distinct capabilities of all involved (Metcalfe and Coombs, 2000). In such distributed and open innovation processes, the company moves away from being the innovator, toward a coordination and integration role for the open innovation process. Open innovation may involve co-innovators from many different groups, such as suppliers, competitors, or NGOs. A particularly powerful outside innovator group appears to be users. User innovation, improving and even creating products, often leads to situations where innovations emerge outside company boundaries, and are freely accessible in the public domain (von Hippel, 2005).

A second crucial group we would like to focus on in this book is managers. Managers may be both innovators, and pioneers in finding exploitation opportunities for innovations. In other words, they may be creators of novelties, "management innovations" (Birkinshaw et al., 2008), and they may be pioneers in applying them in "innovative management" practices (Khandwalla, 1987). As we have learned earlier in this chapter, both novelty and exploitation are constituent parts of an innovation. The idea of management innovation is "the invention and implementation of a management practice, process, structure, or technique that is new to the state of the art and is intended to further organizational goals" (Birkinshaw et al., 2008, p. 825). The most impactful management innovations do not stay within one company, but become part of the repertoire of companies in general. For instance, the balanced scorecard that most companies now use started as a management innovation by Art Schneiderman, a manager in the company Analog Devices (Schneiderman, 2006). The innovation of the Toyota production system has become the basis for most management systems used worldwide. In the realm of responsible business, for instance, it was marketing managers at American Express who created the tool of cause-related marketing,

Figure 16.3: How to become a serial management innovator?

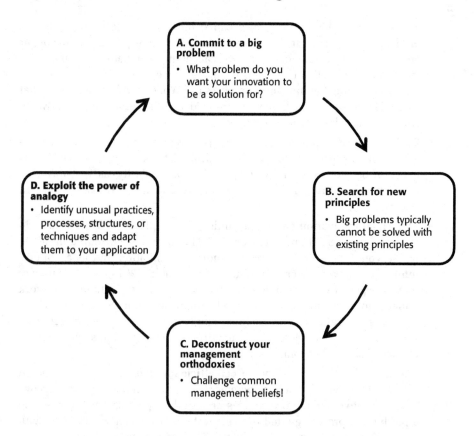

Muhammad Yunus at the Grameen Bank who innovated group lending as a mana-gerial banking practice, and life-cycle assessment started out as a project at the Coca-Cola Company. Imagine you could become a management innovator, trans-forming how companies around the world do business—more sustainably, more responsibly, and more ethically. Figure 16.3 shows a summary of the main steps for becoming a management innovator as outlined by management guru Gary Hamel (2006).

How to innovate?

Now we know everything about innovation, but how do we actually innovate? In this final section we will review a number of innovation methods that are espe-cially relevant for innovating for sustainability, responsibility, and ethics. As you will see in the following list, most of the innovation methods are especially geared toward innovations with an environmental impact. What all of these motivations have in common is a leitmotiv, a theme that serves as orientation for innovation measures:

- The method of **biomimicry**, also called biomimetics, follows the theme of "learning from nature" (Benyus, 2002). This is especially relevant for environmental sustainability, as we can argue that nature is inherently sustainable, given that it sustains itself. When we encounter a problem, the question guiding the innovation process is, "What would nature do?" What examples can we find where nature solved a similar problem and how can we learn from these examples?

- **Backcasting** (as opposed to forecasting) relies on the question, "What innovations do we need today, so that a desired future becomes real?" This question becomes especially relevant for sustainability, as we are trying to do the right thing today to achieve a sustainable future (Holmberg and Robèrt, 2000).

- The **frugal innovation** method is guided by the question, "How would/do we innovate under limited resources?" The idea is to develop a mind-set where you see resource constraints not as a limitation, but as an opportunity to innovate differently (Radjou and Prabhu, 2014). Frugal innovation is especially relevant for two reasons. First, innovations that work under resource scarcity are likely to be applicable to a world where once-abundant natural resources are increasingly depleted. Second, frugal innovation often produces less pricy, but still functional products applicable to the needs of lower income consumers.

- The long-established method of **eco-efficiency**, which was described in Chapter 11, is an approach to incremental innovation that aims to improve the ratio between natural resources used and output achieved. Reviewing a production process guided by the question, "How can we do more with less?" often leads to amazing reductions in resource consumption.

- The **design for environment** method tackles environmental issues by asking, "How can we design things that are better for the environment?" It is guided by the four sub-questions of, "How can we use less material?," "How can we use less toxins?," "How can we make sure the product is recycled?," and "How can we make sure the overall product life-cycle renews environmental, social, and economic capital, instead of depleting it?" (Fiksel, 2010).

Humanize versus naturalize and biomimicry versus humanism?

The idea of biomimicry is based on learning from nature. However, human beings are quite a special animal and do many things differently than what you would typically expect from other living beings. Humanism connects to this idea and the movement around humanistic business is based on our collaborative social nature, compassion, human dignity, and freedom (von Kimakowitz *et al.*, 2011; Melé, 2003). There may be trade-offs and conflict situations between both philosophies, as the most humane thing to do is not always the most natural. One extreme example to consider would be a global disaster that wiped out the majority of humanity from the face of Planet Earth. It would be great for the planet, and is a natural mechanism often observed when there is an overpopulation of one species in its habitat, but it would be a humanitarian catastrophe. What do you think? Should we innovate inspired by the idea of achieving "natural" outputs or "human" outputs? Do you see a potential compromise? What might such a compromise look like?

Exercises

A. Know

Use the multiple choice questions below to test your knowledge. Each answer may be wrong or right and there may be zero to four right or wrong answers per question:

1. The Korean company Biocera has invented "washing balls" that work entirely without detergent. The company highlights its positive effect in terms of less water pollution, economic savings due to the money saved by not buying detergent, and less skin irritations caused by residual detergent in clothes. We may consider this an example of ...

    a. ... frugal innovation, as it provides an answer to the question, "How would we innovate if we had limited fresh water resources?"
    b. ... design for environment, as it provides an answer to the question, "How can we use fewer toxins?"
    c. ... biomimicry, as nature wouldn't use detergent either.
    d. ... of backcasting, as it might be an answer to the question, "For a future where we want to be able to live without contaminating water, what innovations do we need?"

2. Who innovates where? Answers to this question may be ...

    a. ... in open innovation the R&D department innovates, but openly tests the results involving external stakeholders.
    b. ... in management innovation, company managers innovate new practices, processes, structures, or techniques for their own company, but often these innovations are then used across many companies.
    c. ... that it used to be the R&D department driving innovation, but nowadays we typically see a more distributed innovation process.
    d. ... user innovation, where primarily users are involved in pilot-testing to refine new products.

3. The innovation of e-cigarettes involves the innovation of what? Innovation objects are ...

    a. ... product innovation, as electronic cigarettes are radically different than traditional cigarettes.
    b. ... the practice of smoking a cigarette.
    c. ... processes.
    d. ... the supply chain.

B. Think

Identify one strongly held management belief that you think might be open to criticism. Then deconstruct where the belief comes from, what might be wrong with it, and why.

C. Do

Follow the four steps of the management innovation process described in this chapter to come up with one concrete management innovation idea. Then put this novelty to use in order to make it a realized innovation.

D. Relate

Start a small advocacy campaign for an innovation that you think deserves spreading in order to make an impact for sustainability, responsibility, and/ or ethics. Chose whatever medium you think is best, possibly including social networks, emails, involvement in groups, personal conversations, etc.

E. Be

Inform yourself about the story behind one responsible business innovation and the person realizing the innovation. This could be, for instance, how Blake Mycoskie came up with the one-for-one idea, or how Ann Makosinski invented a flashlight powered by the heat in your hands. How does the story relate to you? Do you think you can be an innovator? What would you have done differently? What kind of innovator could you be?

Feedback

A. Know

Question 1

    a. Right: we clearly see the frugal innovation theme of "innovating under scarcity" in this example.

    b. Right: both the emission of toxins into the water and the skin-irritating characteristics of detergents are examples of the toxicity of conventional detergents, which are to be replaced by the washing balls innovation.

    c. Right: in nature, cleaning typically happens with pure water and with mechanical forces—no detergent. This is how the washing balls work.

    d. Right: the washing balls innovation might have resulted from backcasting exercises.

Question 2

    a. Wrong: in open innovation, the innovation itself involves a network of inside and outside innovators, not merely testing the results in such a network afterwards.

    b. Right: this sentence is a rephrasing of the paragraph describing management innovation.

    c. Right: while there are still R&D departments, innovation has become distributed to many more locations and innovators.

    d. Wrong: pilot-testing might be one activity under the umbrella of user innovation, but primarily user innovation refers to users innovating freely, sometimes even without any relationship to a company at all.

Question 3

    a. Right: while both e-cigarettes and traditional cigarettes are ultimately smoked, the product used for smoking is technically entirely different. For instance, tobacco in traditional cigarettes is burnt, while e-cigarettes vaporize a fluid.

    b. Right: the way a cigarette is smoked can be considered a practice, which is innovated through e-cigarettes. For instance, smoking a traditional cigarette involves the use of a lighter.

    c. Right: given the entirely different product, the production processes also have to be innovated.

    d. Right: given the distinct inputs for the e-cigarette, these inputs are supplied by distinct types of company, some of which (e.g., the vaporization liquid) did not exist before e-cigarettes, which makes supply chain innovation necessary.

B. Think

Level	Challenging assumptions and mind-sets	Notes
+	A strong critical argument has been developed, based on a deep understanding of the management belief	
=	A management belief has been identified and an appreciation of its roots has been developed	
–	No management belief worth criticizing has been identified	

C. Do

Level	Innovation-implementation competence	Notes
+	A complete management innovation has been realized, including the idea and putting it to use	
=	An innovative idea has been developed, based on elements of the management innovation process	
–	Neither an innovative idea nor implementation activities have been documented	

D. Relate

Level	Advocacy skills	Notes
+	Evidence of proactive advocacy for the innovation worth promoting	
=	Identification of innovation worth promoting	
–	No innovation worth promoting identified	

E. Be

Level	Developing innovative attitude	Notes
+	Clearly displayed appreciation of own identity as a particular type of innovator	
=	Evidence of emerging attitude to being an innovator	
–	No evidence of developing an innovative attitude	

17
Individual change

[S]ustainable history is propelled by good governance paradigms that balance the tension between human nature attributes (emotionality, amorality and egoisms), on the one hand, and human dignity needs (reason, security, human rights, accountability, transparency, justice, opportunity, innovation and inclusiveness), on the other.

Nayef Al-Rodhan, philosopher, neuroscientist
and geostrategist (Al-Rodhan, 2009, p. 2)

The preceding chapters have focused on what businesses can do to contribute to sustainability. The sobering reality is that businesses can actually not do very much without people. It is single individuals who demand goods, often in a highly unsustainable fashion, it is people who work in companies and make unsustainable decisions, and it is people who, in their citizen function, vote for governments that do not move quickly enough toward a sustainable infrastructure. For this reason, we now look at who we are as individuals and what we need to do to contribute our share to a sustainable world. The constant question in this chapter is, "What does our individuality mean for responsible business?" We illustrate approaches to responsible business that foster the creation of sustainable lifestyles and activism, and show how to benefit from these trends.

The first section takes a close look at what characteristics of human nature are at the root of unsustainable behavior, at understanding how we make decisions, and at what human traits lead us to make decisions that contradict the logic of sustainable development. The second section develops a basic idea of what sustainable lifestyles, consumption, and work patterns might lead to an optimum sustainable lifestyle for the world population. The third section covers how individual activism—actively trying to affect the status quo—can make an important change toward sustainability.

Unsustainable attitudes, behaviors and their origins

Why is it so hard for contemporary human beings to show sustainable behavior? One could dodge the question and blame "politics," "businesses," or even "the system" for today's global unsustainability. Such criticism will be ignored here and the focus will be on the root cause of human nature. Why do we ignore or even deny the disastrous situation humanity is steering toward? Why don't we take action? Why don't we protest? Why don't we at least change our consumption behavior toward more sustainable ways?

Individuals' inertia in accepting the challenge of sustainable development can be attributed to basic elements of human nature. The psychologists Maslow and Kohlberg have both provided staged models, explaining human action and inaction (see Figure 17.1). Abraham Maslow explains human behavior by the needs creating the intrinsic motivation for their actions. The most basic needs are physiological ones, such as hunger, thirst, sex, safety, stability, and routine. These are followed by social needs such as love, belonging, and esteem from others. The ultimate stage of Maslow's needs pyramid is self-actualization. It is in this last

What do sustainability experts think about sustainable consumption?

The consultancy SustainAbility asked more than 500 sustainability experts worldwide about their opinions on sustainable consumption. Interesting outcomes include the following (SustainAbility, 2011):

- Sustainable product lines: "Businesses have a duty to offer sustainable product lines instead of, rather than in addition to, unsustainable ones" (yes: 78%; no: 9%)
- Sustainable consumption means less consumption: "Sustainable consumption must mean less consumption" (yes: 53%; no: 27%)
- Sustainable consumption means degrowth: "There is an inherent conflict between economic growth and sustainable consumption" (yes: 40%; no: 43%)
- Sustainable consumption in emerging countries: "Consumers in emerging countries will adopt sustainable consumption behaviors at a faster pace than in developed countries" (yes: 31%; no: 40%)
- Sustainable consumption is not impossible: "Sustainable consumption is impossible to achieve" (yes: 11%; no: 69%)

Figure 17.1: Classic approaches to explaining human behavior

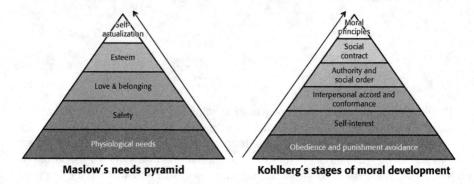

Maslow's needs pyramid   **Kohlberg's stages of moral development**

stage that human beings' greatest need is to fulfill their potential. Maslow suggests that humans fulfill their most basic needs first (Maslow, 1943). Thus, knowing what needs hierarchy an individual is on, or that individual's primary motivation, is crucially important for understanding that person's actions.

Laurence Kohlberg's pyramid of moral development can be used to explain behaviors not by their motivation, but by their capability of moral reasoning. Kohlberg, in contrast to Maslow, does not pose the question, "What do people want to do?," but instead asks what are they morally capable of doing. Kohlberg's lowest stages of moral reasoning are motivated by self-interest and avoidance of punishment. Then follow moralities motivated by interpersonal accord (satisfying the direct social group's expectations) and social order (aligned with the existing social order and authority). The penultimate stage of moral reasoning are the social contract morality, which searches for the greatest happiness possible, and the highest stage is where individuals make decisions based on higher ethical principles. Kohlberg also suggests that human beings usually move from the lowest to the highest stages as they develop (Kohlberg, 1973).

How does sustainability come into the picture? Maslow's needs pyramid is based on people's motivation, asking, "Why do people want to do the things they do?" Most of the behaviors related to sustainable development are actually related to the higher stages of the needs pyramid, especially self-actualization. It is in this final stage where individuals might start to ask themselves, "Why am I really here?" On the one hand, the world's over 4 billion poor are motivated by the short-term physiological needs of safety, love, and belonging. Survival, savings, building family, and community life come before sustainable lifestyles on the needs pyramid of the global poor.

The world's middle class, on the other hand, is to a big degree driven by the need for esteem, which often is satisfied by showing off the newest phone, the biggest car, or the nicest shoes. Such unsustainable consumerism mostly leads to a highly unsustainable footprint. Critics believe that the formerly poor, new middle classes are likely to follow the Western role model of seeking esteem by falling into unsustainable consumerist patterns. The two main change tasks arising from interpretation of the needs pyramid are therefore the following:

1. Improve the lives of poor people up to the esteem level, where they are able to worry about nothing except their own self-actualization

2. Show individuals who seek esteem through consumerist habits how to first achieve self-esteem while adopting more sustainable behavior patterns, and then move to the next level of self-actualization

While Maslow answers questions about people's wants, Kohlberg's pyramid answers questions about what people are able to do if they can actually make moral decisions leading to sustainable living. Unsustainable behavior is usually not punished by law (level 1). Sustainable behavior in most cases is not in individuals' direct self-interest (level 2). Society neither requires (level 3) such behavior, nor is it a fully implemented element of social order (level 4). Thus, sustainable behavior is most likely to be found among individuals on the two highest levels of moral development. On the social contract level, individuals make their decisions based on welfare thinking (level 5). Sustainable development, with its concept of intergenerational equity, is welfare optimization between current and future generations so people on level 6, aligning their decisions and behavior with higher principles, may accept sustainability as a higher principle to be adopted with urgency. Necessary actions for sustainable development resulting from these observations are the following:

3. Support moral development of individuals mostly in economically developed countries

4. Show how sustainable behavior makes sense at each stage of moral development

In addition to the explanations given by these two models, single characteristics of human nature also impede sustainable living patterns:

- **Greed and the insatiable thirst for growth:** human beings seem to have a strong propensity to own more and constantly grow in all aspects of our lives. Unfortunately, both characteristics are hard to align with sustainable development on a finite and crowded planet.

- **Mental disconnect:** people tend to feel isolated from the negative results of unsustainable development. Catastrophes always seem to happen somewhere else to someone else. Contemporary human beings also feel disconnected from nature, and are often not aware of how severe the consequences of their lifestyles are.

- **Present value focus:** people have the tendency to value the present state of affairs more than the future one. Crisis scenarios of an unsustainable future, including the consequences of climate change or an economic meltdown, are usually given less weight than a convenient and sacrifice-free life today. Future events are not perceived as grave enough to make people leave their comfort zone today.

- **Herd-animal man:** it is hard to swim against the current, which means that single individuals are unlikely to change their behaviors to more sustainable ways, if the rest of the group doesn't. Sustainable living has to become a cultural trait before the majority adheres to it.

The psychology of greed

Many people say that greed—wanting more than we really need—is the root cause of human beings' unsustainability. If that is true, to foster sustainable behaviors in us and others, we first need to understand greed. A *Harvard Business Review* article frames greed in the business world and cites Sigmund Freud, the grandfather of psychoanalysis (Coutu, 2003). As the author interprets Freud, there are three types of greed, corresponding to the different phases of infant development: oral, anal, and phallic.

In the oral phase, people just want to swallow as much as they can. Greedy people, corresponding to the anal phase, find pleasure in piling up or splashing around needlessly. The phallic phase is about comparing what you have with others.

Do you see some of these behaviors in the way you consume, do your job, or run your business? Only if we are able to control all three kinds of greed, will we be able to consume corresponding to our true need and in a sustainable manner.

What can business do?

The impediments to sustainable living mentioned in the preceding section are strong, but can be overcome by several tools, most of which work well in a business context. It is important to keep in mind that these human characteristics do not only pose big questions, but also provide immense opportunities for businesses. The following fields of action are just a few places to begin:

- **Responsible marketing** has immense potential to make an impact. If traditional marketing could question its role as a consumption increaser, to stop fueling consumerism and unsustainable behavior patterns, much would be achieved. People would be enabled to make their own decisions on how much and what kind of consumption they need. Interestingly, Philip Kotler, the grandfather of marketing, was already describing the possibility of demarketing as a legitimate strategy in the early 1970s (Kotler and Levy, 1971). If marketing can not only stop fostering unsustainable behavior patterns, but even actively foster sustainable behavior patterns (by using social marketing), its contribution to sustainable behavior can be very powerful.
- **Education:** of course, businesses are not ethics schools. Nevertheless, businesses have an enormous potential to teach sustainable, responsible, and moral competences. Many of the positive learnings from the workplace can

be transferred to private life. Competences as simple as separating trash or as complex as solving moral dilemmas can be learned on the job and applied throughout private life.

- **Human development:** businesses are no development agencies either, but they do automatically contribute to human development. Businesses provide income and healthcare, often improve infrastructure themselves or through tax revenues paid, and provide or support education. Companies can also engage in community involvement and make social investments to strengthen society. The Human Development Index (HDI) provided by the United Nations Development Programme (UNDP) includes all these factors that business can influence. The higher the human development, the higher people climb on Maslow's needs pyramid and the closer they come to a situation where they can truly live a sustainable lifestyle.

Sustainable development, lifestyles and income

An important question that has so far been touched only superficially is: "What happens if economic development eradicates poverty and over two-thirds of the world population who are poor today begin living a rich, but unsustainable lifestyle, as in most fully developed countries?" The second question is: "What happens to the footprint of individuals and whole countries on the way to full economic development?" The concept of the Kuznets curve, named after its inventor Simon Kuznets, provides a powerful analysis tool for both questions (Kuznets, 1955).

The Kuznets curve has been applied to both income inequalities and environmental degradation during the economic development process. Both topics are central considerations in sustainable development. First, income inequality (the gap between rich and poor) is an excellent proxy for the degree of poverty, which in turn is the central factor of socially sustainable development. Poverty and its directly connected conditions, such as exploitation, human rights abuses, and poor health conditions, are crucial factors in achieving socially sustainable development. Second, environmental degradation, such as water and air pollution or deforestation, are central factors in environmentally sustainable development.

As illustrated in Figure 17.2, the Kuznets curve suggests an inverted U-shaped development of income inequality and environmental degradation, along with economic development, measured by the average per capita income of a country. That means countries with a low average income will suffer higher environmental degradation and social inequality once they start developing, but will improve both factors once achieving a high level of average income. Thus, the average sustainability footprint of an inhabitant of these countries would first be increased and finally reduced. In the best case, the reduction would lead back

Figure 17.2: Kuznets curves and sustainable development

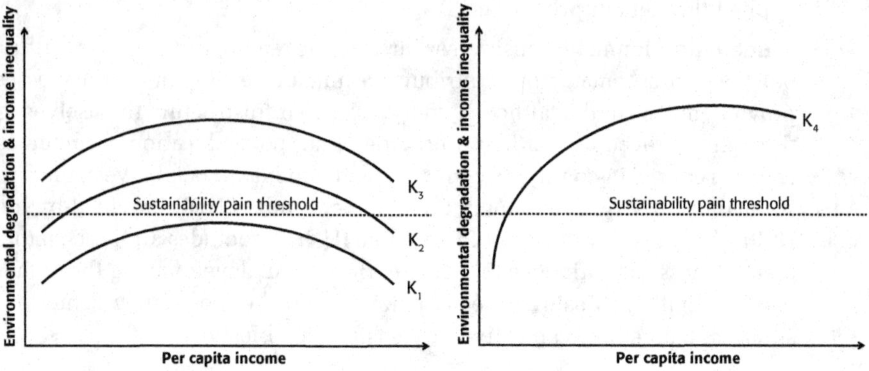

to a low average individual footprint, while maintaining higher income and an accordingly higher level of individual welfare.

There are two important questions when applying Kuznets curves to sustainable development. First, "Will the planet be able to sustain the negative impact during the economic development process?;" and second, "Will the average footprint of the country's citizens, when reaching the point of maximum economic development, be above or below the threshold of the planetary carrying capacity?" One can imagine three possible scenarios, as illustrated in Figure 17.2. Curve K1 describes the optimum situation, where a country develops fully without ever crossing the sustainability threshold. Curve K3 depicts the opposite extreme of a country whose inhabitants, during the development process, are never able to live within planetary resource limits. The global situation looks more like curve

Why does this feel odd?

It sounds too good to be true. If we only make people rich enough, we will solve all our global problems. Unfortunately, there are many reasons why such a beneficial scenario might never be reached, meaning that there is much criticism about the theory of the Kuznets curve itself (Stern, 2004; Yandle *et al.*, 2004). If we assume that the curve properly reflects reality, what are the reasons why countries might not all end up in a sustainable development situation? One salient reason is that the Kuznets curve primarily refers to the situation inside the country. Highly developed countries with little internal inequality and environmental degradation might be outsourcing the negative effects of their wealth to other countries. Another danger is a situation where countries get stuck halfway through their economic development. Such a country and its inhabitants then would constantly exert an unsustainable influence.

K4. The citizens of none of the "developed" countries have achieved a footprint corresponding to the planetary sustainability pain threshold.

What can be learned about sustainable development and how individuals must develop and change in order to reach it? Most urgently, citizens in "developed" countries (curve K4) must learn how to reduce their footprint to a level within the world's resource limits. Second, citizens of these countries must find a personal socioeconomic development path that either never exceeds the planet's carrying capacity (curve K1) or that at least minimizes the length of the unsustainable development section (curve K2). These goals cannot be reached by individuals alone, so there is the need for sound public policies to support these developments, following the clues derived from the Kuznets curve (Panayotou, 2002). The following section will demonstrate ways to achieve both.

Changing lifestyle and consumption

Is it really necessary to change lifestyles? Isn't there a less painful way to reach sustainable development? Western consumerist lifestyles are bound to be unsustainable. The annually published Global Footprint Atlas measured the average footprints of citizens of 156 countries in 2010 and showed that the worldwide average footprint was 1.5 times the Earth's biocapacity per person. The figure varies widely from country to country, with citizens of the United Arab Emirates consuming 5.9 Earths, while for Americans and Australians the figure is 4.4. Even citizens of developed countries considered very advanced in environmental protection score high. Germans, for instance, use up 2.8 Earths, almost double the world average. Only countries such as India, with a population of 2.4 billion people living on an average of 0.5 of the Earth's biocapacity, keep the worldwide environmental footprint from skyrocketing. But what will happen once these countries reach their development goals and join the club of unsustainable consumers? The World Footprint Atlas defines affluence as "consumption per person" and identifies it as one of the three main drivers of the footprint explosion. New lifestyles and alternative consumption patterns are crucial for solving the puzzle of sustainable development (Ewing *et al.*, 2010).

What is an optimum sustainable lifestyle?

A crucial challenge, if sustainable development is to be achieved, is to reach a situation where the average person on Earth is living a lifestyle that is in line with both meeting human needs and the natural carrying capacity of the planet: a footprint of 1. It is also imperative that countries with high and low environmental footprints meet in the middle. Low-footprint citizens, such the Indian population, will only have a minimal margin for increasing their footprints, while high-footprint countries, such as the U.S.A. and Germany, will need to reduce theirs drastically. We are in search of a new sustainable lifestyle for 9 billion people on

The power of awareness, priority, and framing

A young violinist stands in a subway station, playing six classical pieces in 43 minutes. Passers-by hardly notice. Just one person stops while others throw a coin, walking by with an expression of guilt. The financial outcome is US$23, which you might consider decent for a street musician. Only that this man is not an ordinary street musician. The 1,057 people passing by just missed a free concert by the star violinist Joshua Bell. One of the pieces played was Bach's "Chaconne," one of the most difficult violin pieces on Earth. Bell played on a US$3.5 million violin and, just a few days before, thousands of people had paid an average of US$100 for a concert performed by the same person in the same city (Weingarten, 2007). Does the money we need to earn for consumption leave us time to see the free beauty that is surrounding us? If we could only see and cherish the beauty of everything around us, would we be able to forfeit costly consumption and slow down our hectic and unsustainable lifestyles? Would we start to consider protecting the world that surrounds us?

Planet Earth, the population estimate for 2043 (Rosenberg, 2011). What lifestyle(s) might that be? More unsustainable lifestyles have always existed in a wide variety of forms, although no globally significant quantity of people has hitherto lived by them.

Figure 17.3 provides a basic overview of some alternatives to the classic consumerist lifestyle. The figure assumes that the environmental footprint caused by a certain lifestyle depends on both the quantity and quality of consumption. Quantity of consumption refers to how much a person consumes overall. A person owning two cars instead of one will consume more natural resources for the vehicles' production and use, so the individual's footprint will be increased by the quantity of consumption. Other examples of changes in quantity of consumption can be seen in reduced transportation by living closer to the workplace and replacing the cell phone every four years instead of every eighteen months. Quality of consumption refers to the degree of sustainability in an individual's consumption patterns. For instance, both a vegetarian and a nonvegetarian would eat until feeling full (same quantity). Nonetheless, the consumption of the vegetarian is of a more environmentally sustainable quality. Producing meat creates an environmental footprint (greenhouse gases, energy, water, etc.) beyond most vegetarian food alternatives. Thus, a vegetarian's footprint would be decreased due to the quality of consumption. Other examples of improvements in the quality of consumption would be to buy organic goods instead nonorganic, drive an electric car instead of one with a traditional combustion engine, and buy airplane tickets including a carbon offsetting fee. Figure 17.3 shows how different lifestyles, such as a person in a developing country, a LOHAS consumer, or a person living in a sustainable community, score differently in terms of the environmental impact of their consumption quality and quantity. While the figure is an intuitive and

Figure 17.3: Sustainability of lifestyle and consumption styles

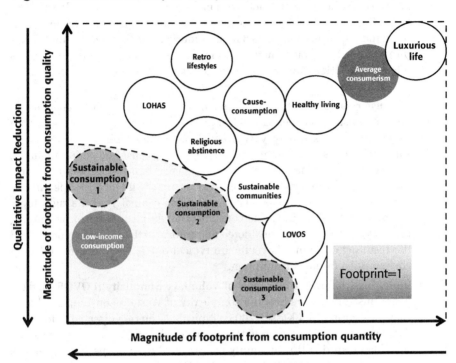

therefore superficial estimate of what different lifestyles might mean in terms of sustainability, it might still provide valuable food for thought and stimulate discussion.

The key criterion for sustainable lifestyles for the future is that their impact per person must be close to a footprint of 1. In the figure, this situation is indicated by the dotted curve. Sustainable lifestyles must not break this sustainability boundary.

Mapping alternative lifestyles

The optimum sustainable lifestyle does probably not yet exist. Nevertheless, a wide variety of lifestyles do already provide alternatives to unsustainable traditional consumerism. What follows is a brief list of prominent alternative lifestyles and consumption patterns to illustrate what might be the starting point for developing an optimum sustainable lifestyle:

- **Lifestyles of Health and Sustainability (LOHAS)** is probably the most-visible sustainable consumption movement. This is probably at least partly due to this group's attractiveness for marketers. LOHAS do not abstain from consumption, but consume differently. They maintain consumption, but replace unsustainable products with more sustainable product alternatives. LOHAS consumers might, for instance, book eco-tourist offers instead of participating in normal unsustainable tourism, or they would buy furniture made of recycled materials instead of tropical woods. LOHAS is often characterized by markets such as sustainable energies or alternative transportation.

- In **cause-related consumption**, consumers base their buying decisions on the relationship between a specific product or its company and a certain good cause. Causes may vary greatly, but so do their contributions to sustainable consumption. Individuals practicing cause consumption might, for instance, buy whatever they can at the local farmers' market to support the cause of local production. Cause consumers might also specifically buy the product of a cause-related marketing campaign, if the right topic is benefited through it. Cause consumers might also abstain from buying certain products that are considered derogatory for the cause supported, and the resulting consumer boycotts are typical outcomes of cause-motivated consumption or nonconsumption.

- Individuals following **Lifestyles of Voluntary Simplicity (LOVOS)** make a conscious choice to reduce the complexity of Western consumption-based lifestyles (Brown and Kasser, 2005). Typical reasons are dissatisfaction with consumerism and the search for nonmaterial benefits, such as personal fulfillment, spirituality, or simply rest. LOVOS individuals usually reduce their consumption drastically and often take jobs that are low in stress and rather distant from the consumerist system. The "slow living" movement is a variant of a LOVOS lifestyle, where individuals leave the "rat race" and reduce complexity by slowing down life's pace (World Institute of Slowness, 2016). The main contribution of LOVOS lifestyles to sustainable development is the reduction in overall consumption per individual.

- **Religious lifestyles** often lead to sustainable behavior patterns. The Amish Christian group is known for its rural lifestyle, characterized by simple living, plain dress, and the refusal of many modern technological comforts. Buddhist belief is based on a simple life, avoiding the distractions represented by consumption. Many animist beliefs and Chinese Taoism base their practices on the nearness to nature.

- **Sustainable communities** are formed by groups of individuals jointly building and running a community that focuses on sustainable infrastructure and practices. In the most extreme case, sustainable communities try to become completely independent from the outside world, produce their own food, clothing, and shelter, and live on social water and energy resources.

Strategic sustainable consumption

The German UTOPIA platform for strategic consumption provides consumers with a Web 2.0 tool for voting how to spend their money. The platform calls itself a tool for "strategic consumption," meaning strategic purchasing decisions for a more sustainable world. The platform offers to its community of subscribers direct contact with leading responsible businesses ("changemakers"), and provides extensive background facts to make cause consumption easier (Utopia Foundation, 2012).

Responsible business and new lifestyles

It would appear that the shift toward sustainable global lifestyle patterns pursued by the majority of the world population is inevitable, either to reach sustainable development (in an optimistic scenario) or to survive the consequences of unsustainable development. How can business connect to this development? As we have already seen, business can have a part in both fostering and harvesting the fruits of new sustainable lifestyles. Adapting to sustainable lifestyles requires substantial transitions in a business's most protected "sanctuaries:" products, core business processes, and even underlying paradigms, such as growth. The following three points are crucial prerequisites for achieving a business transition with the new sustainable lifestyles to be developed.

1. Improve the sustainability quality of products and services. As the slogan "LOHAS means business" (Emerich, 2000) suggests, this prerequisite is probably the most pleasant to be fulfilled. Improving the sustainability quality of products and the processes leading to these products can be a highly attractive product differentiation feature in order to win new customers, or even whole new markets.

2. Be prepared to degrow the quantity of production together with your consumers. As discussed above, the quantity of global production and consumption is already far exceeding the ecological capacity of the planet. Considering how ecosystems decay and their ecological capacity decreases, while population continues to grow, it becomes clear that a purely quality-based reduction in impact from consumption will not lead to sustainable development. The quantity of consumption per capita and as a (planetary) whole needs to decrease. This will only happen if companies transition to lower production volumes. What are the consequences? Does this mean companies need to shut down a major part of their operations and lay off millions of people? If the quantity reduction is properly planned, the negative effects might not be so drastic. For instance, much of the decreased production activity might be absorbed by increased activity in boosting products' sustainability quality. A reduction of quantity might also be achieved by increased servitization, replacing higher-impact products with lower-impact

and less labor-intensive services. Companies should be highly involved in searching for such solutions and facilitating a smooth transition to a low-quantity, low-production economy.

3. Create a mutually beneficial and flexible symbiosis with individuals in their roles as both consumers and employees, sensitive to the needs of new lifestyles. Many of the movements toward sustainable living also involve a change in work patterns and professional preferences. For instance, people searching for voluntary simplicity and a slow life might be very willing to work for a lower salary in a less time-intensive and more flexible position that supports their lifestyle. At the same time their companies could deploy a mutually appreciated reduction of employment, in accordance with both the need for degrowth and the new lifestyle.

See Chapter 18 for more extensive advice on how to achieve this transition at an organizational level.

Activism and change agency

The animal protection activist Ric O'Barry once said, "To me you are either an activist or an inactivist" (Psihoyos, 2009). The previous section addressed consumption and the work aspects of changing an individual's lifestyle toward sustainability. This section goes beyond "minding one's own business" to show how activists (also called "change agents" in responsible business jargon) focus on leaving the boundaries of their own life and actively changing the individuals, social groups, and whole systems around them. In light of the necessity to become a truly sustainable global society, activism is an important catalyst for change.

After-death activism

The Austrian branch of the World Wildlife Fund (WWF) offers specialist support for drafting people's last will for the environment. WWF has even published a last will guide including sound advice ranging from legal to ethical issues (WWF, 2012).

What is an activist for sustainable development?

When we think of activists, very different individuals may come to mind. One might think of famous leaders such as Mahatma Gandhi, Martin Luther King, Che Guevara, or Nelson Mandela. To be an activist, one does not need to be or become famous. Activists share two common characteristics:

1. They display a commitment to a cause
2. They feel nonconformity with the status quo and challenge structures, authorities, institutions, and beliefs

Figure 17.4: Individual activism throughout roles and vehicles

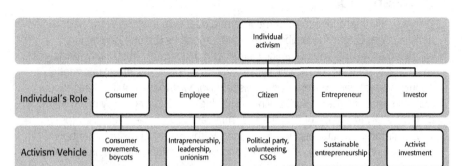

There are two basic groups of activism: grass-roots activism, which emerges naturally and spontaneously from society, and organizational activism, which uses and follows established institutions as vehicles of activism.

As illustrated in Figure 17.4, individuals can be activists in many different roles in life. Even some of the consumer movements, such as cause consumption and related boycotts, can be classified as activism in the individual's role as consumer. They follow a common cause, are nonconforming with the way companies deal with this cause, and challenge the companies by not buying their products. Employees can also be activists inside their employing organization by acting as intrapreneurs and leaders facilitating change toward more responsibility from within. Individuals also find many vehicles for activism in their role as citizens of communities, states, or the world, for they can improve local structures by volunteering and fighting for change as members of a political party or a civil society organization (CSO).

Some individuals might become entrepreneurs to further the cause of sustainable development by business activity, and Chapter 18 will illustrate how to create and manage a business that makes the world more sustainable. A minority of individuals might also further sustainable development through their investment decisions. As an investor, an individual has many opportunities to drive change toward more sustainability. Private angel investors might finance entrepreneurial ventures for more sustainability. Activist investors for responsible business hold shares of companies in order to actively influence their decisions toward more responsible behavior. Even small private investors can invest their money in sustainable development in green technology or microfinance-based funds.

Activism 2.0

Web 2.0, the interactive form of the internet, opens up a whole world of potential activist engagement. Think about the impact made by the one person who uploaded a clip of a parcel service's employee deliberately mistreating packages to YouTube. Think about the WikiLeaks website where confidential information about corporate and governmental misbehavior was made public. Think about websites that call themselves online watchdogs, scrutinizing every move made by potentially irresponsible companies. Think about websites such as https://www.rainforest-rescue.org where you can, with a few clicks, sign a petition against environmentally bad practices and personally influence decision-makers in companies and governments.

What does activism mean for responsible businesses?

Business managers might associate activists with aggressive actions, such as Greenpeace supporters climbing their chimneys. However, activism may take much more collaborative forms than that. Activists may be an invaluable ally in developing new perspectives and even concrete solutions in the process of becoming a responsible and sustainable business.

In order to understand activism and the behavior of activists better, it is important to have an insight into the basic motivations and behavior patterns of activist individuals. Of course, these classifications are extreme stereotypes and activists are in reality a mixture of these and other types:

- **Pragmatist**, motivated by social outcomes
- **Instrumentalist**, motivated by personal benefits
- **Personality**, driven by personal character traits
- **Fanatic**, driven by thoughts of victory and clear image of an enemy

The best activist type to collaborate with is probably the pragmatist, one who is driven by the willingness to solve a pressing social or environmental problem. The pragmatist is results oriented, and will happily collaborate with a business if there is a good chance of mitigating or solving the cause addressed.

By contrast, the instrumentalist uses activism for personal benefit: for instance, politicians are often accused of preying on a good cause to impress voters. Instrumentalists do have an interest in furthering the cause, but only when it helps them to reach their personal goals.

The personality possesses character traits, such as high critical skills or a leader personality, which intrinsically facilitates activist behavior. Personalities might not be as interested in furthering the cause as they are in maintaining their role as "born activist."

It is almost impossible to collaborate with fanatics, for their motivation is the ultimate victory against a self-declared enemy. While the cause of activism might have played a role in shaping the concept of the enemy, the mitigation of the cause becomes increasingly replaced by the motivation to fight against the enemy. Collaboration, if wanted, requires substantial diplomacy and confidence building as prerequisites.

"The beginning is near"

So reads the sign held by an activist protester from the Occupy movement in late 2011. Can activism and protest really be the beginning of a new, more socially responsible and environmentally sustainable economic system? With its criticisms of capitalism, greed, and banking systems in particular, the Occupy movement spread in just a few months to more than 700 cities in over 80 countries worldwide (Rogers, 2011). A worldwide opinion poll revealed that there was minimum opposition to the movement: only 12% did not sympathize with the movement's ideology, while 34% of respondents were undecided, and 53% supported the movement's opposition to "social and economic inequality, corporate greed, the power of the financial sector, and the global financial system" (IPSOS, 2012). Could that be the world citizens' vote for a new industrial revolution?

Exercises

A. Know

Use the multiple choice questions below to test your knowledge. Each answer may be wrong or right and there may be zero to four right or wrong answers per question:

1. Classical approaches to explaining human behavior ...

    a.   ... include Maslow's needs pyramid, which explains human behavior by an individual's needs and motivation.

    b.   ... include Kohlberg's pyramid of moral development, which can be used to explain human behavior by the capacity to make ethical decisions.

    c.   ... can be used to develop recommendations for fostering sustainable human behavior. For instance, Maslow's pyramid leads to the recommendation to focus on the moral development of people especially in developing countries.

    d.   ... features Kohlberg's pyramid of moral development, which might explain the fact that, despite of the negative environmental impact, wealthy people use big cars to gain esteem from others.

2. Characteristics of human behavior impeding sustainable living ...

    a.   ... include greed, because always wanting more does not go in accordance with a planet of finite resources, limiting growth.

    b.   ... include the characteristic of mental disconnect, describing how people are not able to understand the worldwide social and environmental issues on an intellectual level.

    c.   ... include the characteristic of present value focus, which keeps people from leaving their comfort zone and moving toward more sustainable behaviors.

    d.   ... include the fact that individual behavior often does not change before collective behavior does.

3. What business can do to influence people's behavior ...

    a.   ... includes responsible marketing. Responsible marketing here refers only to selling more sustainable products.

    b.   ... always creates costs and can hardly be harnessed as opportunities.

    c.   ... includes the possibility of educating people in the workplace toward more sustainable behaviors, which then might be transferred to sustainable behavior in private life.

    d.   ... does not include contributing to human development, as businesses should not assume the role of development agencies.

4. Sustainable lifestyles …

    a.   … are necessary in order to both reduce the footprint of individuals with medium-to-high incomes and to find viable future consumption styles for the upcoming new middle class in developing countries.

    b.   … need to develop to one or several optimum sustainable lifestyles with a footprint of exactly two per person.

    c.   … may be evaluated by the quantity (e.g., vegetarian meal versus meat-eater's meal) and the quality (e.g., one flight per year versus five flights per year) of consumption of an individual.

    d.   … include the idea that in order to develop a worldwide sustainable lifestyle for the future, the quality of consumption of an average individual has to be increased, independently from the individual's current income level in order to reach optimum sustainable lifestyles.

5. Activism …

    a.   … can be defined by its constituent elements of an individual's commitment to a certain cause, nonconformity with the actual status quo, and an action to change the situation.

    b.   … always comes in the form of a single individual's effort to change the status quo.

    c.   … includes so-called grass-roots activism, which refers to activists who exclusively tackle ecological issues.

    d.   … for sustainable development can be conducted in many of the roles we fulfill as individuals. In responsible business jargon, activists are often called "change agents."

6. Activist roles and vehicles …

    a.   … describe the reality that individuals can be activists in many different ways throughout the different roles taken in their life.

    b.   … do not include an individual's role as an investor.

    c.   … do not include an individual's engagement in political parties.

    d.   … include an individual's role as employee, actively changing the workplace toward more sustainability.

B. Think

Watch a movie on successful activists such as *The Yes Men Fix the World* or *The Cove*. Analyze how the activists in the movie identify a problem and then search for an opportunity to solve it. Think hard to identify one such problem-solving opportunity yourself and plan an action to seize the opportunity.

C. Do

Browse the many causes on online petition sites (e.g., ipetitions, avaaz, change. org), choose one petition you think is worth supporting, and make sure you have enough background information—beyond that given on the site—to cast your vote.

D. Relate

Think about who in your sphere of influence might benefit most from something you could do. Try to truly understand what the other person's situation and needs are, and how that person feels. Then do it!

E. Be

Inform yourself deeply about a lifestyle different than your own (e.g., being a vegetarian or vegan, living a no-waste life, living LOHAS or LOVOS). Organize yourself to lead your life following the principles of this lifestyle for a predetermined period of time. Then do it!

Feedback

A. Know

Question 1

a. Right: Maslow's pyramid is one of the classical approaches we have used in this chapter to explain unsustainable human behavior.

b. Right: Kohlberg's pyramid is one of the classical approaches we have used in this chapter to explain unsustainable human behavior.

c. Wrong: the recommendation given is actually related to Kohlberg's pyramid rather than Maslow's.

d. Right: this is an adequate description of an argument based on Kohlberg's pyramid of moral development.

Question 2

a. Right: greedy behavior by definition will make one's footprint exceed the planetary boundaries.

b. Wrong: mental disconnect refers to the psychological phenomenon that people know about the issues, but do not feel their personal connection to them.

c. Right: present value focus makes us value the current, comfortably unsustainable lifestyle more than future suffering in an unsustainable world.

d. Right: individuals will most likely find it difficult to behave contrary to dominant cultural behavior patterns.

Question 3

a. Wrong: responsible marketing refers to a drastic shift in marketing from promoting consumerism to promoting consumer independence and mature decision-making for consumption.

b. Wrong: businesses can find immense opportunities in influencing people's behavior.

c. Right: such a transfer might be one way businesses may contribute to changes toward more sustainable lifestyles among their employees and their families.

d. Wrong: businesses contribute to human development in many different ways.

Question 4

a. Right: sustainable lifestyles are the solution in both cases.

b. Wrong: a sustainable lifestyle, to be sustainable, has to result in a footprint of 1 or less.

c. Wrong: the examples for quality and quantity are the wrong way round.

d. Right: an increased sustainability quality will help current low-income consumers to not cross the sustainability threshold, and current high-income consumers to move back into the sustainability threshold of their consumption.

Question 5

    a. Right: these are the defining elements of activism.

    b. Wrong: activism does not always need to find its form in a single individual's effort. Organizational activism, such as the environmental activism of Greenpeace, is another form of activism.

    c. Wrong: grass-roots activism refers to activism that emerges naturally and spontaneously in society, without being initiated by existing institutions.

    d. Right: activism and change agency can be rooted in many different roles, such as being an employee, a consumer, or an entrepreneur.

Question 6

    a. Right: activism and change agency can be rooted in many different roles, such as being an employee, a consumer, or an entrepreneur.

    b. Wrong: investors can be activists for sustainable development. Examples are so-called angel investors and activist shareholders.

    c. Wrong: engagement in political parties is the longest-established vehicle for activism. An excellent example of party activism for sustainable development is the Green Party movement, which has achieved important change in many countries.

    d. Right: this is a description of possible activism from the employee role.

B. Think

Level	Social problem and opportunity analysis	Notes
+	Promising action plan grounded in unique social, environmental, or ethical opportunity	
=	Opportunity identified, but no promising action plan outlined	
–	No opportunity identified	

C. Do

Level	Acting with adequate amount of information	Notes
+	Petition decision was made based on sufficient and balanced information from the petition site and other external sources	
=	Decision to sign or not sign the petition was primarily based on information given on the petition website	
−	Specific petition was not identified, or decision to sign or not sign was not made	

D. Relate

Level	Acting on empathy	Notes
+	Action fits the benefited person due to the developed empathy	
=	Credible evidence of empathy for other person	
−	Little evidence of empathy development	

E. Be

Level	Self-organization for action	Notes
+	Lifestyle was lived authentically for the planned period of time	
=	Solid understanding of lifestyle and feasible self-organization efforts	
−	Little appreciation of the lifestyle principles and practices, or little self-organization efforts to live it	

18
Organizational change

> The transformation will bring with it huge shifts in terms of regulation, markets, consumer preferences, the pricing of inputs, and the measurement of profit and loss; all of which will impact business. Rather than follow change, business must lead this transformation.
>
> *Vision 2050* (WBCSD, 2010, p. 5)

Previous chapters have illustrated how to make incremental changes toward the assumption of first responsibilities. But baby steps are not enough. In order to reach a situation where businesses are truly sustainable, it requires disruptive change, a creative destruction and reconstruction of what businesses are and how they work. As early as 1927, Wallace Donham (1927, p. 406) wrote in *Harvard Business Review*, "Unless more of our business leaders learn to exercise their powers and responsibilities with a definitely increased sense of responsibility toward other groups (…) our civilization may well head for one of its periods of decline." Two years later he warned of the dangers of irresponsible economic growth and materialism (Donham, 1929). Have we learned anything since then? The last 80 years have provided ample time to take baby steps and apply theories, but now is the time to change business!

This chapter provides guidance on how to achieve this disruptive innovation of businesses in two basic ways:

1. Businesses may be transformed by strong leaders into more sustainable entities

2. Old unsustainable businesses might increasingly be supplanted by newly created sustainable businesses

Entrepreneurial business creations, boosted by the worldwide sustainability trend, have the potential to quickly grow to a size which can offer sustainability solutions on a global scale. Of course, there are also hybrid forms between transformation and entrepreneurship, such as corporate social entrepreneurship and social intrapreneurship, that will be covered in this chapter.

The first section describes what an optimum sustainable business should look like, providing basic classification schemes along dimensions of impact (unsustainable, sustainable, restorative) and level of responsiveness (from defensive to civic). It also provides clear guidance on what kind of business every organization should finally become. The second section focuses on the transformation of established business through leadership, change management, and sustainability project management. The third section then turns to entrepreneurial approaches to create completely new sustainable businesses or sustainable actions from either inside or outside established businesses. The entrepreneurial approaches covered are social and environmental entrepreneurship, intrapreneurship, and corporate social entrepreneurship.

Developing sustainable business

The responsibility trend among businesses has led to a situation where many businesses and their leaders decide to participate in responsible business, often ignorant of what makes a successful responsible business. What should this change toward a responsible business look like? What should be the goal of responsible business? How do we know how good the business is in its responsibility activities? Answering these questions is instrumental for successfully implementing responsible business. Decision-making for business leaders was comparatively easy before the change toward responsible business. The fundamental criterion for business activity and development, without breaking the law, was increasing profit. Now that the primacy of the profit motive is questioned, many businesses in their responsible activities seem to be drifting aimlessly, trying to find their way in a confusing world of responsible business norms, trends, and activities. This section will structure a basic development path for responsible business and provide clear goals.

Sketching the sustainable business

Throughout the preceding chapters, the focus has been on responsible business, presenting a commitment and the initial actions needed to increase the assumption of business responsibilities. Now the focus will be on developing a roadmap toward the final goal of becoming a sustainable business. What would be the perfect version of a sustainable business? This ideal business would be one that is not only neutrally sustainable (with an overall impact of 0), but also even restoratively sustainable with an overall positive impact, replenishing the Earth's

Eco-bank versus retro-bank

Seeing the flurry of different business models and supposedly sustainable ways of doing business, it is often hard to find out which one is actually responsible or is a sustainable alternative to business as usual. Make up your own mind: here are two competing examples from the German banking industry in the period after the 2007 financial crisis.

The German UmweltBank, which roughly translates as "Eco-bank," exclusively invests its clients' money in opportunities for double profit, a financial one for clients and an environmental one that offers positive environmental impact of investment projects. The bank has had these goals since its foundation in 1997. In 2011 the bank had a working capital of €1.6 billion and employed 150 people (UmweltBank, 2012).

The competing model is the Raiffeisenbank in the small southern German town of Gammesfeld, which we called the "Retro-bank." This operates very much like it would have done several decades ago, with an electric typewriter and calculating machine instead of a computer, and offices that resemble a museum. The bank's only employee, Peter Breiter, who at the same time fulfills the roles of cleaning staff, back-office and front desk manager, and only member of the bank's board of directors, describes "his" bank as the counter-design to what he calls "turbo-capitalism." The bank's investment strategy is rather conservative, for the only type of investment is in safe, but not very profitable, fixed-term deposits. In 2012, the bank had total assets of €25 million with which it achieved an annual profit of €40,000. During the financial subprime crisis, Mr. Breiter received requests from people from all over Germany who wanted to deposit their money at the "safest bank of Germany." All were rejected. Of course the bank does not want to grow. Neither does it want to get rich at the cost of others. Another operating principle predicates that every customer is treated exactly the same, irrespective of whether their deposit is a few euros or millions of euros (Die Welt, 2012).

Which bank do you think is more responsible and closer to becoming a role model for a sustainable banking business? What criteria can we apply to understanding how advanced a business is on the way to becoming truly sustainable and how it is doing in comparison to its peers?

resources. The ideal business that follows the sustainability paradigm would be one that acts as multiplier and inspires sustainability in other actors inside its industry, throughout value chain, and among its broader set of stakeholders.

Figure 18.1 is a roadmap for developing such an optimum sustainable business. The horizontal axis of the chart describes a succession of modes of implementation of responsible business practices, which Zadeck (2004) described as stages in the organizational learning process of becoming a more responsible business. Previous stages are included in the later stages, so a business can only be counted as having achieved the managerial stage if it also fulfills the conditions of the

Figure 18.1: Sustainable business practice and overall output model

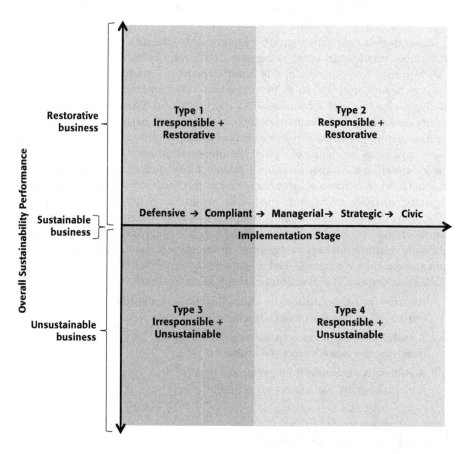

compliance stage, and the highest stage, civic responsibility, can only be counted as achieved if the company has also become a responsible business in its core management and strategic processes. The stages are based on the model of organizational learning for CSR (Zadeck, 2004).

- **Defensive stage:** businesses deny responsibilities to defend the business from reputational damage
- **Compliance stage:** businesses assume all responsibilities that are required by law, norms, and minimum stakeholder expectations by implementing basic policies
- **Managerial stage:** businesses embed responsible management in core management processes and daily operations
- **Strategic stage:** businesses integrate responsible business in core strategies to enhance economic and sustainable value

- **Civic stage:** businesses work as multipliers for sustainability, promoting it among other actors inside the industry and value chain, and among the broader set of stakeholders

These stages of implementation of responsible business can be seen as the input a business provides in order to become first a responsible and then a sustainable business. The outcome of this input, depending on additional external and internal factors, will lead to an impact, which is reflected in the overall sustainability performance of a business. The chart's vertical axis depicts the sustainability performance of a business, which might either be negative (unsustainable), neutral (neutral sustainability), or positive (restorative sustainability). Classifying the company as belonging to one of the implementation stages is less complex than estimating a company's overall sustainability performance. In Chapter 17 the footprint of individuals was compared to the Earth's environmental carrying capacity, whereby a footprint equal to or lower than 1 was defined as sustainable. Assessing and evaluating the footprint of a whole company, throughout the whole product life-cycle, requires an intensive life-cycle assessment and sustainability accounting process as described in Chapters 6 and 12. Once this process and assessment are accomplished, sustainability performance can be divided into three basic degrees of sustainability for any given business:

1. An **unsustainable business** is characterized by a negative overall life-cycle impact exceeding the planet's resource limits
2. A **sustainable business** is characterized by a neutral overall life-cycle impact, matching the planet's resource limits
3. A **restorative business** is characterized by a positive overall life-cycle impact, replenishing the planet's resource limits

---

A restorative business?

The eco-tourist business Amazonia Expeditions organizes tours from a lodge located in the Peruvian Amazon near to the city of Iquitos. A more extensive assessment might reveal that the venture is a great example of a restorative business and even a superficial analysis shows strong evidence for this. Not only is the lodge solar powered, but also most food is locally harvested and fished. Furthermore, the lodge is one of the economically, politically, and organizationally sustaining factors of the surrounding natural reserve. It provides employment and healthcare to local communities through the foundation, Angels of the Amazon, and lodge staff are crucially involved in the creation of micro-enterprises and the protection and restoration of the local ecosystem, including the creation of sustainable agricultural opportunities (Amazonia Expeditions, 2011).

Figure 18.1 does not intend to present a growth pattern of a business's overall sustainability performance, depending on its improvement in modes of implementation. Furthermore, a responsible business is not necessarily a more sustainable business. Indeed, a business at the highest stage of responsibility (the civic stage) is not necessarily a restorative business. Generally, it can be assumed that businesses move toward becoming sustainable in their overall performance the more they develop their modes of implementation for responsible business. Nevertheless, there can be no direct relation between stakeholder responsibilities taken and sustainability performance because far too many other external and internal factors play a role in truly achieving the status of a responsible business. There might be some businesses which are in their basic characteristics so unsustainable that, whatever good implementation practice they try, they will never be able to become completely neutral in their impact. Thus, business leaders aiming to create a responsible business need to understand their organizations' potential and limits. Only with this preparation will it be possible to draft a realistic and effective plan for responsible business development. The following section will provide insight into alternative implementation vehicles, potential drivers, and inhibitors on the way to becoming a responsible business.

Barriers, drivers, and vehicles on the road to sustainable business

What does the road to sustainable business look like? What are typical obstacles and enablers? What are the processes and vehicles available to create a responsible business? Barriers to implementation turn out to be varied (as illustrated in Table 18.1), according to the answers of more than 700 CEOs when asked about the main challenges of company-wide transformation of their business.

Implementation barriers encountered by practitioners can be supplemented by a brief list of bad practices, which inhibit transcendental changes toward sustainable business. Visser (2010) calls these bad practices the "curses" of responsible business:

- **Incremental responsibility:** businesses focusing on incremental possibilities, such as successively improving codes of compliance or continuous improvement in eco-efficiency, might miss the necessary big transformative changes
- **Peripheral responsibility:** businesses focusing on responsible business activities outside the core business will not be able to reach the maximum possible scale and maturity in their activities, thwarting sustainability performance
- **Immediately profitable responsibility:** companies only implementing responsible business activities that pay off immediately, or in the short term, will miss many crucial changes that enable them to become sustainable and that pay off in the long term

It is important to correctly define the word "curse." In fact, each bad practice has a place and valuable function in responsible business and each is a legitimate practice on the way to becoming a sustainable business: bad practices are only curses when businesses are not able to go beyond them.

Table 18.1: Barriers in the way of sustainable business

Barrier	Percentage of CEOs encountering this barrier among their top three obstacles	Approaches to overcoming the barrier
Complexity of implementing sustainability strategy across functions	49%	See Chapters 11 and 12
Competing strategic priorities	48%	See Chapters 8 and 9
Lack of recognition from financial markets	34%	See the finance section in Chapter 12
Differing definitions of responsible business	31%	See Chapters 3, 4 and 5
Difficulty in engaging with external groups	30%	See the stakeholder engagement section in Chapter 6, and Chapters 14 and 15 for stakeholder communication
Failure to recognize a link to value drivers	30%	See "The business case" box in Chapter 8
Lack of skills/knowledge among middle senior management	24%	See the training-related contents in Chapter 14
Lack of effective communication structure	15%	See Chapters 14 and 15
Employee resistance	7%	See Chapters 14 and 15, and the change management section of this chapter
Lack of board support	5%	See the persuasion section in Chapter 14

Source: Lacey *et al.*, 2010

Enablers who are catalysts for successful change are important to a successful path toward sustainable business. The CEO survey mentioned above identifies three main good practices:

1. Develop and launch sustainable products and services for both business-to-business customers and end-consumers. Creating an embedded sustainable implementation throughout internal processes and the external supply chain provides both short- and long-term financial incentives and is likely to

increase competitiveness. New products might range from detergents with reduced toxicity to products that involve fair-trade practices.

2. Make use of new sustainability technologies and innovation to fuel the development of new solutions for sustainable business and development inside and outside the business.

3. Excel at collaboration with all kinds of stakeholder to help tap resources for change inside and outside the company.

Focusing on these three good practices for change toward sustainable business promises a truly transformative responsible business implementation. These three practices are mutually reinforcing—a company should not focus on one practice alone because synergies are lost. For example, Procter and Gamble relies heavily on its "open innovation program" (collaboration) to develop new sustainable innovative products (products and services) and to achieve more sustainable production methods (technology) (Dodgson *et al.*, 2006).

The following two sections describe the main vehicles used for developing responsible business, each of which will provide hands-on insight into the process of creating a responsible business. While vehicle change management transforms a long-established business into a sustainable business, sustainable entrepreneurship creates new businesses that are actively contributing to sustainable development.

Transformational approaches

Transforming organizations of any size is a complex process which involves all systems and subsystems, as well as the interconnections between those systems. For a business to become sustainable, drastic change is often required in spheres as different as the company's organizational structure (power, decision-making, information, etc.), processes, products, values, vision, and even the most basic assumptions in the business and within its management. Imagine a business that realizes its most important input needs to be replaced, because that input is highly unsustainable. Imagine a different business that is forced to reinvent two-thirds of its products. Imagine a third business that realizes its core production technology can never become sustainable and needs to be replaced. These challenges sound overwhelming, even catastrophic, but can be overcome with a well-managed transformational process.

This section illustrates three central elements of transition processes. First, the central role of leadership in times of transition will be described. Second, change management will be introduced as the tool for managing the overall transition process. Third, we present an illustration of project management for successfully managing the manifold subprojects of organizational transitions toward becoming a sustainable business.

Leadership

What is a leader? Can managers be leaders? Aren't entrepreneurs also leaders? It is important to understand the differences and similarities between leaders, managers, and entrepreneurs. It is also important to understand the different roles played by all three groups play in creating sustainable businesses (Fig. 18.2). Leaders for sustainable business follow the basic target of providing guidance for transformation. Important traits of leaders are a clear vision of the sustainable business to be created and the charisma to lead others in achieving this vision. Managers are in charge of the operational aspects of creating effective and efficient departments, resulting in an attractive triple bottom line. To do so they require specialized knowledge in their respective areas of expertise and endurance for the continuous learning and improvement involved. Entrepreneurs for sustainable business take advantage of social, environmental, and economic opportunities to create new sustainable activities, or they may even create new organizations.

No followers, no leader

For the task of leadership it is crucial to understand the "followers" of sustainability leadership and how they can contribute to shifting the company toward sustainable development. There are typically four types of follower as described by Visser (2008):

1. Experts possess technical skills needed for responsible business implementation

2. Facilitators provide excellent interpersonal skills necessary for bringing on board key stakeholders

3. Catalysts have political skills important for assuring progress through times of hardship and opposition

4. Activists usually possess excellent critical skills, that keep the change agenda real and transformative.

These roles may overlap, but not always: for a sustainability leader, certain managerial and entrepreneurial traits will also enrich his transformational task, so it is important not to misunderstand leaders as being purely defined by their job position and institutional power. Some CEOs, who are usually understood as leaders, may in actuality be managers, and individuals at the base of organizational hierarchies may turn out to be great leaders of their respective group. Leaders for sustainability may appear at all levels of the organizational hierarchy (Ferdig, 2007). Such leaders might be the "enlightened" janitor who functions as operational leader of the company's waste separation program, the human resources manager inspiring change toward enhanced employee wellbeing, or the chief sustainability officer. Change happens in many parts of the company through manifold leaders, making leaders the most salient actors of the change

Figure 18.2: Profiles of leaders, managers, and entrepreneurs

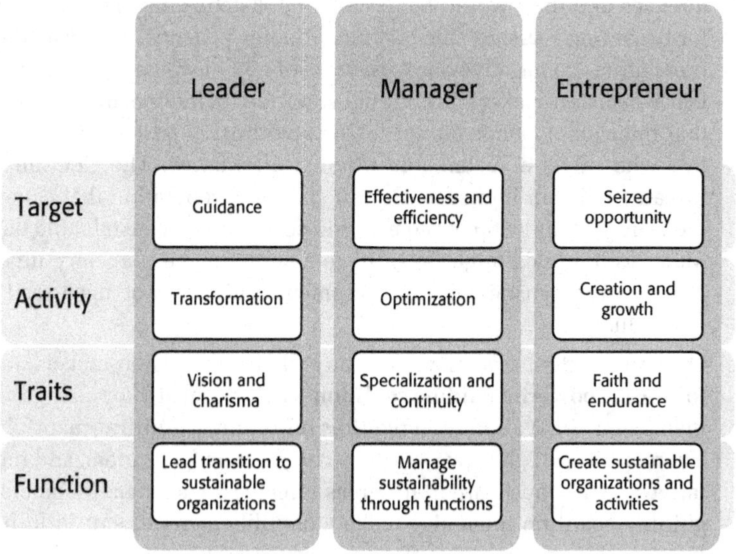

	Leader	Manager	Entrepreneur
Target	Guidance	Effectiveness and efficiency	Seized opportunity
Activity	Transformation	Optimization	Creation and growth
Traits	Vision and charisma	Specialization and continuity	Faith and endurance
Function	Lead transition to sustainable organizations	Manage sustainability through functions	Create sustainable organizations and activities

management process toward sustainable businesses and crucial for its success (Gill, 2003). The following section will highlight the process itself by illustrating the tool of change management.

Change management process

Good news first: the change management process toward sustainable business tends to be easier than other big organizational changes, at least from the following perspective. Typically, employee resistance to change is perceived as the main obstacle to a swift and effective change process, but this resistance is not the case in creating a sustainable business. Only 7% of CEOs report employee resistance among their top three obstacles (Table 18.1). It would appear that employees are enthusiastically inclined to make their business sustainable. Nevertheless, many other obstacles need to be overcome. Kotter (1995) has provided the best-established tool for managing organizational change, and it will be applied in the following steps to highlight the most crucial practices in transforming businesses into sustainable businesses. The tool consists of eight steps going from convincing people to create institutions to anchoring the sustainable business in the organizational structure, divided into three phases—preparation, implementation, and maintenance of change:

A. **Preparation phase**

1. The first step is to "establish a sense of urgency." Key decision-makers (and later all individuals involved in the change) in the organization need

to understand and feel that it is not only important, but also urgent to transform the organization, that there is no alternative and that the consequences of failure would be devastating. Establishing a sense of urgency for becoming a sustainable organization, for instance, can be achieved by translating the negative consequences of non-sustainable development to every decision-maker's individual situation. Marketers might understand that their job depends on not losing one-third of customers to a competitor who offers a sustainable product alternative. The CEO might feel threatened by an immense drop in company reputation that can only be fixed by making people perceive his company as a sustainable business. Many individuals might even have a sense of the planetary urgency to move toward sustainable development and will not necessarily need individual cues.

2. Once the leader has achieved the buy-in of key decision-makers, it is time to **"form a powerful guiding coalition"** in the form of a key change management team. Such a coalition requires individuals fulfilling manifold roles. There must be high-power individuals, knowledge leaders, and representatives of the most important areas affected by change. Members of the guiding coalition must also make a credible commitment to fulfill their function by channeling sufficient resources and personal effort into the sustainable business transformation.

3. Next, the guiding coalition, informed by a broader stakeholder dialog, must **"create a vision"** for the transformation, which in the best case conveys both the sense of urgency and the content of the sustainability shift. General Electric's Ecomagination (General Electric, 2012) or Marks & Spencer's "Plan A—Because there is no plan B" (Marks & Spencer, 2015) visions are excellent examples.

B. **Implementation phase**

4. The first step in this phase is to broadly and credibly **"communicate the vision"** of a sustainable business. The main goal is to motivate not only employees, but also other internal and external stakeholders to do their part in the transformation. In the communication process, it is crucial that the vision is communicated personally by the company's highest leaders, and by each employee's superior not only once, but periodically. Employees must understand that the sustainability transformation is there to last. Once employees and broader stakeholders are motivated to contribute to the shift, the task is to provide them with the necessary tools and power to make a difference.

5. **"Empowering others to act"** may involve activities such as assigning paid work time, allocating budgets or complete job profiles to work on the change, and installing communication channels, committees, and temporary institutions that provide an infrastructure to make a difference. Once employees are able to work on transforming the organization, it is

crucially important to make them see and feel the progress made toward becoming a sustainable business.

6. **"Planning for and creating short-term wins"** aims to provide employees with a sense of achievement that increases motivation and fuels future efforts. In order to communicate these wins credibly, it is important to have started the implementation phase with clear and measurable indicators that can be used to communicate tangible improvements.

C. **Maintenance and consolidation**

7. The first step in this phase should be to build on the first results that were achieved during implementation to **consolidate improvements and create yet more change**. Only when the first wave of change management activities can be translated into a medium- to long-term priority activity can the goal of becoming a responsible and sustainable business be achieved. Companies might define best practices and create working groups with the task to transfer new approaches to scalable results.

8. For the final stage, the salient task is to **institutionalize new approaches** to anchor them in the organization's institutional structure. Institutionalization might consist of the creation of job positions, centers, hotlines, periodical events, and budgets exclusively dedicated to responsible business. Institutionalization might also include periodical sustainability reports, sustainability scorecards, and the inclusion of sustainability-related indicators into every employee's performance evaluation as common good practices.

These eight steps for organizational change toward responsible business provide a basic recipe which then needs to be refined by extensive practice and customized to each company's peculiarities. As with recipes in cooking, all steps are important, for leaving out just one step will inevitably be detrimental to the overall result. Many change initiatives toward sustainable business fail as early as the preparation stage when, for instance, it fails to establish a sense of urgency. Others make the mistake of thinking the change is done with implementation and do not ensure continued maintenance, allowing the business to fall back into its old unsustainable patterns.

Unlike many other change initiatives, change toward sustainable business cannot only be conducted as a top-down process where high-level management decides and lower hierarchies follow. Involving stakeholders at all hierarchy levels, inside and outside the company, is imperative for developing a business that is responsible in all its stakeholder relations and sustainable in its impact. As Figure 18.3 illustrates, a high-level, management-driven, top-down change strategy is just one of many change approaches that in the optimum case must do its part in effecting change throughout the company. A so-called bottom-up change strategy is driven by momentum from the lower hierarchical levels of the company and has strong similarities to the grass-roots activism discussed previously. Nucleus strategies consist of many "cells" of change that effect change in

Is "the PUMA" changing?

The sneaker and sportswear company PUMA hit the headlines for its creative and progressive responsible business conduct in 2010. The company's CEO Jochen Zeitz called it "a transformative year (...) in many ways" and explicitly referred to the next stage of the company's sustainability strategy (PUMA, 2011a).

Did the company actually follow the change management process? Let's go through it step by step:

1. Urgency: PUMA stated that "we feel the one can't go without the other. Sustainability is a necessary lifestyle and not a luxury anymore and is therefore central to our long-term future—not only for PUMA's business success, but also for the environment on which we all rely. Sustainability is key to PUMA's long-term progress as much as Sport and Lifestyle are part of the essence of our brand" (PUMA, 2011a, p. 7).

2. Coalition: responsible business leadership at PUMA involves the company's CEO, support from the company's majority shareholder, the French PPR group's sustainability team (other labels include Gucci and Yves Saint Laurent), and external experts (Liggett, 2011).

3. Vision: the company's vision/mission statement reads as follows: "Our mission to be the world's most desirable and sustainable Sportslifestyle company is driven by the 4Keys: Fair, Honest, Positive and Creative, that guide our work on a daily basis." (PUMA, 2011a, p. 14)

4. Communication: the vision/mission statement, presented as being the company's core purpose, includes sustainability at its heart and this is communicated constantly throughout internal and external communication channels.

5. Enablers: PUMA stated: "PUMA is committed to living these Keys and is focused on empowering employees and suppliers on all levels to take action towards our collective sustainable goals—ultimately helping to provide an authentic and informed customer experience" (PUMA, 2011a, p. 14). An excellent example of the practical implementation of this enabling purpose is the close collaboration with suppliers and the measures described below, which enable consumers to consume more sustainably.

their sphere of influence, and nuclei can be located on any hierarchical level. The wedge-change strategy broadly targets middle managers and enables them as change agents. For change toward sustainable business it is important to complement these internal change initiatives by an outside-in change strategy that allows external organizational stakeholders to participate in change. An inside-out change strategy, where company representatives act as change agents in the company's environment, is also complementary and important. Changing a company toward sustainable business requires extensive adaptation of its environment from technological change to legislation. This change includes a shift in

6. Wins: the years 2010 and 2011 brought a series of sustainability wins for PUMA, consisting of impressive developments toward responsible business which constantly reinforced stakeholders' faith in the overall sustainability efforts of the company. In April 2010, PUMA launched its highly innovative new shoe packaging, replacing the classic shoe box and plastic bag with a reusable design that uses "65% less cardboard, has no laminated printing, no tissue paper, takes up less space and weighs less in shipping" (Gould, 2010). The company's 2010 annual report innovatively included an environmental profit and loss account, including water and CO_2 footprints, not only for PUMA itself, but also for several tiers of suppliers, a worldwide first that made history (PUMA, 2011b). Early in 2011 the company launched biodegradable shoes, promising to revolutionize the waste impact of the very difficult to recycle sneakers (Chua, 2011).

7. Consolidation: it would appear that PUMA was able to continue to innovate high-quality responsible management activities. This was very likely a sign that responsible business had become a part of the company's culture. PUMA now had to show that it would also be able to use the managerial activity to create real-life results for business, society, and environment.

8. Institutionalization: the company had long been creating institutions and reinforcing its sustainability performance. Examples include the code of ethics, the code of conduct for both employees and suppliers, the company-wide sustainability scorecard, and the parent company PPR's "Creative Sustainability Lab" with an annual budget of US$14.1 million (Liggett, 2011).

There is no doubt that PUMA's transformative efforts had gone a long way in establishing the company as a leader in responsible management practices, but was the company truly on the way to becoming a sustainable business? Based on the company's vision ("the world's most sustainable Sportslifestyle company"), PUMA took a best-in-class approach to evaluating its sustainability performance relative to industry peers. The company seemed to be successful in the parameters of this strategy, being ranked as the most sustainable company in its industry by the Dow Jones Sustainability Index in 2010. More than half a decade after Puma's revolutionary moves it appears the Company has gone back to average. Looking at Puma's achievements in sustainability, there is a visible decline in activity after 2013 (http://about.puma.com/en/sustainability) What has happened?

the mind-set of external stakeholders, such as customers and suppliers. The goal is to embed the sustainable company in a sustainable system, which enhances the stability and resilience of both.

Responsible project management for sustainable business

Changing a business toward sustainability involves a myriad of subprojects, each important for the overall process. Projects are different than the overall task of sustainable development because they are usually much shorter in the time

Figure 18.3: Complementary change approaches

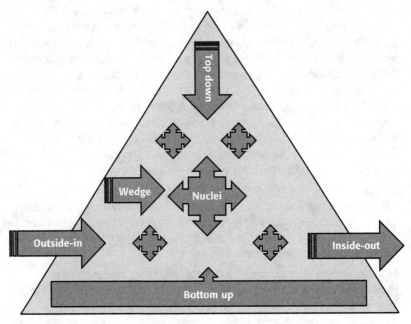

they take to complete. They are also reduced in scale and scope as they focus on subgoals of the overall change to sustainable business (Wysocki, 2009). As illustrated in Figure 18.4, such projects can be classified by the primary project goal (related or unrelated to the responsibility and sustainability of the company) and by the impact made throughout the conduct of the project (responsible/sustainable or not). For instance, if a cosmetic business develops a new skin cream, the primary goal of the project would not be related to the company's responsibility or sustainability. Nevertheless, the project conduct might or might not involve animal testing, for instance, as an environmentally irresponsible practice. If it did, it would be an intolerable project for a responsible business. If it did not, from a responsibility point of view, it would fall into the well-managed project category. If another company used animal testing (conduct) to create a cure for a deadly disease (project goal), it would categorize the project as well-intentioned. A business might decide to conduct well-intentioned projects with a negative conduct for the sake of the final goal. The preferable project type in responsible business is an impact-optimizing project which pursues the goal to further the company's responsibility and sustainability, while also honoring both through the project conduct. In this section we will refer to responsible and sustainable project management when talking about the project's conduct, and about responsibility and sustainability projects when referring to the primary project goals.

Managing projects in responsible and sustainable business requires different consideration than mainstream project management. The following description will provide a quick primer for sustainability project management throughout the three phases of project management (Wysocki, 2009):

1. **Prepare:** define available inputs and intended outputs
2. **Run:** ensure alignment with goals and with principles and sustainability
3. **Close:** communicate transparently and transfer results to organizational process

The project preparation phase determines the potential scope and quality of project goals. For sustainability projects, the project quality especially needs to include concise indicators for not only economic, but also social and environmental project results. The main goal at this preparation stage is to harmonize the available inputs with the desired outputs. Three main inputs need to be considered when preparing a (sustainability) project, which directly influence in the potential scope and quality of project outputs (Wysocki, 2009):

1. The time to completion of the project must be defined. In this context it is important to make sure that, even when projects are of rather short duration, a lasting impact contributing to long-term sustainability is achieved.
2. The economic cost of the project needs to be defined and reflected by assigning an assured budget for all three phases of the project management process. Items to be considered specifically in a sustainability project include costs of assessing social and environmental impacts, and costs of skill development for sustainability or hiring external experts.

Figure 18.4: Categorizing projects by responsibility and sustainability criteria

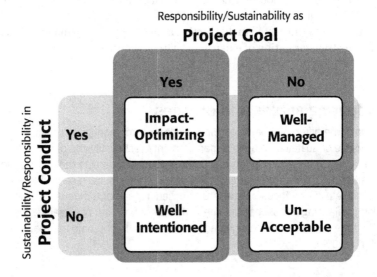

3. Defining resources available might require the hiring of external staff and the reduction of responsibilities for internal staff assigned to the project, including office space assignments, and also communication channels and power given to the sustainability project. As sustainability projects often involve far-reaching change, which may in turn create resistance, the assigning of sufficient resources to assure change in spite of adversity is even more important than in mainstream projects. An important intangible resource is to know exactly where the project goal is ranked on the company's priority list.

To run a sustainability project, the most important task that is different than mainstream projects is ensuring the alignment of all details of the project implementation with values related to responsibility and sustainable development. Negative social and environmental impacts have to be avoided wherever possible. Neglecting "details" of sustainability in project conduct may cost valuable credibility among internal collaborators and the external public. Down-to-earth examples of bad practice are excessive printing (paper footprint), traveling (CO_2), socially irresponsible work conditions (e.g., overtime, contractual issues, hiring and firing), or morally irresponsible behavior of employees (e.g., bullying or embezzlement). The implementation of the project must be a role model for the practices of what the sustainable business is expected to become.

To close the sustainability project, special attention needs to be paid to transparently communicating the process and assuring that project results can be translated into change toward sustainability at an organizational level. Communicating the process, unlike mainstream projects, requires establishing extensive stakeholder dialog, including all groups related to project conduct and outcomes, inside and outside the organization. Projects in this final stage need to be reconnected to the organizational change task of becoming a sustainable business. Project outcomes can be used to communicate short-term wins stimulating the organizational change process (stage six of the organizational change process). Learning from project conduct can be used to increase the efficiency of other sustainability projects.

The approaches illustrated in this section aimed to provide management tools for effecting the transformation of existing activities, products, and whole businesses.

Comparing apples and oranges

So what's the difference between mainstream project management and responsible or sustainable project management? Technically, the difference may not be too big, and might not even be visible from outside the organization. It is rather the details that matter on the inside. For instance, responsible and sustainable projects focus on consensus-based instead of top-down decision-making, balancing a triple bottom line with a predefined set of project goals, and require systemic thinking instead of a linear single-outcome approach (Griffiths, 2007).

The following section focuses on entrepreneurial approaches, involving innovation and new creation.

Entrepreneurial approaches

What is entrepreneurship? Who is an entrepreneur? What do tough business people such as Facebook founder Marc Zuckerberg and the Nobel Peace Prize-winner Muhammad Yunus have in common? However different these two personalities might seem, the answer is simple: they both tackled an opportunity by an innovation and faced significant complexity in bringing their venture to scale. The defining characteristic of entrepreneurs is that they perceive an opportunity that is not necessarily an economic opportunity. In the case of Muhammad Yunus, it was a social opportunity that improved the life of poor women. Both entrepreneurs then seized the opportunity with an innovation: Zuckerberg with his new social networking technology, Yunus with microcredit. The ambiguity involved in creating and implementing innovation automatically brings about more complexity than would be encountered in a management activity. Figure 18.5 summarizes these three defining characteristics of entrepreneurship, with the addition of a further list of variable characteristics.

It is these variable characteristics that open up endless opportunities for entrepreneurship to contribute to creating sustainable businesses and further sustainable development. The motivation of entrepreneurial ventures might be either classic economic value creation or social and environmental causes that contribute to sustainable development. The realized impact of a venture might be a social, environmental, or economic one. The profit motivation might be either

Figure 18.5: Characteristics of entrepreneurship

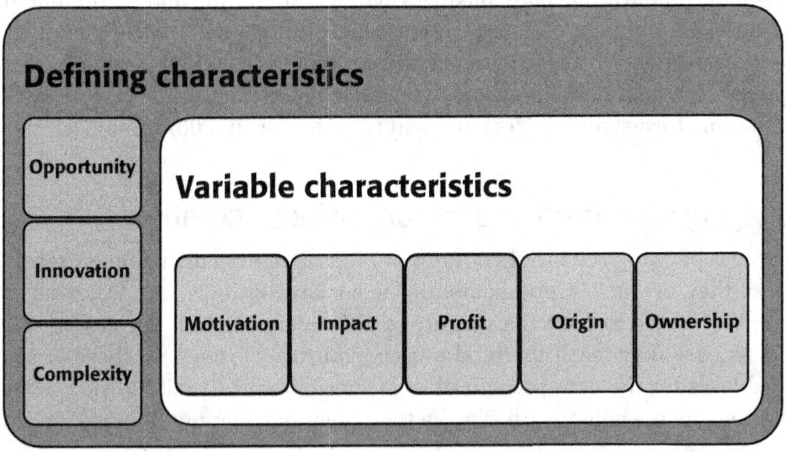

Greenworks versus Grameen

Both companies are entrepreneurial ventures, but could not be more different. Each shares one thing in common: they seize social or environmental opportunities. Greenworks produces natural cleaning products, reducing the environmental footprint, while the Grameen Bank provides microfinance products to reduce poverty. Greenworks is owned by the multinational Clorox Corporation and driven by corporate strategy. Grameen is a cooperative owned by its own customers and driven by Professor Muhammad Yunus's vision of social business (Cate *et al.*, 2009; Grameen Bank, 2010). However different these two ventures are, both share common characteristics, such as seizing an opportunity, complexity in implementation, and innovation as the basis of the venture.

a for-profit or not-for-profit focus, reinvesting profits made into the venture. The origin of ventures might be from an established business or NGO, or from an individual person. The entrepreneurial models resulting from the different combinations of these characteristics can be summarized into two broad types; models embedded in an existing business, and models for the creation of new business. The ownership of an enterprise might lie with single individuals, a broad group (e.g., a cooperative), or an established company.

Models embedded in established businesses can be divided into two main approaches: corporate social entrepreneurship, which highlights the potential of big businesses to seize opportunities for sustainable development in a powerful and scalable way (Austin and Reficco, 2009), and social intrapreneurship, which focuses on individuals and their potential to make a difference for sustainable development, seizing opportunities from within a business (SustainAbility, 2008). Corporate social entrepreneurship focuses on the overall business as entrepreneurial actor, whereas social entrepreneurship is associated with creating a business which has a social cause as its main motivation, and/or creates considerable social value with its main business activity. Environmental entrepreneurship does the same thing, but focuses on creating solutions for environmental causes, whereas sustainability entrepreneurship, sometimes called "sustainopreneurship," takes a more holistic perspective, and aims to further one or a set of causes contributing to sustainable development (Abrahamsson, 2007).

Managing entrepreneurship for business creation

The stages of entrepreneurial ventures are the same in mainstream entrepreneurship as they are in entrepreneurship for sustainable business. After an initial conceptual phase to plan the venture, and implementation and growth phases, the enterprise may reach the final phase, maturity. Throughout these stages, the typical tasks for the entrepreneur change considerably. Crucial to success is that entrepreneurs are able to either make the transition from one stage to another, or to hire people with the necessary skills. The majority of enterprises never reach maturity, and so understanding these different phases is vital for the venture. The following paragraphs characterize each stage, with a special focus on the peculiarities of entrepreneurship in creating a sustainable business.

During the concept stage of development, the entrepreneur's main task is to identify a social, environmental, or economic opportunity and develop a detailed strategy for seizing this opportunity. Problems become opportunities when one holds the key to the solution (or mitigation). The more pressing the problem, the more likely it will be that somebody will finance the entrepreneurial solution. Social and environmental entrepreneurs often use sustainable innovations as a means to seize opportunities. Unlike mainstream entrepreneurial ventures, the main source of income for sustainability ventures does not necessarily need to come from the customers, as such ventures appeal to a greater group of stakeholders due to the social good and environmental benefits created. Governmental institutions, foundations, interest groups, and other stakeholders are often interested in supporting with cash and by making donations in kind. Any social, environmental, and economic issues related to sustainable development have the potential to be an excellent basis for a venture. The conceptual stage is usually summarized by the development of a business plan, which sums up all aspects of the planned venture and is a key reference document for both managing implementation and finding organizational support. Contents typically covered in a business plan are the value proposition, key activities, partners, resources, customer segmentations, relationships, distribution channels, cost structure, and revenue streams (Osterwalder and Pigneur, 2010).

During the implementation phase, the business plan is put into practice. During the conceptual stage, the main entrepreneurial skill is vision and the ability to plan, but for implementation entrepreneurs must be able to show endurance, flexibility, and a strong will to succeed. Implementing a venture is an iterative process, which necessarily includes highs and lows. The primary challenge is financial survival while productive processes and structures are subject to constant change until a working system is implemented. Acquisition of customers and standardization of processes are key activities during the implementation process.

The growth stage involves drafting a strategy for bringing the business to scale. Apart from the financial advantages of company size (e.g., economies of scale), there is a striking argument for quick growth in ventures for sustainable development. The bigger the venture, the bigger the positive sustainable impact to be made. Growth strategies might involve, for instance, sustainability venture capital, partnerships between corporations and sustainability enterprises, mergers and acquisitions, or sustainability franchising (Tracey and Jarvis, 2007).

Once the maturity stage of a business is reached, the opportunity which initially fueled the quick growth of the venture begins to decrease and the business experiences less growth, stagnation or even a decline. The challenge in the maturity stage is therefore to define what the business should become. There are two basic strategic choices: entrepreneurs might either sell their business or innovate to seize a new opportunity. A critical factor in selling a sustainability enterprise is to assure the persistence of sustainability performance and values under new ownership; role model social enterprises such as The Body Shop (sold to L'Oreal) and Burt's Bees (sold to Clorox) have gone down this road with mixed results. Identifying new opportunities might be another viable solution, drawing on the entrepreneurial experience made before, while at the same time leveraging the financial resources of the mature venture. TOMS Shoes, for instance, translated its successful buy-one-donate-one business model from shoes to eyeglasses as a new stream of business (TOMS Shoes, 2012).

Managing entrepreneurship in established businesses

Entrepreneurial approaches to managing responsible business are a promising tool for effecting dynamic change. Such approaches can be divided into corporate social entrepreneurship (CSE), which highlights the potential of big corporations to proactively bring about scalable solutions to major sustainability challenges (Austin and Reficco, 2009), and social or more generalized sustainable intrapreneurship, which highlights how individuals can solve sustainability issues from the inside a company, while still deploying an entrepreneurial process and mindset. Both tools exist in a mutually reinforcing relationship: a company needs intrapreneurs to develop CSE and a company-wide CSE approach to create the most favorable environment for single individuals' intrapreneurial activity for sustainable development.

The intrapreneurial animal kingdom

The SustainAbility guide for entrepreneurs compares social intrapreneurs with four kinds of inhabitant of the animal kingdom, each contributing different important characteristics to the intrapreneurial task. Intrapreneurs must be like donkeys with the capability of carrying the weight of transformation and able to plod along with it. They must also be like giraffes with their head in the clouds (vision to create sustainable business) and their feet firmly on the ground to step over obstacles. Social intrapreneurs must endure periods of loneliness like a wolf during times when their vision of responsible businesses is not shared. Finally, intrapreneurs must be like beavers, reshaping their company's landscape and creating lakes and cascades of opportunities for the business to be changed (SustainAbility, 2008).

The company-internal venture process basically runs through the same stages as external ventures, as already discussed above, and thus does not require repeated illustration. However, one factor that does deserve heightened attention are the collaboration strategies for sustainable intrapreneurship. A guide for social intrapreneurship proposes three different strategies that companies might deploy to facilitate intrapreneurship, depending on the business and venture structure and purpose (SustainAbility, 2008):

1. The **island strategy** allows intrapreneurs to work in isolation from the main business while being on the payroll. Isolation supports the development of innovative, disruptive, or even radical ideas, far away from the usual business rationale, values, and practices. Island strategies require special attention to reintegration of outputs in the mainstream business.

2. A **bridges strategy** provides the intrapreneur with great autonomy, while allowing for some well-defined links for support. Bridges might be communication channels or access to resources and information. The bridges strategy facilitates entrepreneurial outcomes with direct support from the main business.

3. The **symbiosis strategy** aims to locate the intrapreneurial venture right inside the main business, in order to facilitate as many synergetic relationships as possible.

Exercises

A. Know

Use the multiple choice questions below to test your knowledge. Each answer may be wrong or right and there may be zero to four right or wrong answers per question:

1. The different types of sustainable, responsible, and irresponsible business ...
   a. ... include an ideal type of sustainable business that is restoratively sustainable (it even replenishes the Earth's natural capital). Additionally, such a business would work to multiply its good practices among other actors.
   b. ... is a basic classification, involving the business's overall impact (from defensive to civic) and stage of implementation (from very negative to very positive).
   c. ... are related to the business's mode of implementation, describing the different ways a business might manage its responsibilities. For instance, a business might be defensive (fiercely defending its stakeholders and their claims) or strategic (implementing a strategy to avoid responsibilities).
   d. ... relate to a business's overall sustainability performance. Companies can be classified as unsustainable (exceeding the global footprint), sustainable (exactly matching the planet's resource limits), or restorative (replenishing the planet's natural resources).

2. Leaders ...
   a. ... managers, and entrepreneurs all fulfill the same function.
   b. ... for sustainable business primarily need a clear vision of what the sustainable business should look like and the power to lead others toward this vision.
   c. ... of a sustainable business might at the same time also be managers or entrepreneurs.
   d. ... for sustainable business are always representatives of high-level management.

3. Change management ...
   a. ... to create a responsible business is always impeded by very high resistance to change by employees.
   b. ... has been described by Kotter's tool of eight steps for successful change management.
   c. ... ends with the final step of enabling others to act on the vision of sustainable business. From this point on, change will happen automatically.
   d. ... includes creating institutional structures such as budgets, fixed job positions, and official communication channels.

4. Entrepreneurship ...
    a.   ... always refers to creating a new business.
    b.   ... among its defining characteristics has complexity, innovation, and seizing opportunities for profit.
    c.   ... can contribute to sustainable business both from the inside of an established business, and through the establishment of new businesses.
    d.   ... in both of its forms, social entrepreneurship and corporate social entrepreneurship, aims to create new businesses with a social purpose.

5. Entrepreneurship in established businesses ...
    a.   ... may take the form of corporate social entrepreneurship, where single individuals try to change the company from the inside toward more sustainable ways.
    b.   ... may take the form of intrapreneurship.
    c.   ... is related to the island strategy, where social intrapreneurs work in isolation from the main business to develop sustainability ideas for it.
    d.   ... may be achieved by the symbiosis strategy, where businesses aim to establish a mutually reinforcing relationship with a social or environmental cause.

6. Entrepreneurship for creating new sustainable businesses ...
    a.   ... can be divided into four main stages, ranging from the conceptualization of the venture to its maturity.
    b.   ... once it enters the growth stage, is able to magnify its positive social and environmental impact.
    c.   ... in the maturity stage, includes the example of The Body Shop, which was sold to L'Oreal.
    d.   ... means the only possible action, once an entrepreneurial sustainable business venture enters the maturity stage, is to sell it off.

B. Think

Imagine you were in charge of managing the transformation toward sustainability of a company of your choice. Envision what (radical) changes the company would have to go through to become truly sustainable. Then prepare a change management plan according to Kotter's change management process.

C. Do

Conduct a mini-project for sustainability, responsibility, or ethics, either in your private or professional life.

D. Relate

Observe what someone does (for instance, inside a shop, an office, a restaurant, etc.) and identify one practice/activity that appears to be unsustainable to you.

Engage the person in conversation, aiming to both develop an appreciation for why the person does this practice and trying to find more sustainable alternatives. Make sure the person does not feel bothered, pushed, or cornered through the conversation.

E. Be

How do you feel about the possibility of being an entrepreneur? Could you imagine launching and managing an enterprise? Do you feel motivated to drive new ventures, possibly inside in existing company? Are you generally motivated to innovate and pursue opportunities?

Feedback

A. Know

Question 1

    a.   Right: such a business combines the civic stage of business responsibility with a restoratively sustainable output.

    b.   Wrong: the descriptions of overall impact and stage of implementation are the wrong way round.

    c.   Wrong: the descriptions given for defensive and strategic are wrong.

    d.   Right: this is a correct description of the different levels of output in relation to sustainability.

Question 2

    a.   Wrong: while leaders fulfill the function of leading the transformation of an existing business, mangers manage sustainability throughout different business functions, and entrepreneurs create sustainable organizations and activities.

    b.   Right: vision and power to lead are the two main characteristics necessary for leadership.

    c.   Right: leaders may emerge at all parts of the company.

    d.   Wrong: leaders can emerge at all levels of organizational hierarchy.

Question 3

    a.   Wrong: employees have been found to be mostly very supportive of change for becoming a responsible business.

    b.   Right: Kotter's change management process perfectly summarizes the main elements of making large-scale change in a company happen.

    c.   Wrong: enabling others to act is not the final step of change management.

    d.   Right: the institutionalization of the change—making it stick—is part of the change management process.

Question 4

    a.   Wrong: for instance, intrapreneurship and corporate social entrepreneurship describe entrepreneurial activities from inside an established business.

    b.   Wrong: opportunities do not necessarily have to be for-profit opportunities, but can also be of a social, environmental, or ethical nature.

    c.   Right: entrepreneurial ventures may be either embedded into an established business, or lead to the creation of a new business.

    d.   Wrong: corporate social entrepreneurship uses existing businesses to tackle a social opportunity.

Question 5

a. Wrong: corporate social entrepreneurship does not refer to changing the business, but to using the business as a vehicle to seize external opportunities to make a difference for society and environment.
b. Right: intrapreneurship and corporate social entrepreneurship are both types of entrepreneurship located within an established business.
c. Right: the island strategy helps to create entrepreneurial solutions without the restrictions resulting from being deeply embedded in the company.
d. Wrong: the symbiosis strategy refers to intrapreneurs working in close union with the business, in order to achieve synergies.

Question 6

a. Right: the entrepreneurial venture runs through distinct stages, requiring often different entrepreneurial competences per stage.
b. Right: the impact of a business is multiplied through growth and expansion.
c. Right: The Body Shop being sold to L'Oreal is an example of what might happen with sustainability ventures in the maturity stage.
d. Wrong: an alternative action is to restart the entrepreneurial process and use the established business to seize another sustainability opportunity.

B. Think

Level	Strategic thinking	Notes
+	Vision and change process appear deeply thought through and very feasible	
=	A basic vision has been developed, based on the current position of the company, and a basic change process has been outlined	
–	No or a barely feasible change management plan has been developed	

C. Do

Level	Project management skills	Notes
+	Project has come to successful closure from the perspective of both mainstream and responsible management	
=	Project has been planned and initiated based on solid project management skills from the perspective of both mainstream and responsible management	
–	Project has been planned superficially or conducted feebly	

D. Relate

Level	Engaging into meaningful conversation	Notes
+	Conversation has led to learning about sustainability in one or both conversation partners	
=	Conversation has taken place, but did not prove meaningful to learning about sustainability or to improving practices	
–	Conversation has not happened	

E. Be

Level	Entrepreneurial motivation	Notes
+	Strong motivation toward entrepreneurial action	
=	No strong drive toward being entrepreneurial, but it is a possibility	
–	Being entrepreneurial appears unattractive, or even "scary"	

19
Systemic change

> [W]ithin the current international political economic system it would be nearly impossible to adopt development strategies that are conducive to truly sustainable development.
>
> (Carvalho, 2001, p. 61)

Most people assume it is enough simply to change people and businesses, a change which will result in improvements of the economic system. According to systems theory, a system is more than the sum of its elements. Systems have complex internal mechanisms that, in the case of the economic system, can either impede or facilitate the sustainable development of the system as a whole, including the businesses working in it and individuals in their various roles. The economic system is like a machine that needs correct maintenance to produce the intended output: sustainability. This chapter shows that the "rusty wheels" of the machine need oiling and helps to identify the right buttons and levers to speed up the process.

The first section highlights the characteristics of the economic system that can sabotage sustainable development, and shows why the economic system is highly resistant to change. This section also illustrates alternative approaches to traditional capitalism. The second section focuses on transforming subsystems, such as supply chains, industries, or local industry clusters toward sustainability, and emphasizes one potential strategy to make the overall system sustainable. The third section takes the opposite approach by showing how to change the basic conditions and rules of the overall system through public policy instruments, instead of changing subsystems.

Changing systems

A different economic reality

"Economic growth has been decoupled from ecosystem destruction and material consumption, and re-coupled with sustainable economic development and societal well-being. Society has redefined the notion of prosperity and successful lifestyles, as well as the bases of profit and loss, progress and value creation to include more long-term considerations such as environmental impacts and personal and societal well-being" *Vision 2050* (WBCSD, 2010, p. 6).

The economic system has been blamed extensively as the root cause of unsustainable development. This section asks if the system is a mere outcome of the actions of single individuals and organizations, and will it change automatically if people live sustainable lifestyles and companies become sustainable businesses? We assume an economic system can be considered an entity in its own right and that the whole is more than the pure sum of its elements. System elements may be either considerable impediments or positive leverage for achieving sustainable development.

From GNP to GNH for a happy planet

In 2005 the government of Bhutan decided to measure national success by happiness, rather than merely by economic measures. The Gross Happiness Index (GNH) was born and covers nine indicators from Indicator 1, psychological wellbeing, to Indictator 9, time use and happiness (Centre for Bhutan Studies, 2012). The links between economic wealth and happiness are weak, and maybe a change of focus from countries' GDP to their GNH might be a starting point for economic systems that truly serve people's wellbeing instead of their wallets. The Happy Planet Index illustrates the "relative efficiency with which nations convert the planet's natural resources into long and happy lives for their citizens" or, in short, "How much happiness do we get for the resources we use?" (New Economics Foundation, 2012).

What is an economic system and what are sustainable mechanisms within the economy? An economic system consists of interconnected mechanisms and institutions aimed at the allocation of resources to the creation and use of goods and services. A sustainable economic system would lead to an allocation that is socially, environmentally, and economically sustainable in the long term. Achieving this goal implies that both the elements of the system and the connections between those elements are sustainable. As illustrated in Figure 19.1, elements of the economic system are businesses, governmental and

Figure 19.1: Elements, interrelations, and embeddedness of the economic system

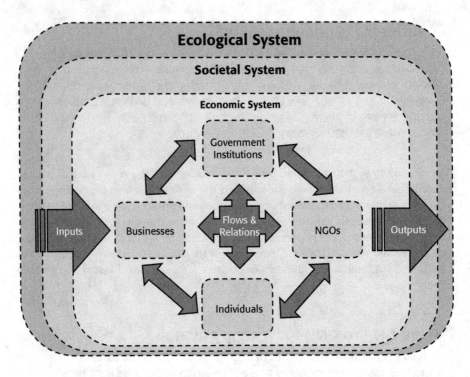

nongovernmental organizations, and individuals as consumers and employees. Connections between the economic system's elements consist of moving flows, such as financial, material, and information flows. The elements of the economic system are also connected by stable relations such as legal responsibilities, norms, values, culture, and power structures. Furthermore, the system is not closed: it requires inputs (e.g., natural resources, labor, ideas) and outputs (e.g., waste, welfare, innovation) to society and the environment. The following sections illustrate how the inherently stable relations that characterize a system need to be understood, influenced, and changed in order to achieve the final goal of a stable sustainable economic system.

Characteristics worth changing

Is the current global economic system truly detrimental to sustainable development? What needs to be changed? How do these changes relate to sustainable business? We covered these ideas extensively in Chapter 1. We now illustrate three of the root causes of the economic system's unsustainability:

1. The **growth imperative** applies to most economic activity inside the system—more is better. Growing a country's GDP, company's revenue, or an individual's income and consumption are just a few examples. Economic growth comes with increased resource consumption, further exceeding the planet's ecological resource-production and waste-absorption capacity. The required systemic change is to **degrow** its planetary impact to a sustainable level of 1, while providing the growing world population with the employment, goods, and services necessary for living a decent life.

2. Neglecting **external effects** creates unsustainable situations as outcomes of the market mechanism. Imagine a fast-food company that would be forced to pay the direct and future environmental cost of destroying the Brazilian rainforest for meat production. This company then would need to include this cost in the price of a hamburger, which might increase to US$50 per piece. Imagine the average price of a car at US$100,000. These figures are fiction, but might not be very far from reality. The change task is to **internalize external costs** in market mechanisms, such as pricing, so that many unsustainable decisions will no longer be made.

3. A long-established preconception is that social **inequality** is built into the global economic system, and that it will always make the rich richer and the poor poorer. However, this might not be completely true: an analysis of recent global developments suggests that there is a sluggish development toward more global wealth equality (Roser, 2015). Nevertheless, it does not go fast enough. The change task is to create a global economic system that redistributes wealth and includes helping the poor in their economic activity and its benefits. This new feature of the economic system might be the remedy for unsustainable population growth as illustrated in Chapter 17.

System resilience

The Kyoto protocol, the United Nations Global Compact, and the Global Reporting Initiative are just some of the manifold, powerful global initiatives for making the economic system more sustainable. In spite of all this effort, change is at best sluggish. One characteristic of systems is to display certain resilience—they are highly resistant to change. In order to change the economic system to more sustainable ways, system resilience needs to be understood and overcome. There are three main reasons why systems are hard to change:

1. Systems exist in a dynamic equilibrium, meaning that the relationships between system elements stabilize the status quo. Examples are values, such as the profit imperative or an irresponsible business morality, which the system reinforces internally.

2. Systems experience leads to path dependence, meaning that past decisions influence the decisions to be made in the present and future. For instance, the past development of a carbon-based economic system goes against current efforts to reorient the economic system toward alternative energy sources.

Economics primer

To understand the relationship between the economic, social, and environmental systems, it is crucial to have a basic working knowledge of central concepts related to economics. These concepts can be divided into the fields of environmental economics (relationship between economy and environment) and welfare economics (relationship between economy and society).

The field of **environmental economics** comprises a wide variety of economic analysis instruments mostly related to idea of external effects (externalities). The idea of differentiating between externalities and internalities was introduced in 1920 by Arthur Pigou (2005), who promoted the idea that any action has a private cost (internal cost) to the actor and a social cost, incurred by society in general (external cost). External costs maybe be social but are primarily environmental, such as pollution through a factory's waste-water being channeled into a river. A so-called Pigouvian tax aims to reduce the effect of negative externalities by internalizing them. Companies are forced to pay a tax, which corresponds to the size of the social costs (externalities) created by their activity. As the company incurs this cost, decision-makers have an incentive to avoid the cost of the tax and to reduce the creation of externalities. The opposite case is a Pigouvian subsidy, where companies are rewarded for any positive externalities created. For instance, the European Union strongly subsidizes renewable energies. This type of internalization provides companies with the incentive to create more positive externalities.

Another way to control externalities is the introduction of a market for externalities, where external effects are traded. This idea has its roots in the work of Ronald Coase, who proposed that the introduction of property rights for externalities would lead to an efficient overall amount of externalities. For instance, the European Union Emissions Trading Scheme gives companies the right to emit a certain maximum amount of CO_2. This right becomes a property of the company, which it can then sell as any other property. These property rights could then be traded in a market. The Coase Theorem states that such a market will create efficient results, no matter the initial allocation of property rights for externalities, in the absence of transaction costs (Coase, 1960). Thus, property rights could lie either with polluters or with the party injured by the negative externalities.

A commons is a resource that is non-excludable, meaning that anybody can use it. Examples of commons are the fish stock in the open sea or air quality. Nobody can be kept from using these, but the more they are used, the less there is left for each user. The term "tragedy of the commons" was coined by Garrett Hardin (1968) and is widely used in environmental economics to describe human behavior which leads to the over-use and final depletion of any commons used to illustrate the unsustainability of current lifestyles.

Environmental economics should not be confused with **ecological economics**. While environmental economics conforms to neoclassical economic theory, ecological economics is rather "revolutionary" in the sense that it rejects many traditional assumptions of neoclassical economics such as the growth paradigm, and the understanding of humans as an egoist and rational *Homo oeconomicus* (Daly and Farley, 2004; Farley *et al.*, 2005).

Welfare economics describes the relationship between economic factors and social welfare, such as the relationship between the overall wealth created by economic activity and how it is distributed. A useful metaphor is that of a cake at a birthday party: the cake should be as big as possible (wealth creation) and the slices should be evenly enjoyed by all attendees (distribution). The Italian economist Vilfredo Pareto (Samuelson and Nordhaus, 2005) defined the efficiency of economic activity as a situation where no individual involved in a certain situation can improve his or her personal welfare without decreasing the welfare of somebody else. This reasoning is called Pareto efficiency, and is in line with the utilitarian "greatest happiness principle" in aiming to maximize the utility and happiness of all involved parties.

The Pareto criterion falls short in assessing equality or the wellbeing of individuals inside a group of people (e.g., a country), as it cannot analyze the distribution of wealth in a country. Instead, the Lorenz curve (Lorenz, 1905) describes how equally wealth is distributed inside a given group, by plotting the percentage of households on the x-axis and the percentage of total income on the y-axis. The reality in countries lies somewhere between two extremes—the most unequal distribution, where one individual is in possession of all income, and the most equal situation, where every person has exactly the same income. The Gini coefficient is a quantitative measurement of income inequality based on the Lorenz curve (Todaro and Smith, 2006).

One important question related to income distribution and economic growth is how income equality develops along with economic development. The Kuznets curve (Kuznets, 1955) is an instrument that describes the relationships between economic development and income equality as a curve in the shape of an inverted "U" (Fig. 17.2). At the beginning of economic development, the possibilities for single individuals to make a fortune (e.g., as an entrepreneur) are large, which increases inequality. The more advanced and mature the economic development becomes, the smaller these possibilities and the stronger the mechanisms for redistributing the fortunes that have already been made. The Kuznets curve has found application in both welfare and environmental economics, where it is applied to the amount of pollution depending on the degree of economic development.

In the most drastic case, the path to carbon dependence can even lead to a lock-in situation, where decision-makers are completely dependent on a single option. For instance, the enormous initial investment and complicated, time-intensive switch-off procedure for a nuclear power plant has led to a technological lock-in of nuclear energy production.

3. Power reinforces power, meaning that powerful players with unsustainable impact use their power to prevent or slow down changes toward costly or even business-harming sustainability initiatives and regulation. Lobbying by the tobacco and petroleum industries, or the agricultural sector in Europe, has led to considerable delays in tackling these industries' sustainability issues.

System resilience is not always bad news. A sustainable economic system, once created, may develop self-reinforcing resilience which stabilizes the new system. The crucial question is: "Will it be possible to change the planetary socioeconomic system before it is too late?" The set of convergent crises illustrated in Chapter 1 leads us to assume that it is likely that we will not be able to avert such a global mega-catastrophe. The best-case scenario, if the global community cannot avert the crises, is highly likely to be a destabilization of the unsustainable economic system to such a degree that it can be changed or rebuilt in more sustainable ways afterwards. If systems are very resilient, the most reliable force for system change is an external shock.

Symptoms of resilience and setback?

Is our economic system moving toward sustainability? Anecdotal evidence casts doubt that it can happen. For instance, in October 2011, British Petroleum regained permission to drill additional oil wells in the Gulf of Mexico, not long after having caused the death of 11 workers and a spill of millions of barrels of crude oil into the Gulf of Mexico, one of the biggest environmental disasters of the new millennium (Krauss, 2011). Can the system become sustainable if we renew the "social license to operate" of a company that has failed so hard? Doubts still remain. Furthermore, in December of the same year, Canada pulled out of the Kyoto protocol because it could not meet the goals set (Guardian, 2011). Is a sustainable economic system possible if an important player bails out of such a crucial commitment? And consider also that, in December 2011, Brazil changed its forest code to drastically reduce protection of the Amazon rainforest compared with the previous legislation (Black, 2011). In February of 2016, the supreme court of the United States of America blocked key elements of Barack Obama's progressive climate change plan (Goldenberg, 2016). Can we reach a sustainable economic system if we accept such drawbacks in legislation?

Envisioning a new system

New economic systems need to solve at least three core problems with the old economic system as mentioned earlier in this chapter. Several approaches for alternative economic systems have been developed in the past, each addressing a different sustainability problem with the economic system. The ecological economics approach aims to create a market system that includes environmental factors, such as the effects that achieve environmental sustainability of the overall system (Common and Perrings, 1992). The Eco-socialism Movement attributes current social and environmental problems to the capitalist system and globalization, and aims to tackle those problems through common ownership by the people and by providing general access to the commons (Pepper, 1993). The social market economy model, created in Germany, occupies the middle ground between socialism and *laissez-faire* economic liberalism by assuring strong social welfare through state intervention, with the minimum possible obstruction of market mechanisms.

Masters of transition

In 2011, Schumacher College in the UK, in association with the New Economics Foundation, the Transition Network and the Business School at Plymouth University, launched a master's program that exclusively focuses on topics related to achieving a transition toward a sustainable economic system (Schumacher College, 2012).

Figure 19.2: Approaches to system change for sustainability

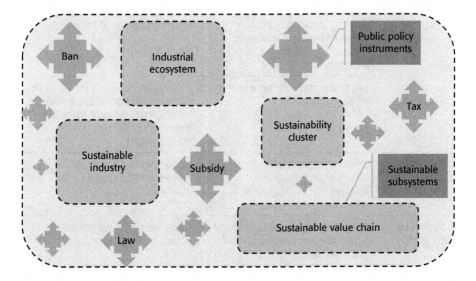

An optimum sustainable economic system might not yet have been envisioned but, whatever it turns out to be, it is important to start change in the right direction right now. The following sections illustrate two approaches to changing the system (see Fig. 19.2). The first is to create sustainable subsystems through sustainability clusters, industrial ecosystems, or sustainable supply chains and industries, which are supposed to change the system from within. The second is to leverage public policy instruments to change the rules of the overall system, which then forces the system to adapt toward more sustainability.

Transforming subsystems

The first step in a bottom-up strategy for changing the overall system is to change economic subsystems. The second task is to grow these subsystems in number and size to transform the overall system from within. Previous chapters have already introduced and discussed these subsystems: the sustainable value chain model in Chapter 13, for instance, can be considered a system of economic actors, coordinating their efforts to become jointly sustainable; similarly, sustainable

Table 19.1: Prominent types of sustainable economic subsystem

Type of system	Aspiration	Entity
Industrial ecosystems	Achieve a locally self-sustaining, zero-waste system	Proximate industrial activities with the potential to connect in their resource usage
Sustainability clusters	Reach maximum synergies, resulting in highest social, environmental, and economic competitiveness among related industries	Similarity and topical relatedness of locally concentrated industries
Sustainable value chains	Create a sustainable value chain of single products	Chain of production and consumption from first raw material extraction to last value extraction from product through ultimate end-consumer
Sustainable industry	Create a sustainable industrial system of production and consumption including several related products	Businesses and consumers connected through the same industry
Sustainable community	Self-sufficiency, social welfare, and sustainable environmental impact of a community	Businesses, citizens, and public actors, shaping a joint community

living communities, mentioned in Chapter 17, can be considered socioeconomic subsystems of social, economic, and political actors, coordinating their varied contributions to make the community system sustainable. Table 19.1 summarizes prominent types of sustainable economic subsystem, their objectives, the basic unit of analysis (entity), and prominent examples of their practice and implementation. The following two sections illustrate the two specific forms of industrial ecosystems and sustainability clusters in greater detail.

Industrial ecosystems

Doesn't the term "industrial ecology" sound like an inherent contradiction? Often industry and ecology are perceived as opposing concepts (Erkmann, 1997) but, interestingly, the intersection of these two terms has given birth to the industrial ecology approach and its main practice application, so-called industrial ecosystems. An industrial ecosystem takes natural ecosystems as an ideal model for industrial organization. Natural ecosystems are usually very resilient and, more importantly, exist in a restoratively sustainable manner. They are circular (perfect recycling), do not create any waste, and are usually able to work with solar power as the only energy input. Even if we could only create a few of these features in an industrial ecosystem, we would have solved many of the environmental problems caused by economic activity.

The highest art of biomimicry

Biomimicry (Benyus, 2002) describes the process of human design being inspired by designs in nature. Biomimicry has been applied in many ways, mainly for product development. Examples are high-speed trains whose aerodynamic characteristics were inspired by the head of a shark, hammers that absorb shocks like woodpeckers, and buildings that "breathe" like termite hives. Biomimicry is ready for the next stage: the big task is now not to just copy single features of ecosystems, but to design whole new economic systems and subsystems following the overall principles of ecosystems. Such systems would restore capital instead of consuming it, eliminate waste, and work within the resource limits of the planet. Achieving such a state of the economic system could be called "the highest art of biomimicry."

Figure 19.3 illustrates the basic mechanisms and objectives of an industrial ecosystem. In contrast to global approaches, such as sustainable supply chain management, industrial ecosystems exist on a local scale with strong local connections. Thus, industrial ecosystems aim to use as many local resources as sustainably as possible to avoid environmental impact from transportation. Industrial ecosystems also aim to minimize waste to a degree that can be absorbed and processed by the local surrounding ecosystem. How can these goals be achieved?

Figure 19.3: Industrial ecosystem mechanisms

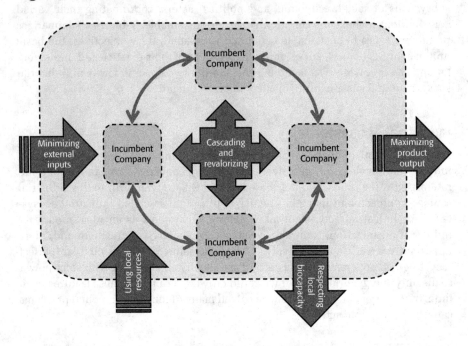

Figure 19.4: Resource cascading and revalorization

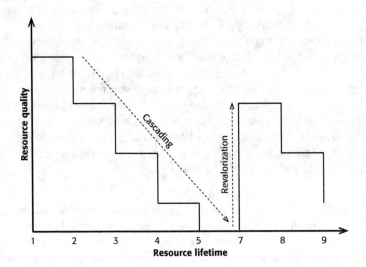

Companies forming part of an industrial ecosystem can develop close links to reach a maximum efficiency in joint resource usage (eco-efficiency).

The two main mechanisms for achieving such efficient resource usage are cascading and revalorizing (see Fig. 19.4). Resource cascading refers to using the same resource several times until all value has been extracted and it is useless. The underlying pattern is to use the resource first for the process that requires the highest resource quality. After every usage the quality of the resource is reduced and can merely be used for processes that suffice with a lower resource quality. For instance, a coal (higher-quality resource) energy plant might capture the fly ash left over after burning (lower-quality resource) and sell it to a gypsum factory, which uses the ash as the main input for its production process. An interesting example of energy cascading can be developed from the same coal energy plant. Coal (highest-energy intensity) is used to heat water in the power generation process. The heated water (lower-energy intensity) can be used for fish farming, which requires warm water all the year round.

While cascading only involves the allocation of lower-quality resources to the correct use, revalorization involves an additional process which increases the resource's quality: its value. For instance, paper will be usable again after recycling. After being treated, waste-water can be used for many purposes. Cascading and revalorization have the strongest effect when combined, so an industrial ecosystem therefore needs a diversity of companies in order to facilitate the processes of both cascading and revalorization.

Although industrial ecosystems have a strong environment focus, they do not yet take into account the creation of social value. A future task is therefore to include the social dimension of sustainability into industrial ecosystem development. The cascading and revalorization concepts do have the potential to be broadened to cover social resource quality, given that industrial ecology in many of its elements is already positively aligned with economic value creation, with increased efficiency in environmental resources often saving companies money.

Growing an industrial ecosystem

The industrial ecosystem in the Danish city of Kalundborg, approximately 100 km from Copenhagen, has been described as the role model for an industrial ecosystem. The system began to form in 1976 when local farmers started using sludge from the town's Novo Nordisk plant as fertilizer (Ehrenfeld and Gertler, 1997). By 2007 the industrial ecosystem involved efficiency-increasing relationships between more than 20 companies, including the exchange of heat, water, fly ash, biomass, all waste for the emitter, and valuable input for the receiver. This industrial ecosystem is also intimately connected with the local natural ecosystems of a local fjord and lake (Cervantes, 2007).

Sustainability clusters

Business clusters are "geographic concentrations of interconnected companies, specialized suppliers, service providers, firms in related industries, and associated institutions (e.g., universities, standards agencies, trade associations) in a particular field that compete but also cooperate" (Porter, 2000). A finance cluster exists in London, a technology and entrepreneurship cluster in California's Silicon Valley, and a diamond cluster in Rotterdam. Clusters support companies and whole regions in developing a competitive advantage, and hone a business's capability to excel in the market by providing strong local competition, highly specialized cluster suppliers, and sophisticated local customers (Porter, 1990). Developing clusters for responsible business is a promising approach, as it involves direct economic benefit from increased cluster competitiveness for both companies and governments involved. Simultaneously, developing responsible business clusters also increases social and environmental competitiveness, jointly creating a responsible competitiveness (Zadeck, 2006). Two different types of cluster are important for responsible business:

1. In **sustainability industry clusters**, companies and industries group locally around a certain sustainability cause, technology, or industry type. A sustainability consulting cluster exists in London, an eco-tourism cluster in the Mexican Riviera Maya, and a sustainable construction cluster around Lisbon.

2. **Responsible mainstream clusters** involve old-established industries that have taken a local turn toward sustainability. The southern German car-manufacturing cluster has developed into a center of excellence for sustainable mobility with companies such as BMW, Audi, and Mercedes shaping a local, more sustainable cluster infrastructure.

Important cluster elements defining the size and quality of a cluster are factor conditions (inputs), demand conditions (customers), a network of related and supporting industries, and the context for firm strategy and rivalry (local laws regulations, incentives, values) (Porter, 1990; Porter and Kramer, 2006). To learn how to create responsible business clusters, it is crucial to understand how each of the cluster elements may contribute to the sustainability of the overall cluster:

*   Factor conditions or inputs determine the functionality of a sustainability cluster in many ways. In order for a food retailer to offer locally grown organic food, this special input needs to be available locally at competitive prices. For a responsible mainstream businesses cluster, it is crucial to find local human resource individuals trained in responsible business.

*   Demand conditions for responsible business clusters are related to customers' attitudes toward responsible business and the degree of sustainability of customers' lifestyles and consumption patterns. When migrating from a mainstream to a responsible business cluster, it is increasingly important to perceive business stakeholders as an important "customer" of the social and environmental component of responsible business

performance. Demanding stakeholders are an additional condition serving to hone responsible business competitiveness.

- Related and supporting industries and businesses include both antagonistic and cooperative relationships. Imagine a green tech cluster. It may be beneficial, for instance, for a solar technology company inside a green tech cluster to have direct competitors nearby, or even to cooperation with competitors on new technology development, industry initiatives, or lobbying. At the same time, the same cluster might include companies developing alternative engine technologies. It might be possible to develop a joint solar-powered engine technology or to jointly invest in battery systems, which are critical to both industries.

- The context for strategy and rivalry for responsible business clusters consists of local public policy factors, such as subsidies for responsible businesses, or high taxation for irresponsible firms. The context factor of local business culture can also have a strong influence.

Which is the world's responsible business capital?

London would definitely be on the list of potential candidates. The city is home to some of the most powerful consultancies and centers dealing with responsible business, such as the SustainAbility or AccountAbility. London is also the world's main hub for socially responsible investments, being the home of the FTSE4Good Index, a stock exchange listing responsible enterprises. The U.K.'s public policy structure is reportedly the world's most advanced (Bertelsmann Stiftung and GTZ, 2007), which gives additional incentives for responsible business development. Both customers and providers in the U.K. are typically highly sensitive to social and environmental issues, and a wide variety of highly renowned universities, such as the London School of Economics, Oxford University, and Cambridge University, have developed specialized degree programs for related sustainability topics, and fuel London's thriving sustainability industries with highly qualified human resources. All of these factors contribute to a conducive climate for the development of clusters related to sustainability and responsibility. No wonder that the city has now become the breeding ground for one of the world's most advanced responsible business clusters, the Green Enterprise District, which will "show the world what the future should look like." This district accumulates businesses and organizations that have a social or environmental purpose and provides them with the infrastructure for low carbon and waste elimination (London Development Agency, 2010).

How should we build and grow responsible business clusters? Zadeck (2006) lists many factors leading to the creation and growth of such clusters, which are all encapsulated by one or another of the cluster conditions mentioned above. Examples include stakeholder pressure (demand conditions), the statutory environment (context for strategy and environment), and business initiatives (related and supporting industries). Once established, a healthy cluster tends to self-reinforce itself with favorable conditions for growth. A high concentration of similar, related enterprises and industries tends to attract a wider variety of specialized factor conditions and vice versa. To actively grow a cluster, an organic growth process is required, simultaneously improving all four cluster conditions. Increasingly, governments become active in creating the necessary context for responsible business cluster creation and growth, and so the following section will provide a quick overview on how public policies can create a favorable environment for not only responsible business clusters, but also a transition to a sustainable economic system.

The role of public policy in systems change

While the preceding section illustrated several ways of creating sustainable subsystems within the overall economic system, this section focuses on changing the economic system's normative infrastructure. The main actors in such infrastructure change are governments (e.g., local administrations, national governments, and regional bodies such as the European Union), supra-governmental institutions (e.g., the United Nations and World Bank) and NGOs with normative "soft" power (e.g., the Global Reporting Initiative and the International Organization

Figure 19.5: Policies and political actors for sustainable development

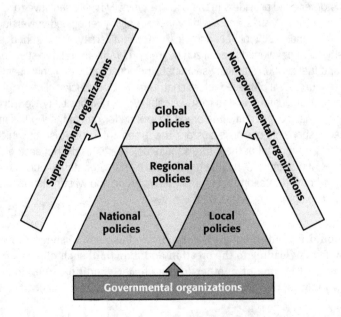

for Standardization). While traditionally only governments are seen as actors of public policies, they are not the only ones with the ability to change "the rules of the game" as, for instance, NGOs are increasingly able to be normative political actors in their own right and influence "world civic politics" (Wapner, 1995).

Responsible business and the sustainability of the world economic system can be achieved by creating efficient institutions governing business conduct (Vanberg, 2007). Creating these institutions will be the primary goal, to be achieved by designing public policies for sustainable world development. In the context of this book, "public policies" has served as a wide umbrella term, including all policies for the creation of an institutional infrastructure for a sustainable economic system. Figure 19.5 illustrates the interconnection between policies and political actors for sustainable development.

Change of the economic system's normative context may be realized on the following four different levels, all of which include different interactions between actors. The goal of sustainable development is allocated at a global policy level. A global issue requires global policies to develop solutions but, as there is no all-embracing, coherent global governance system, policies for sustainable development on a global level are fragmented and partially binding. In the absence of a global government, supranational and global nongovernmental institutions have taken the lead in developing global policies. For instance, the United Nations is leading political efforts in poverty reduction and environmental protection. NGOs such as the Global Reporting Initiative and the World Wildlife Fund press hard to achieve participation in and compliance with global standards of sustainable business and living. Goals for the institutionalization process on a global level are both to create a higher degree of coordination of efforts and to make the standards legally binding.

Is a world government for sustainability possible?

Sustainable development, especially environmental issues, does not have national borders. Global warming, water scarcity, ecosystem damage, and poverty are all problems that require resolute and legally binding actions at a global level. The topic of a potential world government has been both emphasized and criticized. Before the 1993 Rio conference, there was talk of a potential conspiracy by the world's money elite, using environmental topics to reach for world dominance. The Rio+20 congress in 2012 declared the strengthening of an "institutional framework for sustainable development" as one of the two main goals of the event (United Nations, 2012a). Perhaps the conference indicated a move toward a world government for sustainable development?

Regional policies for sustainable development aim to create a sustainable economic system for major global regions such as Latin America or Europe. Regional policies differ greatly in their achievements for sustainable development because of differing levels of regional organization. The European Union is a role model for regional public policies for sustainable development with many policy packages, fostering sustainability clusters, technologies, and sustainable consumption—a landmark document is *Making Europe a Pole of Excellence on CSR* (Commission of the European Communities, 2006). The foremost task for the development of public policies and institutions and promoting a sustainable economic system is to create a higher level of regional coordination and cooperation for sustainable development.

The big advantage at a national and local level (e.g., cities, counties, federal state) is the increasing power of elected governments to create formal public policies for sustainable development. Strategies for developing effective public policies for the creation of sustainable economic systems at a national level can be divided into the three elements of contents (what causes are covered), context (how good is the general infrastructure for sustainable economic system), and maturity (how advanced are the public policy measures taken) (Bertelsmann Stiftung and GTZ, 2007).

Policy instruments to internalize external effects

There is a wide variety of public policy instruments for creating a sustainable economic system. One of the main tasks to be achieved, often called the "silver bullet" for bringing down the unsustainable economic system, is the internalization of external effects. The goal is to achieve a situation where companies pay for negative external effects (e.g., pollution) and are rewarded for positive external effects they create (e.g., reforestation).

The following three instruments all focus on the internalization of external effects and vary in effectiveness and applicability, depending on the situation. (To better understand the underlying justifications and mechanisms, see the "Economics primer" box.) The practice examples given for the three policy measures—prohibition, taxation, and introduction of markets—all refer to public policies related to air emissions in mostly European Union member states. These policy instruments might serve to fulfill two basic purposes. First, policy instruments are designed to change behavior toward the creation of less negative or more positive external effects. Second, the remediation effect of policy instruments aims to mitigate the negative consequences of external effects (e.g., to clean up pollution or to fund the healthcare costs of affected individuals) or to reward the creators of positive externalities:

1. Prohibition and permission aim to control negative external effects by eliminating the sources of the effects. Examples include the prohibition of socially and environmentally harmful products, production methods, or even whole industries. A weaker form of prohibition is to only provide permission to operate in the case of compliance with certain requirements that avoid or minimize negative environmental effects. Cars, for instance, only receive market access to the European Union if complying with emission standards. Many major European cities do not allow the cars of non-residents into the

city centers. Most types of factory do not receive a permission to operate if they do not apply up-to-date filter technologies.

2. Taxes and subsidies aim to put a price on negative externalities (taxes) and a reward on positive ones (subsidies): countries such as Denmark, the U.K., and Germany apply a so-called eco-tax on the use of energy to reduce related CO_2 emissions, for instance, while others, such as Japan, offer eco-subsidies for fuel efficient cars (Kim, 2011). In the optimum situation, the degree of the tax or subsidy should for two reasons correspond exactly to the cost caused by the externality. First, the externality is "internalized," meaning that the company pays the full price or receives the full benefit of its actions. The second reason is that, especially in the case of negative externalities, the harm done can be remediated through the tax income. Unfortunately, it is very difficult to define and attribute the complete and exact external costs and benefits to the actor causing them. Also, the tax income is often not explicitly and exclusively (if at all) dedicated to remediation efforts.

3. Introducing a market on which external effects are traded is the least mature public policy instrument, but has shown great potential and provided the first tangible results. The mechanism is simple and follows the "cap and trade" principle. First, the government decides on the overall amount of external effects (e.g., 500,000 tonnes of CO_2 emissions), the so-called cap. Then an allowance for a maximum amount of external effects is distributed to the main polluters. If they pollute less than their allowed individual cap, they are allowed to trade the difference between actual emissions and allowed emissions to other companies that exceeded their emission limit. These companies can literally buy the right to pollute. However, the overall pollution level would never exceed the initial cap. Regulators may then consider reducing the overall cap in order to reduce the overall amount of external effects in the long term. The best-known and most extensive example of introducing a market for external effects is the European Emission Trading Scheme (ETS).

Trading whales and thick air?

Introducing markets to control external effects may lead to strange schemes. Trading the right to emit CO_2, for instance, is literally trading (thick) air. A little "heavier" is the exchange in the market proposed by an economist and two marine scientists in 2012. The idea was to allocate property rights to whales, which meant whaling countries could buy the right to hunt whales (catch quota) from antiwhaling countries. Vice versa, antiwhaling countries could buy the right to hunt whales from whaling countries, and would then not make use of them (Eilperin, 2012).

Inhibitors of public policies for sustainable development

If there is such a broad choice of effective instruments, why are public policies for sustainable development and a sustainable economic system not yet achieving a far broader level of deployment? An interesting answer might lie in the decision-making process of political actors. The Overton window illustrates that political action in the form of implemented policies is only taken if the general citizen's opinion of the intended policy is very favorable; i.e., the policy to be implemented must be popular. As illustrated in Figure 19.6, many key issues regarding achieving sustainable development are not yet on the popular stage; some, such as degrowth or a world government for sustainable development, might be perceived as outright radical or unthinkable.

Such political action might be explained by political actors only acting in the interest that is reflected in popular opinion. Another less favorable but understandable explanation is the mechanism of blame avoidance, whereby political actors might not want to "lean too far out of the window" when implementing necessary but not commonly accepted policies for sustainable development (Lehman, 2010; Weaver, 1986). What does this mean for the goal of a sustainable economic system as an important pillar for achieving sustainable development? In order to transform the world's economic system to a truly sustainable status, all actors for sustainable development need to actively promote and educate the world's citizens to take big steps toward the sustainability of human beings on Earth.

Another inhibitor of the legislative progress for sustainable development may be lobbying. For instance, the petroleum and tobacco industries have a long history of slowing down political progress toward sustainable development to protect their industries from harsh regulation. However, companies have also been increasingly observed to be lobbying for *stricter* sustainability regulation. This especially makes sense for leading businesses in social and environmental efforts, as it benefits them in their competition against sustainability laggards.

Figure 19.6: The Overton window for selected responsible business topics

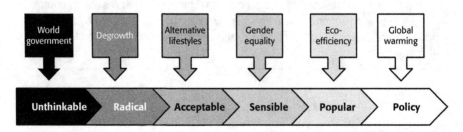

Ready for the next wave?

Changes toward more sustainability do not happen in a linear pattern, but rather in "waves" sweeping over business and society and causing considerable change in little time. After each wave, there is a downphase, during which change might not seem as drastic, but which serves as preparation time for the next wave. The first pressure wave took place from the early 1960s and brought about most of the environmental legislation in place today. The second wave took place over a longer period, from the 1970s to the 1990s, and triggered large-scale criticism of specific companies' misconduct and the creation of most of the international NGOs for responsible business, such as the Global Compact and the Global Reporting initiative. The third wave, in the early 2000s, was characterized by criticism of globalization and multinational business as well as a rapid improvement of supply chain conditions. Now, in the 2010s, the fourth wave shows a rapid increase in entrepreneurial and proactive solutions to global challenges (SustainAbility, 2008). What will be the next wave? Could it bring true sustainability and a profound transformation of the global economic system?

Exercises

A. Know

Use the multiple choice questions below to test your knowledge. Each answer may be wrong or right and there may be zero to four right or wrong answers per question:

1. Changing the economic system ...
   a. ... may be a very complex task, as a system is more than the pure sum of its parts.
   b. ... involves changing the elements of a system, such as the flows of resources.
   c. ... involves influencing the connections between the elements of the system. Examples might be laws, values, and responsibilities between elements.
   d. ... involves considering the embeddedness of the society and environment within the economic system.

2. Root causes of the economic system's unsustainability ...
   a. ... include the fact that the economic system is geared toward growth.
   b. ... require, among other things, the change task of creating mechanisms to internalize external effects.
   c. ... include external effects. External effects if internalized may lead to a situation where people pay the full price for products and this way factor external effects in their buying decision.
   d. ... includes inequality, in the sense that companies should treat all employees equally.

3. System resilience ...
   a. ... refers to systems' high instability.
   b. ... can, among other things, be explained by equilibriums inside the system that are self-reinforcing.
   c. ... can, among other things, be explained by path dependence, which is when organizations inside a system aim to follow the goals recently chosen and therefore leave the system.
   d. ... can, among other things, be explained by power mechanisms. For instance, a powerful corporation with an unsustainable product may have the power to stabilize the system in which it sells such a product.

4. Transforming the subsystems of the overall economic system ...
   a. ... includes the idea of creating industrial ecosystems, which aim to connect a single business with its surrounding natural ecosystem.
   b. ... includes sustainable value chains and clusters. The difference between them is that sustainable value chains aim to create a local network of

companies related to responsible business, while sustainability clusters aim to make all processes involved in producing a single product sustainable.

   c.   … might include creating sustainable communities, involving local individuals, government, and companies jointly in creating a sustainable community life.

   d.   … might include changing a whole industry toward sustainability performance. For instance, the car industry is currently in an industry-wide shift toward more sustainable solutions.

5.   Mechanisms for the efficient use of natural resources …

   a.   … can be divided into resource cascading and revalorization. Both increase the overall useful lifetime of a natural resource.

   b.   … include resource cascading, as in the case of a PET plastic bottle that gets recycled into T-shirts.

   c.   … include revalorization, which requires an additional transformation process before the resource can be reused, while resource cascading only requires reallocating the resource to a use which requires lower resource quality.

   d.   … mean that revalorization and resource cascading cannot be applied to the same resource.

6.   Changing the economic system infrastructure …

   a.   … is necessary to provide public policies, such as legislation, taxation, or subsidies, that support the creation of a sustainable economic system.

   b.   … by public policies can only be done by governments.

   c.   … may be done by mainly three types of political actor: supra-governmental organization (e.g., Greenpeace), nongovernmental organization (e.g., European Union), and local government (e.g., German government).

   d.   … on a global level urgently requires additional coordination of efforts and a local adherence to global norms.

B. Think

The subprime mortgage financial crisis was an excellent example of a malfunctioning of the global financial system. Identify the main forces at play and prepare a causal loop diagram (CLD) explaining "the big picture" of the forces causing and sustaining the crisis. You will find many examples of CLDs, together with advice on how to prepare them, online.

C. Do

Practice either the principle of degrowth or of the internalization of external costs in one aspect of your personal or professional life.

D. Relate

Identify at least two people who have very different disciplinary backgrounds than yourself (e.g., a mixed group of people from natural sciences, philosophy, politics, business). Engage in a discussion with them on what would need to be changed for the economic system to become truly sustainable.

E. Be

Think about one thing that you would like to change toward more sustainability in your immediate production and consumption ecosystem (e.g., to stop your street food stall from using Styrofoam, or your mother from keeping the fridge door open). Attempt to change this aspect until you succeed. If it works with the first try, find another change project that requires a more prolonged effort.

Feedback

A. Know

Question 1

a. Right: systemic complexity is based on this very characteristic of systems.
b. Wrong: resource flows are not the elements (e.g., organizations and individuals) of a system, but a connection between those elements.
c. Right: influencing system elements and the relationships between these elements are both necessary activities for systemic change.
d. Wrong: the economic system is embedded into the society and environment system, not the other way around.

Question 2

a. Right: the growth imperative of the economic system causes problems when considering that we are living on a finite planet with finite resources. So infinite growth is not an option.
b. Right: the internalization of external effects is a main systemic change challenge for creating a sustainable economic system.
c. Right: the underlying idea is that higher (real) prices of products that include all negative external effects throughout the product life-cycle will create a situation where less people buy and use the product, which in turn reduces the negative impact.
d. Wrong: inequality in this chapter refers to the economic system maintaining or even increasing inequalities between rich and poor.

Question 3

a. Wrong: system resilience refers to systems' high stability against forces of change.
b. Right: dynamic equilibriums lead to situations where the system "bounces back" to its original state after it has been influenced externally.
c. Wrong: path dependence refers to how past actions define present actions.
d. Right: power structures with a vested interest in the system may work to maintain the status quo.

Question 4

a. Wrong: industrial ecosystems aim to create a network of connected companies that function like a natural ecosystem.
b. Wrong: the descriptions of sustainable value chains and sustainability clusters are the wrong way round.
c. Right: a sustainable community is an example of a subsystem transformed to become sustainable.
d. Right: a sustainable industry is an example of a subsystem transformed to become sustainable.

Question 5

a.   Right: this is a correct interpretation of the figure and explanation of resource cascading and revalorization.

b.   Wrong: as recycling requires an additional transformation process, it is resource revalorization.

c.   Right: this is a correct interpretation of the figure and explanation of resource cascading and revalorization.

d.   Wrong: combining both mechanisms can extend the lifetime of resources drastically.

Question 6

a.   Right: such public policies are a necessary precondition for creating the global and local infrastructures for responsible and sustainable business and management.

b.   Wrong: increasingly, NGOs create their own public policies, which are as relevant to enterprises as government-made public policies.

c.   Wrong: the examples of Greenpeace and the European Union do not correspond to the organization types mentioned.

d.   Right: global coordination is a crucial task for creating a global infrastructure for sustainable development.

B. Think

Level	Nonlinear thinking	Notes
+	Diagram convincingly captures the main causal loops responsible for the financial crisis, while providing an accessible overview	
=	Feasible causal loop diagram	
−	Diagram does not appreciate the multiple causal mechanisms involved	

C. Do

Level	Principled action competence	Notes
+	Principle has been actioned flawlessly	
=	Principle has partly been converted into action, but still lacks more attention to details that are still not in line with the principle	
−	Principle has either not been understood or not practiced	

D. Relate

Level	Interdisciplinary problem-solving	Notes
+	Multidisciplinary discussion has led to an integrated solution more feasible than the individual solutions of each individual discipline	
=	Discussion reflects multiple disciplinary backgrounds, but an integrated solution approach could not be reached	
−	Discussion has not taken place or reflects a narrow disciplinary background	

E. Be

Level	Endurance	Notes
+	Evidence of multiple attempts to change the same issue with ultimate success	
=	Giving up after multiple attempts to change the same issue	
−	Not tried or giving up after first attempt	

Glossary

A

Accountability
Refers to both assuming a company's responsibilities and being held accountable for these.

Accounting
Refers to the process of measuring and documenting an activity and performance.

Activist
Is committed to a certain cause and shows nonconformity with the status quo by challenging structures, authorities, institutions, and beliefs.

Actors of responsible management activities
Are the individuals (managers) and/or organizations carrying out a particular responsible management process. Organizational actors can be divided into three groups: businesses, civil society organizations (CSOs), and governmental organizations.

Angel investors (= business angels)
Are private investors that use their financial resources to fund entrepreneurial start-ups.

Assurance
Refers to a third-party approval statement of responsible business communications (especially of reports).

B

Biomimicry
Refers to efforts to imitate the designs of nature in order to develop solutions for humanity.

Bottom of the pyramid (BoP)
Is a term coined by Prahalad that refers to (often the market constituted by) the approximately 4 billion people of low income at the bottom of the socioeconomic pyramid.

Business case for responsible business
Describes the manifold advantages that a business can gain when acting responsibility; the business or money sense of responsible business.

Business ethics
Is the study of morally right or wrong decisions in managerial and business contexts. Making morally right decisions is a fundamental precondition for becoming a responsible business. Business ethics is intimately interwoven with the responsible management process and provides the basis for successful ethics management.

Business model
Reflects a company's realized strategy by describing the essence of a business, the underlying logic of everything it does.

Business philanthropy
Is defined by voluntary altruistic contributions of businesses "for the good of mankind." In practice, a business often describes as philanthropic those activities that are not directly related to its main operations, such as donation or volunteering campaigns.

Business plan
Extensively describes the most important characteristics of an entrepreneurial venture.

Business unit strategy
Aims at finding a strategic position inside one core market. Main positions are cost leadership or differentiation. Responsible business activities have potential to create or support both types of position.

C

Cause
A cause is an issue that a company has started to mitigate or solve.

Cause-related consumption
Aims to contribute to a certain cause by strategically consuming or boycotting products, thereby furthering or obstructing the achievement of the cause objective.

Cause-related marketing
Is a responsible management tool that connects sales of a product to contributions to a good cause.

Certifications
Are external approvals of fulfilling predefined criteria.

Change agents
Are individuals successfully contributing to a change process.

Change management
Is a management tool to achieve organizational transitions.

Cluster
Refers to a local accumulation of economic actors, sharing joint characteristics.

Communication barriers
Are circumstances that impede successfully sending, receiving, and understanding a message.

Communication tools in responsible business
Are manifold frameworks, all with the joint purpose of communicating social and environmental business activity and performance to stakeholders.

Compliance officers
Are the highest-ranking official in a company in charge of compliance with hard law and soft law.

Corporate citizenship (CC)
Considers companies as citizens of the community/communities in which they operate. By being another citizen, a business not only has citizen rights, but also the duty to act for the wellbeing and development of the overall community.

Corporate governance
Refers to the rules and institutions governing corporate decision-making. The need for corporate governance stems from principal–agent relationships.

Corporate-level strategy
Is developed for businesses competing in more than one core market with several strategic business units. The main strategic decision at the corporate level is degree and type of diversification. Responsible businesses often aim to reduce the corporation's negative impact by acquiring or developing strategic business units with a very positive social and/or environmental impact.

Corporate social entrepreneurship (CSE)
Describes how whole businesses can apply entrepreneurial activities to tackle social and environmental problems.

Corporate social responsibility (CSR)
The object of CSR is business conduct that acts on the various social responsibilities a business has toward its stakeholders.

Customer relationship management (CRM)
Is the management function in charge of managing the relationship with customers, uniting the traditional functions of marketing, sales, and service.

D

Development objectives for responsible business
Describe the underlying development strategy a business chooses for its responsible business activities. Development activities can broadly be divided into growth and nongrowth objectives.

Diversity management
Refers to the company's inclusion of often marginalized groups, such as elderly employees, women, racial minorities, disabled people, and gay/lesbian/transgender people.

E

Eco-efficiency
Is a management tool developed by the World Business Council for Sustainable Development (WBCSD) that aims to increase efficiency in the usage of natural resources.

Eco-innovation
Describes an innovation that leads to an improved environmental impact.

Economic capital
Can be expressed in monetary terms. It comprises tangible assets such as machines or production facilities, intangible assets such as customer loyalty or brand value, and financial resources such as cash flows or a certain revenue margin. Economic capital can be attributed to an individual company or to the economic system as a whole.

Economic system
Consist of elements (such as businesses, private and governmental organizations, and individuals) and the interrelations between these elements (such as contracts, values, laws, power, and information flows).

Ecosystem services
Are services provided by ecosystems to humanity. Examples include the provision of water, timber, and food, climate regulation, recreational and spiritual functions of nature, and elementary supporting services such as photosynthesis and nutrient cycling.

Employee life-cycle
Describes the different stages of a relationship between employee and company.

Endorsements
Are external statements supporting a company's responsible business activities or performance.

Entrepreneur
Is an individual who takes the initiative to start a venture or enterprise that might involve risk, including environmental entrepreneurship, social entrepreneurship, or sustainability entrepreneurship

Entropy
Refers to fact that resources lose energy (or quality) the more they are used.

Environment, health and safety (EHS) management
Is a management tool that in many countries is required by law in order to ensure the physical integrity of employees and prevent environmental contingencies.

Ethics management
Aims to foster ethically "right decisions" among the actors of responsible management. The main phases of the ethics management process are the

mapping of ethical dilemmas, defining desirable decisions for every dilemma, understanding why people do or do not reach these desirable decisions, and implementing management tools to foster desirable decisions.

Extended chain of responsibility

Refers to the necessity for a responsible business to assume stakeholder responsibilities beyond the factory gate, along both the upstream and downstream supply chain.

External effects

Are the effects of an action that are not incurred by the actor. A smoker, for instance, does not need to pay directly for the damage caused to passive smokers. The opposite term is internal effects, which are incurred by the actor.

F

Fair trade

Refers to a just distribution of the financial benefits of trade between the initial (often "third-world") producer and the (often "first world") distributors of a product.

Financial management

Refers to the process of managing financial resources.

Focal point

Refers to the specific starting point of interest of an analysis. For instance, in supply chain management the focal point is the company of interest in a specific section of the supply chain from where the supply chain analysis starts.

Functional departments (= business functions; = departments)

Refer to certain functions fulfilled by a business, which are anchored in its organizational structure by specific departments fulfilling this function, such as human resources management, and accounting and financial management. Functional departments usually encounter specific functional issues and deploy function-specific management instruments.

Functional issues

Are social, environmental, and ethical issues that specifically occur in a certain function, such as unethical sales practices in the customer relations management function and air pollution in logistics.

Functional strategy

Describes the activities in specific business functions such as marketing or human resources, which aim to support the chosen business unit strategy.

G

Gaia Hypothesis

The Gaia Hypothesis was first proposed by James Lovelock as a means of viewing the planet as a mother system of interconnected subsystems that behave similar to a living organism. The term "Gaia" was borrowed from its eponym, the ancient Greek Earth goddess.

Grass-roots activism
Refers to activist activities that occur at a societal level, not coordinated by existing organizations.

Green supply chain management
Is a management instrument for improving the environmental impact of a product's complete supply chain.

Greenwashing
Refers to a misleading impression about a company's social and environmental performance, created by an imbalance between the company's activities and communication.

H

Hard law
Refers to formalized legislation and is often compared to soft law, which refers to informal norms.

Human development
Refers to a series of indicators (e.g., education, health, income) aiming to assess a human being's overall development.

Human resources management
Is the functional department fulfilling the function of managing employee relations.

I

Ideal speech situation
Refers to a high-quality communication situation, which serves to achieve optimum outcomes of the communication process.

Immediate responsibilities
Aim, in a responsible business, to fulfill the needs of stakeholders currently alive in a humanistic approach of maximizing stakeholder welfare, while at the same time including the rights of natural living beings, objects, and systems.

Inclusive supply chains
Include marginalized groups (mostly poor people) in supply chain activities, such as through the roles of suppliers, employees, or customers.

Incremental responsibility
Refers to making small moves toward responsible business that do not transform the business as a whole.

Industrial ecosystem
Describes a local accumulation of businesses that together imitate the functionality of a natural ecosystem (biomimicry) to jointly reduce their environmental impact. Industrial ecosystems form part of the industrial ecology approach.

Innovation

Describes "the successful exploitation of new ideas" (DTI, 2003, p. 8)

Institutions

Refer to taken-for-granted norms that guide behavior. For instance, institutions may come in the form of a value, a certain way of doing things, a social structure (such as the family), or an organization giving norms.

Integrated communication

Refers to a holistic communication concept integrating communication with all stakeholders, internal and external communication, manifold communication tools, and the activities of many communicating functional departments such as the marketing, public relations, and human resources departments.

Intergenerational responsibilities

Of responsible businesses aim to ensure humanity's survival on Earth and to maintain today's resources for future generations. Intergenerational responsibilities pragmatically follow the question: "What do we need for the future?"

Internal effects

See External effects

Intrapreneurs

Use entrepreneurial measures to either change an organization from within, or using their position within an organization as an instrument to achieve external change.

Irresponsible business

Is a business which, in its mode of responsibility, does not go beyond the compliance stage.

Issues and crisis communication

Is a communication tool aimed at effective communication of critical contingencies, such as issues encountered by a business or during its involvement in crises.

Issues in responsible management

Are understood as areas of potential action to either avoid the destruction of—or foster the creation of—social, environmental, or economic value. An issue being addressed is called a cause. A recent synonym for issue is "subject area," as first proposed by the ISO standard on social responsibility.

K

Kuznets curve

Suggests that, with increasing economic development, the income inequality and environmental degradation of a country follows an inverted U-shaped curve. With initial increasing average income, the income inequality and environmental degradation increase, and then decrease with high average income.

L

Labeling

Refers to the usage of visual symbols to communicate compliance with a predetermined set of criteria.

Leader

In the responsible business context provides vision and guidance for the transformational process toward sustainable business.

License to operate

Describes society's willingness to accept a company's activities. When societal opposition to a company's activity reaches the point at which the business is no longer able to continue operation, society is said to have withdrawn the license to operate.

Life-cycle impact assessment

Is a specialized responsible management instrument that aims to integrate the measurement and management of social, environmental, and economic issues and impacts related to a certain product's life-cycle. The three main product life-cycle phases are production (from raw material extraction to first use by the end-customer), use (by the end-consumer), and end of useful lifetime (disposal or revalorization).

Lifestyle

Describes the way people live, including private and professional life.

Lifestyles of Health and Sustainability (LOHAS)

Characterized by consumption of products and services that increase personal wellbeing and that are at the same time more sustainable than the average comparable product or service.

Lifestyles of Voluntary Simplicity (LOVOS)

Describe a lifestyle characterized by actively making life simpler by reducing consumption and professional workload.

Logistics

Refers to making inputs available to the production process (inbound logistics) and outputs available to customers (outbound logistics).

M

Mainstream responsible management instruments

Are traditional management instruments for economic performance that have been reinterpreted to apply to social and/or environmental performance. Examples are cause-related marketing, social accounting, and sustainable innovation.

Management innovation

Is "the invention and implementation of a management practice, process, structure, or technique that is new to the state of the art and is intended to further organizational goals" (Birkinshaw *et al.*, 2008, p. 825).

Management instrument (= tool)

Is a framework used for a specific management task. For instance, social marketing is used to create behavior change. Management tools can be deployed throughout one or several functional departments. For instance, social marketing may be deployed in both the human resources department and the marketing department.

Manager

In the responsible business context fulfills the task of managing sustainability, responsibility, and ethics in an organization.

Materiality

Describes the overall importance of a certain issue and is a compound value of the importance for an organization's stakeholders and for the organization itself.

Metrics

Are quantifiable indicators.

Microfinance

Is a management tool that provides financial services to a low-income population.

Mode of implementation

In responsible business describes the quality and degree to which responsible business assumes stakeholder responsibilities. The five stages of the mode of implementation are defensive, compliance, managerial, strategic, and civic implementation.

Monetarization

Refers to the process of expressing nonmonetary (social and environmental) values in monetary terms.

Moral development

Refers to an individual's capacity for moral reasoning and for making ethical decisions. According to Kohlberg there are six stages of moral development.

Motivation

Is an individual's reason for action. In the context of sustainable lifestyles, needs and moral reasoning (moral development) are two main motivational factors.

N

Natural (= environmental) capital

Comprises both renewable and nonrenewable natural resources. Resources here should not only be considered as material production inputs, but also as nonmaterial services provided by the natural environment, such as the recreational value realized while enjoying nature, or flower pollination by bees.

Needs

Describe human beings' predominant necessities in a certain situation. According to Maslow, needs are organized hierarchically, with the higher needs (e.g., self-actualization) driving individual behavior only after the lower needs (e.g., physiological needs) have been fulfilled.

Neutrally sustainable
Refers to activities that are exactly within the planet's resource limits: neither unsustainable, nor restoratively sustainable.

O

Ombudsman
Is a neutral person who helps to mitigate conflicts of interest and represents stakeholder interests.

Open innovation
Refers to an approach to innovation where innovators inside and outside the company work together in the same innovation process.

Operations management
Refers to the operational (nonstrategic) level of management. The term is often confused with production management.

Organizational activism
Describes activist behavior deployed through an organization as vehicle.

Organizational structure and design
Refers to the organization's institutions and their interrelatedness through, for instance, power structures and information channels.

Overton window
Explains political decision-making by means of the congruence of the decision to be made with the maturity and public acceptance of the decision topic.

P

Path dependence
Refers to a situation where the breadth of current decisions is limited by decisions made in the past.

Performance indicators
For responsible business performance are social, environmental, and economic performance measures, jointly constituting an organization's triple bottom line. Responsible business indicators may be summarized through a sustainability scorecard.

Peripheral responsibility
Primarily refers to the assumption of responsibilities that are unrelated to the core business and main business activities.

Persuasion
Is a communication tool that aims to convince communication partners of a predefined communication goal.

Planetary boundaries
The critical values that our Earth system should not exceed for humanity to be able to live on Earth in the long term.

Political actors
Refer, in the context of this book, to all organizations and individuals that shape public policies.

Primary functions (= main functions) in the value chain model
Refer to the functional departments of a business that are primarily and directly involved in value creation through a product or service.

Primary motivations
The primary motivations for responsible business describe the main driving forces for a particular business's involvement in responsible practices. Motivations can broadly be divided into profit and non-profit motivations.

Principal–agent relationships
Are situations where on actor conducts a certain action for another actor (e.g., the manager (agent) for the owner of a business or stakeholders (principals)). In the management of such relationships, special attention has to be paid to information asymmetries and diverging interests between both principals and agents.

Production management
Refers to the management of the production process. The term is often confused with operations management.

Public policy
Refers, in the context of this book, to any measure by political actors actively and purposefully changing the infrastructure of the current economic system.

Q

Quality of consumption
Describes the sustainability quality of a particular consumption pattern.

Quantity of consumption
Describes the amount of goods and services consumed by an individual.

R

Resilience
Refers to a system's stability and resistance to change.

Resource cascading
Refers to using the same resource several times until all value has been extracted and it is useless.

Responsible business
Is a business that has committed to ultimately becoming a sustainable business by improving its social, environmental, and economic impacts among its various stakeholders. A responsible business applies responsible management

activities to follow up on the commitment made. To be considered "respon-sible," activities should go beyond compliance.

Responsible business portfolio

Is a list of issues and causes of a business, including an analysis of factors relevant to its management.

Responsible business SWOT analysis

Is a methodology used to analyze the internal and external strategic factors related to social and environmental topics.

Responsible management

Is a process involving tools for managing social, environmental, and economic capital and impact throughout discrete activities and functions. Responsible management aims to achieve sustainable business by influencing its triple bottom line. A synonym for responsible management is "three-dimensional management."

Responsible management instruments

Manage the three constituent elements of the responsible management process and aim to create three-dimensional value. Sub-groups are specialized and mainstream responsible management instruments.

Responsible management process

Consists of the three basic elements—actor, stakeholder, and issue (also called the trinity of responsible management)—and one or several responsible management instruments connecting and manipulating these elements to create a well-balanced triple bottom line.

Responsible management systems

Are sets of rules, values, and procedures that lead to responsible management practices.

Restoratively sustainable

Refers to activities that are not only within the resource limits of the planet, but even contribute to restoring the planet's environmental capacity.

Revalorization

Is the process of increasing the quality of a resource so that it can be used again.

Revalorizer

Is a type of business or business function that in its core operations returns value to formerly depleted resources. Revalorizers are, for instance, maintenance departments or recycling businesses.

S

Second-order supply chains

Are characterized by higher percentages of renewable and renewed resources used than first-order supply chains. For instance, secondhand clothing or recycled paper is managed through a second-order supply chain.

Sensemaking

Refers to the process of creating individual meaning through a communication activity.

Servitization

Describes the replacement of a product by a service. Services often have a lower environmental impact and open up employment opportunities.

Social capital

Is any capital directly embodied in human beings. Social capital on the one hand comprises individual—so-called human—capital, including knowledge, skills, values, and even physical health and personal wellbeing. On the other hand, social capital also comprises capital collectively created by interaction inside groups of human beings, such as joint values, culture, and collective welfare.

Social entrepreneurship

Entrepreneurship with a social purpose and/or following a social opportunity.

Social innovation

Refers to an innovation with added value for society.

Social investment

Is the use of financial resources to strengthen social infrastructure.

Social license to operate

Refers to society's acceptance of a specific business's operations.

Social marketing

Employs marketing instruments to create a behavior change in individuals for the good of society. Examples include nonsmoking or recycling campaigns.

Socially responsible investment

Refers to investment practices with an added value for society.

Soft law

Refers to norms to be obeyed by companies that are not written down in formal law (hard law).

Specialized responsible management instruments

Are three tools specially designed for responsible management, and that are each aimed at the management of one of the constituent elements of the responsible management process.

Sphere of influence

Refers to the area and decisions inside and outside a company that can be influenced directly by the company's actions.

Stakeholder

Are all individuals, groups, living and even nonliving entities that have a relationship with an organization, that are affected by the organization and/or affect it. This means that individuals or even single activities may have stakeholders. Typical stakeholders of businesses are employees, communities, customers, and shareholders.

Stakeholder dialog

Refers to a two-way communication with a diverse set of stakeholders.

Stakeholder management

Is a specialized responsible management instrument that aims to manage a company's stakeholder relations. Stakeholder management can be divided into the phases of stakeholder assessment and stakeholder engagement.

Strategic guidance statements
Define the general parameters for strategy development. The principal statements are vision, mission, values, and codes of conduct.

Strategy evaluation and control
Are mechanisms that aim to track performance and ensure the achievement of a particular strategy's predefined goals.

Subject area
See Issues in responsible management

Supply chain
Consists of a series of companies connected through the joint creation of a product. The supply chain runs from the extraction of the first raw material to the use of the product by the final end-consumer. The supply chain should not be confused with a company's value chain; rather, the supply chain is a *series* of value chains.

Support functions (= staff functions)
Describe all functional departments in a company's value chain that are not primarily and directly involved in value creation through product or service.

Sustainable business
Refers to a single business, industry, or whole economy that has reached a harmonization of its overall social, environmental, and economic capital, and which has achieved sustained neutral to positive impact in all three dimensions. Sustainable business is the business-sector contribution to sustainable development.

Sustainable community
Is a local group of people, companies, and governmental entities that jointly pursues a sustainable overall impact of the community.

Sustainable development
Is a development that achieves a harmonization of economic, social, and environmental capital throughout all sectoral contributions of business, civil society, and government. Sustainable development ensures the long-term quality of life and survival of the human race on Earth. The term "sustainable development" refers to both the process and the achievement of sustainable development.

Sustainable economic system
Operates in the limits of the Earth's natural carrying capacity.

Sustainable governance
Refers to governmental activities creating a neutral or even positive impact in the social, environmental, and economic dimensions. Sustainable governance is the governmental and public-sector contribution to sustainable development.

Sustainable lifestyle
Is a lifestyle not exceeding the planet's resource limits.

Sustainable living
Describes an individual or collective lifestyle characterized by a neutral or even positive impact on business, society, and economy. Sustainable living is the civil society sector contribution to sustainable development.

Sustainable supply chain management
Aims to create supply chains that contribute to sustainable development by paying attention to the supply chain's triple bottom line, assuming an extended responsibility for stakeholders along the supply chain, and creating circular resource flows.

Sustainability accounting
Is a management tool used to measure and document social, environmental, and economic activities and impacts.

Sustainability entrepreneurship
Refers to various types of entrepreneurship that lead to the creation of businesses that contribute to sustainable development.

Sustainability indicators
Are qualitative and quantitative (metrics) categories, aiming to document and control social, environmental, and economic business activity and performance.

Sustainability quality
Refers to the degree of sustainability of an entity (e.g., a product, a consumption style, a company).

Sustainability reporting
Is a communication tool that aims to neutrally, concisely, and completely communicate social, environmental, and economic business activity and performance.

Sustainability scorecard
Uses a set of social, environmental, and economic performance indicators to manage and control an organization's sustainability strategy.

Sustainability strategy
Describes an integrated set of social, environmental, and economic strategies that together aim to achieve the goal of becoming a sustainable business.

T

Testimonials
Are a communication tool involving experience reports of stakeholders involved in a responsible business activity.

Three-dimensional management
Is a characteristic of responsible management that aims to highlight the multi-dimensional (social, environmental, economic) elements of the responsible management process. It also aims to create a neutral term that is not yet complicated by contradictory definitions and understandings. Three-dimensional management is the management process leading to the desired outcome of a well-balanced triple bottom line.

Total responsibility management
Refers to a responsibility management system that aims to achieve maximum quality, for a broad set of stakeholders in responsible management, from all the operations of an organization.

Trade-off
Refers to what one has to give up in order to receive something else.

Trinity of responsible management
Refers to the omnipresent elements—actor, stakeholder, and issue—that are of central importance to any responsible management activity.

Triple bottom line
Refers to balancing the social, environmental, and economic outcome of any activity. Any activity in order to contribute to sustainable development needs to achieve a neutral or even positive triple bottom line. The triple bottom line is the main object of responsible management, and achieving a sustainable triple bottom line is the main characteristic of a sustainable business and the final goal of a responsible business.

U

Unsustainability
Refers to a situation, practice, or object whose negative impact puts a strain on the resource of the planet.

Upcycling
Refers to a recycling process that increases the value or quality of the recycled resource.

V

Value chain
Describes how all functional departments of a company jointly create value through a product or service. The value chain should not be confused with the supply chain, which can be seen as a series of value chains.

W

Whistle-blowing
Is the colloquial name for the process by which a stakeholder (usually an employee) communicates misconduct.

Work–life balance
Refers to creating an equilibrium between private and professional life.

References

Ablett, J., Baijal, A., Beinhocker, E., Bose, A., Farrell, D., Gersch, U., ... Gupta, S. (2007). The "bird of gold": the rise of India's consumer market. Retrieved March 31, 2016 from http://www.mckinsey.com/global-themes/asia-pacific/the-bird-of-gold.

Abrahamsson, A. (2007). *Sustainopreneurship: Business with a Cause* (Unpublished MBA thesis). Växjö University.

AccountAbility (2011). *AA1000 Stakeholder Engagement Standard 2011: Final Exposure Draft*. London: AccountAbility.

Achbar, M., & Abbott, J. (Director). (2003). *The Corporation: The Pathological Pursuit of Profit and Power* [Motion picture]. Canada: Big Picture Media Corporation.

AEA Technology (2008). *Comparative Life-Cycle Assessment of Food Commodities Procured for UK Consumption Through a Diversity of Supply Chains—FO0103*. London: Department for Environment Food and Rural Affairs (DEFRA).

AFL-CIO (2015). Executive paywatch. Retrieved May 20, 2016 from http://www.aflcio.org/Corporate-Watch/Paywatch-2015.

AGA (2010). Life cycle assessment (LGA). Retrieved March 29, 2016 from http://www.etseq.urv.es/aga/Investigacion/LCA.htm.

Aguilera, R.V., Rupp, D.E., Williams, C.E., & Ganapathi, J. (2007). Putting the S back into corporate social responsibility: a multilevel theory of social change in organizations. *Academy of Management Review*, 32(3), 836-863.

Alden Keene (2007). Chili's and St. Jude Children's Research Hospital. Retrieved August 3, 2016 from http://www.causemarketing.biz/2007/08/chilis-and-st-jude-childrens-research-hospital/.

Al-Rodhan, N.R.F. (2009). *Sustainable History and the Dignity of Man: A Philosophy of History and Civilisational Triumph*. Piscataway, NJ: Transaction Publishers.

Amazonia Expeditions (2011). Amazonia Expeditions. Retrieved March 29, 2016 from http://www.perujungle.com.

Ambito.com (2011, August 17). Gas Natural Fenosa consigue la máxima calificación de GRI por segundo año consecutivo [Gas Natural Fenosa achieves the maximum GRI ranking for the second year in a row]. *ámbito.com*. Retrieved March 29, 2016 from http://www.ambito.com/noticia.asp?id=597801.

American Express (2012). American Express Partners in Preservation. Retrieved January 19, 2012 from http://about.americanexpress.com/csr/pip.aspx.

Amnesty International (2013). The Universal Declaration of Human Rights 1948: Simplified version by Amnesty International UK. Retrieved August 3, 2016 from https://www.amnesty.org.uk/sites/default/files/udhr_simplified_0.pdf.

Andersen, M., & Skjoett-Larsen, T. (2009). Corporate social responsibility in global supply chains. *Supply Chain Management: An International Journal*, 14(2), p. 75-86.

Anderson, R. (2012). *Climbing Mount Sustainability*. Atlanta, GA: Ray Anderson Foundation.

Anthes, M., & Verheyen, E. (Directors). (2011). *ARD Exklusiv: Das System Wiesenhof* [Film]. Germany: ARD.

Aristotle (2005). *Politics*. Stilwell, KS: Digireads.com.

Atkins, S. (1999). *Cause Related Marketing: Who Cares Wins*. Oxford, UK: Butterworth-Heinemann.

Austin, J., & Reficco, E. (2009). Corporate social entrepreneurship. *Harvard Business School Working Paper Series*, 101(9).

Baden-Fuller, C., & Morgan, M.S. (2010). Business models as models. *Long Range Planning*, 43, 156-171.

Ballowe, T. (2009, May 20). Google's approach to employee engagement: Surprise! It's an algorithm. *OnStrategy*. Retrieved March 30, 2016 from http://onstrategyhq.com/resources/googles-approach-to-employee-engagement-surprise-its-an-algorithm.

Bandi, N. (2007). *United Nations Global Compact: Impact and its Critics*, Geneva, Switzerland: Covalence.

Barbier, E. (1987). The concept of sustainable economic development. *Environmental Conservation*, 14(2), 101-110.

Barboza, D. (2007a, August 14). Owner of Chinese toy factory commits suicide. *The New York Times*. Retrieved March 29, 2016 from http://www.nytimes.com/2007/08/14/business/worldbusiness/14toy.html.

——— (2007b, August 23). Scandal and suicide in China: a dark side of toys. *The New York Times*. Retrieved March 29, 2016 from http://www.nytimes.com/2007/08/23/business/worldbusiness/23suicide.html?pagewanted=all.

Battilana, J., Lee, M., Walker, J., & Dorsey, C. (2012). In search of the hybrid ideal. *Stanford Social Innovation Review*, 10(3), 49-55.

Bavier, J. (2008, January 22). Congo war-driven crisis kills 45,000 a month: study. *Reuters*. Retrieved March 29, 2016 from http://www.reuters.com/article/2008/01/22/us-congo-democratic-death-idUSL2280201220080122.

BBC (2011, November 8). Australia Senate backs carbon tax. *BBC News*. Retrieved March 29, 2016 from http://www.bbc.co.uk/news/world-asia-15632160.

——— (2014, February 10). Who is behind Mexico's drug-related violence? *BBC News*. Retrieved March 29, 2016 from http://www.bbc.co.uk/news/world-latin-america-10681249.

Beamon, B.M. (1999). Designing the green supply chain. *Logistics Information Management*, 12(4), 332-342.

Bent, D., & Richardson, J. (2003). *Sustainability Accounting Guide: The Sigma Guidelines Toolkit*. London: Sigma Project.

Benyus, J.M. (2002). *Biomimicry: Innovation Inspired by Nature*. New York: William Morrow.

Bertelsmann Stiftung & GTZ (2007). *The CSR Navigator: Public Policies in Africa, the Americas, Asia and Europe*. Eschborn, Germany: GTZ.

Bhattacharya, S.D.C., & Sen, S. (2010). Maximizing business returns to corporate social responsibility (CSR): the role of CSR communication. *International Journal of Management Reviews*, 12(1), 8-19.

Bird Clan of East Central Alabama (2004). Cree Indian prophecy: warriors of the rainbow. Retrieved March 9, 2016 from http://www.birdclan.org/rainbow.htm.

Birkinshaw, J., Hamel, G., & Mol, M.J. (2008). Management innovation. *Academy of Management Review*, 33(4), 825-845.

Black, R. (2011, December 7). Climate targets "risk" from Brazil's forest changes. *BBC News*. Retrieved March 29, 2016 from http://www.bbc.co.uk/news/science-environment-16074628.

Blackburn, W.R. (2007). *The Sustainability Handbook: The Complete Management Guide to Achieving Social, Economic and Environmental Responsibility.* Washington, DC: Earthscan.

Bohman, J., & Rehg, W. (2011). Jürgen Habermas. In *The Stanford Encyclopedia of Philosophy* (Winter 2011 ed.). Retrieved March 29, 2016 from http://plato.stanford.edu/archives/win2011/entries/habermas.

Bones, C. (2006, March 17). Taking over an ethical business. *BBC News.* Retrieved March 29, 2016 from http://news.bbc.co.uk/2/hi/business/4817814.stm.

Boston College & Reputation Institute (2010). *The 2010 Corporate Social Responsibility Index.* Retrieved March 29, 2016 from http://www.bcccc.net/pdf/CSRIReport2010.pdf.

Bowen, H.R. (1953). *Social Responsibilities of the Businessman.* New York: Harper.

BP (2011). *Sustainability Review 2010.* London: British Petroleum.

Branigan, T. (2009, January 22). China to execute two over poisoned baby milk scandal. *The Guardian.* Retrieved March 29, 2016 from http://www.guardian.co.uk/world/2009/jan/22/china-baby-milk-scandal-death-sentence.

Brown, K.W., & Kasser, T. (2005). Are psychological and ecological well-being compatible? The role of value, mindfulness and lifestyle. *Social Indicators Research,* 74, 349-368.

Brundtland, G.H. (1987). Presentation of the report of the World Commission on Environment and Development to UNEP's 14th Governing Council. Nairobi, Kenya.

Buchholtz, A.K., & Carroll, A.B. (2008). *Business and Society* (7th ed.). Scarborough, Canada: Cengage.

Business Library (2002). Missed mission: watch out! Retrieved October 15, 2011 from http://findarticles.com/p/articles/mi_m0DTI/is_5_30/ai_96892217.

Carbon Disclosure Project (2012). Carbon Disclosure Project. Retrieved March 29, 2016 from https://www.cdproject.net/en-US/Pages/HomePage.aspx.

Carr, A.Z. (1968). Is business bluffing ethical? *Harvard Business Review,* 46(1), 143-153.

Carrefour (2013). Working for you. Retrieved August 3, 2016 from http://www.carrefour.com/act-for-you/more-responsible-sourcing.

Carroll, A.B. (1979). A three-dimensional conceptual model of corporate performance. *Academy of Management Review,* 4(4), 497-505.

——— (1991). The pyramid of corporate social responsibility: toward the moral management of organizational stakeholders. *Business Horizons,* July–August, 225-235.

——— (1999). Corporate social responsibility: a definitional construct. *Business & Society,* 38(3), 268-295.

Carson, R. (2002). *Silent Spring.* New York: Houghton Mifflin. (Original work published 1962)

Carter, C.R., & Rogers, D.S. (2008). A framework of sustainable supply chain management: moving toward new theory. *International Journal of Physical Distribution & Logistics Management,* 38(5), 360-387.

Carvalho, G.O. (2001). Sustainable development: is it achievable within the existing international political economy context? *Sustainable Development,* 9(2), 61-73.

Casadesus-Masanell, R., & Ricart, J.E. (2010). From strategy to business models and onto tactics. *Long Range Planning,* 43(2), 195-215.

Cate, S.N., Pilosof, D., Tait, R., & Karol, R. (2009). The story of Clorox Green Works™—in designing a winning green product experience Clorox cracks the code. Retrieved August 3, 2016 from http://www.pdcinc.com/files/sharedimages/visions_march09.pdf.

CBC News (2011, July 7). News of the World to shut down: phone hacking scandal brings end to 168-year-old tabloid paper. *CBC News.* Retrieved March 29, 2016 from http://www.cbc.ca/news/world/story/2011/07/07/newscorp-hacking.html.

cellular-news (2011). Coltan, gorillas and cellphones. Retrieved March 29, 2016 from http://www.cellular-news.com/coltan.

CEMEFI (2011). Responsabilidad social empresarial. Retrieved March 29, 2016 from http://www.cemefi.org/esr.

CEMEX (2012). Centros productivos de autoempleo [Productive self-employment centers]. Retrieved March 29, 2016 from http://www.cemexmexico.com/DesarrolloSustentables/CentrosProductivos.aspx].

Centre for Bhutan Studies (2012). Gross national happiness. Retrieved March 29, 2016 from http://www.grossnationalhappiness.com.

Ceres (2012). The Ceres Principles. Retrieved March 11, 2016 from http://www.ceres.org/about-us/our-history/ceres-principles.

Cervantes, G. (2007). A methodology for teaching industrial ecology. *International Journal of Sustainability in Higher Education*, 8(2), 131-141.

Chamberlain, G. (2011, April 30). Apple factories accused of exploiting Chinese workers. *The Guardian*. Retrieved March 29, 2016 from http://www.guardian.co.uk/technology/2011/apr/30/apple-chinese-factory-workers-suicides-humiliation.

Chappel, V. (1994). *The Cambridge Companion to Locke*. Cambridge, UK: Cambridge University Press.

Chesbrough, H.W. (2003). *Open Innovation: The New Imperative for Creating and Profiting from Technology*. Boston, MA: Harvard Business Press.

Chouinard, Y., & Gallagher, N. (2004). Don't buy this shirt unless you need it. Retrieved March 29, 2016 from http://www.patagonia.com/us/patagonia.go?assetid=2388.

Christensen, C. (2013). *The Innovator's Dilemma: When New Technologies Cause Great Firms to Fail*. Cambridge, MA: Harvard Business Review Press.

Christensen, C.M., Baumann, H., Ruggles, R., & Sadtler, T.M. (2006). Disruptive innovation for social change. *Harvard Business Review*, 84(12), 94-102.

Chua, J.M. (2011). Will Puma be launching compostable clothing, footwear next? Retrieved March 27, 2016 from http://www.ecouterre.com/will-puma-be-launching-compostable-clothing-footwear-next.

Cinépolis (2016). Del Amor Nace la Vista [Love Gives Birth to Eyesight]. Retrieved May 30, 2016 from https://www.fundacioncinepolis.org/.

City of Toronto (2016). Environment and energy. Retrieved July 18, 2016 from http://www1.toronto.ca/wps/portal/contentonly?vgnextoid=fd95ba2ae8b1e310VgnVCM10000071d60f89RCRD.

Clarkson, M.B.E. (1995). A stakeholder framework for analyzing and evaluating corporate social performance. *Academy of Management Review*, 20(1), 82-117.

Climate Counts (2012). Scorecard overview. Retrieved March 14, 2016 from http://www.climatecounts.org/scorecard_overview.php.

Coase, R. (1960). The problem of social cost. *Journal of Law and Economics*, October, 414-440.

Código San Luís (2012). Avanza proyecto del parque industrial "Puro Potosino" [The Puro Potosino industrial park project makes progress]. *Código San Luís*. Retrieved August 3, 2016 from http://www.codigosanluis.com/portal/node/5750.

Cohen, E. (2011). *CSR for HR*. Berlin, Germany: Institute Corporate Responsibility Management, Steinbeis University.

Commission of the European Communities (2006). *Implementing the Partnership for Growth and Jobs: Making Europe a Pole of Excellence on CSR*. Brussels, Belgium: European Union.

Common, M., & Perrings, C. (1992). Towards an ecological economics of sustainability. *Ecological Economics*, 6(1), 7-34.

Conners, N., & Conners Peterson, L. (Director) (2007). *The 11th Hour* [Motion picture]. U.S.A.: Warner Bros.

Corporate Responsibility Magazine (2010). *Corporate Responsibility Best Practices: Setting the Baseline*. Retrieved March 29, 2016 from http://corporateresponsibilityassociation. org/files/CR-Best-Practices-2010-Executive-Summary.pdf.

Costanza, R., d'Arge, R., de Groot, R., Farber, S., Grasso, M., Hannon, B., … van den Belt, M. (1997). The value of the world's ecosystem services and natural capital. *Nature*, 387, 253-260.

Coutu, D.L. (2003). I was greedy too. *Harvard Business Review*, 81(2), 38-44.

Crane, A., & Matten, D. (2010a). *Businesss Ethics* (3rd ed.). New York: Oxford University Press.

——— (2010b). Business ethics. In W. Visser, D. Matten, M. Pohl, & N. Tolhurst (Eds.), *The A–Z of Corporate Social Responsibility* (pp. 45-51). Chichester, UK: Wiley.

CSA (2011). Richard Reed: co-founder of innocent drinks. Retrieved August 3, 2016 from http://www.csaspeakers.com/eng/our-speakers/profile/richard_reed.

Daly, H.E., & Farley, J. (2004). *Ecological Economics: Principles and Applications*. Washington, DC: Island Press.

Darsow, I. (2005). Implementation of ethics codes in Germany: the Wal-Mart case. *IUSL Labor*, volume 3.

Dawkins, R. (1976). *The Selfish Gene*. Oxford, UK: Oxford University Press.

DESD (2011). Decade of education for sustainable development. Retrieved March 9, 2016 from http://www.desd.org.

Design Council (2010). Innocent Drinks: creative culture strengthens brand values and drives profits. Retrieved August 3, 2016 from http://webarchive.nationalarchives. gov.uk/20090903113249/designcouncil.org.uk/case-studies/all-case-studies/innocent -smoothies/.

DiClemente, C.C., & Prochaska, J.O. (1998). Toward a comprehensive, transtheoretical model of change. In W.R. Miller & N. Heather (Eds.), *Treating Addictive Behaviors* (pp. 3-24). New York: Plenum Press.

Die Welt (2010, January 15). Westerwelle mahnt in China Menschenrechte an [Westerwelle warned in China on human rights]. *Die Welt*. Retrieved March 29, 2016 from http://www. welt.de/politik/article5855385/Westerwelle-mahnt-in-China-Menschenrechte-an.html.

——— (2012, January 7). Die Bank in der die Zeit stehengeblieben ist [The bank in which the time stands still]. *Die Welt*. Retrieved March 29, 2016 from http://www.welt.de/print/ die_welt/finanzen/article13802792/Die-Bank-in-der-die-Zeit-stehengeblieben-ist.html.

Dizolele, M.P. (Producer). (2006). *In Focus: Congo's Bloody Coltan* [Video]. Retrieved March 29, 2016 from http://pulitzercenter.org/video/congos-bloody-coltan.

DJSI (2011). Dow Jones Sustainability Indexes. Retrieved August 3, 2016 from http://www. sustainability-indices.com/images/review-presentation-2011.pdf.

Dodgson, M., Gann, D., & Salter, A. (2006). The role of technology in the shift towards open innovation: the case of Procter & Gamble. *R&D Management*, 36(3), 333-346.

Doganovaa, L., & Eyquem-Renault, M. (2009). What do business models do? Innovation devices in technology entrepreneurship. *Research Policy*, 38, 1559-1570.

Donham, W.B. (1927). The social significance of business. *Harvard Business Review*, 5(4), 406-419.

——— (1929). Business ethics: a general survey. *Harvard Business Review*, 7(4), 385-394.

DTI (2003). *Competing in the Global Economy: The Innovation Challenge*. London: Department of Trade and Industry.

Du, S., Bhattacharya, C., & Sen, S. (2007). Reaping relational rewards from corporate social responsibility: the role of competitive positioning. *International Journal of Research in Marketing*, 24, 224-241.

Eco Imprints (2016). Eco Seed Pen. Retrieved March 29, 2016 from http://ecoimprints.com/ ProductDetails/?productId=6288313.

ECOA & ERC (2011). *The Release of Statistics on Ethics and Enforcement Decisions: A Joint Report to the U.S. Department of Justice.* N.l.: Ethics Resource Center.

Edwards, A.R. (2005). *The Sustainability Revolution: Portrait of a Paradigm Shift.* Gabriola Island, Canada: New Society Publishers.

Edwards, J.B., McKinnon, A.C., & Cullinane, S.L. (2010). Comparative analysis of the carbon footprints of conventional and online retailing. *International Journal of Physical Distribution and Logistics Management,* 40(1/2), 103-123.

Ehrenfeld, J., & Gertler, N. (1997). Industrial ecology in practice: the evolution of interdependence at Kalundborg. *Journal of Industrial Ecology,* 1(1), 67-79.

Ehrgott, M., Reimann, F., Kaufmann, L., & Carter, C.R. (2011). Social sustainability in selecting emerging economy suppliers. *Journal of Business Ethics,* 98, 99-119.

Eilperin, J. (2012). Market proposed to end feud over whale hunting. Retrieved March 29, 2016 from http://www.perc.org/articles/article1455.php.

EITI (2009). The EITI Principles. Retrieved March 29, 2016 from http://eiti.org/eiti/principles.

—— (2011). Democratic Republic of Congo. Retrieved March 29, 2016 from http://eiti.org/DRCongo.

El Mundo (2011, August 29). Derechos humanos "a la china" para 2012 [Chinese-style human rights for 2012]. *El mundo.* Retrieved March 29, 2016 from http://www.elmundo.es/elmundo/2011/08/26/solidaridad/1314356293.html.

Elkington, J. (1998). *Cannibals with Forks: The Triple Bottom Line of 21st Century Business.* Gabriola Island, Canada: New Society Publishers.

—— (2010). Triple bottom line. In W. Visser, D. Matten, M. Pohl, & N. Tolhurst (Eds.), *The A–Z of Corporate Social Responsibility* (p. 406). Chichester, UK: Wiley.

—— (2011). Enter the triple bottom line. Retrieved August 3, 2016 from http://kmhassociates.ca/resources/1/Triple%20Bottom%20Line%20a%20history%201961-2001.pdf.

Emerich, M. (2000). LOHAS means business. Retrieved August 31, 2016 from http://www.lohas.com/lohas-journal.

Emerson, J. (2003). The blended value proposition: integrating social and financial results. *California Management Review,* 45(4), 35-51.

EPA (2012). Equator Principles. Retrieved March 29, 2016 from http://www.equator-principles.com.

Erhardt, M.C., & Brigham, E.F. (2010). *Financial Management: Theory and Practice.* Mason, OH: Cengage.

Erkmann, S. (1997). Industrial ecology: a historical overview. *Journal of Greener Production,* 5(1/2), 1-10.

Ernst & Young (2014). *Sustainability Reporting: The Time is Now.* New York: Ernst & Young.

Ewing, B., Moore, D., Goldfinger, S., Oursler, A., Reed, A., & Wackernagel, M. (2010). *The Ecological Footprint Atlas 2010.* Oakland, CA: Global Footprint Network.

Fairtrade International (2011). Fairtrade International. Retrieved March 29, 2016 from http://www.fairtrade.net.

Farley, J., Erickson, J.D., & Daly, H.E. (2005). *Ecological Economics: A Workbook for Problem-Based Learning.* Washington, DC: Island Press.

Farmacias del Ahorro (2013). ¿Quiénes somos? [Who are we?]. Retrieved August 3, 2016 from http://corp.fahorro.com.mx/sections.php?id=29.

Ferdig, M.A. (2007). Sustainability leadership: co-creating a sustainable future. *Journal of Change Management,* 7(1), 25-35.

Figge, F., Hahn, T., Schaltegger, S., & Wagner, M. (2002). The sustainability balanced scorecard: linking sustainability management to business strategy. *Business Strategy and the Environment,* 11, 269-284.

Fiksel, J. (2010). *Design for Environment.* New York: McGraw-Hill.

Financial Times (2010). Global free zones of the future 2010/2011 winners. Retrieved July 20, 2016 from http://www.fdiintelligence.com/Locations/Global-Free-Zones-of-the-Future-2010-11-Winners.

Fincher, D. (Director) 1999. *Fight Club* [Motion picture]. U.S.A.: 20th Century Fox.

Fitch, H.G. (1976). Achieving corporate social responsibility. *Academy of Management Review*, 1(1), 38-46.

Foot, D.K. (2004). *Easter Island: A Case Study in Non-Sustainability*. Sheffield, U.K.: Greenleaf Publishing.

Forest Stewardship Council (2011). The 10 principles. Retrieved August 3, 2016 from https://ic.fsc.org/en/certification/principles-and-criteria/the-10-principles.

Freeman, R.E. (2010). *Strategic Management: A Stakeholder Approach*. Cambridge, UK: Cambridge University Press. (Original work published 1984)

Freeman, R.E., & Reed, D.L. (1983). Stockholders and stakeholders: a new perspective on corporate governance. *California Management Review*, 15(3), 88-106.

Friedman, M. (1970). The social responsibility of business is to increase its profits. *New York Times Magazine*, 13 September.

Friedman, T.L. (2005). *The World is Flat: A Brief History of the Twenty-First Century*. New York: Picador.

Futerra (2008). *The Greenwash Guide*. London: Futerra Sustainability Communications.

Gallisa, R. (2011, August 30). How Pepsi and Coke's plant-based bottle wars affect manufacturers. *GreenBiz*. Retrieved March 29, 2016 from https://www.greenbiz.com/blog/2011/08/30/how-pepsi-and-cokes-plant-based-bottle-wars-affect-manufacturers.

Gas Natural Fenosa (2011). *Informe de responsabilidad corporativa 2010 [Corporate Responsibility Report 2010]*. Retrieved March 29, 2016 from http://www.gasnaturalfenosa.com/servlet/ficheros/1297092433852/35%5C226%5CInformeResponsabilidadSocialCorporativa,29.pdf.

——— (2016). Reports and publications. Retrieved July 22, 2016 from http://www.gasnaturalfenosa.com/en/reputation+and+corporate+responsibility/1285338471576/reports+and+publications.html.

General Electric (2012). Ecomagination. Retrieved March 29, 2016 from http://www.ecomagination.com.

Gill, R. (2003). Change management—or change leadership? *Journal of Change Management*, 3(4), 307-318.

Glanz, J. (2011, September 8). Google details, and defends, its use of electricity. *The New York Times*. Retrieved March 29, 2016 from http://www.nytimes.com/2011/09/09/technology/google-details-and-defends-its-use-of-electricity.html.

Goldenberg, S. (2016, February 10). Supreme court to block Obama's sweeping climate change plan. *The Guardian*. Retrieved July 22, 2016 from https://www.theguardian.com/environment/2016/feb/09/climate-change-supreme-court-barack-obama-plan.

Google (2011). Data centers. Retrieved March 29, 2016 from http://www.google.com/about/datacenters.

Gould, D. (2010). Puma re-invents the shoe box. Retrieved March 27, 2016 from http://www.psfk.com/2010/04/puma-reinvents-the-shoe-box.html#ixzz1kmhUMMw7.

Grameen Bank (2010). Breaking the vicious cycle of poverty through microcredit. Retrieved August 3, 2016 from http://www.grameen-info.org/breaking-the-vicious-cycle-of-poverty-through-microcredit/.

——— (2011). Grameen Bank historical data series: 1976–2011 (in million USD). Retrieved August 3, 2016 from http://www.grameen.com/index.php?option=com_content&task=view&id=1190&Itemid=1016.

Grayson, D., & Hodges, A. (2004). *Corporate Social Opportunity! Seven Steps to Make Corporate Social Responsibility Work for Your Business*. Sheffield, U.K.: Greenleaf Publishing.

Green Works (2011). Home. Retrieved March 29, 2016 from http://www.greenworkscleaners. com.

Greenpeace (2007). 1995: Shell reverses decision to dump the Brent Spar. Retrieved March 29, 2016 from http://www.greenpeace.org/international/en/about/history/the-brent-spar.

Greenpeace UK (2012). *Have a Break?* [Video]. Retrieved March 29, 2016 from http://www. youtube.com/watch?v=VaJjPRwExO8.

Greenwald, R. (Director). (2005). *Wal-Mart: The High Cost of Low Price* [Motion picture]. U.S.A.: Brave New Films.

GRI (2006a). *Sustainability Reporting Guidelines*. Amsterdam, Netherlands: Global Reporting Initiative.

——— (2006b). *GRI Application Levels, 2006*. Amsterdam, Netherlands: Global Reporting Initiative.

——— (2010). *GRI and ISO 26000: How to Use the GRI Guidelines in Conjunction with ISO 26000*. Amsterdam, Netherlands: Global Reporting Initiative.

——— (2014a). *Overview of Changes in Standard Disclosures from G3 to G4 Guidelines*. Amsterdam, Netherlands: Global Reporting Initiative.

——— (2014b). *G4 Sustainability Reporting Guidelines: Frequently Asked Questions*. Amsterdam, Netherlands: Global Reporting Initiative.

——— (2015). *G4 Sustainability Reporting Guidelines: Reporting Principles and Standard Disclosures*. Retrieved July 19, 2016 from https://www.globalreporting.org/ resourcelibrary/GRIG4-Part1-Reporting-Principles-and-Standard-Disclosures.pdf.

——— (2016). Global Reporting Initiative. Retrieved March 29, 2016 from http://www. globalreporting.org.

Griffin, J.J., & Mahoon, J.F. (1997). The corporate social performance and corporate financial performance debate: twenty-five years of incomparable research. *Business and Society*, 36(1), 5-31.

Griffiths, K. (2007). Project sustainability management in infrastructure projects. Paper presented at the 2nd International Conference on Sustainability Engineering and Science. Auckland, New Zealand.

Grosby, S. (2010). The myth of the man-loving Prometheus: reflections on philanthropy, forethought, and religion. *Conversations on Philanthropy*, 7, 11-24.

Grover, S. (2013, March 20). Why one English town created its own currency. *Mother Nature Network*. Retrieved March 29, 2016 from http://www.mnn.com/money/sustainable -business-practices/stories/why-one-english-town-created-its-own-currency.

Guardian (2011, December 13). Canada pulls out of Kyoto protocol. *The Guardian*. Retrieved March 29, 2016 from http://www.guardian.co.uk/environment/2011/dec/13/ canada-pulls-out-kyoto-protocol.

Guggenheim, D. (Director). (2006). *An Inconvenient Truth*. U.S.A.: Lawrence Bender Productions.

Gunningham, N., Kagan, R.A., & Thornton, D. (2002). *Social Licence and Environmental Protection: Why Businesses Go Beyond Compliance*. London: Centre for the Analysis of Risk and Regulation, London School of Economics and Political Science.

H. Ayuntamiento San Luis Potosí (2013). Taller Puro Potosino 2.0 [Purely Potosí Workshop 2.0]. Retrieved August 3, 2016 from http://de.sanluis.gob.mx/taller-puro-potosino-2-0/.

Habermas, J. (2005). *Zwischen Naturalismus und Religion [Between Naturalism and Religion]*. Berlin, Germany: Suhrkamp.

Haeckel, E. (1988). *Generelle Morphologie der Organismen [General Morphology of Organisms]*. Berlin, Germany: Gruyter. (Original work published 1866)

Haigh, N., & Hoffman, A.J. (2012). Hybrid organizations: the next chapter of sustainable business. *Organizational Dynamics*, 41, 126-134.

Hall, J., & Matos, S. (2010). Incorporating impoverished communities in sustainable supply chains. *International Journal of Physical Distribution & Logistics Management*, 40(1/2), 124-147.

Hamel, G. (2006). The why, what, and how of management innovation. *Harvard Business Review*, 84(2), 72-88.

Hands On Network (2011). Skills-based volunteering. Retrieved March 29, 2016 from http://www.handsonnetwork.org/nationalprograms/skillsbasedvolunteering.

Hansen, E.G., & Schaltegger, S. (2016). The sustainability balanced scorecard: a systematic review of architectures. *Journal of Business Ethics*, 133(2), 193-221.

Hansen, E.G., Grosse-Dunker, F., & Reichwald, R. (2009). Sustainability innovation cube: a framework to evaluate sustainability-oriented innovations. *International Journal of Innovation Management*, 13(4), 683-713.

Hansen, E.G., Zvezdov, D., Harms, D., & Lenssen, G. (2014). Advancing corporate sustainability, CSR, and business ethics. *Business and Professional Ethics Journal*, 33(4), 287-296.

Hardin, G. (1968). The tragedy of the commons. *Science*, 162, 1243-1248.

Hargroves, K. & Smith, M.H., 2005. *The Natural Advantage of Nations: Business Opportunities, Innovations and Governance in the 21st Century*. London: Earthscan.

Hartman, T. (2001). *The Last Hours of Ancient Sunlight: Waking Up to Personal and Global Transformation*. London: Hodder & Stoughton.

Hart, S.L., & Milstein, M.B. (1999). Global sustainability and the creative destruction of industries. *Sloan Management Review*, 41(1), 23-33.

Hawken, P., Lovins, A., and Lovins, L.H. (1999). *Natural Capitalism: Creating the Next Industrial Revolution*. New York: Little, Brown & Company.

Heineken (2010). Impact: responsible consumption. Retrieved August 3, 2016 from http://www.sustainabilityreport.heineken.com/2010/brewing-a-better-future/responsible-consumption.html.

———— (2016). HEINEKEN launches a moderation movement. Retrieved May 23, 2016 from http://www.theheinekencompany.com/media/features/dance-more-drink-slow/heineken-launches-a-moderation-movement.

Hitt, M.A., Ireland, R.D., & Hoskisson, R.E. (2007). *Strategic Management: Competitiveness and Globalization* (7th ed.). Mason, OH: Thomson Southwestern.

Hogg, J. (2011, October 4). U.S. buyers shun "conflict minerals" in Congo's east. *Reuters*. Retrieved March 30, 2016 from http://www.reuters.com/article/2011/10/05/congo-democratic-minerals-corrected-idUSL5E7L31S720111005.

Hollender, J., & Breen, B. (2010). *The Responsibility Revolution: How the Next Generation of Businesses Will Win*. San Francisco, CA: Jossey-Bass.

Holmberg, J., & Robèrt, K.H. (2000). Backcasting: a framework for strategic planning. *International Journal of Sustainable Development & World Ecology*, 7(4), 291-308.

Horiuchi, R., Schuchard, R., Shea, L., & Townsend, S. (2009). *Understanding and Preventing Greenwash: A Business Guide*. San Francisco, CA: BSR.

Hornborg, A. (2016). How to turn an ocean liner: a proposal for voluntary degrowth by redesigning money for sustainability, justice, and resilience. *Journal of Political Ecology* (Special issue on Culture, Power, Degrowth). [forthcoming]

HP (2016). Global diversity and inclusion. Retrieved July 22, 2016 from http://www8.hp.com/us/en/hp-information/about-hp/diversity/index.html.

HR Magazine (2012, January 6). Work/life balance ranks higher than stress as the biggest health concern for employers, says GRiD. *HR Magazine*. Retrieved March 30, 2016 from http://www.hrmagazine.co.uk/hro/news/1020665/work-life-balance-ranks-stress-biggest-health-concern-employers-grid.

Hursthouse, R. (1999). *On Virtue Ethics*. New York: Oxford University Press.

Hutchins, G. (2010). *Sustainability and Operational Excellence: One Goal, Not Two.* London: Atos.

IIRC (2013). *The International Integrated Reporting Framework.* London: International Integrated Reporting Council.

IKEA (2003). *IKEA's Position on Forestry.* Gothenburg, Sweden: Ikea Services AB.

ILO (2000). Origins and history. Retrieved March 30, 2016 from http://www.ilo.org/global/about-the-ilo/history/lang--en/index.htm.

——— (2012). International Labour Organization. Retrieved March 30, 2016 from http://www.ilo.org.

IMF (2007). *The Economics of Islamic Finance and Securitization.* Retrieved March 8, 2016 from http://www.imf.org/external/pubs/ft/wp/2007/wp07117.pdf.

Innocent Drinks (2012). Being sustainable. Retrieved March 30, 2016 from http://www.innocentdrinks.co.uk/us/being-sustainable.

——— (2016). Nutrition. Retrieved August 3, 2016 from http://www.innocentdrinks.co.uk/us/nutrition.

InterfaceFlor (2010, November 9). Interface, Inc. raises sustainability bar: Zero environmental impact by 2020 [Press release]. Retrieved March 30, 2016 from http://www.interfaceflor.eu/web/af/about_us/media_centre_landing_page/press_releases/press-Press-Release-Interface-Inc-Raises-Sustainability-Bar.

——— (2016). The Interface story. Retrieved August 4, 2016 from http://www.interfaceglobal.com/Sustainability/Interface-Story.aspx.

Ioannou, I., & Serafeim, G. (2014). *The Consequences of Mandatory Corporate Sustainability Reporting: Evidence from Four Countries.* Harvard Business School Working Paper, No. 11-100. Retrieved July 22, 2016 from http://www.hbs.edu/faculty/Publication%20Files/11-100_7f383b79-8dad-462d-90df-324e298acb49.pdf.

IPSOS (2012). As "Occupy" protesters promise new strategies for 2012: global citizens are in the dark but sympathetic [Press release]. Retrieved March 30, 2016 from http://www.ipsos-na.com/news-polls/pressrelease.aspx?id=5487.

ISO (2010). *International Standard ISO 26000: Guidance on Social Responsibility.* Geneva: International Organization for Standardization.

——— (2012a). ISO 14000: Environmental management. Retrieved March 30, 2016 from http://www.iso.org/iso/iso14000.

——— (2012b). ISO 26000: Social responsibility. Retrieved March 30, 2016 from http://www.iso.org/iso/iso26000.

Jargon, J. (2011, May 18). McDonald's under pressure to fire Ronald. *The Wall Street Journal.* Retrieved March 30, 2016 from http://online.wsj.com/article/SB10001424052748703509104576329610340358394.html.

Jowit, J. (2008, September 7). UN says eat less meat to curb global warming. *The Guardian.* Retrieved March 30, 2016 from http://www.guardian.co.uk/environment/2008/sep/07/food.foodanddrink.

Joutsenvirta, M. (2016). A practice approach to the institutionalization of economic degrowth. *Ecological Economics, 128,* 23-32.

Kant, I., Wood, A.W., & Schneewind, J.B. (2002). *Groundwork for the Metaphysics of Morals.* New Haven, CT: Yale University Press.

Kanter, R.M. (1999). From spare change to real change: the social sector as beta site for business innovation. *Harvard Business Review, 77*(3), 122-132.

Kaplan, R.S., & Norton, D.P. (1996). Using the balanced scorecard as a strategic management system. *Harvard Business Review, 74*(1), 75-85.

Keeble, J.J., Topiol, S., & Berkeley, S. (2003). Using indicators to measure sustainability performance at corporate and project level. *Journal of Business Ethics, 33*(2/3), 149-158.

Kelepouris, T., Pramatar, K., & Doukidis, i.G. (2007). RFID-enabled traceability in the food supply chain. *Industrial Management & Data Systems, 107*(2), 183-200.

Kelly, A. (2016, February 1). Nestlé admits slavery in Thailand while fighting child labour lawsuit in Ivory Coast. *The Guardian*. Retrieved July 22, 2016 from https://www. theguardian.com/sustainable-business/2016/feb/01/nestle-slavery-thailand-fighting -child-labour-lawsuit-ivory-coast.

Kelso, L.O., & Hetter, P. (1973). Corporate social responsibility without corporate suicide. *Challenge*, 16(3), 52-57.

Khandwalla, P.N. (1987). Generators of pioneering-innovative management: some Indian evidence. *Organization Studies*, 8(1), 39-59.

Kim, C.-R. (2011, December 15). Japan auto lobby cheers subsidies, says tax change not enough. *Reuters*. Retrieved March 30, 2016 from http://www.reuters.com/article/2011/ 12/15/japan-autos-idUSL3E7NF00520111215.

Kleindorfer, P.R., Singhal, K., & Van Wassenhove, L.N. (2005). Sustainable operations management. *Production and Operations Management*, 14(4), 482-492.

Kohlberg, L. (1973). The claim to moral adequacy of a highest stage of moral judgment. *The Journal of Philosophy*, 70(18), 630-646.

Kotler, P., & Lee, N. (2004). *Corporate Social Responsibility: Doing the Most Good for Your Company and Your Cause*. Chichester, UK: Wiley.

Kotler, P., & Levy, S.]. (1971). Demarketing, yes demarketing. *Harvard Business Review*, 79(6), 74-80.

Kotter, J.P. (1995). Leading change: why transformation efforts fail. *Harvard Business Review*, 73(2), 59-67.

KPMG (2016). *Currents of Change: The KPMG Survey of Corporate Responsibility Reporting 2015*. Retrieved July 22, 2016 from https://www.kpmg.com/CN/en/IssuesAndInsights/ ArticlesPublications/Documents/kpmg-survey-of-corporate-responsibility-reporting- 2015-O-201511.pdf.

Krauss, C. (2011, October 26). BP to drill again in the Gulf of Mexico. *The New York Times*. Retrieved March 30, 2016 from http://green.blogs.nytimes.com/2011/10/26/bp-to-drill -again-in-the-gulf-of-mexico.

Kravis, H. (2010). Avatar of American finance. Retrieved March 30, 2016 from http://www. achievement.org/autodoc/page/kra0int-2.

Kuznets, S. (1955). Economic growth and income inequality. *The American Economic Review*, 45(1), 1-28.

Laasch, O. (2014). How to develop competencies for responsible management? Retrieved March 8, 2016 from http://responsiblemanagement.net/fostering-competencies-for -responsible-management-by-oliver-laasch.

Laasch, O., & Conaway, R. (2011). "Making it do" at the movie theatres: communicating sustainability at the workplace. *Business Communication Quarterly*, 74(1), 68-78.

——— (2015). *Principles of Responsible Management: Glocal Sustainability, Responsibility, Ethics*. Mason, OH: Cengage.

Laasch, O., & Flores, U. (2010). Implementing profitable CSR: the CSR 2.0 business compass. In M. Pohl & N. Tolhurst (Eds.), *Responsible Business: How to Manage a CSR Strategy Successfully* (pp. 289-309). Chichester, UK: Wiley.

Lacey, P., Cooper, T., Hayward, R., & Neuberger, L. (2010). *A New Era of Sustainability: UN Global Compact-Accenture CEO Study 2010*. Retrieved March 30, 2016 from https://www.unglobalcompact.org/docs/news_events/8.1/UNGC_Accenture_CEO_ Study_2010.pdf.

Lappé, F.M., & Lappé, A. (2002). *Hope's Edge: The Next Diet for a Small Planet*. New York: Tarcher/Penguin.

Lasker, J. (2008). Inside Africa's PlayStation war. *Toward Freedom*. Retrieved August 4, 2016 from http://towardfreedom.com/30-archives/africa/1294-inside-africas-playstation-war.

Laszlo, C., & Zhexembayeva, N. (2011). *Embedded Sustainability: The Next Big Competitive Advantage*. Stanford, CA: Stanford University Press.

Lear, L. (1998). *Rachel Carson: Witness for Nature*. New York: Henry Holt.

Lee, A. (2011, June 5). Apple manufacturer Foxconn makes employees sign "no suicide" pact. *The Huffington Post*. Retrieved March 30, 2016 from http://www.huffingtonpost.com/2011/05/06/apple-foxconn-suicide-pact_n_858504.html.

Lee, M. (2011a, January 13). Analysis: A year after China retreat, Google plots new growth. *Reuters*. Retrieved March 30, 2016 from http://www.reuters.com/article/2011/01/13/us-google-china-idUSTRE70C1X820110113.

———— (2011b, July 21). Fake Apple Store in China even fools staff. *Reuters*. Retrieved March 30, 2016 from http://www.reuters.com/article/2011/07/21/us-china-apple-fake-idUSTRE76K1SU20110721.

Lehman, J. (2010). The Overton window. Retrieved March 6, 2016 from http://www.mackinac.org/12887.

Lehrer, J. (2011). 7 Success Stories from the Journey to Zero Waste. *GreenBiz*. Retrieved March 30, 2016 from http://www.greenbiz.com/blog/2011/11/18/7-success-stories-journey-zero-waste.

Leipziger, D. (2010). *The Corporate Responsibility Codebook*. Sheffield, U.K.: Greenleaf Publishing.

Liggett, B. (2011, March 29). PPR group launches sustainability scheme for Gucci, Yves Saint Laurent, Stella McCartney brands. *Ecouterre*. Retrieved March 30, 2016 from http://www.ecouterre.com/ppr-group-launches-sustainability-scheme-for-gucci-yves-saint-laurent-stella-mccartney-brands.

Local (2009, July 31). Coca-Cola looking to buy Germany's Bionade. *The Local*. Retrieved March 30, 2016 from http://www.thelocal.de/money/20090731-20957.html.

LOHAS Magazine (2010). LOHAS background. Retrieved March 30, 2016 from http://www.lohas.com/about.

London Development Agency (2010). *Green Enterprise District East London*. London: London Development Agency.

Lorenz, M. (1905). Methods of measuring the concentration of wealth. *Publications of the American Statistical Association*, 9(70), 209-219.

Lovell, J. (2007, December 9). Left-hand-turn elimination. *The New York Times*. Retrieved March 30, 2016 from http://www.nytimes.com/2007/12/09/magazine/09left-handturn.html.

Lovelock, J. (1979). *Gaia: A New Look at Life on Earth*. Oxford, UK: Oxford University Press.

———— (2006). *The Revenge of Gaia: Why the Earth is Fighting Back—and How We Can Still Save Humanity*. Santa Barbara, CA: Allen Lane.

———— (2009). *The Vanishing Face of Gaia: A Final Warning*. New York: Basic Books.

Lubin, D.A., & Esty, D.C. (2010). The sustainability imperative. *Harvard Business Review*, May, 1-9.

Malthus, T.R. (2011). *An Essay on the Principle of Population: A View of its Past and Presents Effects on Human Happiness*. London: Forgotten Books. (Original work published 1798)

Mandl, I. (2005). *CSR and Competitiveness: European SMEs Good Practice*. Vienna, Austria: Austrian Institute for SME Research.

Marks & Spencer (2015). About Plan A. Retrieved August 4, 2016 from http://corporate.marksandspencer.com/plan-a/our-stories/about-plan-a.

Marshall, T.H. (1977). *Class, Citizenship, and Social Development: Essays*. Chicago, IL: The University of Chicago Press.

Martin, R., & Kemper, A. (2012). Saving the planet: a tale of two strategies. *Harvard Business Review*, 90(4), 49-56.

Marx, K. (2000). *Das Kapital*. Washington, DC: Regnery.

Maslow, A.H. (1943). A theory of human motivation. *Psychological Review*, 50(4), 370-396.

Matten, D., & Crane, A. (2005). What is stakeholder democracy? Perspectives and issues. *Business Ethics: A European Perspective*, 14(1), 6-13.

Matten, D., & Moon, J. (2004). Corporate social responsibility education in Europe. *Journal of Business Ethics*, 54, 323-337.

McDonald's (2011). *Worldwide Corporate Social Responsibility 2010 Report.* Retrieved August 4, 2016 from http://www.aboutmcdonalds.com/content/dam/AboutMcDonalds/Sustainability/Sustainability%20Library/2010-CSR-Report.pdf.

McDonough, W., & Braungart, M. (2002). *Cradle to Cradle: Remaking the Way We Make Things.* San Francisco, CA: North Point Press.

McGonigal, J. (2010). *Gaming Can Make a Better World* [Video]. Retrieved March 31, 2016 from http://www.ted.com/talks/jane_mcgonigal_gaming_can_make_a_better_world.html.

McIntosh, M. (2010). Citizenship. In W. Visser, D. Matten, M. Pohl, & N. Tolhurst (Eds.), *The A–Z of Corporate Social Responsibility* (pp. 89-93). Chichester, UK: Wiley.

McKinsey (2010). Moving women to the top: McKinsey Global Survey results. Retrieved March 31, 2016 from http://www.mckinsey.com/business-functions/organization/our-insights/moving-women-to-the-top-mckinsey-global-survey-results.

McNamara, C. (2011). Management. Retrieved March 31, 2016 from http://managementhelp.org/management/terms.htm.

Meadows, D.H., Randers, J., & Meadows, D.L. (2005). *Limits to Growth: The 30-Year Update.* London: Earthscan.

Melé, D. (2003). The challenge of humanistic management. *Journal of Business Ethics*, 44, 77-88.

Messerli, J. (2011). Should marijuana be legalized under any circumstances? Retrieved March 31, 2016 from http://www.balancedpolitics.org/marijuana_legalization.htm.

Metcalfe, J.S., & Coombs, R. (2000). Organizing for innovation: co-ordinating distributed innovation capabilities. In N. Foss & V. Mahnke (Eds.), *Competence, Governance, and Entrepreneurship: Advances in Economic Strategy Research* (pp. 209-231). Oxford, UK: Oxford University Press.

Miera-Juárez, B.S. d., Jiménez-Ruíz, J.A., & Reynales-Shigematsu, L.M. (2011). *Las repercusiones del consumo de tabaco en la distribución del gasto de los hogares mexicanos.* Mexico City: Instituto Nacional de Salud Pública.

Millennium Ecosystem Assessment (2005). Overview of the Millennium Ecosystem Assessment. Retrieved August 4, 2016 from http://www.millenniumassessment.org/en/About.html.

Mills, J.S. (2008). *Utilitarianism.* London: Forgotten Books. (Original work published 1863)

Mitchel, R.K., Agle, B.R., & Wood, D.J. (1997). Toward a theory of stakeholder salience: defining the principles of who and what really counts. *Academy of Management Review*, 22(4), 853-886.

Mollenkopf, D., Stolze, H., Tate, W.L., & Ueltschy, M. (2010). Green, lean and global supply chains. *International Journal of Physical Distribution & Logistics Management*, 40(1/2), 14-41.

Moore, M. (Director). 2009. *Capitalism: A Love Story* [Motion picture]. U.S.A.: Dog Eat Dog Films.

Moore, M. (2010, May 27). Inside Foxconn's suicide factory. *The Telegraph.* Retrieved March 31, 2016 from http://www.telegraph.co.uk/finance/china-business/7773011/A-look-inside-the-Foxconn-suicide-factory.html.

Morsing, M., & Oswald, D. (2009). Sustainable leadership: management control systems and organizational culture in Novo Nordisk A/S. *Corporate Governance*, 9(1), 83-99.

Morsing, M., & Schultz, M. (2006). Corporate social responsibility communication: stakeholder information, response and involvement strategies. *Business Ethics: A European Review*, 15(4), 323-338.

Naess, A. (1973). The shallow and the deep, long run ecology movement: a summary. *Inquiry*, 16, 95-100.

Natural Step (2011). The Natural Step. Retrieved March 31, 2016 from http://www.naturalstep.org.

New Economics Foundation (2012). The Happy Planet Index. Retrieved March 31, 2016 from http://www.happyplanetindex.org.

New Statesman (2010). NYT: Cameron's chief media adviser Andy Coulson "actively encouraged" NoW phone-hacking. *New Statesman*. Retrieved March 31, 2016 from http://www.newstatesman.com/uk-politics/2010/09/former-reporter-knew-coulson.

Nidumolu, R., Prahalad, C.K., & Rangaswami, M.R. (2009). Why sustainability is now the key driver of innovation. *Harvard Business Review*, 87(9), 56-64.

NMI (2010). LOHAS Global. Retrieved August 4, 2016 from http://nmisolutions.com/index.php/lohas-global-reports/view_category/6-lohas-global.

—— (2011). Sustainability: a foundation for mainstream growth. Retrieved August 4, 2016 from http://www.nmisolutions.com/index.php/about-nmi/news-a-publications/nmi-trend-insights/121-sustainability-a-foundation-for-mainstream-growth.

O'Dwyer, B. (2003). Conceptions of corporate social responsibility: the nature of managerial capture. *Accounting, Auditing & Accountability Journal*, 16(4), 523-557.

OECD (2004). G20/OECD principles of corporate governance. Retrieved March 31, 2016 from http://www.oecd.org/corporate/principles-corporate-governance.htm.

—— (2009). Impact of the economic crisis on employment and unemployment in the OECD countries. Retrieved March 31, 2016 from http://www.oecd.org/els/emp/impactoftheeconomiccrisisonemploymentandunemploymentintheoecdcountries.htm.

—— (2011). *OECD Guidelines for Multinational Enterprises: 2011 Edition*. Retrieved August 4, 2016 from https://www.oecd.org/corporate/mne/48004323.pdf.

OECD & EU (2005). *Oslo Manual: Guidelines for Collecting, and Interpreting Innovation Data* (3rd ed.). Paris: OECD Publishing.

O'Reilly, T. (2005). What is Web 2.0: design patterns and business models for the next generation of software. Retrieved July 22, 2016 from http://www.oreilly.com/pub/a/web2/archive/what-is-web-20.html.

Orlitzky, M., Schmidt, F.L., & Rynes, S.L. (2003). Corporate social and financial performance: a meta-analysis. *Organization Studies*, 24(3), 403-441.

Ortiz, S. (2008, August 28). Bimbo a la vanguardia en empaques [Bimbo at the forefront of packaging]. *Expansión*. Retrieved March 31, 2016 from http://www.cnnexpansion.com/manufactura/actualidad/2008/08/28/bimbo-a-la-vanguardia-en-empaques.

Osterwalder, A. (2004). *The Business Model Ontology: A Proposition in a Design Science Approach*. Lausanne, Switzerland: University of Lausanne.

Osterwalder, A., & Pigneur, Y. (2010). *Business Model Generation*. Chichester, UK: Wiley.

P&G (2006). *A Company History: 1937–Today*. Retrieved March 31, 2016 from http://www.pg.com/translations/history_pdf/english_history.pdf.

—— (2016). Our approach to innovation. Retrieved August 4, 2016 from http://us.pg.com/who_we_are/our_approach/our_approach_innovation.

Panayotou, T. (2002). Demystifying the environmental Kuznets curve: turning a black box into a policy tool. *The Review of Economics and Statistics*, 84(3), 541-551.

Patagonia (2011). The Footprint Chronicles. Retrieved March 31, 2016 from http://www.patagonia.com/us/footprint/index.jsp.

Pauli, G. (1999). *UpCycling: Wirtschaften nach dem Vorbild der Natur für mehr Arbeitsplätze und eine saubere Umwelt*. Munich, Germany: Riemann.

Pepper, D. (1993). *Eco-Socialism: From Deep Ecology to Social Justice*. London: Psychology Press.

PepsiCo (2016). Diversity and inclusion. Retrieved July 22, 2016 from http://www.pepsico.com/Purpose/Talent-Sustainability/Diversity-and-Inclusion.

Pereira, V., & Alerigi, A. (2011, August 17). Zara supplier accused of slave labor in Brazil. *Reuters*. Retrieved March 31, 2016 from http://uk.reuters.com/article/2011/08/17/zara-brazil-idUKN1E77G18N20110817.

PETA (2016a). Dining with friends and family. Retrieved August 31, 2016 from http://www.peta.org/living/food/making-transition-vegetarian/ideas-vegetarian-living/dining-friends-family/.

PETA (2016b). Ideas for everyday vegan or vegetarian eating. Retrieved August 31, 2016 from http://www.peta.org/living/food/making-transition-vegetarian/everyday-eating/.

Peters, A. (2011, July 3). Using gamification to make the world a better place. *GreenBiz*. Retrieved March 31, 2016 from http://www.greenbiz.com/blog/2011/07/03/using-gamification-make-world-better-place?page=0%2C2.

Phillips, M. (2009, February 26). The world we leave our children [Web log]. Retrieved March 31, 2016 from http://www.whitehouse.gov/blog/2009/02/26/world-we-leave-our-children.

Phills, J.A., Deiglmeier, K., & Miller, D.T. (2008). Rediscovering social innovation. *Stanford Social Innovation Review*, 6(4), 34-43.

PHW (2011). PHW: working for a better life. Retrieved March 31, 2016 from http://www.phw-gruppe.de/company.html.

Pigou, A.C. (2005). *The Economics of Welfare: Volume 1*. New York: Cosimo. (Original work published 1920)

Pohle, G., & Hittner, J. (2008). *Attaining Sustainable Growth Through Corporate Social Responsibility*. Somers, NY: IBM Institute for Business Value.

Porter, M. (1980). *Competitive Strategy: Techniques for Analyzing Industries and Competitors*. New York: The Free Press.

—— (1985). *Competitive Advantage: Creating and Sustaining Superior Performance*. New York: The Free Press.

Porter, M., & Kramer, M. (2002). The competitive advantage of corporate philanthropy. *Harvard Business Review*, 80(12), 56-68.

Porter, M., & Kramer, M. (2006). Strategy and society: the link between competitive advantage and corporate social responsibility. *Harvard Business Review*, 84(12), 78-92.

Porter, M.E. (1990). The competitive advantage of nations. *Harvard Business Review*, 68(2), 73-93.

—— (2000). Location, competition, and economic development: local clusters in a global economy. *Economic Development Quarterly*, 14(5), 15-34.

Prahalad, C.K. (2010). *The Fortune at the Bottom of the Pyramid: Eradicating Poverty Through Profits* (5th anniversary ed.). Upper Saddle River, NJ: Pearson.

Preuss, L. (2010). Codes of conduct in organisational context: from cascade to lattice-work of codes. *Journal of Business Ethics*, 94, 471-487.

PRME (2011). PRME: Principles for Responsible Management Education. Retrieved March 31, 2016 from http://www.unprme.org.

—— (2016). Participants. [Online] Retrieved May 5, 2016 from http://www.unprme.org/participants/.

Psihoyos, L. (Director). (2009). *The Cove* [Motion picture]. U.S.A.: Lionsgate.

PUMA (2011a). *Annual Report 2010*. Retrieved March 27, 2016 from http://about.puma.com/damfiles/default/investor-relations/financial-reports/en/2010/AR-2010-14db11370ece92c7ae49dc5cc15f5604.pdf.

—— (2011b). PUMA completes first environmental profit and loss account which values impacts at €145 million. Retrieved March 31, 2016 from http://about.puma.com/en/newsroom/corporate-news/2011/november/puma-completes-first-environmental-profit-and-loss-account-which-values-impacts-at-145-million-euro.

RAC (2015). How Rent-A-Center works. Retrieved August 4, 2016 from https://www.rentacenter.com/how-rac-works/how-rent-a-center-works.

Radjou, N., & Prabhu, J. (2014, December 10). What frugal innovators do. *Harvard Business Review*. Retrieved March 31, 2016 from https://hbr.org/2014/12/what-frugal -innovators-do.

Randles, S., Gee, S., & Edler, J. (2015). *Governance and the Institutionalisation of Responsible Research and Innovation in Europe: Transversal Lessons from an Extensive Programme of Case Studies*. Retrieved March 31, 2016 from http://res-agora.eu/assets/ Res-AgorA_321427_Del_3-6_final.pdf.

Rawls, J. (1999). *A Theory of Justice* (Revised ed.). Cambridge, MA: Harvard University Press.

Raynolds, L.T. (2002). Consumer/producer links in fair trade coffee networks. *Sociologia Ruralis*, 42(4), 404-424.

RED (2015). What is (RED)? Retrieved August 4, 2016 from https://red.org/about/.

Reed, D. (2002). Employing normative stakeholder theory in developing countries: a critical theory perspective. *Business and Society*, 41(2), 166-207.

Reinberg, S. (2014, July 30). Benefits of e-cigarettes may outweigh harms, study finds. *HealthDay*. Retrieved March 31, 2016 from http://consumer.healthday.com/cancer-information-5/smoking-cessation-news-628/benefits-of-e-cigarettes-may-outweigh-harms-study-finds-690268.html.

Renard, M.-C. (2003). Fair trade: quality, market and conventions. *Journal of Rural Studies*, 19, 87-96.

Rockström, J., Steffen, W., Noone, K., Persson, Å, Chapin, F.S., Lambin, E.F., ... Foley, J.A., (2009). A safe operating space for humanity. *Nature*, 461, 472-475.

Rodrigue, J.-P., Slack, B., & Comtois, C. (2001). Green logistics (the paradoxes of). In A.M. Brewer, K.J. Button, & D.A. Hensher (Eds.), *The Handbook of Logistics and Supply-Chain Management* (pp. 339-350). London: Pergamon/Elsevier.

Rogers, S. (2011, November 14). Occupy protests around the world: full list visualised. *The Guardian*. Retrieved March 31, 2016 from http://www.guardian.co.uk/news/datablog/ 2011/oct/17/occupy-protests-world-list-map.

Roloff, J., & Aßlander, M.S. (2010). Corporate autonomy and buyer–supplier relationships: the case of unsafe Mattel toys. *Journal of Business Ethics*, 97, 517-534.

Roman, R.M., Hayibor, S., & Agle, B.R. (1999). The relationship between social and financial performance. *Business and Society*, 38(1), 109-125.

Rosen, S., Simon, J., Vincent, J.R., MacLeod, W., Fox, M., & Thea, D.M. (2003). AIDS is your business. *Harvard Business Review*, 81(1), 80-87.

Rosen, S., Vincent, J.R., MacLeod, W., Fox, M., Thea, D.M., & Simon, J.L. (2004). The cost of HIV/AIDS to businesses in southern Africa. *AIDS*, 18, pp. 317-324. Retrieved March 31, 2016 from http://info.worldbank.org/etools/docs/library/251038/day9AIDSreprint%20 April9Session%201.pdf.

Rosenberg, M. (2011). Current world population. Retrieved March 31, 2016 from http:// geography.about.com/od/obtainpopulationdata/a/worldpopulation.htm.

Roser, M. (2015, March 27). Income inequality: poverty falling faster than ever but the 1% are racing ahead. *The Guardian*. Retrieved July 22, 2016 from https://www.theguardian.com/ news/datablog/2015/mar/27/income-inequality-rising-falling-worlds-richest-poorest.

Sabbagh, D. (2011, July 8). Phone hacking: how News of the World's story unravelled. *The Guardian*. Retrieved March 31, 2016 from http://www.guardian.co.uk/media/2011/jul/ 08/news-of-the-world-phone-hacking.

SAI (2008). *Social Accountability 8000*. New York: SAI.

Saini, A. (2010). Purchasing ethics and inter-organizational buyer–supplier relational determinants: a conceptual framework. *Journal of Business Ethics*, 95(3), 439-455.

SAM Research AG (2010). *Corporate Sustainability Assessment Questionnaire*. Zurich, Switzerland: SAM Research AG.

Samuelson, P.A., & Nordhaus, W.D. (2005). *Economics* (18th Ed.). New York: McGraw-Hill.

Savage, G.T., Nix, T.W., Whitehead, C.J., & Blair, J.D. (1991). Strategies for assessing and managing organizational stakeholders. *Academy of Management Executive*, 2, 61-75.

Schneiderman, A. (2006). Analog Devices: 1986–1992—the first balanced scorecard. Retrieved March 31, 2016 from http://www.schneiderman.com/Concepts/The_First_Balanced_Scorecard/BSC_INTRO_AND_CONTENTS.htm.

Schumacher College (2012). Economics for transition. Retrieved March 28, 2016 from http://www.schumachercollege.org.uk/courses/ma-in-economics-for-transition.

SGI Network (2015). About the SGI. Retrieved August 4, 2016 from http://www.sgi-network.org/2015/About.

Shiraishi, M., Washio, Y., Takayama, C., Lehdonvirta, V., Kimura, H., & Nakajima, T. (2009). *Using Individual, Social and Economic Persuasion Techniques to Reduce CO_2 Emissions in a Family Setting.* New York: Association for Computing Machinery.

SHRM (2007). *2007 Corporate Social Responsibility: United States, Australia, India, China, Canada, Mexico and Brazil.* Retrieved March 31, 2016 from https://www.shrm.org/Research/SurveyFindings/Documents/2007%20Corporate%20Social%20Responsibility%20Pilot%20Study.pdf.

—— (2011). *Advancing Sustainability: HR's Role.* Retrieved March 31, 2016 from https://www.shrm.org/Research/SurveyFindings/Articles/Documents/11-0066_AdvSustainHR_FNL_FULL.pdf.

Simpson, D.F., & Power, D.J. (2005). Use the supply relationship to develop lean and green suppliers. *Supply Chain Management*, 10(1), 60-68.

Smith, A. (2008). *An Inquiry Into the Nature and Causes of the Wealth of Nations.* Adelaide, Australia: Universty of Adelaide Library. (Original work published 1776). Retrieved March 31, 2016 from http://ebooks.adelaide.edu.au/s/smith/adam/s64w/complete.html.

Sobczak, A. (2006). Are codes of conduct in global supply chains really voluntary? From soft law regulations of labour regulations to consumer law. *Business Ethics Quarterly*, 16(2), 167-184.

Sourcemap (2012). Sourcemap: where things come from. Retrieved March 31, 2016 from http://sourcemap.com.

Spence, L., & Bourlakis, M. (2009). The evolution from corporate social responsibility to supply chain responsibility: the case of Waitrose. *Supply Chain Management: An International Journal*, 14(4), 291-302.

Sprunger, M. (2011). An introduction to Confucianism. Retrieved March 31, 2016 from http://urantiabook.org/archive/readers/601_confucianism.htm.

Spurgin, E.W. (2004). The goals and merits of a business ethics competency exam. *Journal of Business Ethics*, 50(3), 279-288.

Spurlock, M. (Director). (2004). *Super Size Me* [Motion picture]. U.S.A.: Samuel Goldwyn Films.

Starik, M. (1995). Should trees have managerial standing? Toward stakeholder status for non-human nature. *Journal of Business Ethics*, 14(3), 207-217.

Steinberg, S. (2011, January 21). The future of motion-controlled gaming. *CNN*. Retrieved August 4, 2016 from http://edition.cnn.com/2011/TECH/gaming.gadgets/01/21/motion.controls.steinberg/.

Stern, D.I. (2004). The rise and fall of the environmental Kuznets curve. *World Development*, 32(8), 1419-1439.

Stern, N. (2006). *The Economics of Climate Change: The Stern Review.* Retrieved March 31, 2016 from http://webarchive.nationalarchives.gov.uk/+/http://www.hm-treasury.gov.uk/stern_review_report.htm.

Stone, C.D. (1972). Should trees have standing? *Southern California Law Review*, 45, 450-87.

SustainAbility (2008). *The Social Intrapreneur: A Field Guide for Corporate Change Makers.* London: SustainAbility.

—— (2011). *Survey on Sustainable Consumption.* London: SustainAbility.

Sustainable Brands (2010, April 12). Starbucks launches "The Big Picture" campaign for collective action. Retrieved August 4, 2016 from http://www.sustainablebrands.com/news_and_views/articles/starbucks-launches-big-picture-campaign-collective-action.

Sutcliffe, H. (2014). *Responsible Innovation in Business*. London: Matter.

Svensson, G. (2007). Aspects of sustainable supply chain management (SSCM): conceptual framework and empirical example. *Supply Chain Management: An International Journal*, 12(4), 262-266.

——— (2009). The transparency of SCM ethics: conceptual framework and empirical illustrations. *Supply Chain Management: An International Journal*, 14(4), 259-269.

Sweney, M. (2009, April 6). Innocent drinks offer a taste to Coca-Cola. *The Guardian*. Retrieved March 31, 2016 from http://www.guardian.co.uk/business/2009/apr/06/innocent-drinks-sell-stake-coca-cola.

Széll, G. (2004). Environmental Kaizen: Environmental protection as a process. In G. Széll & K. Tominaga (Eds.), *Environmental Challenges for Japan and Germany: Intercultural and Interdisciplinary Perspectives* (pp. 253-268). Frankfurt, Germany: Peter Lang.

Tammilehto, O. (2008). *A Short History of Unsustainability*. Retrieved March 31, 2016 from http://www.ymparistojakehitys.fi/susopapers/Background_Paper_15_Olli_Tammilehto.pdf.

Tata Motors (2010). *Wheeling Innovation: Corporate Sustainability Report 2009–2010*. Mumbai, India: Tata.

Taylor, A. (2006, February 21). Toyota: the birth of the prius. *CNN Money*. Retrieved March 31, 2016 from http://money.cnn.com/2006/02/17/news/companies/mostadmired_fortune_toyota/index.htm.

Terrachoice (2007). *The "Six Sins of Greenwashing": A Study of Environmental Claims in North American Consumer Markets*. Ottawa, Canada: Terrachoice.

Terracycle (2016). Programa de reciclaje de Pan Bimbo [Bimbo Bread recycling program]. Retrieved May 20, 2016 from http://www.terracycle.com.mx/es-MX/brigades/programa-pan-bimbo.

Thielemann, U., & Wettstein, F. (2008). *The Case Against the Business Case and the Idea of "Earned Reputation."* St. Gallen, Switzerland: Institute for Business Ethics.

Timberlake, L. (2006). *Catalyzing Change: A Short History of the WBCSD*. Retrieved August 4, 2016 from http://www.wbcsd.org/pages/edocument/edocumentdetails.aspx?id=74&nosearchcontextkey=true.

Todaro, M.P., & Smith, S.C. (2006). *Economic Development* (9th ed.). Harlow, UK: Pearson.

TogBlog (2008, September 11). The Icebreaker Baa Code. Retrieved August 3, 2016 from http://tog-blog.co.uk/2008/09/11/the-icebreaker-baa-code/.

Tokic, A. (2011, September 28). Fiat 500 pink ribbon limited edition cars support a great cause. *AutoGuide*. Retrieved March 31, 2016 from http://www.autoguide.com/auto-news/2011/09/fiat-500-pink-ribbon-limited-edition-cars-support-a-great-cause.html.

TOMS Shoes (2011). *Giving Report*. Playa Del Rey, CA: TOMS Shoes.

——— (2012). Shop women's sunglasses. Retrieved March 31, 2016 from http://www.toms.com/women/womens-sunglasses.

——— (2016a). Corporate responsibility at TOMS®. Retrieved August 4, 2016 from http://www.toms.co.uk/about-toms#corporateResponsibility.

——— (2016b). What we give. Retrieved July 22, 2016 from http://www.toms.com/what-we-give-shoes.

Tracey, P., & Jarvis, O. (2007). Toward a theory of social venture franchising. *Entrepreneurship Theory and Practice*, 31(5), 667-685.

Transparency International (2009). Business principles for countering bribery. Retrieved March 31, 2016 from https://www.transparency.org/whatwedo/tools/business_principles_for_countering_bribery/1/.

UmweltBank (2012). Geschichte der UmweltBank [History of UmweltBank]. Retrieved March 31, 2016 from http://www.umweltbank.de/umweltbank/index_geschichte.html.

UN ESCAP (2011). What is good governance? Retrieved March 31, 2016 from http://www.unescap.org/pdd/prs/ProjectActivities/Ongoing/gg/governance.asp.

UNEP (2012). United Nations Environment Programme. Retrieved March 31, 2016 from http://www.unep.org.

UNEP & KPMG (2006). *Carrots and Sticks for Starters*. Parktown, South Africa: KPMG Global Sustainability Services.

UNFCCC (2011). Kyoto protocol. Retrieved March 31, 2016 from http://unfccc.int/kyoto_protocol/items/2830.php.

UNGC (2011a). The ten principles of the UN Global Compact. Retrieved March 31, 2016 from https://www.unglobalcompact.org/what-is-gc/mission/principles.

—— (2011b). United Nations Global Compact. Retrieved March 31, 2016 from http://www.unglobalcompact.org.

Unilever (2010). The Unilever Sustainable Living Plan. Retrieved August 4, 2016 from https://www.unilever.com/sustainable-living/the-sustainable-living-plan/our-strategy/.

—— (2015). Unilever sees sustainability supporting growth. Retrieved July 22, 2016 from https://www.unilever.co.uk/news/press-releases/2015/unilever-sees-sustainability-supporting-growth.html.

—— (2016). Sustainable sourcing. Retrieved July 22, 2016 from https://www.unilever.com/sustainable-living/the-sustainable-living-plan/reducing-environmental-impact/sustainable-sourcing/.

United Nations (1987). *Our Common Future*. New York: United Nations.

—— (1997). UN conference on environment and development (1992). Retrieved March 31, 2016 from http://www.un.org/geninfo/bp/enviro.html.

—— (2005). *2005 World Summit Outcome*. New York: United Nations.

—— (2011a). *Agenda 21*. Retrieved August 4, 2016 from https://sustainabledevelopment.un.org/content/documents/Agenda21.pdf.

—— (2011b). History of the document. Retrieved August 28, 2011 from http://www.un.org/en/documents/udhr/history.shtml.

—— (2011c). Millennium development goals. Retrieved March 31, 2016 from http://www.un.org/millenniumgoals.

—— (2012a). Rio +20: United Nations conference on sustainable development. Retrieved January 18, 2012 from http://www.uncsd2012.org/rio20/index.html.

—— (2012b). The Universal Declaration of Human Rights. Retrieved March 31, 2016 from http://www.un.org/en/universal-declaration-human-rights/index.html.

—— (2016). Sustainable Development Goals. Retrieved July 19, 2016 from https://sustainabledevelopment.un.org/?menu=1300.

UNOPS (2011a). *Procurement and the Millennium Development Goals*. New York: United Nations.

—— (2011b). *2010 Annual Statistical Report on United Nations Procurement*. New York: United Nations.

U.S. Environmental Protection Agency (2006). *Life Cycle Assessment: Principles and Practice*. Washington, DC: U.S. Environmental Protection Agency.

—— (2011). Energy Star. Retrieved March 31, 2016 from http://www.energystar.gov.

U.S. Green Building Council (2011). LEED. Retrieved March 31, 2016 from http://www.usgbc.org/leed.

USA Today (2005). The rise and fall of WorldCom. *USA Today*. Retrieved March 31, 2016 from http://www.usatoday.com/money/industries/telecom/2002-07-21-worldcom-chronology_x.htm.

Utopia Foundation (2012). Utopia. Retrieved March 31, 2016 from http://www.utopia.de.

Van der Borght, S., Rinke de Wit, T.F., Janssens, V., Schim van der Loeff, M.F., Rijckborst, H., & Lange, J. (2006). HAART for the HIV-infected employees of large companies in Africa. *The Lancet*, 368, 547-550.

Vanberg, V.J. (2007). Corporate social responsibility and the "game of catallaxy": the perspective of constitutional economics. *Constitutional Political Economy*, 18(3), 199-222.

Vanguardia (2011, August 9). Cambio climático puede incrementar enfermedades: especialista [Expert: climate change may increase dissease]. *Vanguardia*. Retrieved March 31, 2016 from http://www.vanguardia.com.mx/cambioclimaticopuedeaumentarenfermeda desespecialista-1064912.html.

Visser, W. (2008). *CSR Change Agents: Experts, Facilitators, Catalysts and Activists.* Retrieved March 31, 2016 from http://www.waynevisser.com/wp-content/uploads/2012/04/ inspiration_csr_change_agents_wvisser.pdf.

———— (2010). *The Age of Responsibility: CSR 2.0 and the New DNA of Business.* Chichester, UK: Wiley.

Vives, A. (2011, July 11). Chief Reputation Officer, Chief Sustainability Officer ... ¿Y el Chief Responsibility Officer? *Expok*. Retrieved August 4, 2016 from http://www.expoknews. com/2011/07/11/chief-reputation-officer-chief-sustainability-officer%E2%80%A6-y-el-chief-responsibility-officer.

Vogel, D.J. (2005). Is there a market for virtue? The business case for corporate social responsibility. *California Management Review*, 47(4), 19-45.

von Hippel, E. (2005). *Democratizing Innovation*. Cambridge, MA: MIT University Press.

von Kimakowitz, E., Pirson, M., Spitzeck, H., Dierksmeier, C., & Amann, W. (2011). *Humanistic Management in Practice*. New York: Palgrave Macmillan.

von Walter, B. (2012). *MTV Switch: A Global Climate Change Campaign*. Berlin, Germany: MTV Networks Germany.

Waddock, S., & Bodwell, C. (2004). Managing responsibility: What can be learnt from the quality movement? *California Management Review*, 47(1), 25-38.

———— (2007). *Total Responsibility Management: The Manual*. Sheffield, U.K.: Greenleaf Publishing.

Waddock, S.A., Bodwell, C., & Graves, S.B. (2002). Responsibility: the new business imperative. *Academy of Management Executive*, 47(1), 132-147.

Walker, H. (2010). Recapping on BP's long history of greenwashing. Retrieved August 4, 2016 from http://www.greenpeace.org/usa/recapping-on-bps-long-history-of-greenwashing/ .

Waller, R.L., & Conaway, R.N. (2011). Framing and counterframing the issue of corporate social responsibility: the communication strategies of Nikebiz.com. *Journal of Business Communication*, 48(1), 83-106.

Walmart (2009). *Standards for Suppliers*. Bentonville, AR: Walmart.

———— (2011). *Building the Next Generation: Walmart 2011 Global Responsibility Report*. Bentonville, AR: Walmart.

———— (2016). *Fiscal Year 2015 Walmart and Walmart Foundation Giving Report*. Bentonville, AR: Walmart.

Wapner, P. (1995). Politics beyond the state: environmental activism and world civic politics. *World Politics*, 47(3), 311-340.

WBCSD (1999). *Eco-Efficiency: Creating More Value with Less Impact*. Geneva, Switzerland: World Business Council for Sustainable Development.

———— (2002). *The Business Case for Sustainable Development: Making a Difference Toward the Johannesburg Summit 2001 and Beyond*. Geneva, Switzerland: World Business Council for Sustainable Development.

———— (2010). *Vision 2050: The New Agenda for Business in Brief*. Geneva, Switzerland: World Business Council for Sustainable Development.

———— (2011). About WBCSD. Retrieved March 31, 2016 from http://www.wbcsd.org/about. aspx.

Weaver, G.R., & Treviño, L.K. (1999). Compliance and values oriented ethics programs: influences on employees' attitudes and behavior. *Business Ethics Quarterly*, 9(2), 315-335.

Weaver, R.K. (1986). The politics of blame avoidance. *Journal of Public Policy*, 6, 371-398.

Webley (2007). *Use of Codes of Ethics in Business: 2007 Survey and Analysis of Trends*. London: The Institute of Business Ethics

Weick, K.E. (1995). *Sensemaking in Organizations*. Thousand Oaks, CA: Sage.

Weingarten, G. (2007, April 8). Pearls before breakfast. *The Washington Post*. Retrieved March 31, 2016 from http://www.washingtonpost.com/wp-dyn/content/article/2007/04/04/AR2007040401721.html.

Whiteman, G., Walker, B., & Perego, P. (2013). Planetary boundaries: ecological foundations for corporate sustainability. *Journal of Management Studies*, 50(2), 307-336.

Whole Foods Market (2016). Locally grown, raised and produced. Retrieved July 22, 2016 from http://www.wholefoodsmarket.com/local.

Wikipedia (2016). List of Ben & Jerry's ice creams. Retrieved March 19, 2016 from https://en.wikipedia.org/wiki/List_of_Ben_%26_Jerry%27s_ice_creams#Chubby_Hubby.

Windsor, D. (2001). The future of corporate social responsibility. *The International Journal of Organizational Analysis*, 9(3), 225-256.

Wise, J. (2011). There's no such thing as a sustainable business [Web log]. Retrieved March 31, 2016 from http://jonathanwise1.wordpress.com/2011/01/31/theres-no-such-thing-as-a-sustainable-business.

Women's Way (2006). *Power Skills: How Volunteering Shapes Professional Success*. Philadelphia, PA: Women's Way.

World Bank (2001). *Making Sustainable Commitments: An Environment Strategy for the World Bank*. Washington, DC: The World Bank.

—— (2016). World development indicators. Retrieved May 16, 2016 from http://data.worldbank.org/data-catalog/world-development-indicators.

World Institute of Slowness (2016). What is slowness? Retrieved August 4, 2016 from http://www.theworldinstituteofslowness.com/.

Worldwatch Institute (2016). *Can a City Be Sustainable? State of the World*. Washington, DC: Island Press.

WWF (2010). *Living Planet Report 2010*. Retrieved March 8, 2016 from http://www.footprintnetwork.org/press/LPR2010.pdf.

—— (2012). Verändern Sie die Welt ... mit Ihrem letzten Willen [Change the world ... with your last will]. Retrieved March 31, 2016 from http://www.wwf.at/de/testament.

Wysocki, R.K. (2009). *Effective Project Management*. Indianapolis, IN: Wiley.

Yandle, B., Bhattarai, M., & Vijayaraghavan, M. (2004). Environmental Kuznets curves: a review of findings, methods, and policy implications. Retrieved March 31, 2016 from http://www.perc.org/articles/environmental-kuznets-curves.

Zadeck, S. (2004). The path to corporate social responsibility. *Harvard Business Review*, 82(12), 125-132.

—— (2006). Responsible competitiveness: reshaping markets through responsible business practices. *Corporate Governance*, 6(4), 334-348.

Zadeck, S., & Merme, M. (2003). *Redefining Materiality: Practice and Public Policy for Effective Corporate Reporting*. London: AccountAbility.

Zimmer, C. (2011, August 29). Climate relicts: seeking clues on how some species survive. *Yale Environment 360*. Retrieved March 31, 2016 from http://e360.yale.edu/feature/surviving_climate_change_the_story_of_hardy_relicts/2437.

Zott, C., & Amit, R. (2010). Business model design: an activity system perspective. *Long Range Planning*, 43(2), 216-226.

About the authors

Oliver Laasch is the founder of the Center for Responsible Management Education and an assistant professor for strategy at the University of Nottingham, Ningbo Campus. He has worked for more than ten years in academic institutions on topic areas related to business sustainability, responsibility, and ethics. He was a lecturer and researcher at Seoul National University, and director of the Center for Sustainability and Responsibility (CRSE) at the Monterrey Tec. As manager for a European Social Fund project, he developed a training programme for  responsible businesses. He also served as academic coordinator for e-learning at the Institute for Corporate Responsibility Management at Steinbeis University, Berlin. He was formerly a Marie Curie Research Fellow at the Manchester Institute of Innovation Research at the University of Manchester, where he conducted research on business model innovation for sustainability, responsibility, and ethics.

Oliver has published textbooks, case studies, chapters, and journal articles related to responsible management and education. He is editor of the United Nations PRME book collection, and has worked extensively as a coach and consultant with dozens of companies and universities. Oliver has designed and taught a variety of full courses at bachelor, master, PhD, and executive education levels, including blended and massive open online courses such as 'Managing Responsibly,' 'Innovation for Sustainability,' 'Strategic CSR,' 'Leadership for Sustainable Development,' 'Social and Environmental Responsibility,' 'Responsible Management across Functions,' 'Environmental Economics and Management,' 'Social and Cause-Related Marketing,' 'Social Entrepreneurship,' 'Responsible Business Communication,' 'CSR Norms and Institutions,' 'Designing Humanistic Business Models,' 'Design for Environment,' and 'Sustainable Lifestyles.'

Oliver won the 2015 best professional development workshop award of the Management Education and Development Division at the AOM Annual Convention, for the workshop 'Responsible Management Education in Action.' His textbook *Principles of Responsible Management* was reviewed and commended by the Academy of Management Learning and Education in the same year. Oliver received a '100 Most Talented Sustainability Leaders Citation' from the World CSR Day 2014, a Marie Curie Fellowship for 'New Business Models for CSR' in 2013, and the Procter & Gamble Award for the best sustainability-oriented thesis in 2009.

Roger Conaway currently serves as professor of business in the Monterrey Institute of Technology (ITESM), Campus San Luis Potosí, and is a member of the EGADE Business School. He is a faculty member in the doctoral program of Administrative Sciences, Mexico City campus and entered the Mexican National Research Foundation (Sistema Nacional de Investigadores in CONACYT) in 2014 as a Level 1 researcher. He works with a corporate responsibility research team in EGADE and conducts research on environmental responsibility.

He has co-authored *Communication in Responsible Business*, a text which included communication models on developing stakeholder communication and avoiding greenwash. He is coauthor of a recent text, *Principles of Responsibility Management: Glocal Sustainability, Responsibility, and Ethics* (Cengage Learning), which was the first official textbook for the United Nations PRME academic network. His journal articles have published research on reframing CSR issues at Nike and ethical frameworks.

His previous academic experience included a tenured professorship at the University of Texas at Tyler, having appointments in both the Department of Communication and the Department of Management and Marketing. He taught online courses in the Master of Arts in Responsible Management program, Steinbeis University, Berlin, and was Visiting Professor at Florence University of the Arts.

Printed in the United States
by Baker & Taylor Publisher Services

Printed in the United States
by Baker & Taylor Publisher Services